This book is essential reading for anyone who wants to understand the role of management accountants around the world. It provides a fascinating picture of the heterogeneous roles of management accountants in a wide range of countries, including China, Russia, India and Brazil. It illustrates the crucial importance of national history and socio-economic context for understanding the role of management accountants around the world, as well as their different tasks, educational backgrounds and professional structures. In addition, other chapters provide valuable insights into the implications of contemporary global issues, including new communications technology, sustainability and the recent financial crisis.

Professor Robert W. Scapens, *Alliance Manchester Business School, UK, and Birmingham Business School, UK*

Management accountants have guided business decisions for over a century. This book details the emergence of the profession and its relevance today, highlighting global differences and commonalities. It provides a comprehensive overview of how management accountants work in, and influence, today's business environment.

Dr. Noel Tagoe, *Executive Vice President, Association of International Certified Professional Accountants*

There is currently a great deal of interest in the professional role and identity of the management accountant and how various changes in the global business landscape have influenced and continue to influence the role. Research in this area is growing and has the potential to make a significant impact on the accounting profession. This excellent book has achieved a good geographic coverage (including the BRIC countries as well as the UK, US and Europe) and both historical and contemporary perspectives. I recommend it as essential reading for new practitioners and academics in management accounting as well as those with a research interest in this key business role.

Professor Elaine Harris, *University of Roehampton, London, UK*

The Role of the Management Accountant

There is considerable national variation in the professionalization and status of the management accountant. Although researchers from different countries have contributed to our knowledge about tasks and roles, we have limited insights into the development, education, and socio-cultural influences in different countries and surprisingly little is known about the local and national contexts in which these roles are learned and performed.

This book bridges this research gap using two complementary perspectives. The first part explores management accountants in a range of different national contexts, providing information about country-specific historical developments and educational standards as well as specific roles and tasks. The second part focuses on important global developments that will increasingly impact management accountants in the future, such as sustainability, the financial crisis, technology, and changing roles. By combining local context with a global overview, this insightful volume provides an agenda for future research which will be of great interest to scholars and advanced students in management accounting throughout the world.

Lukas Goretzki is currently an Assistant Professor of management control at the University of Innsbruck. His main research interests and publications (e.g. in *European Accounting Review*, *Management Accounting Research*, or *Qualitative Research in Accounting and Management*) are on management accountants' roles, budgeting, and performance evaluation.

Erik Strauss is a Professor of management accounting and control at Witten/ Herdecke University. His main research interests and publications are on the roles of management control systems, management accounting change, influence of technology on management accounting, and management accountants.

Routledge Studies in Accounting

For a full list of titles in this series, please visit https://www.routledge.com/Routledge-Studies-in-Accounting/book-series/SE0715

The Role of the Management Accountant

Local Variations and Global Influences

Edited by
Lukas Goretzki
and Erik Strauss

Routledge
Taylor & Francis Group

LONDON AND NEW YORK

First published 2018 by Routledge

2 Park Square, Milton Park, Abingdon, Oxfordshire OX14 4RN
52 Vanderbilt Avenue, New York, NY 10017

Routledge is an imprint of the Taylor & Francis Group, an informa business

First issued in paperback 2019

British Library Cataloguing in Publication Data
A catalogue record for this book is available from the British Library

Library of Congress Cataloging in Publication Data
Names: Goretzki, Lukas, 1982– author. | Strauss, Erik, 1982– author.
Title: The role of the management accountant : local variations and global influences / Lukas Goretzki & Erik Strauss.
Description: 1 Edition. | New York : Routledge, 2018. | Includes bibliographical references and index.
Identifiers: LCCN 2017020822 (print) | LCCN 2017033059 (ebook) | ISBN 9781315673738 (eBook) | ISBN 9781138941359 (hardback : alk. paper) | ISBN 9781315673738 (ebk)
Subjects: LCSH: Managerial accounting. | Industrial management.
Classification: LCC HF5657.4 (ebook) | LCC HF5657.4 .G674 2018 (print) | DDC 658.15/11–dc23
LC record available at https://lccn.loc.gov/2017020822

ISBN: 978-1-138-94135-9 (hbk)
ISBN: 978-0-367-87426-1 (pbk)

Typeset in Times New Roman
by Wearset Ltd, Boldon, Tyne and Wear

Contents

Figures

Tables

Contributors

Albrecht Becker studied Social Sciences and obtained his PhD and Habilitation at Freie Universität Berlin, Germany. He is Professor of Management Accounting at Universität Innsbruck. His research interests include management accounting and control in not-for-profit contexts and performance measurement in research and academia.

Sebastian D. Becker is Associate Professor of Management Accounting and Control at HEC Paris. His main research interests and publications are on the diffusion, change, and implementation of budgeting and forecasting practices, as well as on the role of controllers.

John Burns is Professor of Management and Accountancy at Exeter University Business School. His broad research interest covers understanding and theorizing both continuity and change in organizations, usually adopting qualitative methods and undertaking theoretically informed case studies. He is co-editor of *Qualitative Research in Accounting and Management*.

Sergey G. Falko is Head of Department Economics and Operations Management and Professor at Bauman Moscow State Technical University and Executive Director NP Partnership "Controller Association" of Russia, member of International Group of Controlling and chief editor of the journal *Controlling*. His interest in science and practice has been controlling as guidance for management. He is author of *Controlling at the Enterprise* and *Controlling for Manager and Experts*, widely cited in Russian books.

Masafumi Fujino has worked at Nihon University since 2004. He holds a PhD from Hitotsubashi University. His recent research explores the use of management accounting in the process of managers' interaction, performance measurement in public sector organizations, and management accounting history in Japan.

Lukas Goretzki is Assistant Professor of Management Control at the University of Innsbruck. His main research interests and publications are on the roles and identities of management accountants, budgeting, planning as well as performance management practices and management accounting change processes.

Rafael Heinzelmann is Associate Professor in Management Accounting and Control at University of Agdar, School of Business and Law, Kristiansand, Norway. Before joining University of Agdar, Rafael was affiliated with NHH Norwegian School of Economics, Bergen. He obtained his PhD from the University of Innsbruck, Austria. Rafael's research revolves around the following topics: IT technologies, role/identity of management accountants, performance management, forecasting/budgeting, and comparative management accounting research.

Jizhang Huang, currently a post-doctoral at the School of Accountancy in Shanghai University of Finance and Economics, earned his PhD on accounting in 2015. He teaches business analysis and management consulting for undergraduates and serves as one of the tutors for the seminar on management accounting research for the PhD program. His research interests center on incentive contracting issues, especially those in Chinese enterprises.

Marko Järvenpää is Professor in JSBE (University of Jyväskylä). He studies management accounting, specifically management accountants' role transformation, performance measurement, strategy, and management accounting change, typically by conducting qualitative case and field studies and employs interpretative theories like institutional, stakeholder, and cultural theories.

Prem Lal Joshi is Professor of Accounting with Multimedia University, Malaysia. Previously, he was Professor of Accounting with University of Bahrain. He has taught in India, Turkey, Kenya, Bahrain, and Malaysia. He has over 90 research articles in international and national journals. He is author of six books in Accounting and Finance. He was the Editor-in-Chief of *IJAAPE* and *AAJFA*. His research interests are diffusions of management accounting practices, budgetary practices, and IFRS compliance practices in developing countries, corporate governance and disclosure and its impact on firm performance.

Vitor Hugo Klein Jr. is Assistant Professor at Cesfi-UDESC, Brazil. He holds a PhD from Helmut Schmidt University, Germany. His research interests include organization studies, leadership, and management accounting. Vitor is currently investigating the relationship between imagination and organizing.

Kip Krumwiede, CMA, CPA, PhD, is Director of Research for IMA. Previously, he spent 18 years as a management accounting professor and worked for two Fortune 500 companies in management accounting related positions. Kip has published over 20 articles in both practice and academic journals.

Tsuilin Kuo is an associate professor at Fu Jen Catholic University. Her research interests include management control systems, performance evaluation, and corporate governance. Professor Kuo's relevant publications covered *Journal of Accounting Review, International Journal of Learning and Intellectual Capital*, and *Journal of Management*.

Caroline Lambert is Associate Professor at HEC Montréal. Her research is interdisciplinary, critically oriented, and focuses on the accounting profession and management control. She has published a dozen articles in major academic journals, including *Accounting, Organizations and Society*, *Management Accounting Research*, and *European Accounting Review*, and several book chapters.

Raef Lawson is Vice President-Research and Policy, Institute of Management Accountants. Previously he served as Professor and Chair of the Department of Accounting and Law at the State University of New York – Albany. Research interests include sustainability, business ethics, and performance management systems.

Kari Lukka's research interests cover a wide range of management accounting and research methodology topics. He is former editor of EAR and currently at the editorial boards of AOS, MAR, ABR, CPA, and BAR as well as an associate editor of QRAM. He is the Chair of the University Collegiate Council of his university and a member of the Board of the TSE.

Matthias D. Mahlendorf is Professor of Managerial Accounting. His research areas are performance measurement and relative performance information. He has published in journals such as TAR, AOS, CAR, EAR, and MAR and has designed and taught seminars for executives of international corporations such as SAP, Bayer, and Henkel.

Martin Messner is Professor of Management Control at the University of Innsbruck. He conducts research on various topics in management accounting and control, including budgeting and forecasting, performance measurement, and the work of management accountants.

Jérémy Morales is a senior lecturer at Royal Holloway. His research interests concern primarily the links between techniques (such as performance indicators or management tools), individuals (organisational members' behaviour, their subjectivity, their morality), and broader macro-sociological trends (financialization, neoliberalism, globalization).

Artur Roberto do Nascimento is Adjunct Professor of Accounting and Control at Universidade Estadual de Feira de Santana. His broad research interest covers management control as organizational and social practice, critical perspectives in accounting theory and control, accounting and society, epistemology and qualitative methodology, social theory (poststructuralism and postcolonialism), qualitative methodology, and critical studies on the interface between accounting, law, and organization.

Fei Pan, Professor of Accounting at Shanghai University of Finance and Economics, earned his PhD on business administration in 1999. He teaches cost accounting and management accounting at the undergraduate, graduate,

MBA, and PhD programs. Mainly concentrating on management accounting, his research has been published in a variety of international and Chinese domestic journals.

Usha Rani Cherukupallis, MCom, MS (Bits, Pilani), BPMA (Hasso Plattner Institute, Germany), MPhil, PhD. She worked as MBA Professor for 29 years in various PG and Degree Colleges. Her paper was presented at the Ninth International Conference on E-business, held by Alfred University, New York, China University of Geosciences, China.

Alan J. Richardson is the Odette Research Chair at the University of Windsor, Canada. His work examines the evolution of professional bodies, standard-setting, and accounting technologies. His work has been published in *Accounting, Organizations and Society*, *Contemporary Accounting Research*, *Journal of Accounting Research*, among others.

Utz Schäffer is Director of the Institute of Management Accounting and Control (IMC) of WHU – Otto Beisheim School of Management in Vallendar. His main research areas are controlling and strategy execution and the roles of CFOs and Controllers.

Stefan Schaltegger is Professor of Management and Head of the Centre for Sustainability Management and the MBA Sustainability Management at Leuphana University Lüneburg. He is a chairman of the Environmental and Sustainability Management Accounting Network (EMAN). His research on corporate sustainability includes sustainability accounting and reporting: www.leuphana.de/csm.

Will Seal has held chairs at the Universities of Essex, Birmingham, and Southampton. He is currently Professor of Accounting and Management at Loughborough University. Will has published extensively in books and in professional and academic journals. His main current research interests are the relationship between theory and practice in management, strategic control, shared services, supply chain management, and lean operations.

Samuel Sponem is Chairholder of the International CPA Chair for Research in Management Control and Associate Professor at HEC Montreal. His research focuses primarily on the use, dissemination, and impacts of management control tools and on the place and role of management controllers. His works have led to publications in peer-reviewed journals (*Comptabilité-Contrôle-Audit*, *Critical Perspectives on Accounting*, *European Accounting Review*, *Management Accounting Research*, *Politiques and management public*).

Leon P. Steenkamp is a senior lecturer at the School of Accountancy at Stellenbosch University, South Africa, who lectures Accounting Information Systems and Risk Management. His research interests include accounting education, transdisciplinary research, accounting information systems, and matters related to the accounting profession as a whole.

Erik Strauss is Full Professor of Management Accounting and Control at Witten/Herdecke University. His main research interests and publications are on the roles of management accountants, management control systems, and management accounting change.

Sophie Tessier is Associate Professor at HEC Montréal. Her main fields of interest are management control and energy efficiency management. She has published articles in *Management Accounting Research, Accounting, Auditing and Accountability Journal, Critical Perspectives on Accounting*, and *International Journal of Qualitative Methods*.

Nachiket Madhav Vechalekar is currently working as Dean-Post Graduate Programs and Research at IndSearch, Pune: 411004. He is a recognized PhD Guide in the subject of Financial Management at Savitribai Phule Pune University. So far four students have completed PhDs under his guidance and five are studying.

Liz Warren is the Director of Learning and Teaching for the Business School, University of Greenwich. She teaches management accounting and strategy across the UK, France, Malaysia, China, and Hong Kong. Her research is based mainly in the energy and banking sector.

Jürgen Weber is Director of the Institute of Management Accounting and Control (IMC) of WHU – Otto Beisheim School of Management in Vallendar. His main research areas are Controllership and Organizational Change.

Philippus L. Wessels (PhD in Accounting), is a full-time Professor at Niagara College in the School of Business and Management Studies. Prior to his joining Niagara College in 2012, he was Professor in Accounting at the University of Stellenbosch, South Africa for 20 years. Philippus specializes in teaching managerial accounting, financial accounting, and information management. He has published widely in academic research journals on a wide range of accounting and business related topics. As a Chartered Management Accountant (member of the Chartered Institute of Management Accountants in the UK), Philippus has also been actively involved in owning and consulting small businesses, mainly in the hospitality industry.

Anne Wu is Chair Professor at National Chengchi University in Taiwan, and is the director of Taiwan Intellectual Capital Research Center. Her current research interests include activity-based costing/activity-based management, balanced scorecard, compensation management, and intellectual capital. She has received an Academic Award from the Ministry of Education and Outstanding Research Awards thrice from the National Science Council (NSC) in Taiwan. She obtained a patent "Strategic Intellectual Capital Evaluation Model (SICEM)" in 2010 and a trademark "Integrative Strategic Value Management System (ISVMS)" in 2012 and 2013 from Taiwan, China, and the USA.

Laura Zoni is currently Professor of Accounting and Control at Università Cattolica del Sacro Cuore and Senior Professor of Accounting and Control at SDA Bocconi School of Management. Among others she has been visiting faculty at Stern – New York University and at Insead. She has published several articles and books on management control, performance evaluation, and incentives. Ms Zoni is Board Member of the Yoox-Net-à-Porter Group.

1 Introduction

Lukas Goretzki and Erik Strauss

The work of management accountants has attracted wide scholarly attention. Research has mainly focused on the heterogeneity of management accountants' tasks and roles, the antecedents leading to the often-observed practice variation as well as its consequences (e.g. Burns & Baldvinsdottir, 2005; Järvenpää, 2007; Lambert & Sponem, 2011; Morales & Lambert, 2013; Mouritsen, 1996; Simon, Guetzkow, Kozmetzky & Tyndall, 1954). Studies show that it is difficult to define *the* role of the management accountant as, empirically, one can basically find management accountants performing different roles ranging from the bean-counter to the business partner, just to mention two ideal types often referred to in the literature. This observed practice variation can, to a certain extent, be explained by internal factors like the organizational structure (centralization vs. decentralization), the internal status or authority of the management accounting function, interaction structures between managers and management accountants, personal characteristics or leadership styles. Additionally, researchers have stressed that country-specific factors have an impact on how management accountants see and interpret their role in the organization and consequently how they interact with managers (Ahrens & Chapman, 2000). An important aspect, hereby, seems to be the degree of professionalization and – associated with this – how management accountants are educated in their countries (e.g. academic education vs. professional training) or how "strong" discursively available social identities are (cf. Down & Reveley, 2009). Furthermore, it appears that the relative status of management accountants (compared to other professional groups) varies between different countries (Lambert & Pezet, 2011) and that even the national culture might have an influence on the role of the management accountant (Granlund & Lukka, 1998).

Furthermore, neither the factors influencing the role of the management accountant nor management accountants' own endeavors to change their role are static and they develop over time. Scholars have paid particular attention to management accountants' development toward an increasing business-orientation and contribution to value-creation (e.g. Burns & Baldvinsdottir, 2005; Goretzki, Strauß & Weber, 2013; Järvenpää, 2007). Researchers described developments of management accountants from 'bean counters' engaged in gathering and analyzing data as well as preparing standard reports for managers (cf. Bougen,

1994; Friedman & Lyne, 1997, 2001; Järvinen, 2009) to 'business partners' who are willing and able to contribute to the management and control of the firm (see, for example, Järvenpää, 2007). One important condition for such developments as emphasized in the literature is technological developments. For example, the introduction of computer-based enterprise resource planning systems unburdened the management accountants from many routine tasks so that they can use their work time for other tasks like more qualitative analyses of variances in the data to provide managers more value-adding information or even concrete suggestions for decision-making (cf. Caglio, 2003; Scapens & Jazayeri, 2003).

In addition to technological aspects as conditions for role change, some studies shed light on management accountants' endeavors to take influence on their own role within the organization (cf. Horton & de Araujo Wanderley, 2016; Morales & Lambert, 2013), sometimes initiated by actors (e.g. chief financial officers, CFOs) trying to establish a particular role (identity) for 'their' subordinates (Goretzki et al., 2013). Efforts of management accountants or financial managers to establish a particular (role) identity for themselves or their subordinates can to a certain extent be considered effects of 'normative pressure' to discard traditional role stereotypes and perform 'innovative' roles. Important players, hereby, are professional associations of (management) accountants that realized the requirement to 'reinvent' the role of management accountants (Picard, Durocher & Gendron, 2014) to, for example, preserve their relevance within the firm. Therefore, professional associations such as the Charted Institute of Management Accountants (CIMA) or the Institute of Chartered Accountants in England and Wales (ICAEW), and also 'quasi-associations' like the German-speaking International Controller Association (cf. Schäffer, Schmidt & Strauss, 2014) started to promote an apparently 'new' role – the business partner role – for management accountants and for providing management accountants with respective symbolic resources (cf. Down & Reveley, 2009) such as role templates. As the existing literature on the (changing) role of the management accountant is often focused on Anglo-Saxon countries it is, however, rather unknown to what extent these developments regarding the role of the management accountant can be taken for granted from a global perspective. In other words, we know rather little whether endeavors, developments or even the rhetoric around the role of the management accountant (e.g. in professional magazines) are similar in different countries.

Taken together, it can be argued that although academic interest has increased tremendously in the last decade, our knowledge about management accountants' actual tasks, roles, organizational status in different countries as well as the different country-specific ways in which they are socialized and educated is still rather limited. However, these insights seem to be necessary to build a comprehensive understanding about the management accounting occupation.

Therefore, this book presents a compendium encompassing detailed accounts about management accountants in different countries (Part I) and global factors that already have or will influence the role of the management accountant (Part II). Summarizing the key insights from Part I, we can say that although a core of activities (like budgeting, forecasting, variance analysis etc.) exists that many management accountants share around the world, the management accounting profession seems more multifaceted than prior research might yet have suggested. Starting from very basis aspects like the name of the profession we can see interesting differences between different countries. For example, management accountants are called, apart from "management accountant" (e.g. in China, India or UK), "controller" (e.g. in Brazil, Canada, Finland or Germany) or "business analyst" (e.g. in Italy) in some countries. The differences between management accountants across different countries (see Chapters 2–13) result to a certain extent also from the very diverse pathways to becoming a management accountant as well as the role that professional associations educating manage-ment accountants play in these countries. Whereas some countries have strong professional associations that have closure about educating management accountants (like CIMA in the UK or Canada) and hence present rather strong social identities for aspirants of this profession, in other societal contexts univer-sities (e.g. China or Germany) or organizations themselves (like in Japan) are responsible for education. Depending (but not exclusively) on the relevance of the professional association and the legal background (in some countries the development of the role of the management accountant was even facilitated by governmental initiatives) management accountants can have very different organizational but also societal statuses around the globe. While in some coun-tries, management accountants have a certain legal back-up (e.g. in Russia) which makes them a prerequisite for management and fosters their strategic role, the status can be described as more traditional (i.e. taking over routine tasks like data gathering) in countries like India or Japan.

The tasks, educational backgrounds and societal as well as organizational sta-tuses of management accountants are quite heterogeneous across countries and the kaleidoscopic landscape of the management accounting profession might also be enforced in the future as various global trends might influence manage-ment accountants' role, tasks and work environments. Nevertheless, the chapters also show that the so-called business partner role seems to constitute a transcon-textual role model with which management accountants in various countries prefer to identity themselves. This fact that business partnering might be associ-ated with very different tasks sheds a rather critical light on those studies that try to identity a distinct or even 'standard' set of tasks, activities or skills that char-acterize business partner management accountants and differentiates them from other stereotypes like the bean-counter (see Chapter 17). It seems that what 'makes' business partners is actually the attitude that management accountants have toward their role but also how others (especially managers) perceive them. The chapter on the influence of economic crises on the role of the management accountant shows, for instance, that in such situations management accountants become more important for managers and are therefore more intensively involved in organizational processes (see Chapter 19). To support managers properly, management accountants should in this respect not unlearn their basic calculative tasks (see Chapter 20), which may be challenging because these tasks are more and more handed over to IT systems (see Chapter 14), fall victim to outsourcing initiatives (see Chapter 15) or taken over by financial accountants (see Chapter 16). A further challenge in the context of the business partner role is that management accountants are expected to stay open to emerging topics or developments such as sustainability (see Chapter 18).

What this book also reveals is that when researchers talk about "the management accountant" they – empirically – refer to very different types of actors. We hope that bringing this diversity to the minds of researchers may create a fertile ground for future studies and routes for further research on local variations and global influences that investigates and exploits differences but also commonalities of "the management accountant."

References

Ahrens, T. & Chapman, C. S. (2000). Occupational identity of management accountants in Britain and Germany. *European Accounting Review, 9*(4), 477–498.

Bougen, P. D. (1994). Joking apart: The serious side to the accountant stereotype. *Accounting, Organizations and Society, 19*(3), 319–335.

Burns, J. & Baldvinsdottir, G. (2005). An institutional perspective of accountants' new roles: The interplay of contradictions and praxis. *European Accounting Review, 14*(4), 725–757.

Caglio, A. (2003). Enterprise resource planning systems and accountants: Towards hybridization? *European Accounting Review, 12*(1), 123–153.

Down, S. & Reveley, J. (2009). Between narration and interaction: Situating first-line supervisor identity work. *Human Relations, 62*(3), 379–401.

Friedman, A. L. & Lyne, S. R. (1997). Activity-based techniques and the death of the beancounter. *European Accounting Review, 6*(1), 19–44.

Friedman, A. L. & Lyne, S. R. (2001). The beancounter stereotype: Towards a general model of stereotype generation. *Critical Perspectives on Accounting, 12*(4), 423–451.

Goretzki, L., Strauß, E. & Weber, J. (2013). An institutional perspective on the changes in management accountants' professional role. *Management Accounting Research, 24*(1), 41–63.

Granlund, M. & Lukka, K. (1998). Towards increasing business orientation: Finnish management accountants in a changing cultural context. *Management Accounting Research, 9*(2), 185–211.

Horton, K. E. & de Araujo Wanderley, C. (2016). Identity conflict and the paradox of embedded agency in the management accounting profession: Adding a new piece to the theoretical jigsaw. *Management Accounting Research*, forthcoming.

Järvenpää, M. (2007). Making business partners: A case study on how management accounting culture was changed. *European Accounting Review, 16*(1), 99–142.

Järvinen, J. (2009). Shifting NPM agendas and management accountants' occupational identities. *Accounting, Auditing and Accountability Journal, 22*, 1187–1210.

Lambert, C. & Pezet, E. (2011). The making of the management accountant – becoming the producer of truthful knowledge. *Accounting, Organizations and Society, 36*(1), 10–30.

Lambert, C. & Sponem, S. (2011). Roles, authority and involvement of the management accounting function: A multiple case-study perspective. *European Accounting Review, 21*(3), 565–589.

Morales, J. & Lambert, C. (2013). Dirty work and the construction of identity: An ethnographic study of management accounting practices. *Accounting, Organizations and Society, 38*(3), 228–244.

Mouritsen, J. (1996). Five aspects of accounting departments' work. *Management Accounting Research, 7*(3), 283–303.

Picard, C.-F., Durocher, S. & Gendron, Y. (2014). From meticulous professionals to superheroes of the business world: A historical portrait of a cultural change in the field of accountancy. *Accounting, Auditing and Accountability Journal, 27*(1), 73–118.

Scapens, R. W. & Jazayeri, M. (2003). ERP systems and management accounting change: Opportunities or impacts? A research note. *European Accounting Review, 12*(1), 201–233.

Schäffer, U., Schmidt, A. & Strauss, E. (2014). An old boys' club on the threshold to becoming a professional association: The emergence and development of the association of German controllers from 1975 to 1989. *Accounting History, 19*(1–2), 133–169.

Simon, H. A., Guetzkow, H., Kozmetzky, G. & Tyndall, G. (1954). *Centralization vs. decentralization in organizing the controller's department*. Houston: Scholars Book Co.

Part I

Management accountants in national context

2 The role of the controller in Brazil

Historical origins, key functions and challenges

Vitor Hugo Klein Jr. and
Artur Roberto do Nascimento

Introduction

Management accounting is a relatively new field of research and education in Brazil (Frezatti, Aguiar, Wanderley & Malagueno, 2015). As a practice comprising an array of ideas and tools, management accounting is affected by the social and political context in which it is situated (see, for example, Hopper, Tsamenyi, Uddin & Wickramasinghe, 2009). In Brazil, periods of high levels of inflation, the creation of its industrial landscape, its colonial past and culture, and its regulatory forms, greatly influenced how management accounting developed as a discipline. Nevertheless, the management accountant position is rare in Brazil, as the practices typically associated with management accountants in western, industrialised countries, are diffusely allocated to analysts, and more prominently, to controllers. A swift search of online recruiters on 27 June 2016 – Catho, Manager and Michel Page – returned just 10 advertisements for management accountants, in contrast to 154 for controllers. Hence, although reliant on the support of other roles (financial analysts, controllership analysts, etc.) in Brazil, the controller takes managerial responsibility for performing management accounting functions. As in Germany, Austria and Switzerland, controllership is defined similarly to management accounting; thus, controller is the nomenclature adopted for this professional in Brazil, and *controladoria* is the Portuguese term describing the functional area within companies.

This chapter continues by offering a contextualised account of the role of the controller in Brazil, discussing pertinent challenges to the controllers' profession and education. The second section describes how accounting education evolved in Brazil, from the inception of Schools of Commerce at the beginning of the nineteenth century to the creation of postgraduate courses in the final quarter of the twentieth century. It examines the historical antecedents of accounting pedagogy in Brazil, highlighting the social, economic and cultural context in which initial controller positions emerged in Brazil during the 1960s. Then, the third section explains the social and political background from which controller positions first emerged in the 1960s, how controllership was established as a practice and discipline in Brazil, and empirical evidence from the last decade detailing the key functions of controllers. The fourth section addresses challenges to the controller's profession and education. The chapter concludes with a brief summary.

The historical origins of accounting pedagogy in Brazil

The historical events leading to the specialisation of accounting education in Brazil can be grouped roughly into three phases. The first covers the establishment of Schools of Commerce in Brazil in 1809, and the respective challenges they encountered during the nineteenth century. The second phase, the first half of the twentieth century, describes the institutionalisation of professional associations and undergraduate courses in accounting. The third phase encompasses developments in undergraduate and graduate courses in the concluding quarter of the twentieth century. While all phases will be contrasted against their respective political and economic backgrounds, the main emphasis in this section is on examining the historical antecedents of accounting pedagogy; this will shed light on the context in which the first controller positions appeared in Brazil in the 1960s.

The first seeds of accounting pedagogy in Brazil can be traced back to the establishment of Schools of Commerce (*Aulas do Comércio*) in 1809, shortly after D. John VI, the King of Portugal, transferred his court to Brazil. Created in Portugal in 1759, amidst the reforms of the Marquis of Pombal, the schools were part of Portugal's plan to regain its importance relative to the more developed European nations (Rodrigues, Gomes & Craig, 2004). As the Head of the Government, Pombal envisioned strengthening the State of Portugal, and fostering economic growth through education. Since the Jesuits – Society of Jesus[1] – exerted significant power and monopoly over education, one of Pombal's first acts was to expel them from Portugal and the colonies. This expulsion reduced the Brazilian educational system to a point of virtual non-existence, a situation that endured until the beginning of the nineteenth century. For Pombal, however, the Schools of Commerce aimed to ennoble the activity of commerce, previously considered by Portuguese society as an affair associated with the lower social strata (Chaves, 2008).

At the time King John and his court arrived in Brazil, the notion of forging a culture of trade remained prominent.[2] Up to that point, however, Brazil had functioned principally as a colony, supplying Portugal with raw goods. Therefore, it lacked an institutional environment able to support economic growth. The first institutions created in Brazil followed the transfer of the Portuguese court. Likewise, the opening of Brazilian ports to friendly nations[3] underscored the need to professionalise the mercantile group on this side of the Atlantic, pushing the royal family to create an administrative structure for the country (Leite, 2005).

In this context, the creation of Schools of Commerce in Brazil opened great possibilities; yet they had to face multiple challenges. As a form of technical and professional education, the schools had, according to Chaves (2008), two main characteristics: an emphasis on practical knowledge and the production of a specific literature through their faculty, the *lentes*. Accounting was central to the schools teaching methods (Chaves, 2008, p. 268), and consisted of shifting from simpler to more complex issues always drawing on practical examples. However, the institutionalisation of the schools was complicated, not only because of the lack of qualified teachers, but also by political quarrels and discontinuities.

The practices and customs of the two territories [Brazil and Portugal] were very different, making it difficult to govern with the same laws and principles. Transforming America into the seat of the empire hardly alleviated the differences and, on the contrary, it accentuated the unequal treatment given to vassals on both sides of the Atlantic. Dealers and especially merchants [in Brazil] wanted to have the privileges granted to the Portuguese with regard to the privileges given to the five classes of merchants. [...] Dealers enrolled in the *Junta de Comércio* [Board of Trade] and in the schools of commerce, but felt that the mercantile group of Portugal continued to have higher privileges.

(Chaves, 2009, p. 179)

For half a century people had had little interest in commercial education, preferring to pursue careers such as engineering, law and medicine (Bielinski, 2015). This was largely due to prejudice against the mercantile professions, an idea rooted in Portugal's culture but reinforced in Brazil by slavery (Bielinski, 2015; Saes & Cytrynowicz, 2001). As manual and technical practices were usually delegated to slaves, a prejudice against practical activities spread both among the ruling class, who considered them paltry, and the poor, who preferred to live in subsistence rather than working for someone else, as a 'slave' (Leite, 2005, p. 53). Despite the limited interest in commercial education, three important events assisted the institutionalisation of accounting education in Brazil. The first of these was the creation of the first Commercial Code in 1850, which demanded companies keep accounting records. This was later followed by the regulation of the first public companies in 1860 (Law 1.083/1860), which demanded companies publically provide their balances; and subsequently by the official recognition of the bookkeeper as a profession in 1870. The Commercial Code of 1850 was thus the first document to regulate accounting and expressly consider book-keepers (*guarda-livros*) and cashiers (*caixeiros*) as auxiliary agents of trade. However, the code did not require these agents to complete any type of formal education.

The second phase in the specialisation of accounting pedagogy occurred in the first half of the twentieth-century. During this period, the creation of professional associations and undergraduate courses bestowed a more prominent role on accounting, helping to regulate it as a profession. In the period 1902 to 1905, two commercial education institutions were created: the *Escola Prática de Comércio*, in São Paulo and the *Academia de Comércio*, in Rio de Janeiro. These institutions represented milestones in terms of management and accounting education in Brazil. The former was created with the support of businessmen and São Paulo companies, and assisted Brazilian firms in a period of economic expansion. Meanwhile, the latter retained close ties with the federal governments, working as consulting partner in matters of industry and commerce. Their curriculum covered both technically oriented courses and more advanced ones, which were expected to prepare the students for high level positions, e.g. consular officers, employees of the Ministry of Foreign Affairs, actuaries in insurance companies and heads of accounting in banks and large companies (Soares, Richartz, Voss & Freitas, 2011, p. 28).

Despite receiving more publicity than technical courses, these advanced courses attracted limited interest from the intellectual elite (Leite, 2005). Nevertheless, the pressures to regulate the accounting profession and the processes of specialisation of management and accounting education were eventually successful. These pressures arose from the creation of professional bodies, and the organisation of conferences in accounting at the beginning of the twentieth-century (Peleias & Bacci, 2004). Changes to the structure of commercial education led to the creation of a Bachelors in Economics in 1931, which attracted a higher status than accounting. Bachelors in Accounting and Management appeared later, in 1945 and 1950 respectively (Saes & Cytrynowicz, 2001; Soares et al., 2011). The specialisations of accounting, management, and economics were a reflection of the favorable environment of the 1930s, in which the hegemony of the landed oligarchies tied to the agro-export model waned, and Brazil started to move towards industrial capitalism.

The third phase in the establishment of accounting pedagogy in Brazil was the creation of courses for graduates. Debates about the development of these courses began in 1961. The first Master's programmes in accounting appeared in the 1970s, one at the *Faculdade de Economia, Administração e Contabilidade da Universidade de São Paulo* and one at the *Fundação Getúlio Vargas*, Rio de Janeiro. While the *Fundação Getúlio Vargas* (EPGE-FGV) transferred its Master's in accounting to Rio de Janeiro University, and the University of São Paulo (USP) advanced as a centre for the diffusion of accounting within Brazil. USP played, and still plays, a key role in the institutionalisation of research on and teaching about accounting in Brazil. The 25 graduate programmes covering accounting in Brazil were largely influenced by USP (from these 25 programmes, 10 include PhD programmes). Their syllabi followed similar lines to USP's, focusing on accounting education, controllership and management accounting, accounting information and the financial and capital markets. Increasing pressures to adopt internationalisation in the last 10 years have, however, begun paving the way for the acceptance of other cultural and institutional influences.

Accounting research is, therefore, considered relatively new in Brazil. The first PhD programme was proposed in 1977 and approved in 1978 by the Federal Counsel of Education. At that time, members of the faculty were unfamiliar with the possibilities for conducting research in the field, highlighting the significance of the efforts of just a few professors to persuade the faculty to open a graduate course:

> [...] the dean himself said he could not approve, because after all graduate courses could only exist where there is a possibility of doing research, and accounting: "where and what do you have to research?" We had to hear that! We began, Professor Sérgio [*Sérgio de Iudícibus*] and I, to search for booklets of American [US] universities, which were the ones to which we had more access. We gathered a lot of booklets from renowned universities, who had PhD programmes. It was a process of personal persuasion of the

dean, to show him that there is indeed research in accounting, and that in Brazil practically nothing is done. It was very interesting to see within the University of São Paulo how unfamiliar people were with the field. So, [our] first try failed. The process only took on later, it was delayed three or four times, because we had to write to the universities asking for their booklets, which came by mail; then he [the dean] approved."

(Prof. Eliseu Martins in: Cunha, Jr. & Martins, p. 17,
translated from Portuguese)

The USP's first PhD programme centred on technical and normative improvements in accounting, which were much needed in that period. Accounting techniques were less developed then, and inflation was a central problem for government and companies. In addition, regulation (Law 6.404/76) introduced a new corporate accounting model and demanded from academics the translation of rules into something practitioners could use. This involved the institutionalisation of technical bulletins in companies. The principal concern of the PhD programme was to debate the technical and practical aspects of accounting. Professors and students decided together on a subject, e.g. standard costing, upon which the students would then develop a thesis. Discussions were based on accounting concepts and examples, which served to support the proposed thesis. Issues such as inflation accounting, assets evaluation, financial analysis and management and cost accounting techniques provoked great interest.

It is worth mentioning that, in the 1970s, Brazil was limited in its openness to the world; thus, many of the sources and materials shared by accounting and management professors originated in the US (Alcadipani & Bertero, 2012). For this reason, management accounting teaching and research focused on quantitative methods for cost analysis, relationships cost-volume-profit, standard costing, operating and capital budgets. During the 1980s, there was little increase in the number of graduate courses, but in the 1990s numbers in higher education soared. In 2007, there were 17 graduate programmes in accounting available throughout the country, although just one PhD programme. However, in management education there were approximately 100 graduate programmes in 2015.

This brief account reveals that an accounting pedagogy in Brazil co-evolved with the development of state institutions (see, for example, Hopper et al., 2009). However, since commercial activities were deemed less noble by Brazilian high society, the schools of commerce did not gain traction until the last quarter of the nineteenth century. In the early decades of the twentieth century, state-led development and industrialisation underpinned the specialisation of accounting education, and, more recently, the creation of graduate courses focused on deepening the understanding of accounting, which was closely connected with practical needs at that time. In the next section, we examine the social and political background from which the first controller positions emerged in Brazil, and explain how controllership was established as a discipline. The section also draws on empirical evidence from the past 10 years to outline the key functions of the controller in Brazil.

The role of the controller in Brazil

The first controller positions in Brazil appeared in the 1960s, due to growth in Brazilian industry (Siqueira & Soltelinho, 2001). Following a period of rising incomes, the industry came under the influence of, among other factors, greater access to credit and the process of import substitution (Furtado, 1972). Between 1947 and 1961, production more than tripled, only being interrupted by political instabilities that resulted in the coup of 1964. In the mid-1960s, capital market reform and tax, and banking reforms paved the way for another period of economic expansion. In this conducive environment, Brazilian academia signalled its interest in developing a 'new' professional role, that of the controller. Here one can identify two triggers that later defined controllership.

Initially scholars sought to define controllership by its functions within companies, and to investigate its connections with business performance (Kanitz, 1976; Nakagawa, 1978; Tung, 1974; Yoshitake, 1982). The definition and functions of controllership are debated until today (Borinelli, 2006; Lunkes, Schnorrenberger & Rosa, 2013; Lunkes, Schnorrenberger, Souza & Rosa, 2012), yet those first studies were important as they afforded legitimacy to controllership (e.g. Messner, Becker, Schäffer & Binder, 2008). Subsequently, another group of researchers, influenced by the *Modelo de Gestão Econômica-Gecon* (roughly: Economic Management System), established a particular orientation to controllership (Almeida, Parisi & Pereira, 2001; Moismann & Fisch, 1999; Peleias, 2002; Santos, 2005). Gecon is a performance management system, which was developed at the end of the 1970s by a USP professor, Armando Catelli. Taking as a basic premise companies strategic planning, Gecon's work concentrates on areas of responsibility when building performance indicators, to assess companies' economic performance. The discourse underpinning the Gecon approach helped shape controllership as a discipline overtly focused on the internal uses of accounting information (Borinelli, 2006), as many related text books underscore (Catelli, 2001; Figueiredo & Caggiano, 2004; Santos, 2005). Comparing Brazilian literature about controllership with German and US literature, Lunkes et al. (2009) defined Gecon as somewhere between operational and strategic approaches to controllership. This classification is, however, not rigid, as many of Gecon's affiliates (i.e. Mosimann & Fisch, 1999; Almeida, Parisi & Pereira, 2001; Peleias, 2002) have, in the words of Lunkes et al. (2009), "sympathies" with the literature that define controllership by its strategic role. The emphasis on the internal uses of accounting within controllership literature must nonetheless be counterbalanced by observations of what controllers do in practice. We next draw on empirical studies that address the role assigned to controllers in Brazil (Borinelli, 2006; Calijuri, 2004; Oro, Beuren & Carpes, 2013; Oro, Carpes, Dittadi & Benoit, 2007; Siqueira & Soltelinho, 2001).

Since the early controller positions of the 1960s (Siqueira & Soltelinho, 2001), the tasks assigned to them have become gradually more complex. During the 1960s, controllers' assignments consisted mostly of producing reports for the government and planning controls. In the 1980s, assignments became more diverse, extending to include the elaboration and interpretation of reports, tax management, performance assessments and evaluations (Siqueira & Soltelinho, 2001). It is important to mention here that between 1960 and 1994 Brazil faced high levels of inflation; in the 1960s and 1970s, Brazil's average rate of inflation rate was 40 per cent. In the 1980s and 1990s, the country faced hyper-inflation, with average rates of 330 (1980) to 764 per cent (1990 and 1994). During this period, management accounting practices had little impact on businesses, since prices changed on a daily basis and it was difficult to separate the effective performance of businesses from the effects of inflation. Hence, while on the one hand companies demanded management accounting reports to be adjusted according to inflation, on the other, the cost-benefits of maintaining complex systems hindered the spread of management accounting practices. The problem of inflation has also been embraced by academics who became interested in developing inflation accounting methods (Martins, Gelbcke, Santos & Iudícibus, 2013). Strongly influenced by the US model, regulation (Law 6.404 enacted in 1976) channelled academia's interests towards regulatory accounting, which concerned issues such as how to account for operations with inventory, and how to determine profits relative to the effects of inflation.

In the mid-1990s, companies increased their interest in management accounting, and the role of controller incorporated a strategic and managerial orientation. After implementation of an economic stabilisation plan in 1994, and with inflation under control, the government, entrepreneurs and sectors of the population came to understand that Brazilian companies were less competitive than their counterparts in developed countries (Coutinho & Ferraz, 1994; Silva & Melo, 2001). Using the so-called Asian Tigers as a benchmark, governmental agencies disseminated the idea of total quality systems. Despite cultural differences, adoption of total quality management (TQM) spurred companies to build performance indicators and cost design systems, underpinned not only by an interest in financial results, but also by concerns about other internal requirements. In the 2000s, tech companies contributed to this discourse by highlighting the importance of intangibles. Underpinned by the idea of innovation, the 'New Economy' – which rendered stronger the emphasis on the management of intangible assets, such as competitiveness, human resources, quality of services, goods, etc., fuelled the interests of companies, encouraging them to adopt broader systems of performance. TQM and innovation were, nonetheless, seeded in a terrain already prepared to receive such notions, as the government built on the public fear of a return to hyper-inflation, to propagate the new public management agenda throughout the country.

The new public management agenda paved the way for the emergence of management accounting practices, as state-led reforms promoted the dissemination of performance and accountability systems (Bresser-Pereira & Spink, 2006). Currently, new public management initiatives can be found at all levels of government. For example, the government promotes interest in cost management by granting awards to students and practitioners aimed at improving practices. The *Internal Revenue Service of Brazil* established best paper awards for students developing ideas on cost management. Similarly, this applies to management control instruments, such as participatory budgeting and indicators, both of which were awarded for practitioners and students. Finally, inspired by the experiences of New Zealand, England and Australia, the *Fiscal Responsibility Law* was an important innovation, establishing metrics and indicators for the management and control of public entities, and thereby increasing the responsibility of controllers employed in public organisations. Implemented in 2000, the *Fiscal Responsibility Law* was at the epicentre of the impeachment of former President Dilma Roussef, as the allegedly creative accounting practices committed under her government are expressly prohibited under this law.

During the last 10 years, therefore, there has been increasing interest among scholars in identifying the key functions and competencies of controllers in Brazil (Borinelli, 2006; Calijuri, Santos & Santos, 2005; Daniel, Vesco & Tarifa, 2006; Fachini, Beuren & Nascimento, 2009; Giongo & Nascimento, 2005; Lunkes, Machado, Rosa & Telles, 2011; Medeiros & Rabelo, 2010; Santos, 2008; Schnorrenberger, Ribeiro, Lunkes & Gasparetto, 2007). According to Lunkes et al. (2012) these studies have identified at least 10 key functions attributable to controllership: accounting, auditing, controlling, tax management, planning, elaboration and the interpretation of reports and internal control. In a detailed study of the practices of controllers in 88 of the 100 biggest companies in Brazil,[4] Borinelli (2006) found the majority of companies had a functional area termed controllership (77 per cent), and of these, most (72.06 per cent) take on management accounting roles. Typical designations for the person responsible for the controllership department are *Diretor de Controladoria* (Head of Controllership), *Gerente de Controladoria* (Controllership Management), Controller, *Controller Corporativo* (Corporate Controller) and *Superintendente de Controladoria* (Superintendent of Controllership). Controllers are typically aged between 36 and 50 years, with an average age of 43 years; 54.41 per cent have majors in Accounting and 27.94 per cent in Management. More than half hold MBAs in Business Management, Finance or Controllership.

Seeking to identify the requirements for hiring controllers, Oro et al. (see also Oro et al., 2013; 2007) surveyed 373 job announcements. They found 241 job offers for controllers related to operational level positions, 22 were for managerial positions and 110 were for strategic level positions. The majority of offers were located in the southeast of Brazil (90–95.45 per cent), which comprises the states of *Espírito Santo, Minas Gerais, Rio de Janeiro*, and *São Paulo*. With a population of circa 80 million inhabitants, the southeast is responsible for more than half of Brazil's GDP. Companies requiring controllers to work at operational level demand skills such as corporate accounting. Regarding financial accounting, the majority of job offers demand skills like closing accounts, accounting routines, knowledge of corporate practices and tax legislation. In the case of management accounting, announcements required operational knowledge of business analysis, followed by management and cost accounting; and mid and strategic levels requirements were directed towards planning and budgeting. The job announcements demanded few skills associated with using modern management accounting tools and techniques, such as Economic Value Added (EVA), Balanced Scorecard, Activity-based costing (ABC), board and management interface, tax planning and informational support. In terms of academic background, management and accounting were evenly distributed. The specifications also requested experience of 1–2 years for operational level, and 5–6 years for managerial and strategic levels.

In an additional study, sponsored by the *Associação Nacional dos Executivos de Finanças, Administração e Contabilidade* (ANEFAC),[5] Calijuri (2004) found 55.2 per cent of executives that returned the survey (29 of 350) were managers and 34.5 per cent were department heads (in Portuguese, *diretores*). In their assignments the controllers listed cost control and accounting closing processes (96.6 per cent), local management reports (93.1per cent), planning and budgeting control (89.7 per cent), tax planning and management systems (82.8 per cent), budgeting (75.9 per cent), feasibility studies for future investments (62.1 per cent), corporate restructuring (55.2 per cent), the creation of internal manuals (51.7 per cent), conversion to US GAAP (48.3 per cent), international management reporting, and relationships with customers, suppliers, government agencies (41.4 per cent) and internal audits (37.9 per cent).

In summary, the controller's role in Brazil is largely focused on budgeting and planning, managerial reports and taxation. The legitimacy of controllership as a practice, and of the controller as a profession, however, is still in the process of institutionalisation. Different from Anglophone countries, in which professional bodies play a key role in raising the value and importance of the management accountant profession (e.g. Willmott, 1986) or the efforts in German controllers towards such professionalisation (Schäffer, Schmidt & Strauss, 2014), in Brazil, the interests of controllers are mainly mediated by, and diluted by, the *Conselho Federal de Contabilidade-CFC* (Federal Accounting Council). In addition, while controllership is now included within the main conferences taking place in the country, such as the USP's Conference on Controllership and Accounting, the *Congresso Brasileiro de Custos*, the Anpcont and the EnANPAD, the number of publications on controllership remains meagre. Hence, the education and professionalisation of controllers in Brazil must still overcome some challenges, as the next section briefly outlines.

Challenges to the controller's education and profession in Brazil

Based on what has been presented, this section explores some challenges for the education and professionalisation of controllers working in Brazil. The challenges addressed in this section include the lack of professional bodies to represent the interests of controllers, the still incipient forums for debating the issues arising within the field, and the difficulties inhibiting knowledge transfer between academia and controllers' practice and training.

The history of accounting in Brazil reveals that accounting education originated in non-academic, technical courses, rather than in universities. Accounting pedagogy resulted from the needs of merchants, and later firms, to comply with tax and commercial law and to maintain companies' records. Technical courses focused on bookkeeping, which was made available to literate people with basic arithmetic skills, making them the first types of institutionalised training. The bookkeeper quoted in the Commercial Code (1850) was essentially responsible for recording accounting information, a practice largely oriented by the bureaucratic demands of legislation. The role of accounting as book-keeping defined the agendas of professional councils, which, continue to only debate management accounting from an academic perspective, focusing instead on accounting regulation and auditing, adherence to tax laws, rules on third-sector institutions and adherence to rules applying to the International Accounting Standard Board (IASB). There have therefore been few efforts, within these councils, to professionalise the controller role.

Hence, in this regard, debates regarding the practices of controllers suffer from councils' narrow agenda. One key limitation concerns their emphasis on regulatory issues. Since their creation, in the middle of the twentieth century, accounting councils have traditionally embraced themes such as financial accounting, taxation and external audits. In general, these matters depend largely on the definition of standards; such as accounting standards. The second limitation refers to councils' focus on tax accounting. Councils provide associates with information, which generally refers to taxation issues. This might relate to the complexity of Brazilian tax legislation, which demands companies expend considerable effort on its interpretation and follow-up. Accounting for taxes requires a significant amount of work in terms of the elaboration of reports and the implementation of controls required by the Brazilian tax authorities. Thus, compliance remains a primary task of controllers.

An attendant challenge, as mentioned above, is the still incipient forums for debating controllers' practice. Brazil recently created spaces for debate, but, similar to the Germanic process of institutionalisation, the controller profession still has little insertion. Recently, a group of professors have been organising meetings to debate the challenges encountered in management accounting as a field of practice and research in Brazil (Frezatti et al., 2015). In the long term, these initiatives might affect the professional development of controllers in Brazil. However, as this very group acknowledges, the gap between academia and practice is a key challenge, responsible for making management accounting more practice-oriented in Brazil. When seeking to establish the professionalisation and education of controllers, this gap tends to be a hindrance, as academic discussions have little influence on accounting councils and tends to minimise the collaboration between practitioners and academics.

Finally, an important challenge refers to how best to bridge discussions within academia and those about controllers' training and education. Issues addressed in conferences are rarely transferred to classrooms. In this regard, the specialisation of controllers has relied largely on the proliferation of MBAs. However, due to the lack of regulation regarding the controller profession, MBA syllabi do not adopt any specific content requirements. The establishment of such content would be relevant in attempts to institutionalise the profession, as the practices performed by the controller only share family resemblances with the different syllabi taught on MBAs.

Conclusion

This chapter has presented an account of the role of the controller in Brazil. Endowed with managerial responsibility, Brazilian controllers are responsible for performing management accounting functions. The social, economic and political contexts from which the controller emerged in Brazil were key to shaping controllership, as a discipline and field of practice. Meanwhile in the 1970s, high levels of inflation in Brazil played an important role in defining the interests of both academia and government regarding accounting, directing it towards finance accounting. The issue of inflation was used to propagate the new public management agenda within the country. As the first positions appeared in the country, around the 1960s, controller's assignments became gradually more complex, and today, studies have shown 10 key functions of the controller: accounting, auditing, controlling, tax management, planning, elaboration and interpretation of reports, and internal control. Some challenges currently associated with the professionalisation and education of controllers in Brazil are the lack of institutional support to represent the interests of controllers, insufficient cooperation between practitioners and academics to promote knowledge transfer and the difficulty translating academic discussions into practice.

Notes

1 The Society of Jesus, or the Jesuit order, is a Roman Catholic Order founded in Rome in 1540 by Ignatius of Loyola, which spread throughout Europe and the world. For a comprehensive account of the Jesuit's accounting practices see Quattrone, 2015.
2 Napoleon demanded Dom John adhere to the Continental blockade. However, because Portugal had a long-standing commercial relationship with England, he decided to adhere to the embargo but continue trading with England in secrecy. Napoleon discovered this betrayal, and invaded Portugal. On 29 November 1807, two days before the Napoleonic forces invaded Lisbon, the Portuguese royal family and the Royal Court departed for Brazil escorted by the English Royal Navy.
3 The opening up of ports was implemented by Royal Charter, dated 28 January 1808, and known as Decreto de Abertura dos Portos às Nações Amigas. In practice, however, British vessels and traders were its main beneficiaries.
4 Controlling interests of companies are concentrated in four countries: Brazil, US, Germany and France. Brazil corresponds to the biggest share.
5 ANEFAC is an association of executives of finance, management and accounting. In its home page it identifies itself like this:

> The association was founded in the same manner as the NAA U.S. to discuss issues that add value to the activity of individual members through technical lectures presented in English, about Comptroller, Public Accounting and Financial Management.

References

Alcadipani, R. & Bertero, C. O. (2012). Guerra fria e ensino do management no Brasil: o caso da FGV-EAESP. *RAE, 52*(3), 284–299.

Almeida, L. B., Parisi, C. & Pereira, C. A. (2001). Controladoria. In A. Catelli (Ed.), *Controladoria: Uma abordagem da Gestão Econômica – GECON* (2nd ed.). São Paulo: Atlas.

Bielinski, A. C. (2015). Educação profissional no século XIX: Curso comercial do Liceu de Artes e Ofícios, um estudo de caso. Retrieved from www.senac.br/BTS/263/boltec263e.htm.

Borinelli, M. L. (2006). *Estrutura conceitual básica de controladoria: Sistematização à luz da teoria e da práxis*. São Paulo: USP.

Bresser-Pereira, L. C. & Spink, P. (2006). *Reforma do Estado e Administração Pública Gerencial*. Rio de Janeiro: FGV.

Calijuri, M. S. A., Santos, N. M. B. F. & Santos, R. F. (2005). Perfil do controller no contexto organizacional atual brasileiro. Paper presented at the XII Congresso Brasileiro de Custos, Florianópolis.

Calijuri, M. S. S. (2004). Controller: O perfil atual e a necessidade do mercado de trabalho. *Revista Brasileira de Contabilidade 150*, 38–53.

Catelli, A. (2001). *Controladoria: Uma abordagem da gestão econômica* (2nd ed.). São Paulo: Atlas.

Chaves, C. M. d. G. (2008). As aulas de comércio no Império Luso-brasileiro: o ensino prático profissionalizante. In A. Doré & A. C. d. A. Santos (Eds.), *Temas setecentistas: Governo e populações no Império Portugês* (pp. 267–276). Curitiba: Fundação Araucária-UFPR.

Chaves, C. M. d. G. (2009). Arte dos negócios: Saberes, práticas e costumes mercantis no império Luso-brasileiro. *America Latina en la Historia Económica, 1*(31), 171–193.

Coutinho, L. & Ferraz, J. C. (1994). *Estudo da competitividade da indústria brasileira – ECIB*. Campinas: Papirus/Ed. Unicamp.

Cunha, J. V. A. d., Jr., E. B. C. & Martins, G. d. A. Pós-graduação: o curso de doutorado em ciências contábeis da FEA/USP. *Revista de Contabilidade e Finanças USP, 19*(48), 6–26.

Daniel, M. M., Vesco, D. G. D. & Tarifa, M. R. (2006). Estudo do perfil, conhecimento, papel e atuação do controller nas cooperativas agropecuárias do Estado do Paraná. Paper presented at the Congresso Brasileiro de Custos, Florianópolis.

Fachini, G. J., Beuren, I. M. & Nascimento, S. (2009). Evidências de isomorfismo nas funções da controladoria das empresas familiares têxteis de Santa Catarina. Paper presented at the XVI Congresso Internacional de Custos, Fortaleza: ABC.

Figueiredo, S. & Caggiano, P. C. (2004). *Controladoria: teoria e prática* (3rd ed.). São Paulo Atlas.

Frezatti, F., Aguiar, A. B. d., Wanderley, C. d. A. & Malagueno, R. (2015). A pesquisa em contabilidade gerencial no Brasil: Desenvolvimento, dificuldades e oportunidades. *Revista Universo Contábil, 11*(1), 47–68.

Furtado, C. (1972). *Análise do 'Modelo' Brasileiro*. Rio de Janeiro: Civilização Brasileira.

Giongo, J. & Nascimento, A. M. (2005). O envolvimento da controladoria no processo de gestão: Um estudo em indústrias do Estado do Rio Grande do Sul. Paper presented at the XII Congresso Brasileiro de Custos, Florianópolis: ABC.

Hopper, T., Tsamenyi, M., Uddin, S. & Wickramasinghe, D. (2009). Management accounting in less developed countries: What is known and needs knowing. *Accounting, Auditing and Accountability Journal, 22*(3), 469–514.

Kanitz, S. C. (1976). *Controladoria: Teoria e estudo de casos* (Vol. 1976). São Paulo: Pioneira.

Leite, C. E. B. (2005). *A evolução das ciências contábeis no Brasil*. Rio de Janeiro: FGV.

Lunkes, R. J., Machado, A. O., Rosa, F. S. & Telles, J. (2011). Funções da controladoria: Um estudo nas 100 maiores empresas do Estado de Santa Catarina. *Análise Psicológica, 2*(29), 345–361.

Lunkes, R. J., Schnorrenberger, D., Gasparetto, V. & Vicente, E. F. R. (2009). Considerações sobre as funções da controladoria nos Estados Unidos, Alemanha e Brasil. *Revista Universo Contábil, 5*(4), 63–75.

Lunkes, R. J., Schnorrenberger, D. & Rosa, F. S. d. (2013). Controllership functions: An analysis in the Brazilian scenario. *Review of Business Management, 15*(47), 283–299.

Lunkes, R. J., Schnorrenberger, D., Souza, C. M. d. & Rosa, F. S. d. (2012). Análise da legitimidade sociopolítica e cognitiva da controladoria no Brasil. *Revista de Contabilidade e Finanças, 23*(59), 89–101.

Martins, E., Gelbcke, E. R., Santos, A. & Iudícibus, S. (2013). *Manual de Contabilidade Societária: Aplicável a todas as Sociedades de Acordo com as Normas Internacionais e do CPC*. São Paulo: Atlas.

Medeiros, C. S. C. & Rabelo, E. C. (2010). O perfil da controladoria em concessionárias de veículos do município de Tubarão (SC). Paper presented at the XVII Congresso Brasileiro de Custos, Belo Horizonte: ABC.

Messner, M., Becker, A., Schäffer, U. & Binder, C. (2008). Legitimacy and identity in germanic management accounting research. *European Accounting Review, 17*(1), 129–159.

Moismann, C. P. & Fisch, S. (1999). *Controladoria* (2nd ed.). São Paulo: Atlas.

Nakagawa, M. (1978). Estudo de alguns aspectos de controladoria que contribuem para a eficácia gerencial. Ph.D, USP, São Paulo.

Oro, I. M., Beuren, I. M. & Carpes, A. M. d. S. (2013). Competências e habilidades exigidas do controller e a proposição para sua formação acadêmica. *Revista Contabilidade Vista e Revista, 24*(1), 15–36.

Oro, I. M., Carpes, A. M. d. S., Dittadi, J. R. & Benoit, A. D. (2007). O perfil do profissional de controladoria sob a ótica do mercado de trabalho brasileiro. Paper presented at the Congresso USP de Controladoria e Contabilidade, São Paulo.

Peleias, I. R. (2002). Controladoria: gestão eficaz utilizando padrões. São Paulo: Sariava.

Peleias, I. R. & Bacci, J. (2004). Pequena cronologia do desenvolvimento contábil no Brasil: Os primeiros pensadores, a padronização contábil e os congressos brasileiros de contabilidade. *Revista Administração On Line – Fecap, 5*(3), 39–54.

Quattrone, P. (2015). Governing social orders, unfolding rationality, and Jesuit accounting practices: a procedural approach to institutional logics. *Administrative Science Quarterly, 60*(3), 411–445.

Rodrigues, L. L., Gomes, D. & Craig, R. (2004). The Portuguese School of Commerce, 1759–1844: A reflection of the "Enlightenment". *Accounting History, 9*(3), 53–71.

Saes, F. A. M. d. & Cytrynowicz, R. (2001). O ensino comercial na origem dos cursos superiores de economia, contabilidade e administração. *Revista Álvares Penteado, 3*(6), 37–59.

Santos, R. V. (2005). *Controladoria: uma introdução ao sistema de gestão econômica*. São Paulo: Saraiva.

Santos, S. (2008). A controladoria como suporte ao processo de gestão das grandes empresas do estado do Ceará: Um estudo em empresas ganhadoras do prêmio Delmiro GOuveia. Paper presented at the XV Congresso Internacional de Custos, Curitiba.

Schäffer, U., Schmidt, A. & Strauss, E. (2014). An old boys' club on the threshold to becoming a professional association: The emergence and development of the association of German controllers from 1975 to 1989. *Accounting History, 19*(1–2), 133–169.

Schnorrenberger, D., Ribeiro, L. M. S., Lunkes, R. J. & Gasparetto, V. (2007). Perfil do controller em empresas de médio e grande porte da grande Florianópolis. Paper presented at the XIV Congresso Brasileiro de Custos, João Pessoa: ABC.

Silva, C. & Melo, L. (2001). *Ciência, tecnologia e inovação: Desafio para a sociedade brasileira – Livro Verde.* Brasília: Ministério da Ciência e Tecnologia & Academia Brasileira de Ciências.

Siqueira, J. R. M. d. & Soltelinho, W. (2001). O profissional de controladoria no mercado Brasileiro: Do surgimento da profissão aos dias atuais. *Revista de Contabilidade e Finanças, 16*(27), 66–77.

Soares, S. V., Richartz, F., Voss, B. d. L. & Freitas, C. L. d. (2011). Evolução do currículo de contabilidade no Brasil desde 1809. *Revista Catarinense da Ciência Contábil, 10*(30), 27–42.

Tung, N. H. (1974). *Controladoria financeira das empresas: uma abordagem prática.* São Paulo: USP.

Willmott, H. (1986). Organising the profession: A theoretical and historical examination of the development of the major accountancy bodies in the U.K. *Accounting, Organizations and Society, 11*(6), 555–580.

Yoshitake, M. (1982). Funções do controller: conceitos e aplicações de controle gerencial. Dissertação (Mestrado em Ciências Contábeis). Departamento de Contabilidade e Atuária-USP, São Paulo.

3 The evolution of management accounting in Canada

Sophie Tessier and Samuel Sponem

Introduction

The timing of this book, and particularly this chapter is very *apropos*. Indeed, the year 2013 marked the end of the 93-year timeline of CMAs in Canada following the merger of the three main Canadian accounting associations (CA, CMA and CGA) into a single association (CPA),[1] thus ending one chapter of the Canadian management accounting history and starting a new one.

Why mention professional bodies regulating accounting in a chapter on management accountants? In Canada, as opposed to many European countries, management accounting is organised as a profession and most management accountants hold a professional designation (Caron et al., 2011). Thus, reviewing the historical development of management accounting in Canada implies reviewing the history of accounting organisations and understanding how these organisations were successful in establishing jurisdiction over management accounting practices.

Each country having its own specificity, it is also important to explain the Canadian context. Canada has 11 jurisdictions of government authority: the federal jurisdiction and ten provincial jurisdictions. Professions (designations and practice rights) and education fall under provincial jurisdiction. As a result, the development of the management accounting profession has evolved differently, to some extent, in each province. Generally speaking, the provincial associations deliver services to and collect revenues from members, while the national association provides coordination and joint services (Richardson & Kilfoyle, 2012). Similarly, accounting education, including management accounting education, has developed differently in the provinces (Richardson, 1992). Hence, national and provincial developments of the profession, as well as professional and educational developments, are intertwined and reflect the changing role of management accountants throughout the last 100 years or so.

The remainder of the chapter is organised as follows. First, the historical development of management accounting profession in Canada is presented. This section provides the development of the profession in terms of status of management accountants, their education and their roles. It is based on a review of public documents, books and articles as well as informal discussions with actors of this development. Second, the state of the profession today is explored in more detail. This section is based on round tables exploring the roles of Canadian financial directors as well as prior literature. The last section offers concluding remarks.

Management accounting in Canada: the making of a profession

The development of the management accounting profession in Canada can be regrouped into five stages: emergence, professionalisation, expansion, legitimisation and rationalisation. These stages represent the 93-year timeline of management accounting as a separate profession as well as the impact the merger had on management accounting.

The emergence of management accounting: moving away from public accounting

The last decades of the nineteenth and first decades of the twentieth century saw the professional emergence of financial accounting with the incorporation of provincial associations and, ultimately, the incorporation of the Dominion Association of Chartered Accountants (DACA) at the national level in 1902 – later renamed the Canadian Institute of Chartered Accountants (CICA) (Murphy, 1986). These newly created associations and institutes had the power to grant the CA designation and focused on the practice of public accounting. Apprenticeships and examinations were based on teaching and testing knowledge of auditing and financial reporting (Richardson & Kilfoyle, 2012). However, very early on, accountants working within organisations wanted "professional training and recognition but without the necessity of articling with a public accounting firm" (Richardson & Kilfoyle, 2012, p. 86).

As early as 1908, a competing association was founded in Montreal, that of the Certified General Accountants (CGA) (Murphy, 1986) with the intended goal to meet this need. CAs saw this new organisation as a direct competitor and a strategic threat (Richardson & Kilfoyle, 2012). Moreover, although CGAs were moving away from public accounting, there was still no accounting organisation specifically overlooking cost accounting. Eight men, CAs from across the country, sought to cater to the specific needs of industrial accountants working in the manufacturing sector by creating in 1920 the Canadian Society of Cost Accountants (CSCA), referred to as "the Society" by its members[2] (Law, 2013). Although the Society was independent from the DACA (Allan, 1982), it had its unofficial blessing (Law, 2013). This organisation did not have the power to hold examinations or establish a designation. Rather, it was "a mechanism to allow cost accountants to share information and improve their craft", without becoming a rival to the CA designation (Richardson, 2000, p. 112).

As the name of the Society suggests, the main concern of industrial accountants was cost accounting. Increased scrutiny over profits of industrial companies, by both the government buying their goods and employees working for them, made cost accounting a popular discipline worthy of its own organisation (Murphy, 1993). The close link with the industry was highlighted by the location of the Society's headquarters itself. Indeed, in 1937, the Society's headquarters were moved from Toronto to Hamilton (Law, 2013), which was an important centre of manufacturing activities. The Society was also concerned with more general topics such as industrial organisation and accounting systems. Hence, according to Georges Edwards, the Society's first president, the Society would "[open] up a field of legitimate endeavor not hitherto covered by either the Chartered Societies or the various existing media for the preparation of young men for industrial pursuits" (Allan, 1982, p. 6).

From the beginning, the Society was concerned with educative objectives. Upon its creation in 1920, the CSCA stated that one of its goal was "to establish and conduct classes, lectures, bulletins, correspondence courses, and other instructional means" (Allan, 1982, p. 7). One of the pedagogical methods it implemented was its *Cost and Management* journal, which was launched in 1926 (Murphy, 1986). During the same period, universities were introducing industrial accounting courses. For example, in 1922, HEC Montréal introduced its first course entirely dedicated to industrial accounting in its commercial licence curriculum. The course covered topics such as cost accounting (raw material, labour and general expenses).[3] A cost accounting course was also added to the Bachelor of Commerce programme at the University of Toronto.[4]

It was in 1927, however, that an official base of knowledge, required for accessing the management accounting profession, saw the light of day when the CSCA adopted the Cost Accounting and Factory Organization examination programme, which led to a Certificate of Efficiency (Allan, 1982, p. 23). The CSCA reached an agreement with McGill University to offer courses allowing students to take these examinations (Cost and Management, 1929, p. 32). This certificate was a first step towards professionalisation.

The professionalisation of management accounting

The birth of the CSCA was a response to "a market demand for professional representation (i.e. an association), and for continuing professional development opportunities" for industrial accountants (Richardson & Kilfoyle, 2012, p. 87). However, at the time, management accounting was not yet a profession. Indeed, the CSCA did not grant any official designation. Moreover, the boundaries between cost accounting and engineering were still not well defined. For example, in 1930, the national Society was renamed the Canadian Society of Cost Accountants and Industrial Engineers (Law, 2013). As White (1930, p. 208) explains in regards to the US context, "since the advent of so-called scientific management, debits and credits have been called upon to an increasingly great extent to furnish facts upon which the decisions of modern industry are made". Hence, he adds, engineers, who were often senior managers, had to familiarise themselves with cost accounting as they were users of this information.

It was not until early 1940s that management accounting became a formal profession. Some people opposed this movement as they feared that professionalisation would move the focus from cost accounting and management to exam preparation (Law, 2013). Specifically, those opposing the professionalisation, who were mostly from Montreal, argued that the Society would shift its focus on candidates occupying lower hierarchical levels, who produced accounting information, as opposed to managers, who used and interpreted this information. Accordingly, these members believed the Society should focus more on management issues (Allan, 1982). The Society nevertheless received designation-granting power in Ontario (Registered Industrial and Cost Accountant, RIA) and in Québec (Licentiate of the Cost and Management Institute, LCMI). Other provinces followed which led to an increase interest in the profession. Although different provincial bodies adopted different names, a clear focus on management accounting emerged. This designation could be granted to members with many years of experience in cost accounting. It could also be granted to members of other accounting associations or to industrial engineers with experience in their field (Richardson, 2002). This inclusive strategy "reflects an attempt to co-opt members of the other professions and thereby gain jurisdiction over the work that they perform" (Richardson, 2002, p. 106). Finally, this inclusive strategy worked, jurisdiction contests between engineers and management accountants were resolved resulting in management accountants being responsible for costing and performance evaluation (Richardson & Kilfoyle, 2012).

The professionalisation of management accounting had a deep impact on the number of members, i.e. it more than doubled between 1938 and 1942, while it had remained stable between 1925 and 1938 notwithstanding some yearly fluctuations (see Table 3.1).

In parallel to this development, efforts were made to expand the offer in regards to education. Indeed, at that time, Montreal was the only city where university courses preparing for the examination were given (Allan, 1982). Thus, these courses started to be offered as evening courses at the McMaster University, in Hamilton were the Society had its headquarters. Topics included book-keeping, accounting, cost accounting, industrial organisation and management,

Table 3.1 Number of members (Ontario and Québec)

Year	Number of members
1925	354
1927	244
1930	359
1932	427
1934	327
1937	266
1938	363
1942	760

Source: Allan (1982).

advanced cost accounting, industrial law and a thesis in cost accounting (Allan, 1982). To reach even more candidates, the CSCA introduced in 1943 correspondence courses (Law, 2013), developed by universities. These courses would prove to be particularly important for smaller provinces, since access to universities was more difficult in these smaller provinces.

With the creation of provincial sections in Alberta (1943) and British Columbia (1945), the national organisation started to reflect the political landscape of the country: a federation of autonomous provincial organisations (Côté, 1992). More than a simple coordination mechanism, the CSCA played a role in the setting up of other provincial societies (Manitoba (1947), Saskatchewan (1948), New-Brunswick (1950) and Nova-Scotia (1950)), by providing administrative support, especially in the smaller provinces. However, one of its biggest role was the standardisation of education and examination. To achieve this, a national committee was created in mid-1940s and was constituted of members of different provincial societies. For the first time, a national view was taken which led to all correspondence courses being revised in 1946. These would continue to be revised every three years afterwards. The Society of Ontario supervised the creation of these courses and in the end provided teaching notes for all the different teaching centres across the country, thus assuring uniformity (Allan, 1982). As a result, the national Society standardised across the country the content of its previously provincial examinations (Richardson, 1992).

To reflect this search for uniformity, a standardised name was also adopted. In 1947, the national organisation was renamed the Society of Cost and Industrial Accountants in Canada (SCIAC) (Law, 2013), abandoning the word "engineer" from its denomination. Provincial organisations were asked to replicate this name by replacing "Canada" with their own provinces' names (Allan, 1982).

Expanding the roles of management accountants

To ensure the advancement of the profession, the national Society gave itself the mandate to innovate. At the beginning of the 1950s, the Society introduced managerial statistics and report drafting courses. It also revised its final cost accounting course to emphasise cost control, budgetary analysis, forecasts and the break-even analysis. During this period, 22 universities and colleges offered courses leading to the title issued by the SCIAC (Allan, 1982). To prepare for their examination, candidates could either enrol in a university and follow lectures in accounting or register to the correspondence courses.

The pedagogical materials developed in the field of management accounting, however, remained inferior to that developed in the field of financial accounting and auditing. This may be explained by the fact that "[m]anagement accounting is a staff position within organizations and, consequently, does not generate funds for its own use. In addition, it is regarded as a 'private good' that benefits only the firm in which it is used" (Richardson, 2002, p. 111). Nevertheless, in the next two decades, the body of knowledge in management accounting and the roles of management accountants would greatly expand.

During the 1960s and 1970s, the Society repositioned the profession to reflect the changing reality of cost accountants (Law, 2013). Indeed, cost accountants expanded their presence beyond industrial cost accountant. The Canadian economy was diversifying itself and becoming more service oriented. Management accountants thus moved away from the manufacturing sector to embrace this new sector of the economy. In early 1960s, 60 per cent of members of the Society were from the manufacturing sector. However, by early 1970s, this percentage had dropped to 40 per cent. Moreover, the proportion of members working in the public sector rose to 25 per cent (Allan, 1982). Accordingly, management accountants also diversified their roles. Following global trends in the field, there was a decline in the development of cost accounting, while operations research techniques, capital budgeting, electronic data processing and simulation methods for budgeting were introduced, in addition to cost-volume analysis which had gained in popularity in the 1950s (Mattessich, 1984). Moreover, management practices, behavioural sciences, communication skills, business law and information systems were now considered as important as accounting techniques (Allan, 1982).

To further fulfil its mandate to innovate, and to respond to members' request for more guidance on management accounting, the Society established a committee whose role was to provide its members with Management Accounting Guidelines (MAGs) and Management Accounting Practices (MAPs). The objective was to create a body of knowledge useful in the management of organisations. Four subcommittees were created: management accounting, financial accounting, legislative issues and thematic studies (Allan, 1982). The research mandate of the Society led to special studies such as capital expenditure appraisal (Special Study #1) or the impact of computers on accountants (Special Study #6). Other research projects included a project on the nature and scope of accounting published in 1968 and a project by Henry Mintzberg on the use of data in decision making jointly sponsored by the Society and the US National Association of Accountants (Mintzberg, 1975). According to Law (2013, p. 26), "continuous research helped the Society keep pace with leading-edge businesses".

During the same period, university education evolved to reflect the development of the profession: teaching focused on using costs to make decisions. These developments were supported essentially by American textbooks adapted to the Canadian context, which are still used today, at least in English-speaking universities (Beaulieu & Lakra, 2005). As Beechy (1980, p. 73) explains:

> The 1962 publication of Horngren's work on cost accounting had a rapid and far-reaching impact on the teaching of management accounting in introductory courses. Students no longer spent the first trimester studying job order costing or process costing in detail. [...] Studying the costs required for decision-making was of the utmost importance in most courses, while the study of processes was delayed until the second course or to the second half of the courses.[5]

In parallel, the two other Canadian accounting associations (CA and CGA) also integrated elements of management accounting into their programmes. At the end of the 1970s, 21,240 students were enrolled in introductory or advanced management accounting courses in Canadian universities (Beechy, 1980).

In search of relevance and legitimacy

In the 1970s, the Society started to reflect on the name of the Society. First, it was believed that, in light of the new extended roles of industrial accountants, the name no longer represented what the members were doing and therefore, that it was no longer relevant. Indeed, by 1975, only 10 per cent of RIA were directly associated with cost accounting.[6] Hence, the word "Industrial", included in the name of the society and the designation of its member, was too restrictive. In addition, issues with the bilingualism of the name surfaced, with the designation not being translatable in French (Allan, 1982). Finally, the term "management accounting" was gaining popularity in the UK and the USA, as well as in universities in Canada. Hence, the Society changed its name to the Society of Certified Management Accountants of Canada (SMAC), and changed the designation to CMAs. This had the advantage of standardising the name of the Society and using the same acronym in both official languages (in French: Société des Comptables en Management Accrédités du Canada, CMA). Accordingly, it also changed the name of its journal *Cost and Management* to *CMA Magazine*, which would later be changed again to *CMA Management* in 1995 (Richardson, 2002).

This, however, was more than a simple name change. It was the promotion of a new field of expertise, that of management accounting, a profession that provided the wisdom of accountants with the audacity of managers.[7] What followed was an intense communication strategy to increase the popularity of CMA, joined by a search for legitimacy through education. Underlying this communication campaign and the increased requirement for education was a latent threat: that of a merger between the different Canadian accounting associations (CA, CGA, CMA). The idea of a merger was not new, with discussion between the different associations in the 1960s and 1970s (Allan, 1982). Being the smallest of the three associations, the Society would not have a lot of negotiation power in the advent of a merger. Therefore, the underlying strategy was to increase credibility and notoriety in anticipation of a merger.

In regards to the communication strategy, it was important to break the image of "cost accountants". This was particularly true in Québec, where the provincial organisation actively promoted the new CMAs as part of a movement called the "Emergence of Quebec Inc." (Normand, 2013). For example, the Society sponsored a book called "Les guerriers de l'émergence" [Warriors of Emergence], in which the CEO of CMA Québec promoted the new management accountant.

The new values promoted by the phenomenon of emergence[8] in Quebec and more particularly by the strategists of this emergence are those corresponding to the mission of the professional corporation of CMAs, a mission first

and foremost focused on pre-eminence in the field of management accounting in Quebec.

True managers, CMA professionals are at the heart of the action and
decision-making in the most diverse organisations. They are part of this
generation, of these actors of the emergence that make things happen. In
addition to the traditional skills of accounting, we recognize this new class
of professional the flair and skill of the manager. That's why the work of
CMAs fits right inside of this emerging phenomenon that is currently experiencing Quebec.

(Renauld, 1986, pp. 18–19)[9]

This attempt to change the image of the Society was supported by an innovative
advertisement campaign. Slogans such as *Pour changer l'ordre des choses*
(1988) (which can be translated as "To change the order of things", a pun in
French with the word *ordre* which is also another word used for Society, i.e.
Ordre des CMA) and *Le M fait toute la différence* (1990) (which can be translated as "The M makes all the difference", meaning that management skills is
what makes the difference between CAs and CMAs). Visuals were also used to
sell the added-value of CMAs. For example, CAs were portrayed as a single
pencil whereas CMAs were portrayed as set of coloured pencils. The aim was to
associate CMAs with decision making and to introduce the notion of business
partners. In order word, CMAs were bilingual: they could talk accounting as
well as management.[10] This proactive strategy was pursued during the 1990s and
2000s. Bob Dye, the president and CFO of CMA Canada stated at the end of his
term in 2006 that "Our critical success factors – from which we have derived our
strategic intent – are market relevance, marketplace recognition, product differentiation, member competence, quality growth, and operational excellence"
(Fletcher, 2003, p. 18). To fulfill this new strategy, it was important to stop training RIA and start training CMAs.[11] Hence, in the 1980s, the Society increased
the development of its members' decision-making skills by including into their
training programmes skills such as team building, leadership, presentation and
communication (Law, 2013). Furthermore, it increased requirements leading to
the CMA designation to improve the credibility of the profession.

The teaching of accounting in Canada has always been characterised by a
"host of educational programs including professional courses, university and
community college programs, correspondence schools and in-house training programs of accounting firms" (Richardson, 1992, p. 263). However, university
education did become increasingly prevalent during the second part of the twentieth century: "the education of accountants evolved from a system of apprenticeships and ad hoc proprietary instruction to an emphasis on university-based
training supplemented by a period of practical experience" (Richardson, 1992,
p. 264). In addition to changing the focus of education, it was important to
increase the credibility of the CMAs designation. For professional associations,
university education was both a source of legitimacy and a means of regulating
access to the profession (Richardson, 1987). It was therefore a major element of

their strategy, and it garnered much attention. Since the Society was the only accounting association that did not require a university degree to obtain the designation, it faced legitimacy issues. Therefore, by the end of the 1980s, the Society made enrolment in its professional programme conditional upon holding a university degree, as had Certified General Accountants (CGA) and Chartered Accountants (CA) (Richardson, 1992). In fact, during this period, the CMA designation evolved from being the one with the least training to the one requiring the most training, since it was the only one that required additional training after completion of an undergraduate degree, a requirement that was eventually copied by the other two associations.[12] The Society also introduced the executive programme designed for managers with professional experience. In partnership with universities, managers could combine an MBA programme with the CMA designation.

Generally speaking, the Society's goal was to develop professional skills through a mix of university training, professional learning, and practical experience. To achieve this, in the mid-1990s, the SMAC began to develop a skills-based learning approach (Boritz & Carnaghan, 2003) based on a competency framework. The CMA competency framework identified 346 skills-related outcomes (Morpurgo, 2015). It was based on three pillars: strategy, accounting and management (Society of Management Accountants of Canada, 2011). The framework identified functional skills (the hard cognitive skills professionals draw upon to do the work required of them) and enabling skills (the softer skills that are required to determine which functional skills and tools should be employed to perform certain tasks, make decisions, lead, communicate and exercise professional and ethical judgement) (SMAC, 2011).

As of 1983, formal education was supported by the publication of MAGs and MAPs based on the various research projects (Cost and Management, 1982) on topics as diverse as the estimation of cash flows for capital expenditure decisions, a framework for internal control, the management of the annual financial statements audit, the strategic schedule for information resource management, the preparation of annual reports (Chlala & Girard, 1993), the implementation of benchmarking, the development of comprehensive performance indicators and the design of the finance function. Forty-six MAGs were published between 1983 and 1998 (Sturge, 1998).

Derrick Sturge, the chair of the board of directors of the SMAC was proud that CMAs were leaders in regards to these guidelines as illustrated by the fact that the Financial and Management Accounting Committee (FMAC) of the International Federation of Accountants (IFAC) used them to draft a new statement of management accounting concepts based on best international practice (Sturge, 1997). Getting recognition on the international scene was part of the Society's international objectives. Indeed, the Society wanted

> to build acceptance for the expanded profile of management accounting as it is practised in Canada, to reinforce the profile of the Society as a standard setter in this sphere of the profession, to establish management accounting

as a distinct and equal branch of the profession along with the field of independent assurance services.

(Stuart, 1997, p. 5)

In addition, the Society published 18 Management Accounting Standard (MASs) in 1998 (Sturge, 1998). While the guidelines looked "at a management accounting issue from a strategic and management perspective" the MASs focused "on narrowly defined topics within three overarching categories – cost finding, cost using, and strategic management control" (CMA Management, 2005). In 2005, the SMAC had a library of 61 MAGs and 50 MASs. The word "standard" would later be abandoned, however, as the Trustees of the Society expressed some concern over this term, considering that the "word standards tends to be misleading to the marketplace, with the connotation of mandated 'standards', whereas these documents in fact aim to be best practices" (Benn, 2007, p. 18).

All these initiatives paid off. Between 1984 and 2012, membership increased from 2,096 members (La Corporation Professionelle des Comptables en Administration Industrielle du Québec, 1984) to 8,180 members (L'Ordre des CMA du Québec, 2012), in Québec alone. In Canada, membership doubled between 1982 and 1992 to reach 23,000 members (Diebel, 1992). In fact, during these years, the Society's growth rate was higher than CAs and CGAs combined.

Rationalising the profession: management accounting and public accounting reunited

As mentioned above, this "golden age" of CMAs was done in conjunction with constant talks of a potential merger. Indeed, negotiation between the three Canadian organisations occurred but failed in 1983–84, 1987–88, 1995–96 and 2004 (Richardson & Jones, 2007). However, by 2010–11, negotiation resumed and succeeded provincially first, and then nationally in 2013.

Several factors contributed to the creation of CPA Canada. First, the differences between the three designations had slowly disappeared (Richardson & Kilfoyle, 2012). According to Caron (2003), there were not really any differences between the three designations when working in organisations. The real distinction was between accountants working in audit firms and accountants working in organisations, notwithstanding their designation (Caron, 2003). On the one hand, CAs increasingly worked outside of public accounting (from 56 per cent in 1991 according to Côté (1992) to 63 per cent in 2009 according to CMA Québec (2009)). On the other hand, while very few CMAs worked in audit firms (only 6 per cent in 2009, (CMA Québec, 2009)), which still reflected the initial *raison d'être* of CMAs, with time, both CMAs and CGAs developed an interest for public accounting (Richardson, 1987). As a result, by the early 2010s, both CMAs and CGAs had obtained the right to practise public accounting (Richardson & Kilfoyle, 2012). A second reason in favour of the merger was that the three Canadian societies needed to regroup to compete against international accounting bodies (Richardson & Kilfoyle, 2012). Finally, the societies felt they needed to be proactive to avoid a government-imposed reform (Richardson & Kilfoyle, 2012), accounting being one of the only professions overseen by more than one association.

After the merger of the three accounting professions, a new competency framework was developed. The CPA framework, which is the one still used today, combines aspects of the CMA, CGA and CA programmes (Morpurgo, 2015). In a similar way to the CMA framework, it distinguishes between technical competencies and enabling competencies (Chartered Professional Accountants Canada, 2012). Core and Elective modules replace the "Strategic Leadership Program" from the CMA programme. The new CPA Professional Education Program (CPA PEP) includes an optional elective module, called "Performance Management" that prepares candidates to management accounting positions. A Capstone module emphasises enabling competencies and includes a team-based written case and board presentation, heavily influenced by the legacy of the CMA programme. The entire CPA certification programme culminates in a multi-day national Common Final Examination, which is a carry-over from the legacy of the CA programme. This new CPA programme seems to be more directed towards younger, inexperienced university undergraduates and MBA/MPacc/MAcc graduates than the previous CMA programme (Morpurgo, 2015).

The Canadian accountant within the organisation

The Canadian accountant can take two paths to reach an organisation. As mentioned above, CPAs starting their career in audit firms often move on to a career within organisations. They thus "opt out" of the practice of external auditing (Caron, 2003). Other CPAs begin their careers directly in an organisation where they often move from a controller position to positions of Chief Accountant or Director of Finance. It is also not rare for accounting professionals to expand their skills beyond accounting and end up in more operational functions (Caron, 2005). Generally speaking, the holder of an accounting designation enjoys strong legitimacy in the Canadian organisations. S/he often sees himself/herself as an actor who "knows more than others" and who can impose her/her knowledge on other organisational actors (Caron, 2003). In addition, accounting technique is seen as a prerequisite to which many accountants do not want to be limited. The knowledge of the business and the development of interpersonal skills are often considered by accountants as essential to the success of their mission (ibid.).

It is worth mentioning that in Canada, the "management accounting" functions are performed under various names. In fact, the designation of "management accounting" per se is quite rare and the one performing the functions of management accounting is more commonly called "a controller". In a study investigating 90 Canadian accountants performing the functions of a controller, five different designations were used to describe this position: "controller", "business manager", "chief accountant", "vice president finance" and "analyst" (Caron, Boisvert & Mersereau, 2011). Caron et al. (2011) show that the controllers they investigated divide their time between six main activities: preparing and disclosing financial statements; ensuring the integrity of the organisation; managing financial resources; analysing and making business recommendations; managing the organisation's performance; and performing transactional or technical activities. Depending on the accountant's profile, managing the organisation's performance, which is the heart of the management accounting trade, occupies between 5 and 25 per cent of the respondents' time. More recently, interviews with CFOs investigating the activities included in their agendas have shown that even at the CFO level, activities associated with management accounting (cost calculation, scorecards and budgeting in particular) represent a substantial part of their role: between 15 and 35 per cent of their time (Jerman & Sponem, 2016).

Concluding comments

During the twentieth century, the SMAC and its predecessors played a key role for the development of the management accounting profession in Canada. Indeed, it standardised and elevated requirements for education, it supported ground-breaking research on management accounting techniques, it published articles in its journal, it provided MAGs and MAPs for its members, etc. All these initiatives paid off and the membership of the Society grew quickly from the 1970s to the beginning of the twenty-first century.

The competition and the diversity of accounting professions in Canada seemed to have cultivated the vitality and the legitimacy of the profession. From the 1980s to the 2000s, the accounting profession and the teaching of accounting was in crisis in the United States (Accounting Education Change Commission and American Accounting Association, 1990; Johnson & Kaplan, 1987). A report from the American Accounting Association expressed worries that the number and quality of students majoring in accounting had been decreasing rapidly, that the students did not perceive an accounting degree to hold the same value it once had, and that both practicing accountants and accounting educators would not major in accounting if pursuing their education today (Albrecht & Sack, 2000). Technological changes, globalisation of business and the increasing power of institutional investors to demand more comprehensive disclosures explained this lack of relevance (Albrecht & Sack, 2000; Johnson & Kaplan, 1987). On the other hand, in Canada, the accounting profession was not affected as much with this crisis since it was able to adapt. Indeed, as explained by William Langdon, who was the Society senior's staff in the 1980s:

> the presence of smaller and thus relatively more agile professional accounting bodies in Canada has meant that the linkages between the identification of customer expectations, the accreditation of accounting professionals, and the content of university accounting curricula are shorter and more responsive. Therefore, the entire chain in Canada from employers to students appears to be more agile at adjusting to changing employer expectations than that found in the United States.
>
> (Langdon, 2002, p. 97)

Although CMAs no longer exist as a separate profession, the push for accountants to become business partners has made its way to the CPA designation. Indeed, a recent article entitled "the Ideal Candidate" (Stefanac, 2016), emphasises the need for future accountants to make decisions, act ethically, have strong communication skills, adapt to change rapidly and be a team player, in addition to having the required technical skills. However, what remains to be seen is whether the innovativeness, pushed by the management accounting Society throughout the twentieth century, which ensured the development of the field, will still be nurtured by CPA Canada.

Notes

1 CMA: Certified Management Accountants; CA: Chartered Accountants; CGA Certified General Accountants; CPA: Chartered Professional Accountants.
2 While the name of the Society has changed throughout the twentieth century, the reference to "the Society" has remained.
3 Annuaire HEC Montréal, 1921–22, HEC Montréal, Fonds du Directorat, A007/ W1,0009.
4 Faculty of Arts and Sciences Calendar, 1921–22, University of Toronto, p. 212, internet archive https://archive.org/details/uoftartsciencecal1921.
5 Our translation.
6 Interview with François Renauld, former CEO of CMA Québec.
7 Ibid.
8 In the original quote, in French, the word "emergence" is used as a noun. The "phenomenon of emergence" is described as a period in Quebec's history characterised by Quebecers becoming more aware of the business world.
9 Our translation.
10 Interview with François Renauld, former CEO of CMA Québec.
11 Ibid.
12 It is worth pointing out that the relationships between universities and the various Canadian accounting associations were complex. In theory, there was no direct link between the associations and the universities, yet the Canadian accounting organisations reviewed and evaluated different university courses that could be credited towards the designation requirements (Etherington & Richardson, 1994). Therefore, the associations and the universities competed with each other to benefit from each other's prestige.

References

Accounting Education Change Commission & American Accounting Association. (1990). *Position Statement Number One. Objectives of Education for Accountants* (Accounting Education Series No. 13) (pp. 307–312).

Albrecht, W. S. & Sack, R. J. (2000). *Accounting education: Charting the course through a perilous future.* Sarasota, Fla.: American Accounting Association.

Allan, J. N. (1982). *History of the Society of Management Accountants of Canada.* Society of Management Accountants of Canada.

Beaulieu, P. & Lakra, A. (2005). Coverage of criticism of activity-based costing in Canadian textbooks. *Canadian Accounting Perspectives, 4*(1), 87–109.

Beechy, T. H. (1980). *L'enseignement de la comptabilité dans les universités canadiennes: tour d'horizon et analyse.* L'Association canadienne des professeurs de comptabilité.

Benn, R. (2007, February). Strength in research. *CMA Management, 80*(9), 17–18.

Boritz, J. E. & Carnaghan, C. A. (2003). Competency-based education and assessment for the accounting profession: A critical review. *Canadian Accounting Perspectives, 2*(1), 7–42.

Caron, M.-A. (2003). *La culture des comptables en organisation: une mise à l'épreuve de leur savoir et de leur pratique* (Thèse). Université de Montréal.

Caron, M.-A. (2005). La socialisation des professionnels comptables dans les entreprises québécoises. *Gérer et Comprendre, 81*, 39–48.

Caron, M.-A., Boisvert, H. & Mersereau, A. (2011). Le rôle du contrôleur revisité: une perspective nord-américaine. *Comptabilité – Contrôle – Audit, 17*(1), 123–154.

Chartered Professional Accountants Canada. (2012). The CPA Competency Map: How to qualify for the Canadian CPA designation. Retrieved from www.cpacanada.ca/en/ become-a-cpa/pathways-to-becoming-a-cpa/national-education-resources/the-cpa-competency-map.

Chlala, N. & Girard, A. (1993, April). Preparing management reports. *CMA, 67*(3), 31–35.

CMA Management. (2005, April). CMA Canada expands resources for management accounting research: Management accounting research will nourish growth of CMA competencies and enhance the competitiveness of leading-edge organizations. *CMA Management, 79*(2), S4.

Cost and Management. (1929). *Advanced Commercial courses in Montréal, 4*(9), September, 29.

Cost and Management. (1982). Management accounting guidelines to be introduced in January. *Cost and Management, 56*(6), 72.

Côté, Y. A. (1992). *La profession comptable canadienne: tour d'horizon.* École des hautes études commerciales, Chaire de sciences comptables.

Diebel, K. R. (1992, June). A word from the President: Before the guard changes. *CMA, 66*(5), 3.

Etherington, L. D. & Richardson, A. J. (1994). Institutional pressures on university accounting education in Canada. *Contemporary Accounting Research, 10*(S1), 141–162.

Fletcher, D. (2003, September). Change agent. *CMA Management, 77*(5), 18–20.

Jerman, L. & Sponem, S. (2016). Chefs des finances et contrôleurs: entre obligation de conformité et leadership stratégique. *Gestion, 41*(2), 30–33.

Johnson, H. T. & Kaplan, R. S. (1987). *Relevance lost : The rise and fall of management accounting.* Boston, Mass.: Harvard Business School Press.

L'Ordre des CMA du Québec. (2009). *Enquête sur la rémunération 2009.* Montréal, QC: L'Ordre des CMA du Québec.

L'Ordre des CMA du Québec. (2012). *Rapport Annuel 2011–2012.* Montréal, QC: L'Ordre des CMA du Québec.

La Corporation Professionelle des Comptables en Administration Industrielle du Québec. (1984). *Rapport Annuel 1983–1984.* Montréal, QC: La Corporation Professionelle des Comptables en Administration Industrielle du Québec.

Langdon, W. (2002). The future of accounting education: The response of Certified Management Accountants. *Canadian Accounting Perspectives, 1*(1), 97–103.

Law, J. (2013). The past. *CMA Management,* November, 15–31.

Mattessich, R. (1984). Management accounting, past, present and future. In R. Mattessich (Ed.), *Modern accounting research: History, survey and guide* (pp. 395–414). Vancouver, BC: Pegassus Press Inc.

Mintzberg, H., National Association of Accountants & Society of Industrial Accountants of Canada. (1975). *Impediments to the use of management information: A study carried* out on behalf of the National Association of Accountants, New York, N.Y., and the Society of Industrial Accountants of Canada, Hamilton, Ontario, Canada. New York: National Association of Accountants.

Morpurgo, M. T. (2015, 26 February). *Beyond competency: The role of professional accounting education in the development of meta-competencies* (Dissertation in partial fulfillment of the requirements for the degree of Doctor of Business Administration). Athabasca University, Canada.

Murphy, G. J. (1986). A chronology of the development of corporate financial reporting in Canada: 1850 to 1983. *The Accounting Historians Journal, 13*(1), 31–62.

Murphy, G. J. (Ed.). (1993). *A history of Canadian accounting thought and practice.* London: Taylor & Francis.

Normand, F. (2013, 23 February). *Les années 1970–1980: naissance et âge d'or du Québec inc.* Les Affaires.

Renauld, F. (1986). Au cœur de l'action. In *Guerriers de l'émergence*, ed. Corporation Professionnelle des comptables en management du Québec, pp. 17–19.

Richardson, A. J. (1987). Professionalization and intraprofessional competition in the Canadian accounting profession. *Work and Occupations, 14*(4), 591–615. http://doi.org/10.1177/0730888487014004006.

Richardson, A. J. (1992). Accounting competence: Canadian experiences. In K. Anyane-Ntow (Ed.), International handbook of accounting education and certification (pp. 263–278). Amsterdam: Pergamon.

Richardson, A. J. (2000). Building the Canadian Chartered Accountancy profession: A biography of George Edwards, Fca, Cbe, Lld, 1861–1947. *The Accounting Historians Journal, 27*(2), 87–116.

Richardson, A. J. (2002). Professional dominance: The relationship between financial accounting and managerial accounting, 1926–1986. *The Accounting Historians Journal, 29*(2), 91–121.

Richardson, A. J. & Jones, D. G. B. (2007). Professional "brand", personal identity and resistance to change in the Canadian accounting profession: A comparative history of two accounting association merger negotiations. *Accounting History, 12*(2), 135.

Richardson, A. J. & Kilfoyle, E. (2012). Merging the profession: A historical perspective on accounting association mergers in Canada. *Accounting Perspectives, 11*(2), 77–109.

SMAC (Society of Management Accountants of Canada). (2011). *The CMA competency map.*

Sturge, D. (1997, December). Society's view of management accounting becoming the world view. *CMA, 71*(10), 4.

Sturge, D. (1998, August). New handbook on Management Accounting Standards. *CMA, 72*(6), 5.

Stefanac, R. (2016). The ideal candidates. *CPA Magazine*, January/February.

Stuart, R. (1997). Accountants in management: A globally changing role, *CMA Magazine, 71*(1), 5.

White, J. C. (1930). Teaching of accounting in schools of engineering. *Accounting Review*, 208–212.

4 Management accountants in mainland China and Taiwan

*Jizhang Huang, Tsuilin Kuo,
Fei Pan and Anne Wu*

Introduction

The purpose of this chapter is to provide an overview and assessment of the roles played by management accountants in mainland China and Taiwan over the last several decades. Specifically, it reviews the history of the management accounting profession in both regions, examines the influence of region-specific factors on the role of management accountants, describes their task profiles and briefly introduces the current status of academic education and professional training for management accountants.

While the focus of this study is on management accountants, this inevitably relates to the historical development of management accounting practices in mainland China and Taiwan more generally, since the roles performed by management accountants in each period have evolved alongside the improvement of the practices implemented in the field. Additionally, a wide variety of management accounting studies are surveyed. On one hand, the topics examined by academic studies in a specific period provide a good reflection of the most popular management accounting practices and the most important issues of the time. Thus, a summary of the topics along the timeline can facilitate the formation of a historical view of the management accounting profession. On the other hand, academic studies have also pushed the development of management accounting in emerging markets like mainland China and Taiwan, as some leading domestic scholars often write papers to introduce advanced ideas and techniques from western countries, which encourages local firms to experiment with and implement them.

The remainder of this chapter is structured as follows. The next section provides a brief history of management accountancy in both mainland China and Taiwan. The third section discusses how the region-specific institutional factors of these two regions affect the management accounting profession. Section 4 describes the task profiles of management accountants in two regions respectively, while section 5 presents the current status of academic education and professional training for management accountants. The chapter concludes with a summary.

The emergence of the management accountant in mainland China and Taiwan

Mainland China

Despite the long-term existence of management accounting in Chinese firms, recorded evidence shows that management accountants were neither viewed as an independent profession nor equipped with a separate position until the early 1990s. The following section reviews the development of the management accounting profession since its emergence in the early 1990s. In general, it was found that the profession evolved through three different stages, each with distinctive characteristics.

Stage one: emergence of the management accountant in mainland China

The economic boom in mainland China in the 1980s stimulated the emergence of the management accountant in Chinese firms. The reforms to the general economic system implemented by the Chinese government in the late 1970s successfully shifted the power of resource allocation from the government to the markets. In particular, this reform led to the blossoming of private sector enterprises. The increasingly severe market competition brought enormous pressure to former state-owned enterprises (SOEs), most of which had operated under the rigid planning imposed by the Chinese central government and had run at low efficiency for quite a long time. These SOEs found that they were unlikely to be able to survive in the competitive marketplace unless they could control their costs and reduce their expenditure. Thus, cost management gradually became a major topic for both practitioners and accounting professors in the late 1980s and early 1990s. Many papers published in the major Chinese accountancy journals shed light on new approaches to cost management. For example, Activity-Based Costing (ABC) was first introduced into mainland China during this period by some leading accounting researchers. Accordingly, Chinese companies also made considerable effort to experiment with novel cost management methods. To deal with more and more complicated costing issues and cost-management practices, those companies realized the urgent need to establish special positions to supervise the whole process. These positions were normally affiliated with the finance department and were usually termed "cost accountant" or "cost manager". The staff members who specialized in analysing and managing costs constituted the earliest form of management accountants in Chinese firms.

Stage two: diffusion of the management accountant in mainland China

The Chinese economy has become increasingly integrated with the world economy since China's entry into the World Trade Organization in 2001, which led to a considerable increase in the implementation of management accounting and the employment of management accountants by Chinese firms. More and more international companies were attracted to entering the Chinese market during this period. On the one hand, this situation stimulated the demand of local companies for advanced management accounting techniques, since they had to improve their operating efficiency in response to the increased market competition in China. On the other hand, it provided Chinese companies with more opportunities to improve their management accounting practices, as the Chinese divisions of international companies could not only be seen as possible benchmarks or role models for local firms to learn from, but also inadvertently served as training camps to produce experienced professional managers for the Chinese job market.

During the early 2000s, more and more Chinese companies began to realize the importance of management control systems. After the Balanced Scorecard (BSC) was first introduced into mainland China in 2001, some firms even raised the implementation of management accounting to the level of strategic importance. Remarkably, the Chinese Ministry of Finance (MOF) issued a series of documents in 2001 and 2002 to advocate the implementation of total budget management in SOEs. In response to the requirements of the MOF, most of the SOEs, as well as many of the non-SOEs, had gradually built up their budgeting systems. Accordingly, special positions, which were normally titled "budget manager" or "planning manager", or working units such as the "budget and planning department", had been set up in these companies to manage the entire budgeting process. For management accountants, budget-related managers were much more influential and significant than the cost accountants who preceded them. Not only were they positioned in the higher levels of the managerial hierarchy, but they also undertook a much broader range of tasks of relevance to firms' operation and management.

Stage three: popularization of the management accountant in mainland China

A nationwide wave of implementing management accounting has taken place in Chinese firms since 2014. The year 2014 is now widely recognized as the opening year of the "Management Accounting Era" in mainland China, because the MoF of the Chinese central government issued a key document entitled "The Guidelines of Widely Implementing and Constructing Management Accounting Systems", with the objective of promoting and encouraging the use of management accounting in Chinese firms. In the document, the government described the severe lack of qualified management accountants as the key issue hindering the development of management accounting in China. It proposed a number of projects to facilitate the training of management accountants for Chinese firms and to push the development of management accounting theory under a Chinese-specific framework. For example, the MoF funds major universities and National Accounting Institutes to provide training programmes for Chinese enterprises and to conduct relevant research projects. Consequently, firms have paid increasing attention to the functions of management accounting in improving a firm's value. According to a joint survey conducted by the Association of Chartered Certified Accountants (ACCA) and the Shanghai National Accounting Institute (SNAI), 39.4 per cent of the sampled firms set up a management accounting department to take charge of planning and control issues in 2014.[1] Some of these departments are affiliated to the finance department, while others might be under the direct leadership of the CFO or one of the vice-presidents. Moreover, firms are highly motivated to seek management accountants in the job market[2] explicitly, and to design special career paths for them to develop related abilities further, because management accountants are widely deemed important in the processes of strategic planning, management control and risk management.

Taiwan

The role of the management accounting profession in Taiwan changed enormously during the period from 1985 to 2015. Generally speaking, the development underwent three different stages. The characteristics of each phase are discussed individually as follows.

Stage one: emergence of modern management accounting

In the mid-1980s, advanced management accounting knowledge was introduced by Taiwanese scholars who had been educated in western countries. Many Taiwanese management accountants tried to learn from American companies or those in other developed countries in order to improve their management accounting skills. From 1985 to 1989, management accountants, such as financial controllers or management controllers, in Taiwan claimed that accountants were considered as managers' "watchdogs", and that management accounting helps with business management and to set up the health diagnosis of an organization. In Taiwan, the most important management accounting and control topics at that time were (1) responsibility centre accounting, (2) budgeting and (3) just in time.

Stage two: initiation of practical implementation

At this stage, Taiwanese scholars who had returned from western countries played an important role in leading the development of management accounting practices in Taiwan between 1990 and 2005. Those scholars not only introduced many novel ideas on management accounting into the classrooms of Taiwanese universities, but also became deeply embedded in the field to help Taiwanese companies implement the most advanced management control tools (such as the ABCM and the BSC) for free. As trust gradually built up between scholars and practitioners in the consulting process, the companies that had received help wished to return the favour to those scholars by providing them with private datasets collected from within their companies to support their academic research. Using these valuable private datasets enables researchers to examine management accounting innovations that suit local companies, and to put those innovations into practice eventually. Everything in this cooperative relationship became a virtuous circle. Several important management accounting practices that were emphasized by management accountants in this period are listed below.

1   ABCM: Many companies have tried to implement ABC and ABM since 1990 to improve the quality of decision-making, understand the approach of cost allocation, as well as to analyse the contribution of profitability of different products or customers and to intensify the competitiveness of the business (Wu 1990, 1991, 1992a, 1992b, 1992c). Accordingly, special positions entitled "cost control manager", "budget manager", "operation manager" or "project manager" have been established in these companies to analyse the actual activity process and provide relevant data.
2   BSC: Many organizations have tried to implement the BSC since the tool was first introduced into Taiwan in 1997. The BSC is regarded as an integrated strategic management tool. Therefore, how to solve performance measurement problems and how to successfully implement the BSC are key issues for management accountants (Wu 1997a, 1997b, 1997c, 2002, 2003a, 2003b, 2003c, 2004a, 2004b, 2007). BSC-related management accountant positions are normally affiliated to the top management team and usually given the job titles "management accounting controller", "chief financial officer" or "strategic manager".
3   IC: The concept of intellectual capital (IC) was introduced into Taiwan in 2002. The topics of interest for management accountants regarding IC include (a) an analysis of intellectual capital (Wu 2002), and (b) the introduction of a strategic intellectual capital evaluation management model and case analysis (Wu 2012). In the knowledge-economy era, Taiwanese companies have made the transition from making cheap and high-quantity products to creating digital and intangible assets. In this scenario, management accountants have not only helped organizations to introduce IC across different departments, but also to find new business models or blue ocean strategies (Kim and Mauborgne 2005) for their companies.

Stage three: integration into globalized communication and the international research community

From 2006 to 2015, two characteristics defined the development of management accountants in Taiwan: (1) the integration of academia and practice, and (2) increased communication between Taiwanese management accountants and the international community. In order to help management accountants better understand the concept of management accounting and to promote the development of management accounting in Taiwan and mainland China, Professor Anne Wu developed a special management accounting framework entitled the "Integrative Strategic Value Management System".[3]

How the institutional context shapes the management accounting profession in mainland China and Taiwan

Mainland China

The evolution and characteristics of the management accounting profession in a specific region are largely shaped by relevant local institutional factors. In mainland China, the active involvement of the government and the form of ownership of the company are likely to have been the main influences. The influences of the two institutional factors are discussed individually as follows.

Active involvement of the government

The MoF of the Chinese central government, the sole authority in charge of setting accounting standards in mainland China, has played a key role in regulating and guiding accounting practices in Chinese firms.

Chinese regulators and professional accountants have made tremendous progress in reforming the financial accounting system and improving accounting standards since the foundation of the market-based economy in early 1990s. However, compared to the rapid development of financial accounting, the promotion and application of management accounting lagged behind in mainland China, which eventually triggered a series of requests for the enhancement of management accounting practices in recent years. Under this scenario, the China Association of Chief Financial Officers (CACFO) organized a series of workshops in July 2014 on the development of Chinese management accounting practices. The financial minister of the Chinese central government, Mr. Jiwei Lou, gave a plenary speech entitled "Upgrading the model of economic growth by speeding up the development of Chinese-specific management accounting". By systematically reviewing the history and functions of management accounting in mainland China, Mr. Lou associated the issues with the current status of management accounting in Chinese firms and expressed his aspiration to popularize the employment of modern management accounting practices throughout the country. Accordingly, as mentioned earlier, the MoF released "The Guidelines of Widely Implementing and Constructing Management Accounting Systems" in October 2014. These guidelines advocate the exploration by researchers and practitioners of the influence of Chinese-specific characteristics on management accounting. Eventually, the guidelines aim to create an integrated framework on management accounting that suits the current economic system of mainland China. The guidelines propose the production of a considerable number of well-trained management accountants in three to five years and a significant improvement in the implementation of management accounting and corresponding information systems in mainland Chinese firms in the next five to ten years.

The government's effort has had a significant influence on the management accounting profession in mainland China. The Association of Chartered Certified

Accountants (ACCA) and the Shanghai National Accounting Institute (SNAI) jointly conducted a series of investigations to depict the development of the management accounting profession in Chinese companies before and after 2014. Figure 4.1 presents some of their statistics. By 2013, 29.4 per cent of their sample firms had set up a management accounting department; the proportion rose to 39.4 per cent in 2014. While only 42 per cent of the sampled firms had clearly defined the task profile of the management accountant in 2013, 63.3 per cent of firms reported a clear definition in 2014.

The property of ownership

The diversity of the type of ownership constitutes one of the most important characteristics in the economy of mainland China. As the Chinese government used to manage its economic system based on the philosophy of central planning, all enterprises were owned by the state by the end of the 1970s. With the implementation of the Reforming and Opening Policy in 1980s, which aimed to transform the central-planning economic system into a market-oriented one, the Chinese government gradually allowed individual investors to enter many sectors in the economy. Since then, private- and foreign-owned firms and various forms of joint ventures have played an increasingly significant role in mainland China.

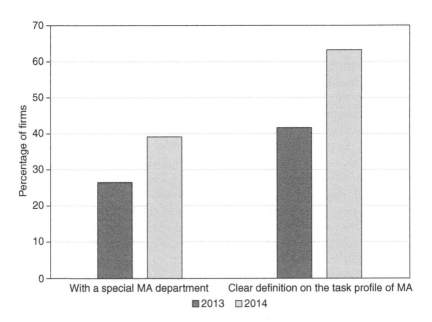

Figure 4.1 Development of MA from 2013 to 2014 in mainland Chinese firms.

Data source: The Association of Chartered Certified Accountants & Shanghai National Accounting Institutes. (2014). *Investigation Report: The Application of Management Accounting in Chinese Enterprises*. Please note this diagram has been reshaped by the authors of this chapter.

The type of company ownership is one of the main institutional factors shaping the management accounting profession. For example, the Chinese central government, as well as all local governments, set up a State-Owned Assets Supervision and Administration Commission (SASAC) in 2002 to evaluate the performance and manage the high-level personnel of government-controlled companies. The roles of the SASAC include: monitoring enterprise operations to protect the rights of the government owner; dispatching supervisors to audit and monitor the enterprise; appointing members of boards of directors and establishing procedures for appointing managers; and reporting on enterprise performance and revenues to the appropriate level of government. The SASAC also issues guidelines to direct strategic pathways for the SOEs.[4] The launch of the SASAC implies that an outside bureaucratic institute undertakes some of the management accounting tasks for Chinese SOEs. A field study of the behaviour of the SASAC by Du, Tang and Young (2012) noted that the performance evaluations conducted by the SASAC suffer from bias originating from superiors' favouritism and the influence of subordinates' activities.

Some of the evidence in the joint study conducted by the Association of Chartered Certified Accountants (ACCA) and the Shanghai National Accounting Institute (SNAI) also sheds light on how the type of ownership affects the management accounting profession in mainland China. As shown in Figure 4.2, while only about 18 per cent of the state-owned and state-controlled enterprises have set up a management accounting department, the proportion is about 40 per cent in foreign-owned enterprises and joint ventures. About 36 per cent of the

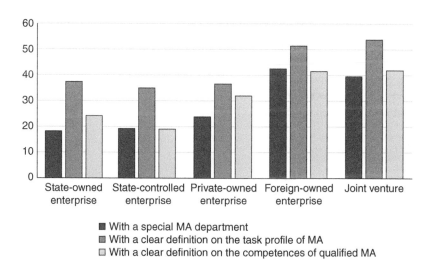

■ With a special MA department
■ With a clear definition on the task profile of MA
□ With a clear definition on the competences of qualified MA

Figure 4.2 Management accounting in Chinese enterprises with different forms of ownership.

Data source: The Association of Chartered Certified Accountants & Shanghai National Accounting Institutes. (2014). *Investigation Report: The Application of Management Accounting in Chinese Enterprises*. Please note this diagram has been reshaped by the authors of this chapter.

sample firms owned or controlled by domestic investors reported a clearly defined task profile for management accountants; the proportions are over 50 per cent for either foreign-owned enterprises or joint ventures. Finally, only about 20 per cent of the state-owned or state-controlled enterprises in the sample have clearly defined the competences of qualified management accountants, whereas over 50 per cent of foreign-owned enterprises and joint ventures reported an explicit requirement.

Taiwan

The influence of the institutional context on the management accounting profession in Taiwan can be explained by the evolution of the industrial development, the institutional context is divided here into four phases: (1) the manufacturing industry; (2) the electronics industry; (3) the services industry; and (4) the technology industry. The influence of the four institutional factors are discussed individually as follows.

Manufacturing industry period

The first economic miracle in Taiwan took place mainly because of the rapid growth of the manufacturing industry. Companies focused on manufacturing high-quantity, low-end and low profit margin products. In the early 1980s, irrespective of GNP, exports or foreign-exchange reserves, Taiwan was always ranked as one of the top countries in the world for manufacturing (Yang, Wang & Hsu, 2013). Using data for 1960 to 1985, economists found out that the fundamental reason for the high economic growth rate in Taiwan at that time was the accumulation of fixed capital and the growth in the workforce, given that the rate of progress in production technology was not outstanding. During this period, management accountants mainly focused on "cost reduction". Since the products generated low gross profit, management accountants had difficulty in creating value and were regarded as general accounting staff.

Electronics industry period

In the late 1980s, with the growth of the electronics industry throughout the world, manufacturing companies in Taiwan were gradually replaced in their dominant economic role by firms from the electronics industry. In 1983, the Industrial Technology Research Institute, Acer and other Taiwanese companies jointly produced the first Taiwanese personal computer, which laid the important foundation for the electronics industry in Taiwan. In the early days, computer production in Taiwan was based on Original Equipment Manufacturers (OEM), the proportion of which increased from 54.8 per cent in 1984 to 72.1 per cent in 1998. The value chain activities of the OEM companies were merely based on manufacture and assembly, and these companies produced products in complete conformity with the specification assigned by their customers. Since the 1990s, the electronic industry in Taiwan has developed strongly, gradually becoming a competitive source of global electronic products, and has transformed from an OEM to ODM (Original Design Manufacturer). The value chain activity of ODM companies includes product design, manufacture and assembly, for which the capability of design, R&D and product assembly are essential. Moreover, ODM companies are able to negotiate with their customers and to design or modify products as required, in contrast to OEM companies. For companies in the electronics industry, product cost and profit are vital information when making decisions. The development of the electronics industry had an impact on the management accountants in Taiwan. Their main tasks were to calculate and control the cost of products, identify cost drivers, decrease invalid waste and increase efficiency. An important task of management accountants was to provide more accurate cost information to assist decision-making, such as pricing and improving the production process. To be more specific, every value chain includes a number of different "activities", from R&D to manufacturing and customer services. An "activity" is the "cell" of a management process; it is the smallest unit and the most vital foundation of a business. Firms should thus focus on the activities that could create value for customers. Accordingly, management accountants should provide information and help analyse each "activity" in the value chain of the company to determine whether it could be improved further. Moreover, management accountants use more intensive non-financial information, such as quality, flexibility and value in their analyses in order to improve competitiveness.

Service industry period

In 1988, the total value produced by the service industry exceeded 50 per cent of GDP in Taiwan. In the same year, the number of employees in the services industry exceeded the number of employees in manufacturing. In the 2000s, the development of services accelerated due to economic liberalization and globalization, as well as the outsourced businesses of traditional industries. The booming service industry largely assisted the upgrading of traditional industries in Taiwan. Intensive knowledge was one of the most important characteristics of the newly developed service industry; companies were successful either because they could design creative commodities with distinctive local features, or provide valuable and highly efficient technical support on operating, marketing or financing to traditional manufacturing companies. In 2012, the services industry accounted for about 68.52 per cent of GDP, and employed 58.57 per cent of the total workforce. In this period, management accountants did not simply analyse financial data, but also needed comprehensively to consider company policies, customer behaviour, and the internal or external environment. As far as services are concerned, under the premise of creating customer value, the key point of customer management was to understand the attributes and profitability of different customers, to decide how to filter customers, set prices and provide differentiated services. Management accountants employed the information generated by the ABC system to compute and analyse the profitability of each individual customer. Furthermore, management controllers also often used the BSC to improve strategy implementation.

Technology industry period

The GDP growth of Taiwan's service industry has slowed since 2001. During the same period, the GDP growth of the high-tech industry (7.4 per cent) has been higher than that of the service industry (3.2 per cent). The high-tech industry, especially the semiconductor industry, has become the backbone of the Taiwanese economy. Technology-intensive products have also become the leading source of exports. A total of 14 items from Taiwan, such as the monitor, motherboard and mouse, now account for the biggest share of the global market (Ho, Wu & Xu, 2011). The production of integrated circuits in Taiwan is the fourth-largest in the world. The output value of the wafer accounts for up to 70 per cent of the world total, and the output of the information industry once ranked third in the world. In the knowledge economy era, intangible intellectual capital, such as the leadership of the management team, the centripetal force of employees, the relationships between customers and suppliers and innovation have created the highest value for companies. For example, in Taiwan's high-tech industry, management accountants emphasize that the accumulation, sharing and integration of knowledge is the main driver to creating value for companies, and that the creation, management, measurement and evaluation of a company's intellectual capital is the key to improving the competitive advantage of a company in the long run. This intellectual capital can help management accountants within organizations reach the goal of sustainable development.

The task profile of the management accountant in Chinese and Taiwanese companies

Mainland China

In 2014, the Association of Chartered Certified Accountants (ACCA) and the Beijing National Accounting Institute (BNAI) jointly conducted a study of management accounting practices in mainland Chinese enterprises. A diversified sample of accounting practitioners from ACCA qualified members and trainees of the BNAI was used, with 552 suitably completed questionnaires eventually collected. Some of the statistics presented in the report depict the task profile of management accountants in Chinese firms, as shown in Figure 4.3. This shows the tasks that are supposed to be undertaken by management accountants and the tasks that they actually undertake in the respondents' firms, from the perspective of managers in the finance department or top-level executives. It is apparent that more than 80 per cent of respondents consider budgeting management, financial forecasting, financial analysis, cost management and performance management to be important tasks for management accountants. More than 70 per cent of

○ Tasks supposed to be undertaken by management accountant
■ Tasks actually undertaken by management accountant

Figure 4.3 Comparison between tasks supposed to be undertaken by MA and tasks actually undertaken by MA.

Data source: The Association of Chartered Certified Accountants & the Beijing National Accounting Institutes. (2014). *Investigation Report: Management Accounting Practices in Chinese Firms.*

respondents think that management accountants should also participate in financial planning, risk management, investment evaluation and strategic decision-making. Additionally, operations management, performance measurement and evaluation and financing decision-making are also considered to be tasks for management accountants in more than 60 per cent of the firms. Some of the respondents even believe that management accounting should play a role in the process of tax planning.

However, since the importance of management accounting has only been realized in mainland China in recent years, many Chinese firms have not been able to take good care of all the perceived management accounting tasks. Thus, such tasks are actually performed by management accountants at a much lower frequency than they are supposed to be in the perception in mainland Chinese firms. Only four of the listed tasks, namely budgeting management, financial prediction, financial analysis and cost management, are undertaken by management accountants in more than 50 per cent of the surveyed firms. Only slightly more than 20 per cent of the sample firms let their management accountants play a role in strategic planning and operations management. Less than 30 per cent of firms involve their management accountants in risk management practices, which have also become increasingly important in recent years. Overall, as the investigation shows, Chinese companies still have a long way to go in making better use of management accountants' professional skills and knowledge so as to fully explore their potential in improving the efficiency of management and the firm's value.

Taiwan

A literature review by Kuo and Wu provides an overview of management accounting research published in Taiwanese academic journals; it sought to identify trends in various characteristics of the task profile of Taiwanese management accountants (Wu, Peng, Kuo & Chan, 2016). This began by identifying all of the management accounting articles published in 23 local journals between the beginning of 1984 and the end of 2014. A total of 257 articles are of relevance to the tasks typically undertaken by management accountants in Taiwanese companies. After identifying all of the articles that met the criteria for inclusion, each one was grouped using three to five keywords drawn from the title, abstract and conclusion. Each article was also coded using three dimensions (task profiles).[5] Figure 4.4 shows the tasks that are mainly undertaken by management accountants in Taiwanese firms, including the three task profiles: designing management control systems (144 articles), cost management (69 articles), and strategy formulation and implementation (44 articles). Some examples are presented below.

The task profile under the "designing management control systems" heading includes performance measurement and evaluation (79 articles, 55 per cent), incentives and compensation (36 articles, 25 per cent), operational and capital budgeting (17 articles, 12 per cent) and organizations and management control systems (12 articles, 8 per cent). Specially, management accountants in Taiwan emphasize how relative performance evaluation affects the performance of a company and employee satisfaction; how incentives and reward systems impact team and individual performance; how to effectively implement a performance evaluation system and strengthen a governance mechanism; how to predict and manage risk through budget planning; and how the management control system can bring about change and innovation within the organization. Management accountants combine the management control system and management accounting information to provide a detailed decision-making basis for top managers. In addition, they need to develop good performance evaluation and incentive compensation systems to motivate employees to create value for the organization.

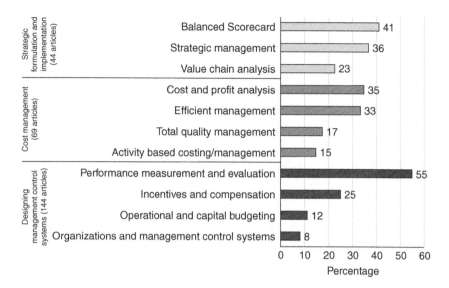

Figure 4.4 Tasks of the management accountant in Taiwanese companies.

The tasks usually performed by Taiwanese management accountants in the "cost management" field are cost and profit analysis (24 articles, 35 per cent), efficiency management (23 articles, 33 per cent), total quality management (12 articles, 17 per cent), and activity-based costing/management (10 articles, 15 per cent). All of the task profiles for management accountants focusing on cost and profit analysis deal with how different cost allocation methods affect communication and employees' behaviour among departments. Furthermore, the duty of cost controlling is also described, including: (1) transfer pricing; (2) just in time; and (3) target costing. In addition, the task related to efficient management focuses on applying enterprise resource planning (ERP) systems in daily operations or project management. Efficient management can prompt management accountants to make efficient use of limited resources, to increase the utilization of capacity and to reduce costs. Tasks related to total quality management (TQM) concern the impact of this and service quality on business performance. The activity-based costing/management (ABCM) tasks are concerned with explaining the concepts and contents of ABCM and how it should be implemented.

The task profile that comes under the "strategy formulation and implementation" heading includes the BSC (18 articles, 41 per cent), strategic management (16 articles, 36 per cent) and value chain analysis (10 articles, 23 per cent). More than 40 per cent of the articles analysed focus on the BSC, emphasizing it is an important tool that also helps management accountants in Taiwanese companies to create links with the strategic and operational levels of the firm. The strategic management tasks pertain to the analysis and implementation of strategies, not only in enterprises but also in governmental or non-profit organizations.

Management accountants emphasize strategic planning and control, and how to create added economic value for enterprises. The tasks linked to value chain analysis encompass the comparison of financial and other non-financial performance on their association with the value chain.

Academic and professional institutions and their relevance for management accountants

Mainland China

The implementation of the reform and opening policy in mainland China in 1978 led to rapid growth in the Chinese economy over the past 30 years. The huge demand for professional accountants because of the booming number of enterprises stimulated the development of accounting education in Chinese universities (Sun & Li 2014). By the end of 2015, 401 Chinese universities had set up an accounting major for college students. According to the ranking developed by the Research Centre for China Science Evaluation, Wuhan University, and the Network of Science and Education Evaluation in China, 20 out of 401 undergraduate accounting programmes were rated as A+ level, while 60 have been rated as level A.[6] With regard to graduate programmes, by the end of 2015, 35 Chinese graduate schools had set up an accounting PhD programme, and 155 graduate schools offer a Master's degree in accounting.

Besides colleges, some practical institutions also exert significant influence on the education of management accountants in mainland China. Their roles are summarized below.

National Accounting Institutes

Under the strong support of former Chinese Premier Zhu Rongji, three National Accounting Institutes were established consecutively in Beijing (1998), Shanghai (2000) and Xiamen (2002) as public service institutions affiliated to the MOF. These three institutes are now able to provide three different kinds of accounting education and training services in mainland China. They have their own MPAcc, EMBA and EMPAcc programmes,[7] which are authorized to issue degrees to students, and operate a variety of training programmes to serve individual-level and enterprise-level customers to facilitate the development of executives and professional managers. As a third-party business education provider, they also deliver distance education via the Internet for managerial staff and accounting practitioners in western China. To date, the three National Accounting Institutes have trained over 3 million trainees in total.

These three National Accounting Institutes have also made tremendous contributions to training management accountants and advocating the improvement of management accounting practices in Chinese firms. For example, many of the programmes, such as the National Leading Accounting Talents Programme, which is for chief accountants of SOEs, place significant emphasis on MA-related courses and seminars in their training curricula. They have set the education and promotion of management accounting in China as one of their major purposes. The Shanghai National Accounting Institute (SNAI) organized an annual management accounting symposium since 2013 to bring together academics and practitioners and facilitate the improvement of management accounting research and practice in greater China. Moreover, SNAI set up the Amoeba Research Centre in 2015, which aims to facilitate the efficient application of advanced management accounting techniques in Chinese firms.

Association of Chartered Certified Accountants (ACCA)

ACCA is a global body for professional accountants. It offers business-relevant, first-choice qualifications to people of ability and ambition around the world who seek a rewarding career in accountancy, finance or management. ACCA has been active in mainland China since 1988. It mainly cooperates with major Chinese universities to improve the quality of higher education in accounting. To date, about 100 accounting departments in Chinese universities have set up an ACCA major, and it has more than 24,000 licensed members in mainland China, 48 per cent of whom serve as CFOs or management accountants in various types of Chinese enterprises.

Chartered Institute of Management Accountants (CIMA)

As the world's largest leading professional body of management accountants, CIMA has been active in mainland China since 2004. Since then, CIMA has cooperated with many local education institutes in the training of management accountants. For example, CIMA sponsors the National Leading Accounting Talents Programme, which has been supported by the MOF of the Chinese central government and run by the three National Accounting Institutes for five years. CIMA has also cooperated with about 40 local universities and colleges on the education of MA at both undergraduate and graduate levels. So far, CIMA has more than 10,000 registered learners and more than 1,000 licensed members in mainland China.

Taiwan

In Taiwan, there are 49 universities with accounting departments. These include 10 public universities, 18 private universities, 6 public vocational colleges and 15 private vocational colleges. All these universities and colleges have included cost accounting and management accounting as part of their curriculum. Most of those universities and colleges run programmes to issue specialized Master's degrees in accounting and five schools have set up a PhD programme in accounting, including managerial accounting.

In addition to the above-mentioned institutions, there are some other representative academic institutions in Taiwan. Their roles for management accountants are summarized below.

Taiwan Accounting Association (TAA)

The TAA was established in 1995 with the objective of improving the professional level of Taiwanese accountants, and promoting knowledge creation and sharing in the accounting community. In recent years, it has supported accounting education development and cultivated the employment of professionally skilled people in managerial accounting. Moreover, in order to facilitate communication between domestic and foreign academics and practitioners, the TAA conducts academic as well as practice-oriented research projects and holds regular meetings or conferences.

Taiwan Strategic Cost Management Association (TSCMA)

Established in 2003, the purpose of the TSCMA is to innovate, integrate, accumulate and spread integrative strategic cost management techniques to support domestic and foreign companies and non-profit organizations. It shares experiences in classes and helps Taiwanese organizations to implement tools like the BSC, ABC, modern incentive systems and intellectual capital.

Accounting department of National Chengchi University (NCCU)

The accounting department of NCCU is the only department in Taiwan that has acquired the certification of the Association to Advance Collegiate Schools of Business (AACSB), which represents the courses and teaching quality that have achieved recognition from the international accounting industry. National Chengchi University became the first contracting school with CIMA in Taiwan, and is to date the only cooperation partner. CIMA signed a joint contract with the NCCU College of Commerce in 2015 to establish the course to improve the capabilities of management accountants in Taiwanese companies. As long as the students complete the assigned courses and pass the examination, they can acquire the CIMA certificate, which helps management accountants to find jobs.

Chinese Strategic Management Accounting Institute

The Chinese Strategic Management Accounting Institute is the Taiwanese branch of the IMA. Its mission is to promote world-class management accounting knowledge as well as its certification in Taiwan and other places in the Greater China area. The Chinese Strategic Management Accounting Institute has held the authentication test for CMA since 2007, which serves to evaluate and diagnose management accountants' professional knowledge as well as their abilities to employ this knowledge in practice on the right occasions. Participants who pass the series of examinations can earn a certificate of being a qualified management accountant.

Conclusion

This chapter has provided an overview of management accountants in both mainland China and Taiwan. The economic growth in Taiwan the 1970s and in mainland China in the 1980s both played a dominant role in driving the emergence of management accountants in the two regions. With the aid of the institutional background, the active involvement of the government and the form of ownership of enterprises have been found to exert significant influence on the management accounting profession in mainland China, whereas in Taiwan, the development of the profession has been mainly shaped by the development of different industries. The authors' investigation of the task profiles of management accountants show that, in both mainland China and Taiwan, management accountants are widely supposed to be involved in a variety of management activities, such as strategy formulation and implementation, and cost management. Finally, both mainland China and Taiwan have developed a multi-layer and comprehensive education system for the management accounting profession.

To conclude, the authors have considerable confidence that management accounting will continue develop well in the long term in both mainland China and Taiwan. Both scholars and practitioners will continue to gain experience from western countries and to cooperate closely with international management accounting researchers to develop a good foundation for management accounting research and practice in the two regions.

Notes

1 Source: Association of Chartered Certified Accountants and Shanghai National Accounting Institutes (2014). Investigation Report: *The Application of Management Accounting in Chinese Enterprises*. More detailed information is presented in Figure 4.1.
2 An online search found many job advertisements explicitly calling for management accountants (for example, www.51job.com). For example, the Marifor technology company in Shanghai is offering 15,000 RMB (a decent salary) to hire a management accountant; the job description states that the new employee will be required to manage the budgeting process for the company, make financial predictions and perform financial analysis, analyse the cost model for each product and provide precise cost information to senior executives.
3 In 2010, Professor Wu took out a patent for her "Strategic Intellectual Capital Evaluation Model (SICEM)" and a trademark called the "Integrative Strategic Value Management System (ISVMS)" in 2012 and 2013 from Taiwan, China and the USA. Professor Wu subdivided the management accounting of an organization into five systems: strategy-forming system, strategy implementation system, activity-oriented management system, activity-oriented value management system and strategic value creation system. Further information on the frameworks can be found in ISVMS. These products allow her as a researcher to gain access to corporate practice and thus establish close cooperation.
4 See Du, Tang, and Young (2012) for a more detailed description of the supervision of SASAC on SOEs.
5 If an article pertains to various tasks that can be categorized into different dimensions listed, the authors tried to select a main topic (task) of the article using its title and listed keywords.
6 Source: www.nseac.com.
7 MPAcc stands for Master of Public Accountant; EMBA stands for Executive Master of Business Administration; EMPAcc stands for Executive Master of Public Accountant.

References

Association of Chartered Certified Accountants & Beijing National Accounting Institutes. (2014). *Investigation Report: Management Accounting Practices in Chinese Firms.*

Association of Chartered Certified Accountants & Shanghai National Accounting Institutes. (2014). *Investigation Report: The Application of Management Accounting in Chinese Enterprises.*

Du, F., Tang, G. & Young, M. (2012). Influence activities and favoritism in subjective performance evaluation: Evidence from Chinese state-owned enterprises. *The Accounting Review, 87*(5), 1555–1588.

Ho, J., Wu, A. & Xu, S. (2011). Corporate governance and returns on information technology investments: Evidence from an emerging market. *Strategic Management Journal, 32*(6), 595–623.

Ministry of Finance, People's Republic of China. (2014). *The guidelines of widely implementing and constructing management accounting systems.* (Speech scripts).

Kim, W. C. & Mauborgne, R. (2005). *Blue Ocean Strategy: How to create uncontested market space and make the competition irrelevant.* Boston: Harvard Business School Press.

Sun, Z. & Li, Z. (2014). The trend and path of the reform of higher accounting education. *Accounting Research, 11,* 3–15 (in Chinese).

Wu, A. (1990). The spirit of ABC system: Increasing the competitiveness of enterprises. *Accounting Research Monthly, 62,* 92–95 (in Chinese).

Wu, A. (1991). Activity-based costing system. *Accounting Research Monthly, 68,* 29–31 (in Chinese).

Wu, A. (1992a). The application for the combination of ABC and quality costing system. *Budget, Accounting and Statistics Monthly, 73*(4), 49–54 (in Chinese).

Wu, A. (1992b). Services of activity-based management system: A case study of the accountancy firm (1). *Accounting Research Monthly, 81,* 17–24 (in Chinese).

Wu, A. (1992c). Services of activity-based management system: A case study of the accountancy firm (2). *Accounting Research Monthly, 82,* 59–66 (in Chinese).

Wu, A. (1997a). BSC: Transfer strategy to action (1). *Accounting Research Monthly, 134,* 133–140 (in Chinese).

Wu, A. (1997b). BSC: Transfer strategy to action (2). *Accounting Research Monthly, 135,* 102–116 (in Chinese).

Wu, A. (1997c). BSC: transfer strategy to action (3). *Accounting Research Monthly, 136,* 108–118 (in Chinese).

Wu, A. (2002). An analysis of intellectual capital. *Accounting Research Monthly, 204,* 57–66 (in Chinese).

Wu, A. (2003a). The essence, category, and the integration of balanced scorecard (1). *Accounting Research Monthly, 211,* 45–54 (in Chinese).

Wu, A. (2003b). The essence, category, and the integration of balanced scorecard (2). *Accounting Research Monthly, 211,* 45–54 (in Chinese).

Wu, A. (2003c). An analysis of implementation of government institutions on balanced scorecard. *Bimonthly Journal for Research, Development and Evaluation, 237,* 45–61 (in Chinese).

Wu, A. (2004a). The prior development direction of balanced scorecard. *Accounting Research Monthly, 224,* 98–108 (in Chinese).

Wu, A. (2004b). The study of feasibility of promoting the balanced scorecard by banking. *Sinopac Financial Journal Quarterly, 27,* 47–80 (in Chinese).

Wu, A. (2007). The activity-based costing system for the direction of development and integration. *Accounting Research Monthly, 263*, 60–76 (in Chinese).

Wu, A. (2012). The introduction of strategic intellectual capital evaluation management model and case analysis. *Accounting Research Monthly, 314*, 100–113 (in Chinese).

Wu, A., Peng, H., Kuo, T. & Chan, A. L. (2016). A literature review of accounting academic research in Taiwan. *Journal of Management, 33*(1), 1–49 (in Chinese).

Yang, C., Wang, M. & Hsu, M. (2013). The footprints of Taiwan industrial history: A case of umbrella making industry. *Sun Yat-Sen Management Review, 21*(2), 369–412 (in Chinese).

5   Management accountants in France

A range of fragile, open-ended positionings

Caroline Lambert and Jérémy Morales[1]

Introduction

It was only in the 1970s that the position of management accountants "flourished" in French firms and French organizations more broadly. Today, many management accountants occupy relatively strategic positions given their direct contact with the CFOs, who are becoming more important as financial methods of management become generalized (Zorn, 2004). Contrary to what was sometimes predicted in the past, they look unlikely to disappear in the foreseeable future (Bouquin & Fiol, 2007). However, the occupation covers such a heterogeneous collection of activities, roles and profiles that it can be difficult to define what they have in common. Management accountants' work is always affected by its organizational setting, and this explains the diversity of positionings observed. Yet certain features connected with historical and cultural backgrounds have an influence on the occupation, and although it would be an exaggeration to talk of a "French-style" management accountant, France does have a certain national tradition that goes some way to explaining the practical expressions of management accounting observed in French business. The dominance of engineers and the "honor principle" (d'Iribarne, 1989, 1994) help to grasp the environment in which management accountants work in France. As we shall see, this context often forces management accountants in France to position themselves in relation to competing functions and "sell their work to the operationals."[2]

Historical background to the function's emergence: the dominance of engineers

In the United States, the emergence of management accounting dates back to the 1920s. It was marked from the outset by a clearly financial orientation. Alfred Sloan and Donaldson Brown were both qualified engineers, but what made them famous was the introduction of financial ratios (the famous ROI pyramid) and control of a primarily budgetary and profit-driven nature at General Motors and DuPont (Sloan, 1963). In the United Kingdom, cost accountants appeared as early as the First World War and soon gained significant influence, under the explicit model of the accounting profession in the UK (Loft, 1986). In France, the principles of "*contrôle de gestion*," literally "management control," spread essentially from the 1960s, chiefly through engineers (Bhimani, 1998). The struggles between engineers and accountants to have sole competence for management accounting happened in different ways in France and the United States.

In France, the management accounting field had long been the preserve of engineers,[3] especially graduates of the prestigious *Ecole Polytechnique* (Moutet, 1984), some of whom headed projects that were accounting, industrial and political in nature all at once (Bouquin, 1995, 2008, 2011). Lieutenant-Colonel Emile Rimailho (inventor of a method for allocating indirect charges called the "homogeneous sections" method) and Auguste Detoeuf (the first president of Alsthom and promoter of uniformized cost calculation methods), are good examples (Bouquin, 1995, 1997; Lemarchand & Le Roy, 2000). The dominance of engineers, with their talent for complex numerical reasoning, doubtless explains the level of sophistication found in the management accounting methods adopted by French firms (Bhimani, 1998; Bouquin, 2008).

Also, French management committees have not been affected by the "rising power" of the accounting function as much as observed in the United Kingdom and United States. Referring to a 1972 study by the British Management Institute about management committee membership, Armstrong (1985, p. 129) underlined that more British Chairs and CEOs had a banking or accounting background than a technical engineering-type background. Fligstein (1990) reported similar observations for the United States. In contrast, a study of French employers from 1912 to 1973 by Levy-Leboyer (1979) showed the dominant role played in management bodies by engineers, many of them graduates of the top engineering schools, particularly the *Ecole Polytechnique*. Even today, the top French engineering schools supply close to 50 percent of the managers of the largest French firms (Gomez & Guedri, 2014).

In a context where technical development of control systems and management accounting was attributable to engineers, the principal managers were for a long time reluctant to appoint management controllers, whom they did not perceive as providing any added value. In the first edition of *Echanges*, the principal journal for management accounting practitioners in France, de Fréminville (1967) rejected the idea of using the services of a management accountant, arguing that "control" was the CEO's responsibility and "no-one else can do it for him." The title of "management controller" was also "hard to accept for the management, who find it too ambitious," and "the people who might bear the title, because it does not give them the degree of prestige and authority to which they believe they are entitled" (de Fréminville, 1967).[4] Furthermore, as Martin (1969) observed following a study conducted for the *Association Nationale des Contrôleurs de Gestion* (ANCG)[5] of French management accountants (who in this study were called *contrôleurs d'affaires* or "business controllers") in French subsidiaries of US firms, "French business controllers still often wonder what their role is."

Cultural context: French specificities in hierarchical relations and performance assessment

D'Iribarne's (1989) analysis of national management methods brings out the tensions and contradictions that exist between the French way of management and the principles and methods of management accounting. These contradictions have a significant impact on the work of management accountants in France.

The honor principle

D'Iribarne (1989) describes French organizations as being founded on an "honor principle." Some of the rules applicable in a "French-style management model," particularly the vision of responsibilities and judgment criteria, but also hierarchical relations inside organizations, are not without impact on the place and role of management accountants.[6]

According to d'Iribarne (1989), French society is marked by strong corporatism (which Bourdieu (1989) calls the "esprit de corps"). Every individual is defined by his or her "status," which confers certain prerogatives but also obligations:

> Each of the groups I observed appears to be not only attached to prerogatives, but also duties. Each "status" is marked by a demanding idea of the responsibilities incumbent on its members solely by virtue of belonging to it, without having to be required by some authority; there are many duties that must be fulfilled above and beyond any legal and contractual obligations, and any formal sanction threatening the man [*sic*] who shirks them. Far from being incompatible with the defense of particularisms and privileges, this vision of duty is closely associated with it.
>
> (d'Iribarne, 1989, p. 57)

D'Iribarne outlines a connection between this view of responsibility as independent of any legal, hierarchical and contractual framework and the concept of honor as defined by Montesquieu in *The Spirit of the Laws*:

> What every group considers honorable or contrary to honor is not defined by reason, or by law, or by the prince. It is a "prejudgement." It depends "on its own caprice," not the will of any other person. Only a tradition can set it. It is less "what we owe to others than what we owe ourselves"; it is not "so much what calls us towards our fellow citizens as what distinguishes us from them." It is closely bound up with pride in one's "rank" and the fear of being deprived of it."
>
> (d'Iribarne, 1989, p. 59)

This logic of responsibility founded on honor means that each individual wishes to work (or feels they work) for an objective that reaches beyond the sphere of their own direct interest. The organization thus benefits from "the intensity with which each person applies themselves to their work, as long as he [*sic*] feels honored" (d'Iribarne, 1989, p. 98). But "height," "rank" and "distinction" lead people to refuse anything that could reduce them to a servile condition. Since honor is what everyone "owes themselves," the forms of incentive will only be effective if they preserve a feeling of independence, and servile submission is contrary to honor.

In their idea of work, French management accountants appear to follow the national culture. But that culture is not totally convergent with a management accounting logic founded on a view of the organization that tends to be associated with an Anglo-American idea of responsibilities and relations at work in which the contract plays a central role. While the two logics are not totally opposed (both, for example, stress the notion of independence), they do sometimes conflict. This has an effect on the work, position and role management accountants may hope for in French firms. We examine four points of tension: the service relationship, the concept of control, the concept of accountability and the relationship with financial data.

Helping without becoming servile

Hopper (1980), in a UK setting, presents the service role for management accountants as prestigious, but the French view of the relationship to work sees more ambiguous connotations in the idea of "service." In a logic of honor, service is perceived as low-prestige when it is considered equivalent to a situation of servitude (d'Iribarne, 1989). This is a general concern for all support functions (Lambert, 2005). They often try to avoid being perceived as "at the service of" others, which can easily be considered as a relationship of servility in which everyone must know their place. Instead, they present themselves as "helping" and "cooperating" with managers in a relationship of exchange between individuals who consider themselves peers. As d'Iribarne (1989, p. 109) notes: "It is perfectly honorable to do voluntarily, 'to help,' something that would be humiliating to do under the obligations of a position where one is 'at the service of'." This idea also means managers with whom good informal relationships have been built up will be less reluctant to respond to management accountants' requests for information (Morales & Lambert, 2013). "Cultivating" relationships by personalization and special arrangements, opening the door to cooperation in a give-and-take dynamic that extends over time, can limit the asymmetry of service relationships and encourage mutual trust and cooperation (Bigus, 1972). Gaining acceptance in units they are supposed to work with and developing interpersonal relationships with managers becomes an integral part of management accountants' work.

The ambivalence of control

The second tension for French management accountants derives from their name of "management controllers." The French word "*contrôle*" can mean "check" or "inspection" and carries negative connotations of checks by the police, or the tax or legal authorities. In France, as in Germany and Austria (but unlike the United Kingdom), control is perceived as a form of subordination (Scheytt et al., 2003, p. 531). While the British tend to see control as an opportunity for personal development, the French generally consider it related to an embarrassing, awkward situation: being "controlled" is perceived as being a victim of a power structure (Scheytt et al., 2003, p. 532). In such a context, controllers are often caricatured as following "ridiculous" behavior (Scheytt et al., 2003, p. 526).

The very fact that a superior can closely control, or monitor, a junior seems inappropriate in France. It is interpreted both as a sign of distrust and as despicable behavior by the superior (d'Iribarne, 1989). This is even truer when an outsider asks a member of the group for explanations. In a corporate spirit, "solidarity" must reign between all the members of the group, including between superiors and juniors. This means that the person sent by the finance division is no more welcome in the operational departments than the external auditor in the very same finance division: each person is careful not to disclose any information that might put their superior (or junior) in difficulty without prior consent, which would be perceived as a form of denunciation. This leads certain business partner-style management controllers who are strongly involved in the business units to collude with managers to subvert hierarchical control (Lambert and Sponem, 2005; Lambert & Sponem, 2012).

The limits of accountability

This ambivalent attitude toward control is hard to reconcile with the central importance of accountability processes in Anglo-American systems of management accounting. In France, asking a junior for explanations can easily be experienced as a humiliation if the junior feels the request is an implicit accusation of incompetence, or indicates a lack of trust. Compliments remain implicit and encouragements and congratulations are rarely expressed. The bonus and promotion periods are interesting. Asking for a pay rise is coherent with a conception of performance in which everyone must advertise themselves; talking about one's own achievements is much more problematic under an honor principle that sanctions individuals who do not "know their place" and are too "self-interested" or "proud" (Weber, 1989). It is often considered more "natural" in the French business culture to receive a promotion without having actively sought it.

Accountability processes also raise questions in a context where intelligence is reflected less in the ability to achieve the objectives set than in the ability to find new ways to get round procedures in order to lighten the workload, simplify the task, change the rules of the game or divert the attention of distant controllers (Crozier & Friedberg, 1977). In a culture where rules and monitoring are perceived as contrary to the honor principle, and resistance and circumvention are readily celebrated, such compromises are rarely considered illegitimate, but rather seen as a clever way to "play the system," or make up for the absurdity or complexity of hierarchical or bureaucratic directives that are issued by remote authorities or are "unreasonable." And conversely, anyone who simply "does as he's told" is perceived as naïve and lacking in ambition, mediocre, unworthy of honor.

Asking for proof of the results achieved, holding long meetings where everyone must promote their recent achievements, making no secret of successes and failures: the whole accountability process is often perceived by the French as a fool's game or a sham, because such exercises appear hard to reconcile with the honor principle, *esprit de corps* and rank.

Financial data versus "useful" data

In this situation, figures are accepted, but only if they are useful for understanding "how things work" (d'Iribarne, 1989, p. 106), if they enable everyone to understand their own scope of intervention and act on that. Technical data are more easily accepted than financial data. Financial data, particularly if they are used to "judge" "individual performance," can elicit rejection and bafflement. It is not unusual to hear a manager say that "you can't do anything with" accounting data (Morales, 2009). However, collecting and using technical data is accepted when the aim is to improve procedures, and the manager remains completely in control of them. Figures are thus considered useful, but must not come into conflict with the sense of duty and autonomy claimed by individuals in the French model of society. To achieve this, figures must help the manager "steer" the activity rather than enabling the superior to assess his/her juniors (even if the manager and superior in this example are one and the same person); inform him/her about the activities managed, but not inform the people to whom he/she is accountable. This tricky relationship with figures is central to the safeguarding function of French management accountants (Lambert & Sponem, 2012). The data produced and used by management controllers, perceived by engineers as less robust than the data they themselves produce, and incorporated into a reporting system that shows little congruence with the honor principle, are particularly difficult to legitimize in the eyes of French managers.[7]

Problematic positioning: neither accountant, nor manager

Non-specialist training and various career trajectories

In contrast to their British and American counterparts, French management accountants, like the Germans, are not formally organized into a profession. Theses on the subject of French management accountants, although they are not free of bias,[8] provide a picture of their training (Demaret, 2014; Lambert, 2005, Legalais, 2014; Morales, 2009; Redslob, 2012). The vast majority of people interviewed followed general management studies, and did not opt for any specialization in accounting or management accounting. Legalais (2014) observes that specialist management accounting courses are finding it difficult to attract students, both in universities and business schools. It is extremely rare to find a management accountant who is a qualified accountant (or has any other professional certification). However, most of them have a qualification equivalent to five years of higher education, and generally have "*cadre*" or executive status. Some engineers round off their studies with an MBA or one-year master's in management before they become management accountants. Management accountants may complete an internship in management accounting during university, in certain cases complemented by experience in auditing which they see as a kind of finishing school. Both students and practitioners appear to value an education that combines general management knowledge (acquired through a postgraduate course in the case of engineers) with practical specialization in management accounting.

Ahrens and Chapman (1999) show that the difference in educational background has a strong influence on perception of the role that management accountants are prepared to play in organizations. Auditing experience also influences the management accountants' view, making them more inclined to perceive themselves as guardians of internal control and objectivity in figures, while engineers are generally more interested in the "realities of the business." Redslob (2012) and Legalais (2014) show that as their careers progress, management accountants in France often seem to have to choose between their organizational identity and their occupational identity. As a result French management accountants follow a varied range of career trajectories that are open-ended but lack uniformity. Puyou (2015), for example, sees a distinction between management accountants from the operational side of business and their counterparts who consider themselves primarily as financial specialists (and move between group companies, or between groups); this places them in separate professional networks, with different expectations and consequences as regards the nature of the reporting information sent to the upper echelons. Legalais (2014) and Redslob (2012) also demonstrate differences in perspective: some have a career plan built around management accounting (the ultimate goal generally being to reach a CFO post) while others only see it as a transitional phase (a few years as management accountant will give them financial skills that will later be useful for operational or general management posts).

This diversity of profiles is not without impact on the boundaries of the occupation's jurisdiction, which are much vaguer in France than in countries where the regulated management accounting profession has considerable influence (Canada, UK, USA, New Zealand, Australia, etc.). French management accountants thus have more latitude, but their positioning in the organization appears to be more tenuous than in these English-speaking countries, in relation to both managers and competitors of the function.

The function and its "competitors"

French management accountants seek to define their work in relation to, and by differentiation from, various organizational groups. The literature, for example, has demonstrated their connections with marketing (Farjaudon, 2007; Farjaudon & Morales, 2013), purchasing (Sebti et al., 2015), quality (Demaret, 2014) and R&D (Morales, 2009). But the most significant connection is their relationship with the accounting departments.

French management accountants make it a point of honor that they should not be taken for accountants. This is a recurrent finding in the theses written on the topic (Lambert, 2005; Morales, 2009; Demaret, 2014; Legalais, 2014). The distinction is doubtless explained by the negative stereotypes of the accounting profession (Bougen, 1994; Friedman & Lyne, 1997, 2001), which are particularly marked in France where being an accountant does not carry the same prestige as in other countries. But it is also coherent with the cultural analysis presented earlier. When asked what differentiates them from accountants, French management accountants often say "considering the bigger picture" (as opposed to accountants who are believed to focus on the detail) and producing figures that are useful for decision-making, in contrast to accounting documents that are useful for their detail and precision rather than for their influence on operational decisions. Accounting figures are perceived to be associated with an aim of monitoring, assessment and self-justification, while management accountants want to supply instruments managers could use for their own purposes, and which are "really" useful for "steering" the activity. This symbolic distinction between the autonomous (and thus honorable) manager and the (negatively perceived) hierarchical supervisor is what explains their desire to avoid becoming too closely associated with the accountant's role.

One relationship that is perhaps less studied is the management accountants' relationship with the IT departments. Yet they increasingly interact with the IT team,[9] who are sometimes specialized in accounting and financial systems (Morales, 2009). This is because management accountants need to be familiar with the information systems (in many cases, they were involved in development of the system architecture) just as much as they need to understand operational processes.[10] They also have to monitor major IT projects, which are sometimes extremely expensive. They regularly ask the IT division to develop "solutions" that are useful for the finance division. But in addition to all this collaboration, management accountants may find themselves positioned more clearly as competitors to the IT specialists when a control system for operational managers is to be designed. Such systems are built on accounting and operational data, involving mechanisms that relate to management accounting but operate through an IT medium, and for these reasons they are often produced in collaboration with the IT specialists. Meanwhile, the IT specialists occasionally develop financial competence that means they are able to respond directly to requests from operational staff, bypassing the management accountants. As a result a degree of competition can emerge around this activity.

Although they are far from any form of social closure (Sarfatti Larson, 1977), French management accountants are keen to establish a certain monopoly: for example, they want to be the only people able to determine the legitimate measures of performance (Farjaudon & Morales, 2013). Their scope of activity depends broadly on a definition that is locally situated, because it is influenced by power struggles, personalities and organizational traditions. Due to their personal view of their post, they seek to delegate tasks considered non-relevant to other departments, but also want to appropriate or "take over" certain other tasks (Lambert, 2005). Delegation, here, is a way to reduce the workload or avoid the "dirty work" (Morales & Lambert, 2013), but also involves the loss of a zone of responsibility. This situation is particularly sensitive as regards interaction with operational staff.

Selling their work to the operationals

In France as in many other countries, the "business partner" myth prevails (Morales & Lambert, 2013). Management accountants are encouraged to "leave their desks and spreadsheets" (their "ivory tower") and bring "added value" to the managers. But French management accountants are not always very warmly received by "the operationals" (Morales & Lambert, 2013). Oriot (2004), for example, shows that while management accountants and operational staff can have a complementary relationship, they can also become locked into an undermining or broken relationship. This happens because management accountants suffer from a rather negative image (Redslob, 2012; Legalais, 2014) and have to gain acceptance by showing that they are not "spies from the general management," helping the people they deal with to "overcome the fear of surveillance" – which is contrary to honor.

Even when the management accountants are accepted and manage to overcome their function's negative stereotypes, cooperation with operational staff often remains relative. The management accountants must also legitimize their work itself (Morales, 2009; Demaret, 2014). They often say they have to "sell their work," "charm" the operationals and spend their time "educating" managers to explain why it is in their interest to refer to them. And yet discussions with operationals primarily concern reporting and budgeting activities, and are thus moments of hierarchical accountability (Morales & Lambert, 2013). The management accountants would prefer to play the roles of coordinator and advisor, which require regular cooperation independently of assessment processes. But that is a very specific role for management accountants, and one that certain managers and organizations do not necessarily want to encourage.

From a qualitative study of 93 management accountants working in multinational firms that are leaders in their respective markets, Lambert (2005) has shown that while certain management accountants benefit from authority in decision-making and have "equal-footing" relationships with managers, this is by no means always the case. "Discreet" functions, which appear to concern the majority of the people interviewed, and "safeguarding" functions suffer from a lack of recognition and several tactics are used to try and obtain greater authority (Lambert, 2005; Lambert & Sponem, 2012). At the other end of the spectrum, in the rare cases of organizations that have to implement a structural cost-killing strategy, management accountants can become central links in the organization, monitored guards in a panopticon, set up as truth-tellers within the organization (Lambert & Pezet, 2011). This makes them direct competitors with managers, in some cases taking their place.

The "business partner," the mythical figure of the modern management accountant that is often presented as a magical cure-all, has not become established as an uncontestable norm in organizational practices, however efficient the organization (Lambert & Sponem, 2012). Rather than a generalization of the "business partner management accounting function," we are seeing the emergence of a new segment within the function, the "business partner" assisted by other management accountants who specialize in production of reporting (Morales, 2009).

This combination is presented as a solution to the problem of manager accountability: the business partner who is friendly with operationals is counterbalanced by a guardian who guarantees validity in the figures. To guarantee their credibility with operationals, business partners must demonstrate their awareness of the potential side-effects of short-term, opportunistic management accounting which is too inflexible and encourages "gaming" and blame avoidance – a system based on "naming and shaming" rather than giving people control over their operations generates "irresponsible behaviors" (Bouquin, 1998, p. 12). They promote the idea that their objective is not to produce information (an activity that is delegated to the reporting team), but to analyze and interpret that information, i.e. relate it to an operational event (Morales, 2013). Management accountants thus position themselves within a discourse of their added value lying in their "neutrality": the fact that they are independent of line management guarantees all parties a viewpoint, thus ensuring objectivity in the numbers produced, whereas operationals seek to defend an interpretation that is favorable to them. The management accountants are positioned at the interface between senior management and operational departments: for the operationals they "translate" the hierarchical constraints expressed in accounting language by the management, and for the remote managers they report on operational events that give meaning to the figures (Legalais & Morales, 2014).

This positioning strategy does not always work, and may lead to the disappearance of the business partner, as the management accountant's only remaining function is to supply and guarantee the reporting. Some people even talk of "pre-consolidation," thus stressing their role as guarantor of the figures, which appears to have become more important than all other roles.[11] Managers may also become the management accountants' primary competitors. In mass consumption industries, for instance, brand managers spend most of their time analyzing past returns and estimating potential ones. In the automotive industry, pricing specialists spend most of their time in tasks that could perfectly fit management accountants' duties. These positions do not report to the financial management but often directly to a line manager, and need hybrid skills to understand both operations and accounting. Although they may be reluctant to deal with accounting data, engineers are not afraid of figures and produce many indicators to monitor their work, including measures for costs and margins where necessary. These indicators are based on categories that are often more relevant for the engineers than the categories used by management accountants (Morales, 2009; Redslob, 2012). The French *tableau de bord* (Bourguinon et al., 2004) is thus often constructed without any input from management accountants.

Conclusion

In contrast to the British cost accountants described by Loft (1986), French management accountants (or "management controllers") are not formally organized into a profession, and have not based their occupational aims on the model of chartered or certified accountants. For a long time they were more similar to engineers, but they have gradually sought to differentiate themselves and avoid competition with engineers, of the kind experienced in the United States (Abbott, 1988). However, accounting and finance departments do not share the prestige of engineers in France. Management controllers usually have a relatively humble reputation, which affects the occupation's identity construction. They must find (and defend) a position in relation to other competing groups and demonstrate their relevance to other people, beginning with the operational managers. Doubts are sometimes cast on their technical skills and legitimacy (Demaret, 2014). The traditional tools of management accounting, but above all their use as a measure of individual performance, are clearly marked by a specific culture. The sacred dimension of figures and their systematic use in individual performance assessment are coherent with the American pattern of action, in which the contract and the associated limited liability play a central role. In France, figures are not sacred and their use as a measure of performance conflicts with the conception of responsibility. In this environment, the use of figures can appear legitimate as long as the individuals perceive themselves as being in control of the figures, and the figures concerned are useful for improving their entity's operation.

The challenge facing management accountants in France is thus how to carve out a place where they can supply interpretations that reincorporate elements of context, reading "between the figures" in a detached but positive way, to give managers the control and enlightenment that makes them wholly "responsible" in coherence with the honor principle. This is not an easy position, since direct intervention by a management accountant into what (in France) is perceived as the manager's responsibility could be equivalent to relieving the manager of some of his or her duties. An expert who helps to decode accounting language may be welcome, but a representative of the distant authority (a "spy") will easily be kept out of the information channels (until he or she must beg for the figures needed to prepare the reporting). Also, while the mythical figure of the "business partner" is presented as the ideal model, it must not bring about a loss of independence that would place the management accountant "at the service of" the operationals. A partner who "helps" without "removing responsibility," who succeeds in putting across "tough messages" without losing the "trust" of the people he or she deals with – such a position is naturally unstable, ambivalent and unsettled. The French management accountants' major ambition is to demonstrate that their specific expertise is relevant for managers (Lambert, 2005; Morales, 2009; Redslob, 2012; Demaret, 2014; Legalais, 2014). This ambition remains largely unfulfilled to date.

Notes

1 We would like to thank Laetitia Legalais, Ludivine Redslob and Hicham Sebti for offering instructive comments on an earlier draft of this chapter.
2 This is an ambiguous expression. French management accountants generally talk of "operationals," a term that seems to cover anyone who does not work in the finance division. The primary aim is to distinguish bookkeeping tasks, which can be done from the desk, from decision support tasks, which need management accountants to spend more time with people up and down the hierarchical line.
3 In the sense that the term is commonly used, engineers in France form a homogeneous group of people who have a high level of studies certified by a qualification, and enjoy high status. Historically, engineers have been part of the country's economic and political elite (Bourdieu, 1989).
4 All English translations of French quotations are the authors' own.
5 This association, now renamed the *Association Nationale des Directeurs Financiers et de Contrôle de Gestion* (DFCG), is not a professional association in the Anglo-American sense, as it originated in the Cegos, a private vocational and in-service training center set up by French employers in 1926 to spread the principles of scientific management. Since 1967, the association has published the journal *Echanges* (whose editorial board and authors are business executives). In practice, this association is a network that does not issue any qualifications and has few connections with higher education and research.
6 The idea of a "national culture" is necessarily an over-simplification (McSweeney, 2002; Scheytt et al., 2003). Firm managers can be considered as a homogeneous group since they have been through various selection processes that are particularly discriminating as they are based on "elective affinity" (Boltanski, 1982; Bourdieu, 1989). However, we should not ignore the diversity of practices and perceptions, which have in fact evolved substantially under the influence of Anglo-American management methods (Djelic & Zarlowski, 2005). We use the cultural analysis proposed by d'Iribarne (1989) because it brings out certain features that are coherent with the perceptions of the people we interviewed for empirical studies. We thus draw inspiration from this analysis "pragmatically and as a heuristic device" (Scheytt et al., 2003, p. 520), while remembering that it is simplistic to want to describe the whole of French society in just a few clearly-defined concepts.
7 Once again it is important to note that this view covers a range of disparities. Many French managers, particularly business school graduates but also many engineers, make extensive use of accounting data. Our aim here is simply to highlight the more fragile legitimacy of financial data in French organizations than other settings.
8 The people interviewed for management accounting theses are not necessarily representative of the general population of French management accountants. The bias tends to be conservative: it is possible that management accounting doctoral students can more easily contact practitioners who at some point in their career had some education in management accounting (either because they are on the alumni lists, or through personal connections); engineers, on the other hand, are probably underrepresented (particularly engineers who do not hold the title of management accountant even though their work is similar).
9 The time spent with IT teams is rarely mentioned in the literature, even though the parameters of an enterprise resource planning (ERP) system cannot be set without IT

specialists. This is because this relationship is not "operational," but between two functions. The management accountants' attitude to IT colleagues is very similar to the attitude they criticize in operationals toward themselves.

10 Management accountants' work has been strongly affected by the generalization of certain IT software packages (Puyou & Faÿ, 2015), from data warehouses to ERP systems, via consolidation, budgeting and investment management software. These types of software have made it possible to automate a large number of tasks, although some tasks are still performed manually, as reflected in the extensive use of spreadsheets. Some people complain that they spend less time collecting data but more time correcting it, for example when they have to find data input errors that have led to irregular figures (Morales & Lambert, 2013).

11 Some people emphasize the pressure from institutional investors and financial markets, which impose reporting deadlines that are becoming harder to meet and require control systems focusing primarily on creation of value for the shareholder. Their work is thus shaped by the needs of financial reporting. Paradoxically, the financialization of organizations does not necessarily result in a broader role for management accountants.

References

Abbott, A. D. (1988). *The system of professions: An essay on the division of expert labor*. Chicago: Chicago University Press.

Ahrens, T. & Chapman, C. (1999). The role of management accountants in Britain and Germany. *Management Accounting*, May, 42–43.

Armstrong, P. (1985). Changing management control strategies: The role of competition between accountancy and other organisational professions. *Accounting, Organizations and Society, 10*(2), 129–148.

Bhimani, A. (1998). Knowledge, motivation and accounting form: An historical exploration. *European Accounting Review, 7*(1); 1–30.

Bigus, O. E. (1972). The milkman and his customer: A cultivated relationship. *Urban Life and Culture, 1*(2), 131–165.

Boltanski, L. (1982). *Les cadres: la formation d'un groupe social*. Paris, Minuit,

Bougen, P. D. (1994). Joking apart: The serious side to the accountant stereotype. *Accounting, Organizations and Society, 19*(3), 319–335.

Bouquin, H. (1995). Rimailho revisité. *Comptabilité, Contrôle, Audit, 1*(2), 5–33.

Bouquin, H. (1997). Management accounting in its social context: Rimailho revisited. *Accounting, Business & Financial History, 7*(3): 315–343.

Bouquin, H. (1998). *Le contrôle de gestion pousse-t-il les managers à des comportements irresponsables?* Working paper 9801 & 9802. Paris: CREFIGE.

Bouquin, H. (2008). *Le contrôle de gestion: contrôle de gestion, contrôle d'entreprise et gouvernance*. Paris: Presses Universitaires de France.

Bouquin, H. (2011). *Les fondements du contrôle de gestion*. Paris: Presses Universitaires de France.

Bouquin, H. & Fiol, M. (2007), Le contrôle de gestion: repères perdus, espaces à retrouver, paper presented at 28th annual conference of AFC, Poitiers.

Bourdieu, P. (1989). *La noblesse d'État: grandes écoles et esprit de corps*. Paris: Les Éditions de Minuit.

Bourguignon, A., Malleret, V. & Nørreklit, H. (2004). The American balanced scorecard versus the French tableau de bord: The ideological dimension. *Management Accounting Research, 15*(2), 107–134.

Crozier, M. & Friedberg, E. (1977). *L'acteur et le système: les contraintes de l'action collective.* Paris: Editions du Seuil.

de Fréminville. C. (1967). Qu'est-ce qu'un contrôleur de gestion? *Echanges,* 1(1).

d'Iribarne, P. (1989). *La logique de l'honneur: gestion des entreprises et traditions nationales.* Paris: Editions du Seuil.

d'Iribarne, P. (1994). The honour principle in the "bureaucratic phenomenon". *Organization Studies, 15*(1): 81–97.

Demaret, J. (2014). *Le processus de construction de légitimité des contrôleurs de gestion.* Unpublished PhD, Tours: Université de Tours.

Djelic, M.-L. & Zarlowski, P. (2005). Entreprises et gouvernance en France: perspectives historiques et évolutions récentes. *Sociologie du travail, 47*(4), 451–469.

Farjaudon, A.-L. (2007). *L'impact des marques sur les modes de pilotage de l'entreprise.* Unpublished PhD, Paris: Université Paris Dauphine.

Farjaudon, A.-L. & Morales, J. (2013). In search of consensus: The role of accounting in the definition and reproduction of dominant interests. *Critical Perspectives on Accounting, 24*(2), 154–171.

Fligstein, N. (1990). *The transformation of corporate control.* Cambridge, Mass.: Harvard University Press.

Friedman, A. L. & Lyne, S. R. (1997). Activity-based techniques and the death of the beancounter. *European Accounting Review, 6,* 19–44.

Friedman, A. L. & Lyne, S. R. (2001). The beancounter stereotype: Towards a general model of stereotype generation. *Critical Perspectives on Accounting, 12,* 423–451.

Gomez, P. Y. & Guedri, Z. (2014). *Qui sont les patrons français? Évolution des dirigeants des entreprises cotées 1992–2012, Preuves à l'appui.* Les cahiers de l'IFGE, 4.

Hopper, T. M. (1980). Role conflicts of management accountants and their position within organisation structures. *Accounting, Organizations and Society, 5*(4), 401–411.

Lambert, C. (2005). *La fonction contrôle de gestion. Contribution à l'analyse de la place des services fonctionnels dans l'organisation.* Unpublished PhD, Paris: Université Paris-Dauphine.

Lambert, C. & Pezet, E. (2011). The making of the management accountant: Becoming the producer of truthful knowledge. *Accounting, Organizations and Society, 36*(1), 10–30.

Lambert, C. & Sponem, S. (2005). Corporate governance and profit manipulation: A French field study. *Critical Perspectives on Accounting, 16*(6), 717–748.

Lambert, C. & Sponem, S. (2012). Roles, authority and involvement of the management accounting function: A multiple case-study perspective. *European Accounting Review, 21*(3), 565–589.

Legalais, L. (2014). *La construction de l'identité professionnelle des contrôleurs de gestion. Les trajectoires professionnelles et leur influence sur la financiarisation des organisations: Le cas Saint-Gobain.* Unpublished PhD, Paris: Université Paris Dauphine.

Legalais, L. & Morales, J. (2014). Interfaces, narrations et légitimations de la financiarisation. *Revue Française de Gestion, 40*(240), 165–184.

Lemarchand, Y. & Le Roy, F. (2000). L'introduction de la comptabilité analytique en France: de l'institutionnalisation d'une pratique de gestion. *Finance, Contrôle, Stratégie, 3*(4), 83–111.

Levy-Leboyer, M. (1979). Le patronat français, 1912–1973. In Levy-Leboyer, *Le patronat de la seconde industrialisation* (pp. 137–188). Paris: Les Editions Ouvrières.

Loft, A. (1986). Towards a critical understanding of accounting: The case of cost accounting in the U.K., 1914–1925. *Accounting, Organizations and Society, 11*(2), 137–169.

Martin, J.-A. (1969). Le contrôle de gestion dans les filiales françaises de sociétés américaines. *Echanges*, Avril.

McSweeney, B. (2002). Hofstede's model of national cultural differences and their consequences: A triumph of faith – a failure of analysis. *Human Relations, 55*(1), 89–118.

Morales, J. (2009). *Le contrôle comme dynamique de gouvernement et de socialisation. Une étude ethnographique des contrôleurs de gestion.* Unpublished PhD, Paris: Université Paris-Dauphine.

Morales, J. (2013). Le projet professionnel des contrôleurs de gestion: Analyser des données pour aider les managers à prendre des décisions rationnelles? *Comptabilité-Contrôle-Audit, 19*(2), 41–70.

Morales, J. & Lambert, C. (2013). Dirty work and the construction of identity: An ethnographic study of management accounting practices. *Accounting, Organizations and Society, 38*(3), 228–244.

Moutet, A. (1984). Ingénieurs et rationalisation: dans l'industrie française de la Grande Guerre au Front Populaire. *Culture Technique, 12*, 137–153.

Oriot, F. (2004). L'influence des systèmes relationnels d'acteurs sur les pratiques de contrôle de gestion. *Comptabilité-Contrôle-Audit, 10*(3), 237–255.

Puyou, F. R. (2015). Saisir les frontières des groupes de sociétés au travers de la dynamique des trajectoires professionnelles des contrôleurs de gestion, Comptabilité, Contrôle et Audit des invisibles, de l'informel et de l'imprévisible, 36th Annual Congress, Toulouse: Association Francophone de Comptabilité.

Puyou, F. R. & Faÿ, E. (2015). Cogs in the wheel or spanners in the works? A phenomenological approach to the difficulty and meaning of ethical work for financial controllers. *Journal of Business Ethics, 128*(4), 863–876.

Redslob, L. (2012). *Construction de l'identité professionnelle des contrôleurs de gestion dans un milieu où la performance financière est en quête de légitimité: le cas des armées françaises.* Unpublished PhD, Paris: Université Paris Dauphine.

Sarfatti Larson, M. (1977). *The rise of professionalism. A sociological analysis.* Berkeley: University of California Press.

Scheytt, T., Soin, K. & Metz, T. (2003). Exploring notions of control across cultures: A narrative approach. *European Accounting Review, 12*(3), 515–547.

Sebti, H., Gérard, B. & Perray-Redslob, L. (2015). Utilisation identitaire des dispositifs de contrôle par les membres d'un groupe professionnel: le cas des acheteurs. *Comptabilité, Contrôle, Audit, 21*(2), 13–32.

Sloan, A. P. J. (1963). *My years with General Motors.* New York: Currency Doubleday.

Weber, F. (1989). *Le travail à-côté: étude d'ethnographie ouvrière.* Paris: INRA-EHESS.

Zorn, D. M. (2004). Here a chief, there a chief: The rise of the CFO in the American firm. *American Sociological Review, 69*(3), 345–364.

6 The role of the controller in Germany

Utz Schäffer and Jürgen Weber

Introduction

In Germany, you will hardly find anyone with the job title of "management accountant." In fact, German management accountants consider it important to note that they are by no means accountants, instead referring to themselves as controllers. As such, they are typically part of a controlling unit, which can easily comprise several hundred controllers in a large DAX 30 company and typically reports to the CFO or – especially in smaller companies – to the CEO (Schäffer & Weber, 2015a).

According to data from the German Federal Employment Agency (Bundesagentur für Arbeit), there were approximately 100,000 controllers in Germany in 2014. This figure comprises 69,000 controllers with compulsory social insurance (not including freelance and staff controllers), and 21,000 cost accountants (who are usually also associated with controlling) as well as controllers with management responsibilities within the controlling function. In total, this corresponds to roughly 0.3 percent of compulsory social insurance employees and is more or less equivalent to the number of employees in the HR function (cf. Grunwald-Delitz et al., 2014). Controllers as a group possess a higher level of education and vocational training than employees in other professions within the finance function (cf. Grunwald-Delitz et al., 2014).

Demands on controllers are high, as a glance at the relevant skill profiles in textbooks and practice-oriented publications shows (cf. Gänßlen et al., 2013; Küpper et al., 2013; Weber & Schäffer, 2016). They range from a sound knowledge of measurement and control systems, analytical skills, a wide set of soft skills such as interpersonal and communication skills, steadfastness, and, last but not least, a solid understanding of the underlying business model. Interestingly, at least some former controllers tend to be successful outside the finance function. This is evident in the fact that the number of CEOs of German DAX companies with a controlling background is remarkably high.

In this chapter, we describe the profile of controllers in Germany. We discuss how their tasks and roles have changed over time as well as the extent to which they differ from the profile of management accountants in other parts of the world. In addition, we attempt to identify the drivers of controller-specific idiosyncrasies and provide an outlook on the forthcoming transformation of the controller profession.

Emergence of controller positions

In Germany, the term "controller" long remained unknown. This changed, only slightly at first, when travel experiences in the USA stimulated discussions in the 1950s (Auffermann, 1952) and then with a (small) number of seminal newspaper articles on US controllers (e.g. Gretz, 1965). However, rejection and misunderstanding still prevailed (Goossens, 1959). Even in the late 1960s, controllers were usually only found in the German subsidiaries of large US multinationals (Weber & Schäffer, 2008).

The combination of three factors contributed to the picture changing relatively rapidly (Binder, 2006; Schäffer et al., 2014).

- The shift from a seller's to a buyer's market and, in particular, the first oil crisis in 1973 led to increasing cost pressure and a stronger need for carrying out future-focused analyses.
- The increasingly felt need for a greater proximity to markets and the rising complexity of companies led to divisionalization and the formation of profit centers. These organizational forms in turn required adjustments to information supply and management control.
- The development of information technology and increasing prevalence of cost accounting concepts in the 1950s and 1960s (especially marginal planned cost accounting) enabled the realization of increased demands for transparency and economically informed decisions.

In the eyes of cost accountants and managers of the time, these developments appear to have required and enabled a greater integration of planning, control, and information supply, which often fell to the newly-created (or renamed) controller positions (cf. Schmidt et al., 2016). Not surprisingly, the number of such positions began to grow. According to a survey by McKinsey, 90 percent of companies with a turnover greater than 1 billion DM already had controller positions in 1974, even if they were not always named as such (Henzler, 1974). Other cross-sectional studies in the 1970s and 1980s provide a similar picture (for an overview, see Richter, 1987).

The task profile of controllers

An analysis of job advertisements in the leading German daily newspaper (the *Frankfurter Allgemeine Zeitung*) for the period from 1949 to 1994 illustrates the development of controller tasks (Weber & Kosmider, 1991; Weber & Schäffer, 1998). Most job advertisements show a marked prevalence of the simultaneous presence of budgeting and budget control as well as target-performance comparisons, variance analyses, and cost control. While controller positions were initially only offered by subsidiaries of American parent companies, the number of advertised positions increased significantly and progressively. In addition, the analyses of Weber and Kosmider (1991) as well as Weber and Schäffer (1998) indicate a certain change of tasks over the course of time (e.g. toward a stronger involvement of controllers in project work and strategic management), nonetheless without changing the fundamental profile.

A current task profile of controllers in the German-speaking area is provided by a series of surveys of the WHU Controller Panel[1] (cf. Schäffer & Weber, 2015a). As shown in Figure 6.1, the work of controllers from 2008 to 2014 appears to be characterized by a triad of (1) reporting and information supply, (2) planning and control, and (3) project-related work and advisory activities:

- At 21–23 percent, the majority of controller resources are allocated to reporting. Traditional cost accounting, on the other hand, occupies only 8–14 percent of controllers' time.
- Controllers, on average, spend 31 percent of their time on project-related and advisory activities.
- Planning and control related tasks constitute 32–36 percent of controllers' time. Here, budgeting dominates with 14–16 percent, followed by medium-term planning and control (mid-term) at 7 percent, strategic planning and

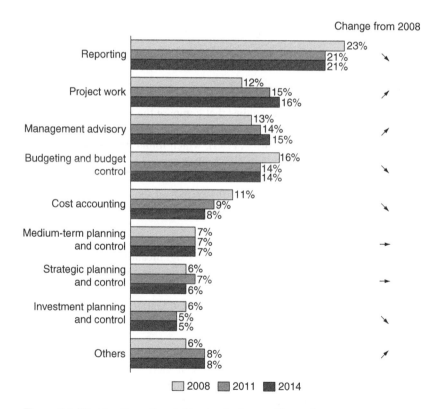

Figure 6.1 Working time allocated to standard controlling tasks.

Source: Schäffer and Weber (2015a, p. 13).

control at 6–7 percent, and planning and investment related planning and control (capital budgeting) at 5–6 percent.

Taken together, our results show that the fundamental task profile of controllers is still evident. However, the working time spent on cost-related tasks has decreased, whereas the share of project-related and advisory activities has gone up relative to earlier studies. A similar picture emerges over the six years of observation in the panel study: we note a slight decrease in the proportion of time for reporting, cost accounting, and budget planning and control, as well as an increase in project work and other management advisory activities. The basic task profile also remains largely stable if we allow for other contingencies. We can observe no differences across industries and only small differences due to company size and performance. More specifically, the results show that controllers in large companies are slightly less occupied with cost accounting than controllers in small companies; however, the more complex structures in large companies seem to imply more involvement with projects as well as operational and strategic planning tasks. With respect to company performance, a significant difference between high and lower performing companies is evident: controllers in companies with better performance invest a larger share of their working time in strategic planning and control, but less in reporting (cf. Schäffer & Weber, 2015a).

Tasks in a comparative perspective

Unfortunately, there are very few studies that compare the tasks of management accountants and controllers between countries. The likely first survey-based comparison was conducted by Stoffel (1995), which found three key differences of German controllers relative to their US counterparts:

- US controllers are responsible for a major part of budgeting activities, but they share the responsibility for budgeting tasks with other staff or support units.
- The position of US controllers in volume and quality-related operational planning processes that precede budgeting is significantly weaker.
- In information supply and reporting, US controllers focus strongly on the informational needs of parties external to the company. This leads to additional fields of activity, for which controllers in Germany are only responsible in exceptional cases, such as liquidity management, corporate taxation, debtor accounting, and company insurance.

Overall, in this study the tasks of controllers in Germany appear to be less limited to accounting and finance and more oriented towards management. At the same time, US controllers tend to have a much broader financial task profile, which is also evidenced by the fact that they are generally part of the finance department.

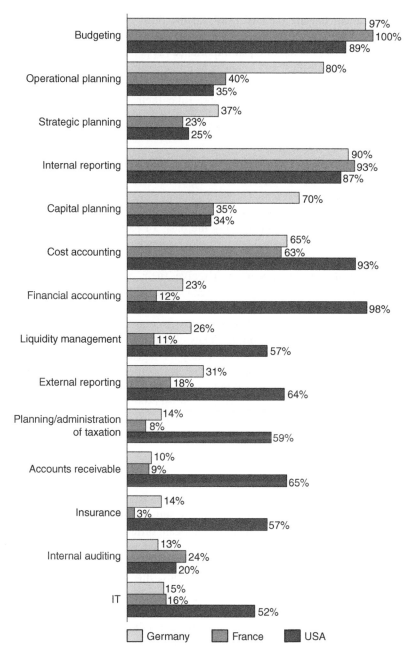

Figure 6.2 Management accountant's tasks in Germany, France, and the United States of
America.

Source: Stoffel (1995, p. 157).

Stoffel also finds that management accountants in France usually report to the finance department but are (at most) only at the third management level and therefore have little influence. Where planning, control, and information supply tasks tend to be seen as being of equal importance (as is the case in Germany), a significant part of controllers' tasks consist of influencing and accompanying the planning process itself. Correspondingly, controllers are ranked at a higher level in the company's organizational structure. Like their German counterparts, French management accountants are consistently not responsible for the additional accounting and finance-related tasks that occupy the majority of controllers' attention in the United States.

While Stoffel and most other authors with a German-language affiliation focus on their observation that the tasks of controllers in Germany are different in scope and more oriented toward management (rather than accounting), Ahrens' (1999) work focuses on cultural differences between German and British management accountants. On the basis of participant observation, interviews, and document analysis, he gives a somewhat different impression of their respective differences. Whereas controllers in the German breweries participating in the study appear to perceive their company through the concept of plans, and accordingly view accounting as being an abstract and operationally detached form of expertise, management accountants in Britain and the operational managers they cooperate with tend to seek early involvement in emerging operational proposals. They claim a substantial – as opposed to a mere formal – influence on the day-to-day management of organizational activities. Correspondingly, Ahrens states that companies appear primarily as technical units in the case of German breweries, where controlling is responsible for ensuring that technical processes are profitable. In the British breweries, on the other hand, accountants have a stronger position and make sure that managers stay within the budget framework laid out by accounting and meet profit expectations.

With these older studies in mind and against the backdrop of a global homogenization of processes, systems, and training content (Granlund & Lukka, 1998), as well as increasingly international controlling teams, the questions arise how differences between controlling in Germany and common practices in other countries have evolved as well as whether significant differences remain.

Management accounting systems might be considered as a first potential source of country-specific differences. In the case of Germany, we find a particularly rich tradition in cost accounting, which is directly reflected in relatively sophisticated accounting and costing practices. Here, the instrument of *Grenzplankostenrechnung* is of particularly high importance. The concept was developed by Wolfgang Kilger (1976, 1980), a professor, and Hans-Georg Plaut (1953), a consultant. It is usually translated as "flexible standard costing" and is characterized by a separation of variable and fixed costs (based on production theory), the concept of contribution margin as revenues minus variable costs (based on decision theory), and a focus on the control of efficiency in cost centers. To the extent that cost accounting and calculation are more frequently components of internationally standardized software packages and textbooks in the field of cost accounting are increasingly oriented towards an international, English-language standard, this difference in management accounting systems should have a decreasing effect. Even if there is no large-scale empirical evidence, management accounting systems and associated processes, at least in larger companies, appear to be increasingly globally interchangeable.

Anyone searching for differences in the working practices of controllers must thus turn to individuals and the micro-level (Granlund & Lukka, 1998) and ask if there are relevant differences in the use of given systems and the interaction of management accountants and managers. These might be due to different management cultures, as the aforementioned study of Ahrens shows.

In an interview with the *Frankfurter Allgemeine Zeitung*, Klaus Kleinfeld, former CEO of Siemens and current CEO of the US corporation Alcoa, provides some anecdotal evidence on the difference between the management culture in the USA and in Germany (Meck, 2014): an American CEO has greater discretion, is less likely to receive less open critique within the company, and is further removed from production than his/her German counterpart. This has direct consequences for the role of a controller and the way controllers and managers interact. In a similar vein, the predominant self-image of managers in Chinese companies appears to deviate strongly from what is common in Europe. In China, managers in charge are typically undisputed, absolute rulers, who, in cases of doubt, govern in all operations. Existing transparency and information asymmetries tend to be a fundamental part of their power base, which they only reluctantly relinquish or share with subordinate managers and controllers. Depending on management culture, identical systems and processes will thus be used differently, and the supporting role of the controller will deviate despite similar management accounting systems.

Such cultural differences are also reflected in a more recent study by Weber (2008). Thirteen years after Stoffel's study, he conducted interviews with the group controllers of German DAX 30 companies, finding that their experiences suggest significant differences between the tasks as well as the mindsets of German controllers and their counterparts in other countries:

> I often have the impression that people with operational responsibility in British companies show a higher level of commercial thinking than one would see with the so-called technicians in German companies, and when this commercial thinking is available to a sufficient and reliable degree in people with operational responsibility, then I don't need many of the things that German controllers do.
>
> (p. 273)

> In America, controllers have much less influence, they are really just the reproducers. Their basic focus is to translate decisions into figures and that's it. It is more the mechanical part. One has to say this quite clearly. They just

reproduce numbers and when we tell them about our approach to controlling, where controllers sometimes say "no, not like that," then this is
something completely foreign to them and also unheard of. It is very difficult for someone coming from a different culture to accept this.

(p. 273)

The controlling environment ... is characterized by an enormous degree of
detail, extremely high accuracy, not very critical. The controlling function
plays second fiddle to the other functions. In Japan, sales is king, then
there's nothing for a long time ... and right at the end you find administration and the people who deal with numbers. According to Japanese understanding, they are really just data capturers.

(p. 274)

In addition to the aforementioned differences in the interaction of controllers
and managers, controlling in Germany has been characterized by a comparatively close relationship between operations and the business side, on the one
hand, and a financial valuation perspective, on the other. This is also indicated
by the adaptation of the figures from external accounting to the needs of internal
management and a clear separation of cost accounting and financial accounting
in the German-speaking area (Schildbach, 1997; Mattessich, 2008), which ultimately stems from the need to adapt figures from external accounting to the
needs of internal management. Internationally, we generally experience a much
more distinct separation of operational business and the primarily outward-
oriented finance function.

Organization of controllers' activities

The comparatively close relationship between the operational business and the
financial perspective also has organizational consequences. In particular, German
controllers view themselves not only as part of the finance function within the
company but as an independent unit that reports directly to the CFO or the CEO.
While a DAX 30 company is characterized by a controlling organization with
several hundred employees, the organizational setup of management accountants, performance analysts, and controllers in English speaking countries is often
less pronounced. A comparable management accounting organization generally
does not exist.

Larger German companies regularly distinguish between corporate and local,
or decentralized, controlling. While corporate controlling is primarily concerned
with tasks relating to governance and assurance, the purpose of the decentralized
controller, in contrast, is largely to carry out all routine controlling tasks close to
the business and advisory activities for management on-site (Hahn &
Hungenberg, 2001; Weber & Schäffer, 2016). Typically, both share a common
controller model and staff development process (Weber & Schäffer, 2016).

Decentralized controllers can in principle report to both decentralized management or to central controlling. In practice, double subordination predominates in the form of a so-called "dotted-line" (Schäffer & Weber, 2015a). The decentralized controller is subordinate to one of the aforementioned instances in a professional context and to the other in a disciplinary context. This solution aims to strike a balance between corporate requirements and decentralized business competence, and thus addresses the underlying tension between involvement and independence (Sathe, 1983).

Professional associations

A further peculiarity of Germany lies in the fact that the country has no professional association for controllers in a stricter sense that would take charge of standardized training, certification, and so on (Schäffer et al., 2014; Luther, Jones & Saxl, 2009; Ahrens & Chapman, 2000) and international associations such as IMA and CIMA have so far found it hard to establish themselves. While institutions do exist that offer professional training for controllers (such as the Controller Akademie) and contribute to knowledge development (such as the Schmalenbach Gesellschaft or the Center for Controlling and Management at WHU – Otto Beisheim School of Management), only the International Controller Association (ICV) comes close to being a professional association (Schäffer, 2013; Schäffer et al., 2014). It has 6,000 individual members in Germany, Austria, Switzerland, and, increasingly, other European countries as well as more than 100 corporate memberships, 60 work groups, and an "Idea Factory" as controlling think tank. Every year, the ICV organizes the largest convention for controllers in the German-speaking world in Munich. The other noteworthy association, the Bundesverband der Bilanzbuchhalter und Controller, is – despite its name – focused more on bookkeepers than controllers.

However, even the ICV was not intended to be an official professional union or association with a role in a regulatory process, as is explicitly stated in its charter. To date, it sees itself more as a loose association of "working controllers" that has neither the mission nor the financial capacity to be concerned with issues such as standardized exams, certification, and professional training (Schäffer et al., 2014). In addition, membership is by no means mandatory for professional controllers (as it is for public accountants and lawyers in most countries).

Therefore, the normative isomorphism associated with institutions such as the Chartered Institute of Management Accountants (CIMA) and the Institute of Management Accountants (IMA) has been largely lacking in Germany. The founding father of the International Controller Association and the associated Controller Akademie, Albrecht Deyhle, as well as professors at both universities and universities of applied sciences (*Fachhochschulen*) have, however, adopted some of the traditional roles of a professional association by providing education for controllers and normative guidance to practitioners relating to, for example, the concept of controlling and the role of the controller (Schäffer, 2013).

Conceptual foundations

Albrecht Deyhle, in particular, has greatly influenced the conceptual thinking of German-speaking controllers. As early as the beginning of the 1970s, he acted as a professional trainer for controllers and developed a concept of controlling that did not define controlling as the work of controllers, but rather as the result of the interaction between controllers and managers (Deyhle, 1984). In his "classic" set diagram of intersection, Deyhle suggests that controllers should take on the role of a neutral and objective counterpart, providing a third-party perspective based on analytical rigor and an intimate knowledge of metrics and processes (cf. Figure 6.3). In this perspective, the controller complements a manager, who is primarily characterized by his entrepreneurial judgment and his task to motivate employees and execute decisions. Ideally, the controller is involved in decision-making processes on equal footing with management, sharing clear responsibility for the outcome.

Based on his experience in training and executive education, Deyhle focused on the combination of – as he calls it – "logic and psycho-logic" (Deyhle, 1984), or the behavioral dimension of controlling. In addition, it appears that he coined the term "controlling" for the German-speaking world. Deyhle asserts that the term was invented as an analogy to "marketing," a term that became popular in Germany at the same time: while marketing means managing from the market, controlling means managing for results (Schäffer et al., 2014).

In addition to the work of Albrecht Deyhle and the Controller Akademie, German university professors have extensively attempted to explain why controllers are doing what they are doing (Messner et al., 2008). They have developed normative concepts on the nature of controlling and on controller tasks (for an overview, see Scherm & Pietsch, 2004). Küpper and Horváth, for instance, define controlling as a function aimed at coordinating different managerial functions (such as reporting, planning, and control in the case of Horváth;

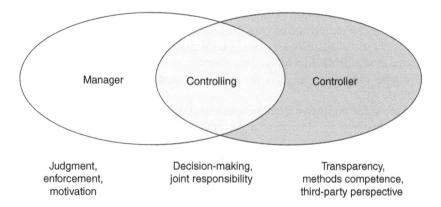

Figure 6.3 Set diagram of intersection.

Source: adapted from Deyhle (1984), see also Gänßlen et al. (2013).

Küpper adds organization and a human resource perspective; cf. Horváth 1978; Küpper, Weber, & Zünd, 1990; Küpper et al., 2013). Schäffer and Weber, as a second example, define controlling as a function aimed at assuring management rationality (Weber & Schäffer, 1999; Schäffer & Weber, 2002).

According to their concept, controllers support managers by carrying out three fundamental types of tasks: unburdening, complementing, and constraining managers (cf. Weber & Schäffer, 2008; Gänßlen et al., 2013). First, they unburden managers by relieving them of specific tasks (e.g. coordinating the planning process, or preparing and supplying information). These are tasks that, in principle, managers could do themselves; however, controllers provide the advantages of experience, specialization, and cost.

Second, controllers complement managers by constructively challenging their business activities and acting as critical counterparts. This differs significantly from the unburdening task: managers have a limited ability to complement themselves, which requires a certain distance and independence that is generally more easily provided by a second party, namely controllers with their profound knowledge of numbers and systems as well as their analytical perspective. In addition to a certain distance, providing complementing tasks effectively requires controllers and managers to operate on an equal level. This makes it clear that controllers face a quandary: they are expected to unburden managers in terms of traditional task delegation while, at the same time, assuming an equal footing as a critical counterpart and business partner. Given the diversity of the tasks at hand, this is no small feat. In the traditional scheme of things, controllers are only able to provide complementing tasks if they also fulfil the unburdening tasks. In this way, controllers gain not only an intimate knowledge of numbers and processes but also the trust and respect of managers – which allows them to

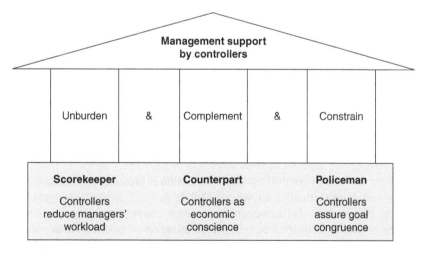

Figure 6.4 Support role of controllers according to Weber and Schäffer (2008) (see also Gänßlen et al. 2013).

complement managers in a competent manner in the first place. One task is dependent on the other.

Finally, the complex interaction between managers and controllers includes a third category of tasks: controllers constrain managers, for instance, by preventing uneconomic decisions that managers may try to push through for their own interests or for those of the department. Controllers thus act as central agents, adopting a third role as a police officer or watchdog; a role which does not make the trusting collaboration of complementing and unburdening any easier. Here too, the tasks are interdependent, since the constraining tasks cannot be effectively fulfilled without detailed knowledge of the other areas of activity (Sathe, 1983).

In the perspective of Weber and Schäffer, unburdening, complementing, and constraining managers contributes to ensuring the rationality of management as an overall objective of a controlling function. The individual components of the controllers' supporting roles, however, may change in importance. Currently, there are at least two major developments that can be distinguished here: an increasing industrialization of controlling and a growing focus on complementing tasks.

Transformation: quo vadis?

In recent years, controlling processes in large companies have become increasingly standardized as a result of standard software, increased efficiency, and globalization (Schäffer & Weber, 2014, 2015b). Standardization, in turn, is a prerequisite for a growing automation or centralization of the respective processes in "centers of excellence" or "shared service centers." As unburdening tasks are increasingly automated or migrate over to shared service centers, the huge gains in efficiency that can be achieved leave the management of the controlling function with two alternatives: either considerably reduce the controller capacity and/or significantly increase complementing ("business partnering") tasks. The latter is dependent not only on the controller possessing the appropriate skills but also on the management having sufficient need for and acceptance of a counterpart. In view of the fact that many management teams appear to be chronically overworked and face the challenge of a volatile environment, the need for such counterpart services should generally be present.

At the same time, three developments in information technology are expected to change the way that controllers and managers work together: the trend towards self-service analysis enables managers to gain direct access to information without the help of controlling; this information is increasingly accessible in real-time and from (virtually) anywhere. Mobile devices, such as smartphones und tablet PCs, ensure that managers enjoy even greater flexibility. Together, these trends should facilitate a certain democratization of information access in organizations and make managers more discerning partners for controllers (Wiegmann, Schäffer, & Weber, 2016). At the same time, the average finance and accounting qualification of managers has risen slowly but constantly over the last decades and data science centers start to be involved in the analysis of big data. Therefore, it seems reasonable to assume that the task of effectively complementing managers as a business partner will tend to become more challenging in the years ahead (Schäffer & Weber, 2015b).

As for the status quo, in 2014 almost one in ten respondents reported that the controllers in their organization do not generally act as business partners (cf. Figure 6.5). More than a third of respondents place the concept of business partner firmly at the senior management level or see only some of the controllers below senior level acting as business partners. Only 16 percent of respondents state that all controllers act as business partners in their organization. At least according to the expectations of the CFOs and controllers surveyed by Schäffer and Weber (2015b), this might change over the next years. Whereas more than a third believe that business partnering is the domain not only of senior controlling managers but also affects some controllers below senior level, almost half of the respondents believe that all controllers (left) in their organizations will be acting as business partners in five years. For those controllers who have spent many years, or even decades, crunching numbers in the back office, however, it might be quite a challenge to morph into a more complementing business partner role.

Conclusion

In Germany, approximately 0.8 percent of all employees in large companies are controllers. While it is not obvious whether these controllers should be primarily considered as accountants or managers, their role-set constitutes a unique approach to organize learning and critique in organizations, which we consider worthwhile to study. In observing the management accounting practices in Germany and comparing them with the respective practices in other countries,

In our organization

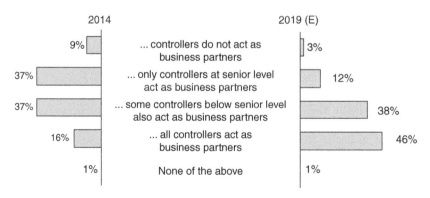

Figure 6.5 Implementation of the business partner concept in the German-language area over time.

Source: Schäffer and Weber (2015b, p. 190).

we find it difficult to disentangle the effects of different cultures, business traditions, general economic conditions, industry and size effects, and other potential drivers of the respective practices. In addition, the roles of controllers have changed over time, and will likely continue to change in the coming years. The digitalization of the processes associated with management accounting and control as well as the increasing digitalization of the underlying value chain of the corporation, globalization, and increasingly better qualified managers appear to be the prominent drivers of this development (Schäffer & Weber, 2016). As a result, we expect to see not only a smaller number of more qualified controllers and even more homogenization in management accounting practices across the globe but also new career paths and likely changes in the identity of the controller profession.

Note

1 The WHU Controller Panel was founded in 2007 in association with the International Controller Association (ICV) for the purpose of creating benchmarking information about controlling practices in the German-speaking countries as well as supporting field research in this area. Today, more than 1,000 controllers and CFOs from Austria, Switzerland, and Germany participate in the panel.

References

Ahrens, T. (1999). *Contrasting involvements: A study of management accounting practices in Britain and Germany*. Amsterdam: Harwood Academic Publishers.

Ahrens, T. & Chapman, C. S. (2000). Occupational identity of management accountants in Britain and Germany. *European Accounting Review, 9*(4), 477–498.

Auffermann, J. D. (1952). Preface. In Rationalisierungs-Kuratorium der Deutschen Wirtschaft (RKW) (Ed.), *Rechnungswesen im Dienst der Werkleitung*, RKW-Auslandsdienst, 9, 6.

Binder, C. (2006). *Zur Entwicklung des Controllings als Teildisziplin der Betriebswirtschaftslehre*. Wiesbaden: Deutscher Universitätsverlag.

Deyhle, A. (1984). *Management- und Controlling-Brevier. Vol. I: Manager und Controller im Team* (3rd ed.). München: Gauting.

Gänßlen, S., Losbichler, H., Rieder, L., Schäffer, U., & Weber, J. (2013). The essence of controlling: The perspective of the Internationaler Controller Verein (ICV) and the International Group of Controlling (ICG). *Journal of Management Control, 23*(4), 311–317.

Goossens, F. (1959). Der "Controller": Chef des Unternehmens ohne Gesamtverantwortung. *Mensch und Arbeit, 11*, 74–77.

Granlund, M. & Lukka, K. (1998). It's a small world of management accounting practices. *Journal of Management Accounting Research, 10*, 153–179.

Gretz, W. (1965, November 17/18). "Mädchen für alles" in amerikanischen Firmen: der Controller. *Frankfurter Allgemeine Zeitung* – Blick durch die Wirtschaft, Artikelserie "Das amerikanische Rechnungswesen als Führungsinstrument," October 28, 1965–March 17, 1966, Folge VII.

Grunwald-Delitz, S., Schäffer, U., & Weber, J. (2014). Wie viele Controller gibt es in Deutschland? *Controller Magazin, 38*(3), 48–52.

Hahn, D. & Hungenberg, H. (2001). *PuK, Planung und Kontrolle, Planungs- und Kontrollsysteme, Planungs- und Kontrollrechnung, Wertorientierte Controllingkonzepte* (6th ed.). Wiesbaden: Springer.

Henzler, H. (1974). Der Januskopf muß weg. *Wirtschaftswoche, 28*, 60–63.

Horváth, P. (1978). Controlling-Entwicklung und Stand einer Konzeption zur Lösung der Adaptions- und Koordinationsprobleme der Führung. *Zeitschrift für Betriebswirtschaft, 48*(3), 194–208.

Kilger, W. (1976). Kostentheoretische Grundlagen der Grenzplankostenrechnung. *Zeitschrift für betriebswirtschaftliche Forschung, 28*, 679–693.

Kilger, W. (1980). *Einführung in die Kostenrechnung*. Wiesbaden: Gabler.

Küpper, H. U., Weber, J., & Zünd, A. (1990). Zum Verständnis und Selbstverständnis des Controlling. *Zeitschrift für Betriebswirtschaft, 60*(3), 281–293.

Küpper, H.-U., Friedl, G., Hofmann, C., Hofmann, Y., & Pedell, B. (2013). *Controlling: Konzeption, Aufgaben, Instrumente* (6th ed.). Stuttgart: Schäffer-Poeschel.

Luther, R., Jones, T., & Saxl, A. (2009). *Experiencing change in German controlling: Management accounting in a globalized world*. Amsterdam: Elsevier.

Mattessich, R. (2008). *Two hundred years of accounting research: An international survey of personalities, ideas and publications*. London: Routledge.

Meck, G. (2014) Amerikaner reden dem Chef mehr nach dem Mund, Interview mit Klaus Kleinfeld, *Frankfurter Allgemeine Sonntagszeitung*, February 16, 2014, p. 21.

Messner, M., Becker, A., Schäffer, U., & Binder, C. (2008). Legitimacy and identity in Germanic management accounting research. *The European Accounting Review, 16*(2), 129–160.

Plaut, H. (1953). Die Grenzplankostenrechnung. *Zeitschrift für Betriebswirtschaft, 23*, 347–363.

Richter, H. J. (1987). *Theoretische Grundlagen des Controlling: Strukturkriterien für die Entwicklung von Controlling-Konzeptionen*. Frankfurt am Main.

Sathe, V. (1983). The controller's role in management. *Organizational Dynamics, 11*(3), 31–48.

Schäffer, U. (2013). Management accounting research in Germany: From splendid isolation to being part of the international community. *Journal of Management Control, 23*(4), 291–309.

Schäffer, U. & Weber, J. (2002). Thesen zum Controlling. In J. Weber & B. Hirsch, (Eds.), *Schriftenreihe des Center for Controlling & Management (CCM) an der WHU: Bd. 7. Controlling als akademische Disziplin – Eine Bestandsaufnahme* (pp. 91–97). Wiesbaden, Germany: Gabler.

Schäffer, U. & Weber, J. (2014). Controller: eine gefährdete Spezies. *Harvard Business Manager, 36*(7), 86–90.

Schäffer, U. & Weber, J. (2015a). *Controlling Trends and Benchmarks* (English version). Vallendar, Germany: WHU – Otto Beisheim School of Management.

Schäffer, U. & Weber, J. (2015b). Controlling im Wandel – Die Veränderung eines Berufsbilds im Spiegel der zweiten WHU-Zukunftsstudie. *Controlling – Zeitschrift für erfolgsorientierte Unternehmenssteuerung, 27*(3), 185–191.

Schäffer, U. & Weber, J. (2016). Die Digitalisierung wir das Controlling radikal verändern. *Controlling and Management Review, 60*(6), forthcoming.

Schäffer, U., Schmidt, A., & Strauß, E. (2014). An old boys' club on the threshold to becoming a professional association: The emergence and development of the association of German controllers from 1975 to 1989. *Accounting History, 19*(1–2), 133–169.

Scherm, E. & Pietsch, G. (Eds.) (2004). *Controlling – Theorien und Konzeptionen.* München: Vahlen.

Schildbach, T. (1997). Cost accounting in Germany. *Management Accounting Research, 8*(3), 261–274.

Schmidt, A., Schäffer, U., & Strauß, E. (2016). *Professionalization inside multi-professional bureaucratic organizations: The case of German controllers.* Working paper.

Stoffel, K. (1995). *Controllership im internationalen Vergleich.* Wiesbaden: Deutscher Universitätsverlag.

Weber, J. (2008). *Von Top-Controllern lernen.* Weinheim, Germany: Wiley VCH.

Weber, J. & Kosmider, A. (1991). Controlling-Entwicklung in der Bundesrepublik Deutschland im Spiegel von Stellenanzeigen (Special Issue). *Zeitschrift für Betriebswirtschaft, 61*(3), 17–35.

Weber, J. & Schäffer, U. (1998). Controlling-Entwicklung im Spiegel von Stellenanzeigen 1990–1994. *krp Kostenrechnungspraxis – Zeitschrift für Controlling, 42*(4), 227–233.

Weber, J. & Schäffer, U. (1999). Sicherstellung der Rationalität von Führung als Aufgabe des Controlling? *Die Betriebswirtschaft, 59*(6), 731–747.

Weber, J. & Schäffer, U. (2008). *Introduction to Controlling* (1st ed.). Stuttgart: Schäffer-Poeschel.

Weber, J. & Schäffer, U. (2016). *Einführung in das Controlling* (15th ed.). Stuttgart: Schäffer-Poeschel.

Wiegmann, L., Schäffer, U., & Weber, J. (2016). IT statt Interaktion. *Controlling and Management Review, 60*(4), 36–42.

7 The changing role of management accountants

An Indian perspective

Prem Lal Joshi, Usha Rani Cherukupallis, and Nachiket Madhav Vechalekar

Introduction

In recent years, management accounting and the role of the management accountant (MA) has expanded. The MA is now expected to have a deep understanding of business activities, the ability to manage the performance of each unit in a business line, focusing on being a value-adding consultant. Several such activities link performance measurement to unit's short- and long-term targets, bringing operating and financial performance measurements together, and identifying and managing risk and uncertainties in advance. MAs provide strategic information to create value and enhance the position of stakeholders. They protect the interests of investors and target the optimum utilisation of resources, and minimisation of wastage. Prasad (2015) argues that in future, businesses in India will have to make strategic choices to maintain global standards. A shift towards progressive methods and practices are needed to advance management accounting in a globalised context. While each country has different laws, practices, traditions, cultures, etc., due to recent fast-paced developments in the field of information technology, almost every nation expects to routinely trade with multiple other nations. Since laws and practices vary from nation to nation, 'adaptability' is key. Efforts are being made worldwide to enhance uniformity of practice in many economic domains. One area of importance, therefore, is accounting, which includes the presentation of financial statements in regions that have adopted the International Financial Reporting Standards (IFRS). Meeting the requirements of the IFRS is generally considered beneficial for a company's stakeholders, when its interests are global.

As management accounting is converging with local practices and global requirements, Indian MAs need to be aware of developments in the wider world and the impact of such developments on local businesses. For example, the slowdown of the economies in the US, Europe, and China might be expected to affect the business practices of an entity in India. In India, MAs are expected to facilitate the organisation of information pertaining to global events, i.e. detailing the likely impact of external change on the organisation and developing strategies to neutralise that impact. The ultimate aim of management accounting is to support businesses as they take crucial decisions, by providing accurate and pertinent information. Hence, an MA plays a key role in providing apposite information, 'suited to the varied needs of different stakeholder in various locations across the globe' (Interview excerpt, Sanjay Swarup, AICWA, Working at Bharat Electronics Limited, Bangalore). When performing a management function, the role of an MA is crucial, as explained in Figure 7.1.

The areas of cost and management accounting have recently undergone rapid growth in India. MAs work in taxation and internal auditing areas, which offer tremendous scope for further growth. India has been witnessing a change in industrial leadership, and the manufacturing sector is expected to grow increasingly rapidly under Prime Minister Modi's 'Make in India' campaign. It is argued that the manufacturing sector is likely to expand in the same way as information technology and other services sectors have already grown. Thus, in an interview, Durga Prasad, President of ICAI stated: 'CMAs role is vital to 'Make in India' campaign a success. We envisage a major role towards achieving the right cost competitiveness' (Prasad, 2015, p. 7).

The aforementioned objective of this chapter, to review the changing role of MAs in the Indian context, will be achieved by describing and reviewing the local variants and global factors responsible for that change. The chapter reviews the evolution and current status of MA systems, the education system that is

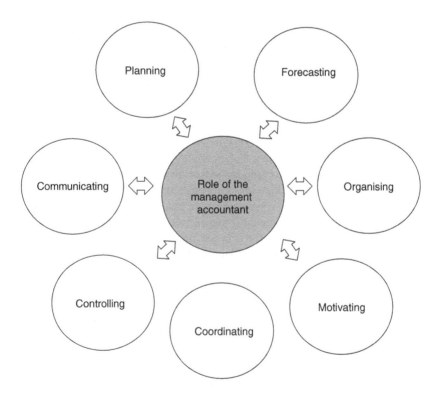

Figure 7.1 Role of management accountants.

contributing to the changing role of MAs. Additionally, it reports the findings of a questionnaire survey examining the extent to which major categories of core functions of MAs have adapted.

The remainder of the chapter is divided into the following sections: section 2 describes the history and evolution of MA systems; section 3 describes the commerce education system and how it is contributing in reshaping the role of an MA; section 4 explains the recently introduced 'Make in India' campaign and the likely role of the MA; section 5 addresses the interaction of culture and management accountancy; section 6 provides a detailed literature review; section 7 discusses the survey results; finally, section 8 concludes the chapter.

Evolution of cost and management accounting in India: pre-independence era

According to Indian scriptures, 'Vishnugupta Chankiya Kautilya' can be accorded the credit as the originator of the Indian accounting system; he prepared a manuscript recognisable as a financial management book during the period of the Mauryan Empire. His book, entitled *Arthashasthra* ('The Science of Material Gain' in Sanskrit), contained several detailed aspects concerning how to maintain the account books for a sovereign state. It is claimed that Kautilya developed the principles of modern accounting, specified the scope and methodology of accounting, codified financial rules, and explicated the role of ethics in accounting. During the era of British rule in India, when companies started to expand, accountancy obtained a higher status, and accountants were recognised as important because of the need to maintain records of expanding trading operations and to meet the demand for audits.

In 1886, the School of Madras (Chennai) introduced Commerce education to India, and in 1903, the Presidency College of Kolkata was opened. In 1913, the College of Commerce and Economics was established in Mumbai with the objective of introducing accounting at postgraduate level. Subsequently, to promote and develop accounting education further, the Institute of Cost and Works Accountants (ICWAI), the Institute of Chartered Accountancy of India (ICAI) and the Institute of Chartered Secretary (ICS) were started as professional bodies for overseeing accountancy and financial management in India.

A wider audience for the use of accounting information emerged following the development of Joint Stock companies. This development divided accounting systems into internal (management accounting) and external (financial accounting purposes), and electronic data processing played a role in the development of cost and management accounting system in India. Joshi (2009) states that until the 1930s, the accounting system in India, with the exception of that for Ordinance Factories, was designed primarily to produce final accounts. The need for cost accounting and qualified cost accountants was deeply felt in British India during the Second World War. During this period, the Government set up an Advisory Panel of Accountants to advise on war contract pricing, as it wanted war materials to be delivered quickly, and to avoid excessive pricing. Furthermore, the economic policy of the government emphasised a planned economy, aiming to achieve economic goals. This led to cost reduction programmes, and the establishment of a National Productivity Council in 1958, and the Statutory Nature and Scope of Cost Accounting accelerated management accounting systems in India (www.new agepublishers.com/samplechapter/000882.pdf).

Post-independence era: role of the Institute of Cost Accountants of India (ICAI)

The ICAI was introduced in 1944 under the Companies Act, with a directive to promote, regulate, and develop the profession of Cost Accountancy. On 28 May 1959, the Institute was established as a statutory professional body by a special act of Parliament, namely, the Cost and Works Accountants Act, 1959. This Act provided further impetus to installing cost accounting systems in Indian industries (http://icmai.in/icmai/aboutus/history.php).

The chart in Figure 7.2 explains the stages for becoming a CMA under ICAI. ICAI has introduced a number of cost and management accounting programmes and recently signed a memorandum of understanding (MoU) with the Chartered Institute of Management Accountants in the UK (CIMA-UK). ICAI is also the professional examination body for CMAs in India. There are three levels of Cost Accountancy: Foundation, Intermediate, and Final, accompanied by a compulsory three years of practical training. While admission to Foundation level requires a pass of Class 10 or equivalent from a recognised board, the admission

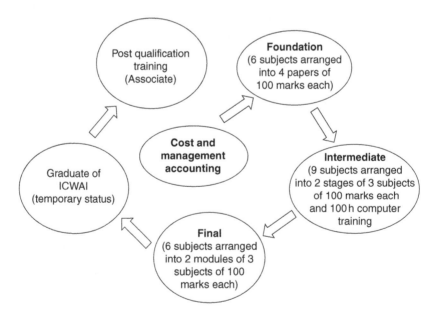

Figure 7.2 Stages in CMA course.

for Intermediate level requires a pass at Senior Secondary School and a pass in the CMA Foundation course. Alternatively, a graduate candidate $(10+2+3)$ (see Figure 7.2) is eligible to advance directly to Intermediate level.

It is mandatory to obtain a Certificate of Practice (CP) from ICAI to practice as a CMA in India, whether independently, in a partnership, or in a Limited Liability Partnerships (LLP). CMA professionals can work as Internal Auditors and Cost Auditors for a company, as Investment Advisers under the Securities Board of India (SEBI) regulation, as an Auditor under the Value Added Tax (VAT) act pertaining to various states and central excise, as an authorised representative under various statutes, and as a tax auditor. To comply with the requirements of the International Federation of Accountants (IFAC), a CMA must undergo compulsory and continued training by ICAI.

Cost Accounting Standards (CASs)

The institute recognised the need for a structured approach to the measurement of cost in the manufacturing and service sector, constituting the Cost Accounting Standards Board (CASB) in 2001 to fulfil this purpose. It has since identified 39 areas for CASs development, and developed 22 CASs. With the introduction of 'The Companies (Cost Audit Report, CAR) Rules, 2011', the scope and application of the Statutory Cost Audit (u/s 233B of the Companies Act, 1956) was widened considerably. The said rules also introduced a new concept, called a 'Performance Appraisal Report' (PAR), to be submitted with the Statutory Cost Auditor to the company along with the CAR. The new Companies Act, 2013 redefined the CAR and now companies engage in producing certain types of goods in strategic sectors, operating in areas of public interest, ensuring the production of certain medical devices, in sectors regulated by a Sectoral Regulator or a Ministry or Department of Central Government, responsible for maintaining CAR (www.mca.govt.in).

Chartered Accountants (CAs) from ICAI have also contributed to the development of management accounting practices, extending their competencies through training in production costs and learning about processes at different operational levels when manufacturing products. The Institute of Chartered Accountants of India has been recognised as a 'partner-in-nation-building'. Bharat Ratna and Dr. A. P. J. Abdul Kalam bestowed this honour by recognising chartered accountants' contribution to the nation. Mr. Lal Bahadur Shastri claimed that accountants should play an important role in public as well as in private sectors, emphasising their integrity and the creation and sustenance of public confidence in the market. To achieve such a development, ethics are an integral part of any professional endeavour. As members of a 'noble profession', it is the moral responsibility of CAs to promote ethics and integrity in society, and they act as guides to excellence within the profession. Through consultancy services, CAs also play role in assisting businesses and organisations to utilise their resources effectively, to develop management information systems, design budgetary and control systems, measure the effective utilisation of capital, install cost accounting systems, review operational controls, and devise solutions to specific business problems, such as product mix and pricing decisions. Anderson and Lanen (1999) argued that the policy of liberalisation after 1991 intensified international competition, thereby changing the internal data requirements of Indian managers, and also the role of the MA.

Indian education system and the management accountant

Fundamentally, Indian higher education for accountants emphasises the attainment of skills in cost effectiveness through the maximal utilisation of resources. CMAs are expected to play an important role in accounting evaluation, resource allocation, and distribution, within the jurisdiction of regulatory bodies, and to obtain cost efficiency and resource optimisation. Table 7.1 depicts some statistics relating to the status of higher education in India during 1950–2015.

When India attained its independence, the number of universities in the country was 20, it has since increased to 677 (figures for 2014–2015). The number of colleges has also increased by a similar proportion. The importance of CMAs has been crucial to the development of educational institutions/universities, including costings at the strategic level, so that every student, institution, university, and the government yields returns for every rupee invested. The education department in India (in collaboration with foreign educational institutions) can help drive enterprises ethically globally and also create value for stakeholders. Table 7.2 presents some statistics regarding the courses offered by leading institutions in India. These courses are intended to educate professionals to drive organisations ethically, by creating value for society, shareholders, and stakeholders (Bhowmik, 2014).

As per regulations produced by the University Grants Commission (UGC), CMAs, Chartered Accountants and Company Secretaries with First Class Degrees may be appointed as principals/directors/heads of the institution,

Table 7.1 Status of higher education in India

Institutes/universities	1950–1951	2010–2011	2011–2012	2013–2014	2014–2015
Number of universities	20	554	642	692	677
Colleges	500	17,023	34,852	36,671	37,204
Standalone Institutes	–	5,713	11,126	11,445	11,443
State (private)		178	142	195	201
Total enrolment	4 million	27.5 million	29.9 million	30 million	31 million
Gross enrolment ratio (GER)		19.4 times	20.8 times	22.3	21.1
Student enrolment in Commerce (UG) (%)		13	15	20	29

Source: All India Survey on Higher Education (2011–2012), MHRD, Department of Higher Education, Government of India (2013).

Table 7.2 Courses offered by premier institutions in India

Organisations offering Cost and Management Accountancy in their curricula	PG level MBA	PG level MCom	UG level BCom	UG level BBA
1 Institute of Cost & Works Accountants of India	Inter and Final		NA	NA
2 Institute of Chartered Accountants of India	Inter and Final	NA	NA	NA
3 Institute of Company Secretaries of India	Inter	NA	NA	NA
4 Indian Institute of Management, Ahmadabad	FPM, PGP, PGP-FABM, PGPX, FDP, AFP	NA	NA	NA
5 Indian Institute of Management, Bangalore	PGP, PGPPM, PGPEM, EPGP, FPM	NA	NA	NA
6 Indian Institute of Management, Calcutta	PGP, PGPEX, PGDBA, FPM	NA	NA	NA
7 Xavier Labor Relation Institute School of Management (XLRI), Jamshedpur	PGDM (BM) PGDM (GM) PGDM (BM), (JSR) PGP (Dubai) PGDM (Global BM)	NA	NA	NA
8 Faculty of Management Studies, Delhi	PGPM, FPM, PGFB	NA	NA	NA
9 Indian School of Business Management, Hyderabad	PGPM, PGP(ABM, PGP(SM), FPM, EFPM	NA	NA	NA
10 Indian Institute of Management, Lucknow	PGPM	NA	NA	NA
11 Management Development Institute, Gurgaon	PGPM			
12 Indian Institute of Technology, Madras	MBA, PGPEX	NA	NA	NA
13 Department of Management Studies, IIT, Delhi	MBA, Ph.D	NA	NA	NA
14 SP Jain Institute of Management Studies, Mumbai	MGB, GMBA, EMBA	NA	NA	BBA
15 Jamnalal Bajaj Institute of Management Studies, Mumbai	MBA/MMM, MFM, MIM, MHRDM	NA	NA	NA
16 Narsee Monjee College of Commerce and Economics, Mumbai	MBA, ICWAI, ICAI, ICSI	MCom.	BCom.	BBA
17 ICFAI Business School, Hyderabad	MBA, PhD	NA	LLB	BBA
18 Shri Ram College of Commerce, New Delhi	PGDGBO	MCom	BCom (Hons)	–
19 Symbiosis College of Arts and Commerce, Pune	–	MCom	BCom	BBA/BBM
20 Indian Institute of Foreign Trade, Delhi	MBA(IB)	–	–	–

Associate and Assistant Professor in universities and colleges in the area of management/business administration and management accounting. Today, in India, 36 universities recognise the CMA qualification for the purpose of admission in Ph.D. in commerce. These courses enable CMAs, Chartered Accountants, and Company Secretaries to pursue a Ph.D. without previously obtaining a Master's degree. Additionally, uniformity in course curricula will also promote the efforts of CMAs to attain global standards through a design-thinking process as they develop accounting education. Alongside professional bodies like ICMAI, CFAI, IFAI, ICAI, ICSI, IIMs, and IITs (see Table 7.2), colleges have contributed to the attainment of uniformity. Therefore, the education system has been continually reshaping the role of management accounting and that of MAs in India.

The subjects included in course curricula demand a design-thinking process to assist students and institutions to make their choices. The thinking processes involved in highlighting courses may lead organisations towards growth and economic development when educating people. The institutions listed above cover all these factors, as indicated in Figure 7.3.

The 'decision tree' in Figure 7.3 conveys ideas to students interested in pursuing a management accountancy course. In any educational system, in addition to knowledge and experience, ethics, morals, and values are important components for both faculty members and students. A regular course curriculum with an internship and article publications, group discussions and student-teacher interactive sessions benefits individuals and supports organisational growth and development. Frequently, results are adversely influenced by a lack of organisational strength and poor quality of internal resources such

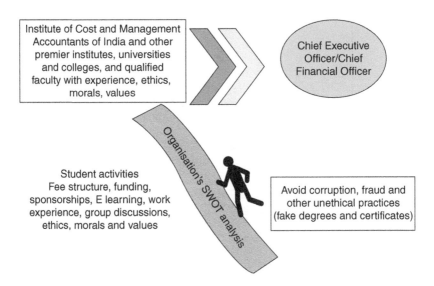

Figure 7.3 'Accounting Tree of Management' (ATOM).

as inefficient faculty, lack of interest in studies, egoism, poor health conditions, family responsibilities, and other personal problems. The professional institutes named in this chapter cover all the factors indicated in Figure 7.3, and are used to overcome different types of risks and uncertainties. Thus, the present study assists students interested in pursuing the above courses before they seek admission into an organisation. The number of colleges run under UGC regulations is too great to cover them all in our study; however, the general ideas conveyed in Figure 7.3 might nevertheless be of interest to students.

In recent years, accounting education in India has been integrated into the course curriculum, with multiple changes. Areas relating to accountancy and finance now include digital accounting, e-accounting, e-learning, e-commerce, and e-finance, or e-costing methods. Many students are choosing these courses, with the intention of forging careers in corporate and government sectors. An application-oriented system assists students, and keeps pace with technological development. The traditional system of accounting should be taught based on global standards to ensure students are then in a position to design their course framework, to become experts in accountancy based on their thinking process. The framework shown above should ensure accounting education effectively supports students to face and overcome future challenges to the global economy in the fields of business and industry.

The 'Make in India' campaign and the role of the management accountant

On 25 September 2014, Indian Prime Minister Narendra Modi launched the 'Make in India' campaign, to revive the Indian manufacturing sector and give the Indian economy global recognition. The 'Make in India' campaign is asking companies to manufacture high quality and low cost products in India. The focus is increasingly on shifting the manufacturing of products from China to India, considering the survival of countries is based on imports and exports. The role of MAs is likely to change with the 'Make in India' campaign, as India's market size is predicted to increase. It is anticipated that MAs will play a major role in achieving competitiveness at the right price, ensuring quality improvement and effective outsourcing decisions, as well as enabling enterprises to focus more on core activities and resources. Furthermore, MAs might also be expected to play a role in achieving 'zero defect' and 'zero effect policies', sustainability and environmental management accounting areas, or risk management. Overall, the most important role they will be expected to perform involves the development of KPIs to evaluate the manufacturing sector's performance, particularly involving non-financial measures to examine the value chain analysis. The use of ABC and ABM will grow, and MAs will consequently play a bigger role by designing and implementing an ABC system that can successfully identify the accurate cost of products and reduce costs (http://icmai.in/upload/Institute/Journal/February_2015.pdf).

Culture and the role of the management accountant

In the last two decades, manufacturing and service sectors have faced dramatic changes to their business environments. There has been a significant reduction in the product life cycle arising from technological innovations, and companies have adopted new management approaches, changed their manufacturing systems, and invested in new technologies. However, due to cultural differences, there are notable variations in the application of management accounting techniques. Hofstede's cultural framework is commonly applied by management accounting researchers to explain variations between different nations and their cultures (Carr and Tomkins, 1998: 217).

Hofstede (1980) identified cultural dimensions around which people in various countries might be clustered, and groups have been formed exhibiting identical behaviours. These dimensions are power distance, uncertainty avoidance, individualism and masculinity, and long-term orientation. According to Hofstede's cultural dimensions, Indian culture may encourage constraints in the adoption of innovative management accounting practices to change the role of MA (see also Joshi, 2001). For example, in India, decisions are taken by the highest ranking officials. Indian managers are usually risk averse and hence may be reluctant to use modern management accounting techniques including ABC or target costing, unless they have been tested elsewhere previously. Resistance to change is demonstrable, and hence Indian companies might be slow to modernise (see also Joshi, 2001).

Gray (1988) advanced Hofstede's ideas, developing accounting values and cultural dimensions: professionalism referring to judgements, and self-regulation under legal requirements; uniformity as the level of enforcement based on standards and consistent accounting principles; conservatism describing a vigilant approach to measuring accounting values to avoid risk; secrecy highlighting that confidentiality but also transparency to achieve public accountability. He emphasised that societal values lead to the growth and development of institutions within a society, including educational, legal, political, corporate financial, and accounting structures. Figure 7.4 indicates how Hofstede's cultural and Gray's accounting dimensions are interrelated.

Furthermore, Indian society includes many castes and communities and cultural differences vary across these communities. Some communities are more customer focused, and hence are willing to invest money to achieve future cost reductions and obtain orders from customers. In professionally managed companies, as well as in MNCs operating in India, cultural factors do not influence management accounting techniques. The influence of culture is mitigated by business practices and behaviours. Various techniques, such as target costing, ABC, budgetary control, and standard costing, are applied objectively as the cultural background does not affect their application. Gupta (2005) argues that Management accounting per se is principle-based. Its approach is not influenced by cultural differences. The focus is on attaining real-time relevant information for facilitating managerial decision making. Management accounting mirrors

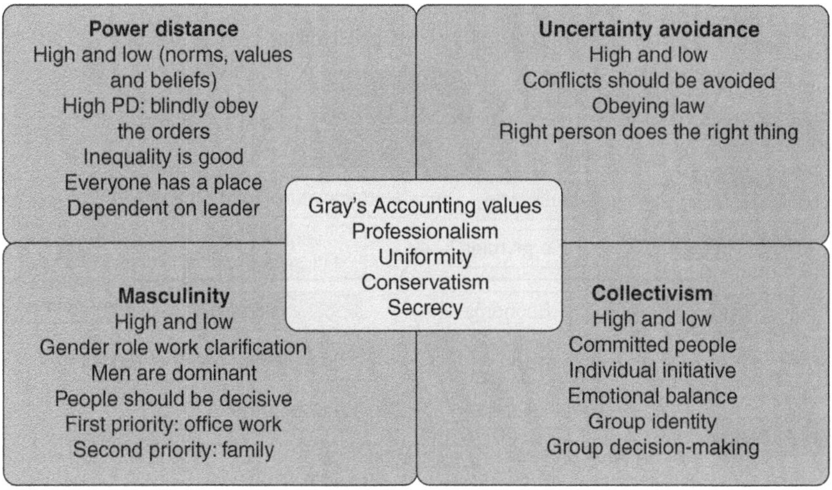

Figure 7.4 Hofstede's cultural and Gray's accounting dimensions and their interdependence.

Source: adapted from Hofstede (1980) and Gray (1988).

Indian culture's focus on the efficient utilisation of scarce resources through ethical means to benefit all (Van Dyck et al., 2005). The roles of an MA in relation to cultural dimensions are depicted in the fishbone diagram displayed in Figure 7.5.

This diagram depicts values linked to cost and management accounting, and used for measuring performance. These disciplines include new approaches, such as total quality management, re-engineering, group dynamism, Kaizen costing, etc. Additionally, to measure businesses' performance, CMAs use what is termed a Value Based Management (VBM) approach, which helps create value globally. The VBM approach requires people with a mind-set to maximise financial value to pursue the objective of goal accomplishment. A deep cause and effect analysis involving all the activities in the fishbone diagram might help the CMA's VBM performers and Value Management Advisers, which are the most important cultural activities.

Literature review: the role of management accountant

Traditionally, the role of MA was principally seen as offering a direct contribution to the planning and control of organisational operations (Milne, 1996; Parker, 2002). Recently, this role seems to have evolved (Albelda, 2011) and expanded from mere score keeping, bean counting, and cost controlling to wider multidisciplinary and strategic roles (e.g. Emsley 2005). To perform these new roles, MAs serve internal customers as business partners (Rahman and Ahmed, 2011). Additionally, Turnbull and Neumann (2014) mapped the roles of MAs

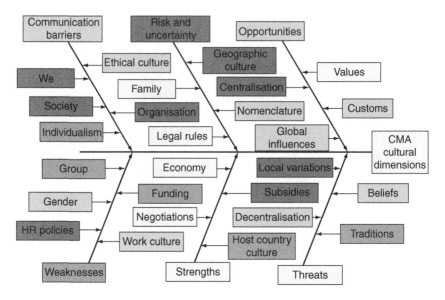

Figure 7.5 The role of management accountants, cultural dimensions (cause and effect relations).

into four broad categories: strategic apex, specialist unit, business partner, and support staff. They report that MAs are experiencing changes in all four roles. Furthermore, managers of the organisations are customers of the MA, proffering accounting information (Kariyawasam, 2009), as MAs assist in the formulation and implementation of organisational strategy (Emsley, 2005). Ahid and Augustine (2012) state that MAs are equipping themselves with the necessary skills to become significant decision makers, strategic planners, and market analysts. However, Clinton and White (2012) report that MAs strategic role and initiative in the area of cost management has not developed over a period of nine years (2003–2012). In a similar vein, Sunarni (2013) reports that the MA's role is still perceived as one of operational manager, and Pietrzaka and Wnuk-Pel (2015) identify budgeting, cost control, and performance measurement as the most important tasks performed by MAs. Moreover, Clinton and White (2012) report that cost management was important to 66 per cent of respondents in 2012, but in 2003 was important to just 80 per cent. The top three initiatives for both 2003 and 2012 involved the implementation of enterprise resource planning (ERP), new budgetary procedures, and business intelligence software. Sunarni (2013) reports that the development of accounting information technology was considered the most important factor by large-scale companies (68.8 per cent) in Indonesia

With regard to factors that might affect the role of MAs, Burnett and Hansen (2008) report that the relationship between environmental and economic performance has increased, affecting MAs' role. They found that this stronger relationship is as a facilitator of decision making, with new performance measures and analysis tools integrating environmental issues into their roles. This influence on the role seems also to be fostered by MAs' educational background, Indeed, Collins et al. (2011) report that CIMA members had a higher participation rate in sustainability strategies. Additionally, changes in technology in large-scale companies are an important driver for change in the role of MAs. Meanwhile Saravanan and Sankararan (2011) report the role of the MA is changing in the rapidly evolving in Indian Telecom environment.

It is apparent that the role of MAs in certain environments remains traditional, while in others it has changed and broadened in recent years. Practitioner's literature suggests a radical change in the role of the MA has been occurring at CFO level and below (e.g. KPMG, 2006). In the Indian context, Bhattacharya (2009) argues that there is no culture of systematic field studies to capture the evolution of management accounting, and most companies do not use it to its full potential. Therefore, there has been a paucity of research into the role of MA in India.

Survey results methodology

To understand whether the role of MAs has been changing in the Indian context, we conducted an online questionnaire survey of CMAs. (See Appendix for a sample questionnaire.) We conducted this survey using a convenience sample, i.e. non-probability sampling, which involves collecting information from members of the target population who are readily available to provide information (Sekaran, 2003).

The sample for this study was taken from the Members Practice Directory, 2014 and the ICAI's Members Directory, 2014. In the first week of October 2015, we sent emails to 540 CMAs with the survey link. However, 82 emails bounced back. One month was allowed for respondents to complete the questionnaire, and reminders were sent in the second and third week. We received replies from 56 CMAs, delivering a 12 per cent response rate. Five questionnaires were incomplete and so were dropped from the final analysis. The number of usable questionnaires was 51. Early and late responses were compared and the t-test showed no significant difference, indicating an absence of non-response bias.

The questionnaire contained demographic information and 22 core functions of MAs. These 22 core functions were taken from CIMA and other prior studies. In responding to the open-ended questions, the respondents were asked to provide information regarding the challenges they faced, and the global factors influencing their roles. The respondents were then asked to rate these core functions using the 5-point Likert scale (with 5 denoting changed significantly and 1 not changed at all) to indicate the extent to which they perceive the core functions identified have changed the role of MAs.

Findings

The demographic characteristics for the responses are presented in Table 7.3, which reveals that 54.9 per cent of the respondents hold the position of MA and 13.7 per cent that of controller. Interestingly, 86.3 per cent possess the CMA qualification and 11.8 per cent have both CA and CMA. The Cronbach Alpha coefficient value is 0.918, which indicates an acceptable internal consistency estimate of reliability (the acceptance level is 0.90 and over, as suggested by Nunnally, 1978).

Based on the work experience of respondents employed by industrial and non-industrial organisations, a significant difference was observed in 'cost transformation and management' ($t=2.21$; $p<0.05$). The mean value for respondents with industrial experience is higher than that for non-industrial units, indicating that cost transformation and management change the role of MA more than non-industrial units do (see Table 7.4). Other functions found to be significant are 'internal control' ($t=2.30$; $p<0.05$), 'evaluation and adoption of information technology' ($t=2.05$; $p<0.05$), 'performance management' ($p=3.85$; $p<0.01$), 'social and environmental cost management and reporting' ($t=2.33$; $p<0.05$). The 'risk management' also indicates a significant difference at 0.10 level.

Furthermore, we asked four experts to categorise the 22 core functions of the MA into six major categories, namely cost management, performance management, strategic management, operations management, risk management, and information

Table 7.3 Demographic characteristics of responses

Demographic characteristics	Frequency	Percentage
1 Respondent's position		
Management accountant	28	54.9
Controller	7	13.7
Cost accountant/Manager	5	9.8
Others	11	21.6
Total	**51**	**100.0**
2 Professional qualifications		
CMA	44	86.3
CA and CMA	6	11.8
Others	1	2.0
Total	**51**	**100.0**
3 Respondent's total work experience		
Less than 5 years	13	25.5
5–10 years	7	13.7
10–20 years	8	15.7
20 and more years	23	45.1
Total	**51**	**100.0**
4 Major part of work experience has been in:		
Industrial	36	70.6
Non-industrial	15	29.4
Total	**51**	**100**

Table 7.4 Core functions that are changing the role of MAs in India

Functions	Mean	SD	Rank	T test by industrial G1 = 36; non-industrial G2 = 15		
				G1 mean	G2 mean	T value (equal variance)
Cost transformation and management	4.118	0.9518	1	4.44	3.92	2.21**
Product mix decisions	4.039	0.8237	2	4.09	3.92	0.59
Financial strategy	3.922	0.9347	3	3.94	4.00	0.21
Pricing of products	3.882	1.1072	4	3.85	4.23	1.07
Internal control	3.863	1.1665	5	4.11	3.31	2.30**
Evaluation and adoption of information technology	3.784	1.1192	6	3.68	4.31	2.05**
Internal audit	3.745	1.1462	7	3.79	4.15	1.03
Regularity adherence and compliance	3.725	1.0213	8	3.65	3.85	0.57
Information management and internal reporting	3.667	1.0708	9	3.71	3.77	0.21
Adoption of new management accounting techniques such as ABC/ ABM, Target costing, JIT, TQM, Balanced Score cards etc.	3.627	1.0576	10	3.65	3.77	0.34
External reporting	3.608	1.1845	11	3.68	3.92	0.66
Management of budgeting and control	3.569	0.9221	12.5	3.62	3.61	0.01
Risk management	3.569	1.0818	12.5	3.47	4.00	1.76***
Contract negotiations and management	3.529	1.0070	14	3.59	3.69	0.35
Project management	3.490	1.1895	15	3.56	3.62	0.15
Performance management	3.412	1.0616	16.5	3.24	4.31	3.85*
Outsourcing decisions	3.412	1.2357	16.5	3.32	3.92	1.59
Investment appraisal	3.392	1.0785	18	3.53	3.46	0.20
Strategic tax management	3.353	1.1632	19	3.38	3.54	0.43
Resource management	3.333	1.1776	20	3.21	3.77	1.64
Social and environmental cost management and reporting	3.235	1.1591	21	3.12	3.92	2.33**
Treasury and cash management	3.137	1.0587	22	3.23	3.39	0.47

Notes
*p < 0.1, **p < 0.05, ***p < 0.01.

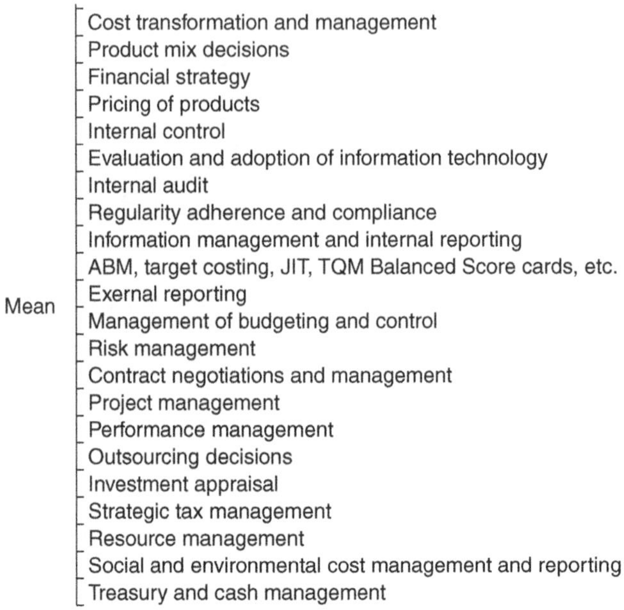

Mean
- Cost transformation and management
- Product mix decisions
- Financial strategy
- Pricing of products
- Internal control
- Evaluation and adoption of information technology
- Internal audit
- Regularity adherence and compliance
- Information management and internal reporting
- ABM, target costing, JIT, TQM Balanced Score cards, etc.
- Exernal reporting
- Management of budgeting and control
- Risk management
- Contract negotiations and management
- Project management
- Performance management
- Outsourcing decisions
- Investment appraisal
- Strategic tax management
- Resource management
- Social and environmental cost management and reporting
- Treasury and cash management

Figure 7.6 Ranked functions based on mean values.

technology management (see Table 7.5). This was done manually to assess which category of functions indicated a significant change in MA's role in the organisations.

The mean value (25.88) for 'strategic function' was the highest ranked category, followed by 'performance management' and 'cost management' respectively. The strategic function category included the pricing of the products, product mix decisions, financial strategy, project management, strategic tax management, investment appraisal, and adoption of new management accounting techniques (such as ABC/ABM, target costing, JIT, TQM, BSC). Based on respondents' total experience in industrial versus non-industrial units, the t-test reveals that the category, strategic oriented functions ($t=2.02$; $p<0.05$) is significant and may have the highest impact on changing the role of MAs in an Indian context. The changing role might also seem to be reflected more in industrial units than non-industrial units, as the mean scores are higher for industrial units. Therefore, it may be inferred that strategically oriented functions are shifting the MA role.

We also asked respondents whether the role of MAs has changed to that of catalyst and advisor in India. The responses are presented in Table 7.6. The table shows that if we exclude those who were undecided, half the respondents believe that the role of the MA has transformed into a catalyst and advisory one. Since there is a significant difference ($p<0.05$), it may be inferred that the role is changing, targeting a higher decision-making level as a catalyst. Burns and

Table 7.5 Categories of functions of MA

Categories of functions	N	Mean	SD	Rank	T value (df=49)	Mean		Significance
					Based on major experience in industrial and non-industrial. units	*G1 (n=36)*	*G2 (n=15)*	
Cost management	51	14.33	3.01	3	1.30	14.69	13.47	$p>0.05$
Performance management	51	14.49	2.23	2	0.44	14.36	14.80	$p>0.05$
Strategic management	51	**25.88**	4.90	**1**	**2.02**	**26.75**	**23.80**	**$p<0.05$**
Operations management	51	13.86	3.07	4	1.52	14.28	12.87	$p>0.05$
Risk management	51	3.57	1.08	6	1.01	3.67	3.33	$p>0.05$
Information technology management	51	7.45	2.00	5	1.19	7.67	6.93	$p>0.05$

Yazdifar (2001) report that few skills are needed for MA to perform strategically oriented functions, such as analytical/interpretive, IT/system knowledge, broad business knowledge, integrating financial and non-financial information etc. Conversely, Cokins et al. (2015) state that the notion that MAs are expanding their role and supporting the executive team as strategic advisers, is hype and fantasy on the part of MAs.

In another question, we asked respondents to state whether the role of MAs is expected to change considerably under the 'Make in India' campaign. The responses are presented in Table 7.7, which reveals that aside from those who were undecided about the possible change in the role of the MAs under 'Make in India' campaign, a significant percentage of respondents believed that it would change considerably, compared to those who stated 'no'. Since there was a significant difference ($p < 0.05$) in the responses, there is a significant likelihood of change to the role of MAs under the 'Make in India' campaign. Several respondents also provided reasons for this change, as given below:

> This gives impetus to manufacturing and hence the role of management accountant in not only cost efficacy but also in the management of resources.

> Costs of manufacturing, segment-wise and product-wise will gain importance as we need to compete in the global market. Each element of cost needs detailed analysis and ways and means to optimise it. ABC shall gain momentum as each activity shall need to link with the final product/service in order to identify wasteful areas and activities.

Table 7.6 Change of role of the MA

Statement	Yes	No	Can't say	Chi square	Df	Significance
Do you think that, in the Indian context, the role of management accountant has changed to catalyst and advisory?	25 (50%)	10 (20%)	15 (30%)	7.00	2	p<0.05

Table 7.7 Expected change of role of the MA

Statement	Yes	No	Can't say	Chi square	Df	Significance
Under 'Make in India' campaign, do you think that the role of MA will change considerably?	20 (42.6%)	7 (14.8%)	20 (42.6%)	7.191	2	p<0.05

Global factors

In terms of the changing role of MA in India, global factors also apparently play a key role. The changes in MA started after the Indian economy was deregulated during the 1990s. In the open-ended question, the respondents were asked, based on their experiences, to identify important global factors that are changing their role. Their responses are presented in Table 7.8.

Parker (2002) states that a number of studies have been undertaken or commissioned by professional accounting associations around the globe, which have generally agreed on the key driving forces of change in the role of MAs. These include business internationalisation and globalisation, the knowledge-based economy, information technology, and changing work patterns and attitudes. The respondent's stated that 'global competition and quality assurance' are forcing MAs to apply new management methods and techniques to manage product and services costs to guarantee their survival. Increasing compliance with governance codes at the global level and 'financial statement audit requiring strengthening of internal control and its reporting' are additional factors contributing to this process of change (Parker, 2002).

Challenges

We also asked the respondents to specify the most critical challenges they are facing today. Seven respondents stated 'government and industry recognition' of their profession, while four mentioned 'fee structure and remuneration of CMAs' as significant challenges. 'Lack of research and development in MA field' is also a concern. The 'Government takes no action on the reports submitted by CMA

Table 7.8 Important global factors that are changing the role of MA

Global factors	Frequency
Globalisation (leading to cost competitiveness)	9
Advances in technology	8
Advances in information technology	4
Emerging and innovations in MA techniques	3
Adoption of global uniform accounting policies such IFRS/IAS	2
Adoption of corporate governance practices and its impact on firm performance	2
Knowledge-based economy	2
Global economy uncertainty	2
MNCs are establishing their businesses in India given new opportunities to apply a few MA practices	2
Sometimes MAs are not updating themselves on changing global accounting practices	2
Global competition and quality assurance are forcing the MAs to apply new management methods and techniques to manage product and services costs for survival	2

auditors', 'difficulties in recognising new policies', and 'changes in the legal environment' were also mentioned. In addition, there has been some resistance from CAs in relation to the function of MA in the organisations.

Conclusions and implications

The objective of this chapter has been to analyse the changing role of MAs in India. The MAs' roles and responsibilities are so crucial that a single miscalculation or underestimation in a business plan can put a company's future at risk. Business internationalisation and globalisation are facilitating the transfer of capital and information across national borders, and this is also influencing the role of MAs. Our survey revealed that 42.6 per cent respondents supported the view that the role of MAs is changing to become more advisory in nature. Approximately 50 per cent of respondents stated that under 'Make in India', the role of the MA will also change considerably. Among the core functions of an MA, it seems that cost management, internal control, evaluation and adoption of information technology, performance management, social and environment cost management, and even risk management (to a certain extent) are influential. The major categorisation of core functions is tilting towards the strategically oriented, which may continue to prompt changes in their role and necessitate MAs to update their knowledge and skills to meet new challenges.

Drivers contributing to this process of change include local variants. The Indian commerce education system has facilitated a transformation by reshaping the roles of MAs. CMAs can now be appointed as Lecturers and Principals/ Directors at colleges and universities. CMAs are also allowed by many universities to pursue their Ph.D.'s. Other local factors include the ICAI, which has played a significant role as a professional body in bringing about change. The institute renders valuable services by providing up-to-date curricula to CMAs, and guides them in continuing education and conducting other professional activities. It approves their practice licences and monitors ethical conduct. The regulations that strengthen and change the practices of MAs in India include ICWAI's Cost Accounting Act, Government notifications for the coverage of Cost Accounting and Cost Audit, self-initiatives by industry associations, and practical training while completing a CMA course.

Despite cultural differences across the various communities, in professionally managed local companies as well as MNCs operating in India, cultural factors either do not come into play, or their influence is mitigating. Among global variants, global competitiveness, advances in technology, advancement in information technology, emerging and innovative management accounting techniques, and globalisation of accounting standards may also be contributing to changing MAs' role. Under the 'Make in India' campaign, MAs are expected to play a key role in cost transformation and management. 'Make in India' improves thought processes and provides a systematic method of implementing quality in the education system that is on a par with global standards.

Among the core functions of MAs, strategically oriented functions might also be changing roles as novel functions pose new challenges to them. These changes are more often reflected in industrial units. Therefore, we might foresee more changes slowly coming to pass in their roles in the future.

The implications of the theoretical descriptions and survey findings presented here might be that the government and industry need to afford due recognition to MAs as highly valuable professionals. The Government and ICAI need to improve training and placement programmes to enhance the capabilities of CMAs, so that they are equipped with up-to-date knowledge and skills. Professional associations like the ICAI should also focus more on online training programmes, aimed at bridging the gap in interdisciplinary technical and qualitative skills among CMAs.

Appendix: sample survey form

Personal particulars

Sanjay Swarup
B.Com, SAS (Com), CAIIB, AICWA
Worked at:

C&AG of India at Dehradun from March 1982 to September 1984, auditing Central Governement Companies and Corporations.
Allahabad Bank, Lucknow from September 1984 to March 1988.
HMT Limited at Srinagar (J&K) and at Nainital from March 1988 to June 1996.
Bharat Electronics Limited at Bangalore and Pune from June 1996 till date.
Presently heading Finance function at Electronic Warfare & Avionics SBU of Bangalore Unit.

It is an admitted fact that every country has different laws, practices, traditions, culture etc. However, thanks to the enormous development in the field of Information Technology, the world has become a small village. Due to this almost every nation has to deal with almost every other nation. Since laws, practices etc. vary from nation to nation, 'adaptability' is the key word. Efforts are being made world wide to enhance the uniformity level in many areas. One such important area is the accounting and presentation of financial statements by adopting IFRS. Similarly, in order to meet the requirements of various stakeholders, spread across the globe, Management Accounting has to converge on local practices and global requirements. Also, it has to be aware of developments in the world and the impact of such developments on business in India. For example, slowdown of economies in US, Europe and China may cause impact on business of an entity in India. Management Accountant has to facilitate the Organisation to have information of such global events, their likely impact on the Organisation, its strategy to neutralise the impact of such situation etc. The ultimate aim of Management Accounting is to facilitate businesses take crucial decisions based on proper information. Hence, Management Accountant has to play a key role in making available proper information, 'suited to the varied needs of different stakeholder in various locations across the globe'.

Questionnaire

Objective of this survey

'To describe and assess the changing role of the management accountant in Indian perspective and to identify the factors/influences in such a change.'

1 Respondent's position:
   a   Management Accountant
   b   Controller
   c   Cost Manager
   d   Any other (please specify … Finance Head of a Strategic Business Unit in a Manufacturing Organisation.)

2 Your age (please tick)

Less than 30 years	
30–40 years	
40–50 years	
50 years and more	✓

3 Your professional qualifications (please tick):

CA	
CMA	✓
CA and CMA	
Others (specify …)	

4a Respondent's total working experience as Management Accountant or in Management Accounting area:

a Less than 5 years	
b 5–10 years	
c 10–20 years	
d 20 years and more	✓

4b Major part of your working experience have been in (please tick):

Industrial ☑ Non-industrial ☐

If you are working in a listed company, please also answer Questions 5 and 6, otherwise, please move to Question 8.

5 **Total sales turnover of your company (for 2014):**
   a Less than Rs 300 crore
   b Rs 300 crore–Rs 600 crore
   c Rs 600 crore–Rs 1,200 crore
   d Rs 1,200 crore and more ✓

6 **Total assets of your company (for 2014):**
   a Less than Rs 300 crore
   b Rs 300 crore–Rs 600 crore
   c Rs 600 crore–Rs 1,200 crore
   d Rs 1,200 crore–Rs 2,400 crore
   e Rs 2,400 crore and more ✓

7 **Your company is:**

Industrial ☑ Non-industrial ☐

8 The following is a list of possible core functions of the Management Accountants in the organisations. We are interested to investigate to what extent each of these functions **are changing the ROLE OF MANAGE-MENT ACCOUNTANT** in the contemporary business environment.

   Please use the following rating scale ranging from 5 to 1:

   • Changed significantly (5) ✓
   • Changed moderately (4)
   • Changed somewhat (3)
   • Changed insignificantly (2)
   • Not changed (1)

Core functions that are changing the role management accountants in India:

Functions	Changed significantly	Changed moderately	Changed somewhat	Changed very little	Not changed
Cost transformation and management	5	4	3	2	1
Adoption of new management accounting techniques such as ABC/ABM, target costing, JIT, TQM, Balanced Score cards, etc.	5	4	3	2	1
External reporting	5	4	3	2	1
Financial strategy	5	4	3	2	1
Internal control	5	4	3	2	1
Investment appraisal	5	4	3	2	1
Management of budgeting and control	5	4	3	2	1
Pricing of products	5	4	3	2	1
Product mix decisions	5	4	3	2	1
Project management	5	4	3	2	1
Regularity adherence and compliance	5	4	3	2	1
Resource management	5	4	3	2	1
Risk management	5	4	3	2	1
Strategic tax management	5	4	3	2	1
Treasury and cash management	5	4	3	2	1
Internal audit	5	4	3	2	1
Performance management	5	4	3	2	1
Evaluation and adoption of information technology	5	4	3	2	1
Contract negotiations and management	5	4	3	2	1
Information management and internal reporting	5	4	3	2	1
Social and environmental cost management and reporting	5	4	3	2	1
Outsourcing decisions	5	4	3	2	1
Any other (specify)	5	4	3	2	1

9 **Do you think that, in Indian context, the role of management accountant has changed to catalyst and advisory?**
   - Yes ✓
   - No
   - Can't say

Any comments:

_____

_____

_____

10 In your opinion, what are the FIVE most challenges that the management accountant is facing today?

   I   High expectations from stakeholders
   II High level of compliance with statute
   III Change from Controller to Facilitator
   IV Fast changing economic scenario
   V Impact of global changes

11 Specific culture, societal culture and company culture have changed the Management Accountant's role:

  a Any **FOUR** cultural predispositions MNC's tend to have towards managing in global context:

     I   Global requirements
     II Convenience of company's parent country put first
     III Implementation of best practices of different countries
     IV Local laws and traditions to be respected

  b What are the challenges in communicating across cultures?
     The language, traditions, customs, understanding of requirements, lack of standard terminology in many areas, varied timings at various places.

  c Techniques used (if any):

_____

_____

12 In your opinion, which are the FIVE factors or influences of government and its polices in changing the role of the management accountant:

   I   Change and synchronisation of various laws
   II IT revolution
   III Stringent compliance requirements
   IV Government's stress on growth

   V Survivor of fittest

  a Any major statutory challenges before CMAs:
     Fast Changing statutes, e.g. Companies Act, 2013, Companies (Cost Records and Audit) Rules, Ind AS, GST etc. require CMAs to keep themselves updated all the time.

  b Regulations which strengthen Practices of CMAs:

     I   Companies Act, 2013
     II Companies (Cost Records and Audit) Rules

  c Industry specific norms complementing Cost Accounting Standards:
     No such specific norms for our industry

13 In your opinion, HOW university education system has changed this role when in from undergraduate to master's level, only 3–4 courses in cost and management accounting are taught:

In my opinion, the university education system does not have major impact on the profession. This is because the courses at university level are not that stringent. Also, the professional seriousness is seldom observed at university courses with the same intensity as is observed in professional courses.

a   Objectives behind introducing cost and management accountancy as one of the subjects in university education system:

I   Making students aware of the professional requirements
II   Preparing foundation for future professional course

14 Any factors or contributions by ICMA how it has changed the role of management accountants and management accounting practices in India:

a   Major operational initiatives taken during your tenure in your organisation:

I   Implementation of ERP – SAP
II   Receivables Management, with complete stress on time value of money
III Inventory Management
IV   Cost Reduction

b   Improvement practices (as CMA practices in your organisation):

I   Process improvement in all the areas
II   Close attention to Audit observation and ensuring preventive and corrective actions
III Six sigma projects
IV   Bar coding of fixed assets for easy verification

15 Whether technology is used in your management accountancy practices?

(a) Yes or (b) No

Yes   ☑   No   ☐

I   If yes, what is the cost of the technology used and its impact on global perspective?

The cost of technology used in accounting practices in our company is towards usage of ERP called SAP. Approximate cost is Rs 60 crores. The adoption of this software has helped us to to achieve highest level of capabilities in preparation of accurate and timely accounts, MIS, Analytical reports etc. Even the offices outside India are well connected and integrated. Globally, it enhances the image of the Company regarding its capabilities.

16 **Based on your experiences, in your opinion, what are the FIVE most important Global factors that are changing the role of management accountant in India?**

    I   Further opening up of economy by India has accelerated the pace of foreign investment

    II   In view of global competition, Indian organisations have to be more efficient and effective

    III The slowing of Chinese, US and European economies

    IV 'Make in India' policy of Govt. of India

    V   Massive Defence modernisation programme of India

Any comments:

CMAs play a vital role in maintaining and improving inner health of the organisation, thereby enhancing the value for all the stakeholders. CMAs' role in identifying the symptoms and raising alarm before things go out of control cannot be ignored.

Thanks for your kind participation in this small survey. Your responses will be strictly treated as confidential.

References

Ahid, M. & Augustine, A. (2012). The roles and responsibilities of management accountants in the era of globalization. *Global Journal of Management and Business Research, 12*(15), 430–453.

Albelda, E. (2011). The role of management accounting practices as facilitators of the environmental management: Evidence from EMAS organizations. *Sustainability Accounting. Management and Policy Journal, 2*(1), 76–100.

Anderson, S. W. & Lanen, W. N. (1999). Economic transition, strategy and the evolution of management accounting practices: The case of India. *Accounting Organization and Society, 24*(5), 379–412.

Bhattacharya, A. K. (2009). Evolution of management accounting. *Business Standard*, New Delhi, July 13.

Bhowmik, A. (2014). Financial and cost management of universities in the information age. *The MA Journal, 49*(4), 16–27.

Burnett, R. D. & Hansen, D. R. (2008). Eco-efficiency: Defining a role for environmental cost management. *Accounting, Organizations and Society, 33*(6), 582–602.

Burns, J. & Yazdifar, H. (2001). Tricks or treats? *Financial Management*, March, 33–35.

Carr, C. & Tomkins, C. (1998). Context, culture and the role of the finance function in strategic decisions: A comparative analysis of Britain, Germany, the U.S.A and Japan, *Management Accounting Research, 9*(2), 213–239.

Clinton, B. D. & White, L. R. (2012). The role of management accountant 2003–2012. *Management Accounting Quarterly, 14*(1), 1–36.

Cokins, G., Cherian, J., & Schwer, P. M. (2015). Don't be stuck in the last century. *Strategic Finance*, October (1), 1–10.

Collins, E., Lawrence, S., Roper, J., & Haar, J. (2011). Sustainability and the role of the management accountant. *CIMA, 7*(14). Retrieved from: www.cimaglobal.com/Documents/Thought_leadership_docs/Sustainability%20and%20Climate%20Change/Management-control_NZICA.pdf.

Emsley, D. (2005). Restructuring the management accounting function: A note on the effect of role involvement on innovativeness. *Management Accounting Research, 16*(2), 157–177.

Gray, S. J. (1988). Towards a theory of cultural influence on the development of accounting systems internationally. *Abacus, 24*(1), 1–15.

Gupta, K. (2005). *Contemporary auditing*. Delhi: Tata McGraw-Hill.

Gupta, S. K., (2015). Value added to value management: Role of CMAs. *The Management Accountant, 50*(1), 96–97.

Hofstede, G. (1980). *The cultural consequences: International difference in work related values*. London: Sage.

Joshi, D. V. (2009). *Cost and management accounting profession in India: A Reminiscence*. Pune, India: CMA Priyamwada D. Joshi, Erandwana Co-op Hsg. Society.

Joshi, P. L. (2001). The international diffusion of new management accounting practices: The case of India. *Journal of International Accounting, Auditing and Taxation, 10*(1), 85–109.

Joshi, P. L. & Bremser, W. G. (2004). Changing dimensions of accountants' role and skill requirements in organizations: Findings from the corporate sector in Bahrain. *International Journal of Accounting, Auditing and Performance Evaluation, 1*(3), 363–384.

Kariyawasam, U. (2009). Changing role of the management accountant. Achievers. CIMA Graduation Ceremony, Sri Lanka, 1–13.

KPMG (2006). *Being the best: Insights from leading finance functions*. London: KPMG.

Milne, M. J. (1996). On sustainability; The environment and management accounting. *Management Accounting Research, 7*(1), 135–161.

Nunnally, J. C. (1978). *Psychometric theory* (2nd ed.). New York: McGraw-Hill.

Parker, L. D. (2002). Reinventing the management accountant. Lecture delivered at Glasgow University, 15 March. Retrieved from: www.cimaglobal.com/Documents/Thought_leadership_docs/VisitingProfessor/tech_presnot_reinventing_the_manage ment_accountant_mar02.pdf.

Pietrzaka, Z. & Wnuk-Pel, T. (2015). The roles and qualities of management accountants in organizations: Evidence from the field. *Procedia – Social and Behavioral Sciences, 213*, 281–285.

Prasad, P. (President of ICAI). (2015). Emphasis on 'Make in India' and 'Make India' competitive points: The direction towards CMAs. *The Management Accountant, 50*(1), 7–9.

Rahman, S. & Ahmed, J. U. (2011). An evaluation of the changing role of management accountants in recent years. *Indus Journal of Management and Social Sciences, 6*(1), 18–30.

Saravanan, P. & Sankararan, S. (2011). Emerging role of management accountant in the Telecom Space. Retrieved from: http://papers.ssrn.com/sol3/papers.cfm?abstract_id= 1737448.

Sekaran, U. (2003). *Research methods for business: A skill building approach* (4th ed.). New York: John Wiley.

Sunarni, C. W. (2013). Management accounting practices and the role of management accountant: Evidence from manufacturing companies throughout Yogyakarta, Indonesia. *Society of Interdisciplinary Business Research Review, 2*(2), 616–626,

Turnbull, K. J. & Neumann, J. (2014). *Management accountant as change*. Cranfield: Cranfield University.

Van Dyck, C., Frese, M., Baer, M., & Sonnentag, S. (2005). Organizational error management culture and its impact on performance: A two-study replication. *Journal of Applied Psychology, 90*(6), 1228–1240.

8 Management accountants in Italy

Economic, institutional and educational environment, and evidence from the job market

Laura Zoni

Introduction

The interpretation of the management accountant's role in organisations and society has recently been widely debated in efforts to untangle the multiple intertwined factors influencing management accountants' ability to participate in the value creation process (Caglio & Cameran, 2016). In recent research, Pitcher (2015) provides an effective summary of three sets of drivers when explaining the role of management accountants in value creation (Figure 8.1). The first set of factors is organisational in nature, including considerations of the level at which the management accountant operates within the organisation, the culture of the organisation and the relationship between the CEO and the accountant. In

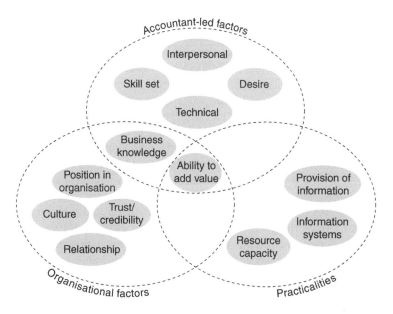

Figure 8.1 Factors enabling management accountants to add value.

Source: adapted from Pitcher (2016).

relation to the second set of factors, Pitcher includes all practicalities involved in enabling accountants to perform their roles; namely, the provision of information, resource capacity and the availability of information technology. Management accountant-led factors, which are a third subset of factors, are also considered critical to explain the role of management accountants in the value generation process. Within this category Pitcher identifies the management accountant's interpersonal skills, e.g. the quality of being a 'people's person', their technical skills and the desire to become involved in the business and take a genuine interest in business issues.

The aim of this chapter is to provide a local view of the management accountant's role, by illustrating how the Italian economic and institutional-legal environments and educational setting uniquely affect the management accountant's role in value creation.

Italian economic environment

The economy of Italy is constructed on the success of small enterprises; 95 per cent of the approximately 4.5 million companies employ fewer than 10 employees each, equating to 47 per cent of national employment (ISTAT, 2010). Of these companies, 65.2 per cent (approximately 3 million) have no employees, as they are sole proprietorships. Wide economic differences exist between regions: northern regions such as Lombardy, Piedmont, Veneto and Emilia Romagna are the most developed, and are where the headquarters of most of the largest Italian companies can be found.

Despite their indisputable role in value generation for the Italian economy, micro companies are characterised by several distinctive features, which are not necessarily beneficial to their further development and sustainability. First, the presence of an entrepreneur and founder of a company is central to the management of that firm. S/he usually makes all managerial decisions and manages issues across functions (finance, production, sales). The entrepreneur is the main vehicle for both technical and managerial knowledge transfer. Second, the organisation of the firm is very simple and informal, both due to the limited number of individuals involved in the company, and because the presence of managers (not owners) is limited. Third, the ownership structure itself, and the top management team, is dominated by the owner and his/her family members. Frequently family members, as part of the top management team, are under-skilled for the roles and positions they hold. As can be seen from Table 8.1, Banca d'Italia (Navaretti, Bugamelli, Cristiadoro & Maggioni, 2012) reported that in a sample of European Firms in a Global Economy (EFIGE), 85.6 per cent are firms with a dominant shareholder: the family. The percentage is somewhat comparable to that in France, Germany, Spain and the United Kingdom, but the main difference between Italian family firms and other European family firms is the low propensity to hire managers external to the family. In Italy 66.3 per cent of companies feature a top management team, entirely comprised of family members. The percentage in other countries is significantly lower.

Table 8.1 Family owned and managed firms

Country	Family firms as a proportion of all firms	Family firms only	
		CEO is a family member	Top management team comprised of family members only
France	80.0	62.2	25.8
Germany	89.8	84.5	28.0
Italy	85.6	83.9	66.3
Spain	83.0	79.6	35.5
United Kingdom	80.5	70.8	10.4

Source: Bugamelli et al. (2013).

Notes
Family members in top management is a dummy variable equal to one if all members of the top management team belong to the same family.
Numbers are expressed as percentages.

Ownership and control habitually overlap. Frequently, the entrepreneur is also the founder. Generational change is seldom managed, and sometimes there is no generational change at all; no delegation is in place. The absence of formalised mechanisms of accountability mean that the owner frequently makes decisions that are not necessarily knowledge-based, or in the firm's best interests. The owner applies his/her own intuition and preconceived knowledge to the decision-making process optimising his/her utility function. Intuition and preconceived knowledge are frequently substituted for managerial accounting techniques and tools such as cost analysis, budgeting and reporting (Cortesi et al., 2004). An additional draw-back of the lack of a clear definition of tasks and responsibilities among the firm's employees is the loss of efficiency in organisational processes and the lack of time devoted to business analysis and strategic designs (Pencarelli, 2010).

Small and medium-sized firms are unable to offer structured career paths and attractive remuneration that is comparable to that offered by large companies. Moreover, the personnel at small and medium-sized firms are frequently less qualified and competent, when compared to the personnel at large companies. Additionally, the founder-owner of the small firm can be very reluctant to acknowledge that professional work and services are essential to improve the company's management. This perpetuates a negative loop, and does not contribute to the development of the job market for professional managers and professionals (Cortesi et al., 2004).

A degree of informality in interpersonal communications and relations is a key element of the family workplace environment. Whilst the family atmosphere leads to effective coordination and integration based on values and beliefs, it also explains the absence of managerial performance measurement mechanisms. A formal mechanism of performance evaluation is not considered appropriate, being inconsistent with a culture of trust and friendship.

Management control in small and medium-sized firms

According to Stocchetti (1996, p. 113), and more recently Ballucchi and Fornaciari (2015), management control is rarely implemented in Italian small and medium-sized firms, although a few exceptions emerged during the recent economic crisis in 2008. Italian entrepreneurs are technically highly skilled, very competent in terms of product development, engineering and production, but are underprepared to deal with financial matters, due to clear knowledge gaps in financial management. As a consequence, Italian small and medium-sized firms do not effectively use financial planning tools such as budgeting and medium-term planning. Half of the population surveyed by Ballucchi and Fornaciari (2015) employs external consultants to perform management control tasks; but, in one-third of the surveyed firms, management control tasks are assigned to employees, while in the remaining firms, the owner "takes care" of management control. These external consultants are mainly certified professionals or *dottori commercialisti*. The role of the *dottori commercialisti* will be further investigated in the section devoted to the institutional context.

In the above mentioned survey (Ballucchi & Fornaciari, 2015), the authors reported that more frequently used management control tools are financial statements prepared for statutory purposes, financial statement analysis and interim reporting. Cost accounting is designed and used mainly to determine the cost of products, and to support pricing decisions, but only rarely to assign responsibility or to influence behaviour. When available, budgets typically consist of a profit plan only. The profit plan supports estimations of financial resource requirements. "Errors" in cash budgeting are frequently absorbed by stretching the days payable outstanding (DPO). The budget is almost never used to assign financial responsibility targets and is almost entirely disconnected from operations planning. This is true in medium-sized companies as well as small ones (Zoni & Stamerra, 2009). Very frequently, the owner is the only person providing input to the profit plan, and there is no formal approval of plans and budgets. Hence, there are no formal checks that the assumptions contained therein are reasonable and consistent with the firm's strategic choices (Gatto & Ciabattoni, 2015). Variance analysis is popular, at least at the stage of a line-by-line comparison of items included in the statutory income statement. Variances are rarely investigated, and flexible budgets are not used. It is rare (applying to less than 15 per cent of cases) that small and medium-sized firms employ more than one individual to carry out cost accounting tasks; typically the person in charge of cost accounting holds a high school diploma, with a specialisation in accounting (Gatto & Ciabattoni, 2015). There is evidence, however, that Italian small and medium-sized firms equip themselves with more systematic and more formalised management control systems in certain situations: generational transition, rapid growth, sale of business and business venture aggregations (Broccardo, 2014).

Management control in large firms

Large companies do exist in Italy. There are approximately 3,000 such firms, employing about 19.7 per cent of the labour workforce, and producing 31 per cent of national value added (ISTAT, 2010). Approx. 300 of these are listed on the Milan stock exchange. Large companies are highly exposed to global economic trends. Although they exhibit distinctive features, both national and of their own making, international management business practices are relatively widespread among large Italian corporations.

In a recent study of CFO roles and finance function features in large Italian industrial corporations, Zoni (2013) studied nine cases, carefully selected to assure comparability to non-Italian large corporations. The companies were headquartered in the most industrialised regions in Italy: Lombardy, Tuscany, Emilia Romagna and Veneto, and their turnover ranged from €480 million to close to €4 billion. They outperformed their peers in terms of organisational outcomes (competitive, social and financial results). All the observed companies had a finance unit that met the specifications of "standard" international archetypes of finance units (IBM, 2010): unsophisticated finance organisations; strong, administrative-focused finance organisations striving for finance efficiency; administratively unstructured finance organisations with advisory ability; and finally, administratively mature finance organisations with an ability to *read* the business. All of the finance units were specialised, with competence sub-units in charge of cost accounting, budgeting and controlling, and had been decentralised to suit specific company needs. In some cases, the finance unit included planning staff.

Italian institutional environment

Within the institutional framework, two elements are worth mentioning as drivers of a role for Italian management accountants in the value creation processes. The first relates to the accounting qualification(s) available in Italy; the second to the accounting legal and regulatory environment, as applicable to statutory financial statements.

Accounting certification(s)

The accounting qualification available in Italy is *dottore commercialista*, which can be translated as 'certified public accountant' (CPA). The *dottore commercialista* becomes such after gaining a Master's of Science in Economics and Management (300 ECTS credits and five years of study), completing an internship period of 18 months (three years to become certified auditors) and successfully passing public examinations. The examinations test a broad body of knowledge, including accounting (both financial and managerial), taxation, business law, bankruptcy law, valuation, financial management and foundations of information technology. The qualified *dottore commercalista* is required to follow a programme of continuing education to maintain his/her qualification.

In Italy, in many instances the *dottore commercialista* is the external consultant at small and medium-sized companies, offering basic accounting and tax filing services. The *dottore commercialista* resembles a northern European CPA. In several cases, the *dottore commercialisti* associated themselves with professional practices, so that they could serve medium-sized firms. Associated practices assist medium-sized firms in tax litigation, bankruptcy proceedings, valuation and financial restructuring proceedings, and IT software package implementation.

Management accountants in Italy do not receive this title when qualified; they hold the qualification *dottore commercialista*, which covers an extensive array of disciplines and technical skills, including management accounting practices. Nonetheless, associations of financial controllers do exist, such as the Controller Associati di Ancona, International Group of Controllers, Assocontroller or Association of Italian (Financial) Controllers (AIC). Of these, the AIC, founded in 2010, is the best-established. Within the context of public debate into the roles and qualification of professionals not organised into formalised professional bodies, AIC has been the most active association urging legislation for the public recognition of financial controllers. AIC successfully supported the passing of two pieces of legislation. The first, Italian law no. 4/2013, applying European legislation (no. 765/200–9 July 2008), governs the qualifications of professionals not organised into formalised professional bodies. This legislation enabled FacCertifica to certify controllers and senior controllers based on two written exams and one oral exam. Before applying for the qualification, an individual must meet minimum requirements, which are differentiated between financial controllers and senior controllers. These qualifications are valid for a period of three years and require at least 10 hours of continuing education a year. The second, UNI 11618, is a voluntary norm enacted by UNI (Ente Nazionale Italiano di Unificazione) and approved on 7 January 2016, becoming effective on 28 January 2016. This norm is not compulsory, as its application is voluntary. UNI 11618 defines and details financial controller's skills and competencies. The norm states that a controller should be able to: design and implement the architecture of a management information system; run internal audits; support management control through the design and use of control tools and processes; communicate financial results inside and outside a firm, while disseminating a culture of financial discipline; evaluate financial performance at all organisational levels; provide input for strategic planning; and provide support to top management leaders as a business partner. UNI 11618 appears to describe the abilities required of a CFO working in the organisational environment of a large company, rather than those needed by a financial controller employed by a small or medium-sized company. UNI 11618 does not address the issue of the certification of such abilities.

In summary, in Italy there is currently no organised institute of management accountants; financial controllers are organised into associations (e.g. AIC), and the certification of financial controllers is still in an initial phase.

Legal and accountancy framework of statutory financial statements

Johnson and Kaplan (1987) warned against financial accounting requirements undermining the purposes and practices of management accounting, and we believe that this is particularly true in the case of Italy, where the role of the management accountant has been influenced negatively by financial accounting regulations. The law regulates the content and format of financial statements, and is based on: Civil Code (art. 2423 and subsequent articles); decree no. 127/1991 adopting EU directives in terms of accounting harmonisation; decree no. 38/2005 introducing IFRS for listed companies; the latest development included in decree no. 139/2015 adopts EU directive 34/2013 on the convergence of local GAAPs to IFRS, effective from the beginning of 2016. The Organismo Italiano di Contabilità (OIC) is the Italian accounting standards setter. The OIC is comprised of certified professional accountants, "preparers" (members representing different industries' regulatory bodies), analysts and financial investors, and security exchange commission representatives.

In Italy, listed companies and banks are currently required to report using IFRS, while all other legal entities registered in Italy adopt Italian accounting standards. The IFRS and Italian accounting standards, used until January 2016, show major differences. These differences will be partially bridged by the introduction of new IFRS-compatible accounting standards (see below). Italian firms (except those adopting IFRS) are required to use *uniform* financial statements, e.g. external reporting formats are compulsory and rigidly determined, regardless of company size, industry and any other specific information needs; line-items cannot be changed. The income statement, whose upper section is presented in Table 8.2, requires a statement of the "value of production", subsequently listing all the costs of production. The value of production consolidates revenues with changes to the inventory of work in progress, semi-manufactured products and finished goods (A.2 and A.3), and the capitalisation of previously delineated costs, relative to internal job/constructions (A.4). Costs of production are classified by nature (vs. stages of production); the consumption of raw materials and goods is identified by combining "B.6 Purchases of raw materials, other materials and consumables" and "B11 Changes in inventory of raw materials and other materials, consumables and goods for resale". An intermediate result is that value of production net of costs of production approximates to the profit from operating activities. Under the same regulation, a cash flow statement is not required, although the OIC suggests cash flow statement would be of some importance.[1]

Whilst uniform financial statements can effectively assist in data collection at the national level, they offer limited information to entrepreneurs and owners, who incur the costs of their preparation. Scepticism about why financial statements should be prepared and to the advantage of whom is widespread among small and medium-sized company owners.

The layout of statutory income statements assumes an accounting flow that does not require any management or cost accounting classifications or techniques. The classification of operating costs by nature does not require any effort to determine why certain resources were employed and at which stage of production. Furthermore, positioning in the list of costs of production of items B.6 "Purchases of raw materials, other materials and consumables" and B.11 "Changes in inventory of raw materials and other materials, consumables and goods for resale" denote an assumption of a periodic inventory method (versus a perpetual method). The periodic inventory method is frequently associated with rudimental operating information flows and simplified cost accounting systems. Overall, the "cost of goods sold", a key item of managerial information, is neither determined, nor determinable.

These factors lead us to conclude that the legislation in place in Italy has provided little incentive for Italian firms to adopt management accounting systems. Failure to provide incentives for the adoption of management accounting results in financial statements that are not sufficiently informative, increasing scepticism among the owners and entrepreneurs of small and medium-sized firms towards financial measurements (see section on management control in small and medium sized firms above). This results in an unavoidable cost, due to legal requirements, rather than acting as a means to support management in financial decision making.

Table 8.2 Standard format of statutory income statements for Italian firms adopting Italian GAAPs (upper section)

A Value of production
   1 Changes in inventories of work in progress, semi-manufactured products and finished goods
   2 Changes in inventories of work in progress made to order
   3 Capitalisation of internal work
   4 Other income and revenues

Total value of production

B Production costs
   5 Purchases of raw materials, other materials and consumables
   6 Services received
   7 Leases and rentals
   8 Payroll and related costs:
      a Wages and salaries
      b Social security contributions
      c Employee termination indemnities
      e Other costs

Total payroll and related costs
   9 Amortisation, depreciation and write-downs:
      a Amortisation of intangible fixed assets
      b Depreciation of tangible fixed assets
      c Write-down of fixed assets
      d Write-down of current receivables and liquid funds

Total amortisation, depreciation and write-downs
   10 Changes in inventory of raw materials and other materials, consumables and goods for resale
   11 Provision for risk reserves
   12 Other provisions
   13 Other operating costs

Total production costs
A–B Difference between value and cost of production

Italian educational environment

A third variable to consider when explaining the role of the Italian management accountants is the Italian educational environment. Managerial accountancy is traditionally taught at Italian universities and business schools. In a comparative survey, Pistoni and Zoni (2000) compared and contrasted management accounting courses across different European countries using a questionnaire sent to members of the European Accounting Association network.[2] Their results showed Italian universities do not differ significantly from their European counterparts in terms of topics covered and time devoted to management accounting topics; additionally, both core and advanced courses are comparable. Their research supported the supposition that in Europe, management accounting is perceived as part of the fundamental background to be completed by any student hoping to pursue a career in management. On the contrary, at the undergraduate level courses in management accounting would not always be recommended to accounting specialists, confirming the adoption of a users' approach rather than a specialists' approach to the delivery of management accounting content. To train specialists, universities offer courses in accounting in the form of specialised master's degrees, although until the beginning of the century this was a feature of Anglo-Saxon countries. Master's level courses were introduced in Italy only after 2001, following university reform and the Bologna process.[3] Other changes have since occurred in Italy, and the offering of managerial accounting courses has increased both at undergraduate and the newly introduced graduate level.

In the top 10 private and public Italian universities (CENSIS,[4] 2015), managerial accounting is taught at undergraduate level, in four cases as an elective course. A Master's of Science in Accounting and Control is offered by four institutions: Alma Mater Studiorum, Università Luigi Bocconi, Università Cattolica del Sacro Cuore and Università Luiss, Guido Carli. The emphasis of the course is on taxation, financial communication and governance structures, and financial management, rather than the design and use of performance measurement systems. SDA Bocconi School of Management, the leading business school in Italy, offers executive training in management accounting to benefit managers and small and medium-sized company owners. An Executive Master's in Accounting, Control and Finance was formerly offered, but it has now been discontinued and substituted with shorter and more specialised programmes.

Management accountants: evidence from the job market

To provide evidence of the job market for management accountants in Italy, we analysed job offers drawn from various sources: specialised websites such as Linked-in and Monster, and the 'Career' or 'Work with us' sections of companies listed on the Milan stock exchange, in the months of September and October 2015. Out of 950 job offers analysed we found 66 positions (approximately 7 per cent of the total) related to management accounting (and controlling).

The 66 job offers of interest were distributed across industrial sectors (designer clothing, energy, health care, food and beverages, telecoms) and also included the providers of financial services. The companies represented in the pool were very heterogeneous in terms of size and financial and competitive results. In some cases, the jobs offered were issued by the Italian subsidiaries of international companies, and in other cases by medium-large-sized Italian companies.

For each of the 66 positions surveyed, information gathered when available included: the name of the company posting the job offer, the function/organisational unit where the applicant would be employed, the function or role to whom the applicant would report, a brief job description providing the activities to be performed, the skills and competencies required, and the compensation range. Some information was often missing, including the person to be reported to and the compensation being offered.

Interestingly, none of the 66 positions used the job title 'management accountant'; the most frequently given job title was either 'business analyst' (28 out of 66 cases, approximately 42 per cent), or 'financial controller' (in another 28 out of 66 cases, approximately 42 per cent). 'Planner' was the heading of the job postings in the remaining 10 cases (approximately 16 per cent). An English term to express job title was used in the majority of cases. In Italian, 'financial controller' is very seldom translated, while 'business analyst' and 'planner' have Italian equivalents.

The activities to be performed according to the job descriptors, are summarised in Figure 8.2, wherein relative frequencies are also reported. Reporting activities (74 per cent) and financial analysis (70 per cent) were the most frequently mentioned activities. Budget preparation (59 per cent) was second, together with process management and cost containment activities (52 per cent). It is important to observe that the requirement for defining the budget target was seldom mentioned (14 per cent), meaning the management accountant is required to support the budgeting process technically rather than organisationally. Capital budgeting (3 per cent) and M&A identification (9 per cent) do not distinctively identify the management accountant role. Design activities are rarely mentioned (cost allocation design is mentioned in 27 per cent of job postings).

Figure 8.3 reports the frequencies with which the main technical skills were requested. A degree in Management seems to be a standard requirement (73 per cent of cases). It is, however, interesting to note that more and more companies value a quantitative background developed in engineering and statistics when mentioning university programmes. The requirement for a degree in engineering is not surprising: in Italy as in other continental European countries, engineers serve as management accountants in manufacturing plants. The requirement for degrees in statistics (15 per cent of cases) is more recent. Statistics is in great demand among digital companies, where big-data analytics are needed to provide business insight. Previous work experience is required for this role (70 per cent of cases), although in approximately one-third of the cases (35 per cent), fewer than three years' work

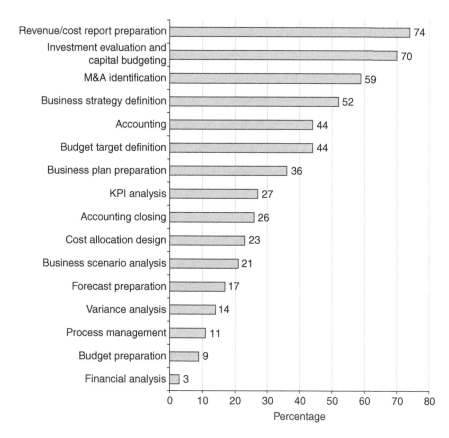

Figure 8.2 Job offers: activities required (frequencies).

experience would be deemed adequate. More than five years' experience is rarely required (17 per cent of cases). The evidence from the job-post listings is that there is not a very active market for senior positions in Italy. This is consistent with findings reported by Zoni (2013), who in recent research observed that the majority of Italian Chief Financial Officers were internally promoted to the position. Knowledge of the English language and the basic Microsoft Office package is required in almost all cases, respectively 80 and 76 per cent of cases. Knowledge of SAP and other software packages is mentioned in approximately 40 per cent of cases. More specific language requirements are made in 24 per cent of cases; these related to positions in Italian companies that are expanding internationally into non-English speaking countries.

Figure 8.4 reports the positions' requiring personal skills. Analytical skills are in high demand (83 per cent), and this is not surprising. If we pair the former with the requirement for communication skills (42 per cent) and flexibility (38 per cent), we perceive a need for a management accountant who can take on the

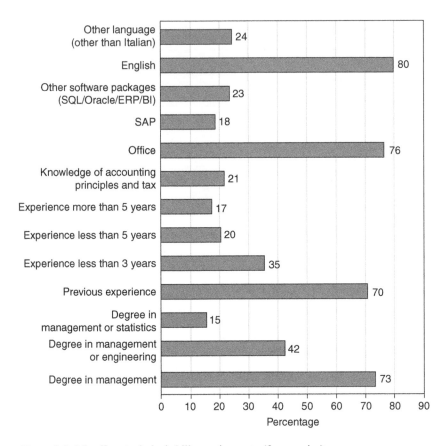

Figure 8.3 Job offers: technical skills requirements (frequencies).

role of business partner rather than merely 'bean counter'. Further requirements are teamwork skills (30 per cent), results-based approach (30 per cent) and proactivity (30 per cent). Skills less frequently mentioned include accuracy, problem solving and organisational skills, ability to work under pressure and self-motivation.

Although the number of observations is limited, an attempt was made to gather evidence by performing statistical data analysis. The analysis was conducted as it follows. We codified each job posting's requirements in terms of activities and technical and personal skills as a series of dummy variables (one if the job posting mentioned the activity/requirement, and zero otherwise). The first step consisted of calculating three Pearson's correlations matrices among the activities required, technical skills and personal skills. This analysis was intended to examine how each set of variables was combined in the job postings. We then created three categories based on job title: we attributed the value of

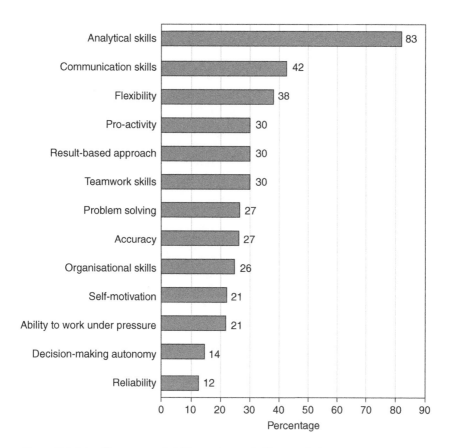

Figure 8.4 Job offers: personal skills requirements (frequencies).

one to 'controller', two to 'business analyst' and three to 'planner'. We ran an ordered Logit regression, whereby the dependent variable was the job title, and the independent variables were in turn: activities required, technical skills and personal skills. This analysis was intended to examine if each job title was distinctively defined in terms of activities and technical and personal skills. Lastly, we regressed the three sets of requirements onto firm size (total revenues in the most recent year) to check if the requirements were distinctive in this regard. Not all the analyses were equally significant, and so we report only the most significant findings in the following subsections.

Management accountant's technical skill requirement

Table 8.3 illustrates the Pearson correlation matrix for technical skills required of business controllers (1), business analysts (2) and planners (3). The significant

Table 8.3 Pearson correlation matrix technical skills requirements

	1 = controller 2 = business analyst 3 = planner	Degree in management	Degree in management or engineering	Degree in management or statistics	Previous experience	Experience less than 3 years	Experience less than 5 years	Experience more than 5 years	Knowledge of accounting principles and taxation	Office	SAP	(SQL/ Oracle/ ERP/BI)	English	Other languages
1 = controller 2 = business analyst 3 = planner	1													
Degree in management	-0.022	1												
Degree in management or engineering	-0.022	0.113	1											
Degree in management or statistics	0.002	0.069	0.321**	1										
Previous experience	-0.003	-0.182	0.032	0.095	1									
Experience less than 3 years	-0.090	-0.123	-0.113	-0.043	0.413**	1								
Experience less than 5 years	0.103	0.132	0.192	0.216	0.327**	-0.362**	1							
Experience more than 5 years	-0.038	-0.183	-0.055	-0.076	0.295*	-0.327**	-0.221	1						
Knowledge of accounting principles and taxation	0.116	0.068	0.080	-0.013	0.100	-0.068	0.023	0.166	1					
Office	-0.042	-0.029	0.056	-0.155	-0.065	0.043	-0.164	0.063	-0.225	1				
SAP	-0.129	-0.152	-0.087	-0.199	0.140	-0.097	-0.036	0.316**	0.236	0.083	1			
Other software packages (SQL/ Oracle/ERP/BI)	-0.124	0.007	-0.100	0.275*	0.122	0.286*	-0.087	-0.049	-0.193	0.138	-0.162	1		
English	0.056	0.039	0.040	-0.109	0.005	-0.038	0.054	0.017	-0.023	0.431**	0.135	-0.004	1	
Other languages (other than Italian)	0.042	-0.051	0.301*	0.057	0.219	-0.043	0.075	0.221	0.139	0.073	-0.083	-0.307*	0.191	1

Notes
N = 66.
* Correlation is significant at the 0.05 level (2-tailed).
** Correlation is significant at the 0.01 level (2-tailed).

correlations among technical skills required in the job postings are scattered; input data on the length of work experience is sometimes mutually exclusive, showing a negative significant ρ. The most meaningful positive correlations are the association of previous work experience with less than three years of work experience (ρ=.41; p<.05), and the knowledge of English with the Office package (ρ=.43; p<.05).

To complement our analysis, we also ran a regression to check the probability that some technical skills would be distinctive in each of the three itemised roles. The ordered Logit regression conducted on 66 cases, and reported in Table 8.4, shows only three technical skills are statistically related to the role and position, as reported in the job postings: previous work experience, its length and knowledge of SAP. Previous work experience has a higher likelihood of being associated with planners than with controllers, while longer work experience and knowledge of SAP have a lower likelihood of being associated with planners than with controllers.

Management accountant's personal skill requirements

Table 8.5 shows the Pearson correlation matrix for the personal skills required of business controllers (1), business analysts (2) and planners (3).

We observed some significant correlations among activities required in the job postings. Flexibility is correlated with analytical skills (ρ=.27; p<.10), communication skills (ρ=.28; p<.10), organisational skills (ρ=.50; p<.05) and results-based approach (ρ=.30; p<.10). Proactivity is correlated to accuracy (ρ=.34; p<.05), results-based approach (ρ=.43; p<.05), flexibility (ρ=.26;

Table 8.4 Ordered Logit regression conducted on a sample of 66 cases of job titles and technical skills requirements

		Estimate	Sig.
Threshold	[1=controller; 2=business analyst, 3=planner=1.0]	−0.452	0.604
	[1=controller; 2=business analyst, 3=planner=2.0]	1.603	0.075
Location	Degree in management	−0.445	0.441
	Degree in management or engineering	−0.455	0.415
	Degree in management or statistics	0.252	0.748
	Previous experience	17.984	0.000
	Experience less than 3 years	−18.130	0.000
	Experience less than 5 years	−17.607	0.000
	Experience more than 5 years	−18.152	0.000
	Knowledge of accounting principles and taxation	0.806	0.221
	Office	0.098	0.886
	SAP	−1.529	0.056
	Other software packages (SQL/Oracle/ERP/Business Intelligence)	−0.394	0.594
	English	0.412	0.556
	Other language (other than Italian)	−0.019	0.978

Table 8.5 Pearson correlation matrix personal skills requirements

	1 = controller 2 = business analyst 3 = planner	Team work skills	Accuracy	Analytical skills	Communication skills	Organisational skills	Results-based approach	Flexibility	Reliability	Problem solving	Ability to work under pressure	Pro-activity	Decision making autonomy	Self-motivation
1 = controller 2 = business analyst 3 = planner	1													
Team work skills	-0.135	1												
Precision	0.069	0.040	1											
Analytical skills	0.094	0.295*	0.274*	1										
Communication skills	0.021	0.234	-0.250*	0.384**	1									
Organisational skills	0.056	0.139	0.106	0.263*	-0.015	1								
Results-based orientation	0.141	0.067	0.262*	0.206	-0.099	0.215	1							
Flexibility	-0.062	0.097	0.083	0.265*	0.278*	0.397**	0.301*	1						
Reliability	0.092	0.361**	0.398**	0.166	0.057	0.100	0.260*	0.189	1					
Problem solving	0.116	0.114	0.160	0.183	-0.181	0.028	0.114	-0.057	-0.019	1				
Ability to work under pressure	-0.143	0.222	0.098	0.133	0.155	0.118	0.222	0.206	0.148	-0.068	1			
Pro-activity	0.233	0.211	0.336**	0.206	0.101	0.064	0.426**	0.029	0.260*	0.114	0.303*	1		
Decision making autonomy	0.168	0.218	0.153	0.178	0.016	0.271*	0.218	0.145	0.394**	0.153	-0.098	0.122	1	
Self-motivation	-0.039	0.222	0.098	0.133	0.005	0.033	0.303*	0.130	0.034	0.098	0.275*	0.303*	0.442**	1

Notes
N = 66.
* Correlation is significant at the 0.05 level (2-tailed).
** Correlation is significant at the 0.01 level (2-tailed).

$p<.10$) and ability to work under pressure ($\rho=.30$; $p<.10$); self-motivation further correlates results-based approach ($\rho=.30$; $p<.10$), ability to work under pressure ($\rho=.28$; $p<.10$), proactivity ($\rho=.30$; $p<.10$) and decision making autonomy ($\rho=.44$; $p<.05$). From the above correlation, we conclude that flexibility, proactivity and self-motivation imply a set of the management accountant's skills that describe both role and position.

To complement our analyses, we also ran a regression to check the likelihood that some personal skills would be distinctive of each of the three itemised roles. An ordered Logit regression was conducted for 66 cases, and reported in Table 8.6, showing that only two personal skills relate statistically to role and position as reported in the job postings: teamwork skills and proactivity. 'Teamwork skills' has a lower likelihood of being associated with planners than with controllers, whereas proactivity has a higher likelihood of being associated with planners than controllers.

Firms' size and management accountants

Finally, we ran three Logit regressions setting the firm size, as measured against total revenues in the most recent year as dependent variable, and sets of activities to be performed, technical skills requirements and personal skills requirements as independent variables. The activities described in the job postings did not provide details of the difference in company size, whereas some technical skills requirements (knowledge of accounting principles and taxation, and SAP) and some personal skills requirements (ability to work under pressure, proactivity and self-motivation) were suggestive of differences in the firms' sizes.

Table 8.6 Ordered Logit regression conducted on a sample of 66 cases of job titles and personal skills requirements

		Estimate	*Sig.*
Threshold	[1=controller; 2=business analyst, 3=planner=1.0]	0.202	0.739
	[1=controller; 2=business analyst, 3=planner=2.0]	2.458	0.000
Location	Team work skills	−1.362	0.052
	Accuracy	−0.628	0.398
	Analytical skills	0.573	0.500
	Communication skills	0.264	0.696
	Organisational skills	0.125	0.857
	Results-based approach	0.303	0.650
	Flexibility	−0.571	0.377
	Reliability	0.799	0.449
	Problem solving	0.424	0.485
	Ability to work under pressure	−0.718	0.333
	Pro-activity	1.523	0.030
	Decision making autonomy	1.050	0.301
	Self-motivation	−0.702	0.406

Conclusions

In Italy, management accountants are not codified. There are several reasons why management accountants have not been formally recognised traditionally. The first relates to the Italian economic environment, which features small and micro firms with no experience of management accounting practices. Additionally, only a few large Italian corporations exist where management accountants could and have been serving under different job titles. In addition, the institutional environment has not assisted in the recognition of management accounting as a profession. The role of the *Dottori commercialisti*, certified financial accountants, has prevailed over that of management accountants in the same way that binding and compulsory financial accounting rules have undermined the development of management accounting practices. Lastly, whereas in Italy management accounting is recognised as a core subject of a degree in management as in the rest of Europe, specialised master's degrees in accounting were only introduced their recently.

Our survey of 66 job postings leads us to conclude that, nonetheless, a job market exists for controllers, business analysts and planners. Some technical skills (length of previous work experience and knowledge of SAP) and personal skills (teamwork skills and proactivity) are distinctive of job titles, which are frequently used interchangeably. Large and medium-sized companies require personnel to support value creation by preparing revenue and cost reports, running financial analyses, preparing budgets and forecasts, mapping processes and managing costs. From the survey, it also emerges that while management accountants need to be technically skilled, they must also possess softer personal skills if they are to contribute to their fullest potential.

Notes

1 The preparation of cash flow statements became compulsory under decree no. 139/2015.
2 The following limitations should be considered when interpreting the results: three European countries, Germany, Greece and Ireland, were not represented; the number of institutions contacted in each country was not always proportional to the number of institutions delivering undergraduate education; EAA membership was not evenly distributed across countries.
3 The Bologna Process involved a series of ministerial meetings and agreements between European countries, designed to ensure comparability in the standards and quality of higher education qualifications. Through the Bologna Accords, the process created the European Higher Education Area, in particular under the Lisbon Recognition Convention. It is named after the place of its proposal, the University of Bologna, with the signing of the Bologna declaration by Education Ministers from 29 European countries in 1999 forming a part of European integration.
4 CENSIS stands for *Centro Studi Investimenti Sociali*. The Italian institute of socio-economic research, founded in 1964, works for the Italian Government and publishes influential research.

References

Ballucchi, F. & Fornaciari, L. (2015). *La diffusione degli strumenti di pianificazione e controllo nelle PMI. Analisi Empirica in Emilia Romagna.* Working Paper, Dipartimento di Economia Università di Parma, Parma.

Broccardo, L. (2014). Management Accounting System in Italian SMEs: Some Evidences and Implications. *Advances in Management and Applied Economics, 4*(4), 1.

Bugamelli, M., Cannari, L., Lotti, F. & Magri, S. (2013). Il gap innovativo del sistema produttivo italiano: radici e possibili rimedi. In A. Arrighetti & A. Ninni, (editors), *La trasformazione "silenziosa".* Dipartimento di Economia Università di Parma, Collana di Economia Indutriale ed Applicata, Parma.

Caglio, A. & Cameran, M. (2016). *Is it shameful to be an accountant? GenMe perception(s) of accountants' ethics.* Abacus, forthcoming.

CENSIS. (2015). *Quarantanovesimo rapporto sulla situazione sociale del paese 2015.*

Cortesi, A., Alberti, F. & Salvato, C. (2004). *Le piccole imprese. Strutture, gestione, percorsi evolutivi.* Carocci: Roma.

Gatto, F. & Ciabattoni, M. (2015). *Il processo di pianificazione e controllo e il ruolo del Controller: logiche funzionali e commento degli esiti della survey svolta su un campione d'imprese del corso CUOA "Il controller",* Working Paper, CUOA Foundation, Padova.

IBM Institute for Business Values. (2010). *The new value integrator.* Insights for the Global Chief Financial Officer Study, IBM Global Business Services, Somers.

ISTAT. (2010). *Noi Italia: 100 statistiche per capire il paese in cui viviamo.* Rome: Istituto Nazionale di Statistica.

Johnson, H. T. & Kaplan, R. S. (1987). The rise and fall of management accounting. *IEEE Engineering Management Review, 3*(15), 36–44.

Navaretti G. B., Bugamelli, M., Cristiadoro, R. & Maggioni, D. (2012). Are firms exporting to China and India different from other exporters? Available from: www.bancaditalia.it/pubblicazioni/qef/2012-0112/QEF_112.pdf.

Pencarelli, T. (2010). *La valorizzazione dei prodotti tipici nell'economia delle esperienze.* Esperienze d'Impresa: Dipartimento di Studi e Ricerche Aziendali, Università di Salerno.

Pitcher, G. S. (2015). Management accounting in support of the strategic management process. *CIMA Executive Summary Report, 11*(1), 1–18.

Pistoni, A. & Zoni, L. (2000). Comparative management accounting in Europe: An undergraduate education perspective. *European Accounting Review, 9*(2), 285–319.

Stocchetti, G. L. (1996). *Il controllo di gestione nella piccola impresa.* Milano: EGEA.

Zoni, L. (2013). *Amministrazione, Finanza e Controllo: costo o valore? La trasformazione della Funzione AFC nelle imprese italiane.* Milano: EGEA.

Zoni, L. & Stamerra, G. (2009). Il ruolo del budget in tempi di crisi: perché non si può rinunciare alla formalizzazione dei piani di azione. *Economia & Management, 4,* 57–76.

9 Management accountants in Japan

Masafumi Fujino[1]

Introduction

Contemporary management accountants in Japanese companies are expected to play a greater role in strengthening the connection between management accounting and strategy (Hiromoto, 1991). Literature about Japanese management accounting also suggests management accountants communicate closely with operational managers (Daniel & Reitsperger, 1991; Hiromoto, 1991), and that to a substantial extent this shapes their strategic role.

Close communication between management accountants and working people is one of the characteristics of a decentralized management accounting function (Simon, Kozmetsky, Guetzkow, & Tyndall, 1954). However, organizational context is not the only factor that may have an effect on the role of the management accountant. Literature illustrates that the origins of this close interaction between management accountants and operational managers can be identified in the process of the historical development of Japanese management accounting (Okano & Suzuki, 2007). In addition, it is fostered by the Japanese collectivistic culture that creates environments in which people are motivated by group interests, and emphasizes the maintenance of interpersonal harmony (Hofstede, 1991). A further important factor is the education of management accountants. In light of this, this chapter explores what effects historical and educational contexts have on the interaction between management accountants and managers in Japanese companies.

The next section explains the current role and status of management accountants in Japanese companies. The focus then moves on to describe the historical development of the management accounting function in Japan, and the educational environment for Japanese management accountants. Finally, a summary and conclusion is provided.

Current roles and status of management accountants in Japanese companies

Kato, Ishikawa, Oura and Arai (2007) argued that no single department fulfils the management accounting function in Japanese companies entirely. Indeed, the management accounting function is usually shared between at least two different departments: the accounting department and the corporate planning department (Tsumagari & Matsumoto, 1972; Sakurai, 1997; Kato et al., 2007; Yoshikawa, Takahashi, & Manabe, 2016). In addition, management accountants are sometimes employed in other departments, such as the human resources department (taking responsibility for disaggregating corporate performance goals into departmental goals), the purchasing department (taking responsibility for target costing practices), and the production engineering department (taking responsibility for capital expenditure programs) (Kato et al., 2007). Furthermore, the different management accountants in these horizontally differentiated departments report to top management via different channels. No single senior management accountant integrates and controls the management accountants dispersed throughout the organization.

Generally, the head of the accounting department is responsible for financial accounting and reporting, management accounting, and taxation. Thus, their role is similar to that of a controller, and in some cases, that of a treasurer. Some companies, however, assign the responsibility for the collection of receivables to the sales department (Sakurai, 2015). Typically, management accountants in accounting departments are only responsible for budgeting and cost management. Other management accounting tasks, such as middle-range planning and capital budgeting, are often assigned to management accountants located within the corporate planning department.

The task of budgeting overlaps between the accounting department and the corporate planning department (Tsumagari & Matsumoto, 1972). In some cases, management accountants in the corporate planning department are in charge of budget setting, and management accountants in the accounting department take responsibility for compiling actual results and developing variance analyses. In other cases, the former conduct both budget setting and variance analyses, whilst the latter compile actual results and then only transmit them to the corporate planning department. The head of the corporate planning department serves various roles and is involved in several tasks, such as the evaluation of subsidiaries, M&A negotiations, assisting the board of directors, legal affairs, and so forth (Toyo Keizai, 1999).

Moreover, both the accounting and the corporate planning department are given various vernacular titles in Japanese companies. The accounting department (*keiri* in Japanese) is also known as *zaimu* (finance), *kanri* (administration), *shukei* (paymaster), and so on. Some companies might use two of these titles simultaneously; for example, the *zaimu* section is sometimes a sub-unit of the *keiri* department (Sakurai, 2015). An investigation conducted by Nishizawa (1995) revealed that over 80 percent of Japanese companies use the name *keiri* for the accounting department or its sub-units. Meanwhile Keizai (1999) demonstrated that 44 percent of companies listed on the Tokyo Stock Exchange call the corporate planning department *keiei kikaku* (corporate planning). The corporate planning department also has alternative names such as *sohgo kikaku* (general planning), *shacho shitsu* (president's office), or *keiei kanri* (business administration).

It appears from the organizational charts of Japanese companies that the accounting department and the corporate planning department are often functionally differentiated and associated with different career paths. The members of the accounting department receive several years of training, in particular, accounting training programs,[2] before they move up the promotional ladder within the accounting department. Job rotation between the accounting department and the corporate planning department is relatively rare, and the size of the corporate planning department is often smaller than that of the accounting department. In about 75 percent of listed companies, the corporate planning department has only 10 staff members or fewer (Toyo Keizai, 1999).

According to findings reported by Keizai (1999), the most valued skill of a corporate planner is the ability to collect information, specifically from the various functional departments. Since a wealth of experience and personal connections proceeding from the position of functional manager are considered helpful for collecting information, corporate planning departments typically recruit experienced people from functional departments such as sales, research and development, and production. Corporate planning staff often attain their positions by following various career tracks. In contrast with accountancy training programs, most companies do not offer specialized training programs to their corporate planning staff.

Figure 9.1 illustrates vertical decentralization within the accounting function. Large manufacturing companies often have a three-layered structure: corporate, divisional, and factory accounting departments. This decentralized structure strengthens horizontal communication between divisional/factory managers and accountants respectively (Simon et al., 1954). In order to communicate frequently with divisional managers, divisional accountants need to understand the products, customers, and market environment within the division. In most companies, divisional accountants are involved in the middle-range planning process.

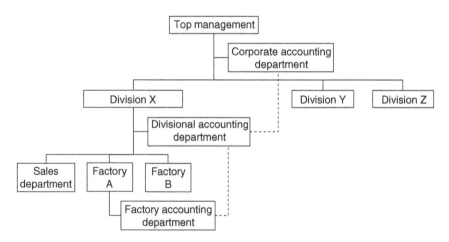

Figure 9.1 Structure of the accounting function.

As mentioned above, middle-range planning is usually assigned to the corporate planning department. Involvement in the planning process at the divisional level can facilitate co-operation between the corporate planning department and the accounting department.

Accountants at the divisional and factory level usually serve two 'bosses' (i.e. the corporate accounting department head, represented as the dotted lines in Figure 9.1, as well as divisional or factory level management). In this context, the role of the accounting career track system is to ensure loyalty toward the corporate accounting department (Hiki, 1997; Ikenaga, 2005). This system grants the head of the corporate accounting department the power to reposition accounting personnel within the accounting function and its different sub-units and levels. The human resources department cannot reposition accounting personnel without the approval of the head of the corporate accounting department. Through this rotation, the corporate accounting departments in Japanese companies design the in-house careers of accounting personnel, allowing them to gain the necessary experience to become accounting managers, whilst also strengthening their loyalty toward the accounting function.

Moreover, as a member of the accounting function, the accountants at the divisions and factories are required to act in line with the corporate missions and values (Hiki, 1997; Kawai & Matsuda, 2015). If they observe divisional managers behaving inappropriately, they are expected to highlight the particular problem and inform their divisional managers (Hiki, 1997). However, even when the divisional accountants are in conflict with the opinions of the divisional managers, the accounting career track system does not allow the divisional manager to transfer the accountant to another department. Thus, this system provides some guarantee of the status of the accountants.

The historical development of management accountants in Japan

In the previous section the current status of management accountants in Japanese companies was explained. This section examines the history of the Japanese management accountant and provides further insights into the origins, as well as the important factors that shape interactions between management accountants and operational managers in Japan.

Management accountants in the early stages: engineers as factory accountants

As explained briefly above, the origins of management accountants in Japan can be traced to factory accountants in the mid-1920s. At that time, Japan had experienced heavy industrialization years after the West. Japanese companies actively introduced advanced technologies, including management accounting techniques such as budgeting and standard costings (Hasegawa, 1936; Kato, 1958). However, these techniques were not called 'management accounting' at that time, but simply 'budgeting' or 'standard costing,' and the researchers found that engineers, in particular, were engaged in the design and use of these systems (Fujino, 2010; Toyoshima, 2005). The following paragraphs detail the case of Mitsubishi Electric to illustrate how engineers came to undertake management accounting tasks. Mitsubishi Electric was selected here because it was one of the earliest adopters of budgeting in Japan, and because the engineers involved in the implementation of the budgeting system also participated in governmental efforts as pioneers in later years, and by doing so, influenced subsequent management accounting practices.

Mitsubishi Electric launched the design of a budgeting system in 1927. During the early stages of its design, accountants (not engineers) at the headquarters and external consultants learned from textbooks published in the United States and prepared a draft of the budgeting system (Mitsubishi Electric, 1927). However, since the accountants at headquarters had only been in charge of keeping general accounts and preparing external reports, they did not have the necessary capabilities to design and use the budgeting system. The draft was then sent to the factory to gather input from factory managers and accountants (Noda, 1928). The majority of these were engineers who had graduated from higher educational institutions of engineering. The factory managers from different departments and the accountants held a cross-functional meeting to compile their responses to the draft. From a user perspective, they proposed some modifications in the documents and procedures of the budgeting system; for example, the terminology used in some of the budget sheets and the procedure for calculating factory financial performance (Noda, 1928). In reality using the modified budgeting system, whenever further modification was needed the factory managers and accountants repeatedly arranged cross-functional projects to discuss how to redesign the budgeting system (Mitsubishi Electric, 1951).

Although the engineers who took up positions as factory accountants were not known as 'management accountants' at that time, they performed virtually identical roles to those currently undertaken by management accountants. In addition to setting budgets, they engaged in factory-wide cost reduction projects together with other functional managers, joined product design meetings on how to achieve specific cost targets, and were involved in negotiations with suppliers for discounts. Notably, at that time, their role was already not to simply control operations at a distance, but to build close relationships with, and support, factory functional managers. The Japanese collectivistic culture seemed to foster, shape and, to some extent, even characterize the interaction between factory managers and accountants. For example, even when management accountants faced a strong argument from a design engineer over the use of high-quality components, they usually managed to persuade him to accept the use of low-cost components by appealing to the consensus that priority should be given to the achievement of cost targets for the factory as a whole (Mitsubishi Electric, 1951).

The close co-operation and somewhat smooth communication between functional managers and accountants was based on their shared beliefs and experiences as engineers. Some engineers at Mitsubishi Electric shared the experience of importing and then adapting Western technologies to their own manufacturing environment on the shop floor (Mitsubishi Electric, 1951). They believed that work experience at the actual operational sites should be one of the qualities needed to be a 'real' engineer. Literature on business history suggests that this belief was rooted in university curricula that included an apprenticeship program at the factory (Morikawa, 1988). Thus, it can be argued that one important reason for the close interaction and co-operation between management accountants and operational managers that can still be observed in Japanese companies is that both groups share experiences at the actual sites and professional beliefs that these experiences should be valued.

Cost accounting regulation during wartime

The governmental regulation of cost accounting during wartime triggered the further diffusion of management accounting knowledge, particularly to accountants at headquarters who had mainly engaged in financial accounting. In the 1940s, under the controlled economy, the Japanese government required companies to implement cost accounting in order to set product prices and increase efficiency. The government announced the Cost Accounting Rules for the Manufacturing Industry in 1942, and issued a series of industry-specific rules over the following few years. Moreover, not only accounting academics, but also many practitioners from various industries, including the factory accountants at Mitsubishi Electric, participated in the development process of these specific rules. Through their joint efforts, they learned a great deal from Western publications on cost accounting and, in this vein, the diffusion of cost accounting knowledge was rapidly promoted in Japan (Kurosawa, 1980). In addition, to widely enforce the governmental cost accounting policies, The Japan Cost Accounting Institute was established. Its founding board consisted of government and military officials, accounting scholars, and practitioners. The institute rapidly established regional branches nationwide, and each branch offered cost accounting seminars for business persons, students, and military people. According to the records, every seminar was full (Japan Industrial Management and Accounting Institute, 2003).

Furthermore, the institute established the Training Center for Cost Accountants as a permanent educational institution. The course at the center took six weeks (six days per week) with approximately 200 course hours in total. Military accountants, accounting academics, and pioneering practitioners served as lecturers. The subjects in the course were not limited to the cost accounting techniques required by the governmental rules, but also covered issues such as factory management, budgetary control, statistics, auditing, tax, and economic laws (Japan Industrial Management and Accounting Institute, 2003). This broad coverage indicates that a Training Centre can be regarded as the first educational institute specializing in training management accountants. Unfortunately, there is no historical material indicating what positions the graduates on the course held in their companies. However, during this period 'management accountants' and even 'management accounting' were unfamiliar terms generally in Japan. Indeed, with very few exceptions, even accounting academics did not use the term 'management accounting' in their publications. Accountants who performed cost accounting and budgeting tasks were usually known as cost accountants or budgeting managers.

Introduction of the controller from the United States following World War II

Budgeting and costing managers became recognized or labelled as 'management accountants' only after the government announced two associated reports entitled *On Internal Control in Companies* (1951) and *Guidelines for the Implementation of Internal Control* (1953).[3] (Hereafter, these two reports are referred to simply as 'the Reports.') In order to produce the Reports, the government created the Financial Management Committee in the Ministry of International Trade and Industry (MITI). This committee consisted of leading accounting academics and practitioners. The Chairperson of the committee joined the design of the Mitsubishi Electric budgeting system in the late 1920s. He and other committee members had also engaged in pre-war and wartime governmental policies.

Although the term 'internal control' is included in the title, the main body of the Reports relates to the roles of the controller and the procedures for budgetary control. The words 'management accounting' were not used in the Reports, but one of the committee members explained at the Japanese Accounting Association symposium on the Reports that "[the committee] understands internal control as management accounting" (Oota et al., 1951, p. 71). Following World War II, the term 'management accounting' was widely used in accounting textbooks and professional journals.

The Reports highlighted four basic functions of the controller: budgeting, accounting, statistics, and auditing. Figure 9.2 shows an organizational chart used as an example in the Reports. The Reports proposed a separation between the treasurer and controller function, because the committee members recognized that accountants spent too much time doing the work of a treasurer. In that sense, the Reports advocated the introduction of the American-style controller. The Reports stated that "nowadays, the controller function is widely established in U.S. companies" (MITI, 1951, p. 13). They also argued that Japanese companies "need to introduce the controller at all costs" (MITI, 1951, p. 13).

When the Reports were issued, the Japanese economy had just undergone the return from a controlled economy to a market economy. The committee continued on the premise that to deal with quite unstable market demands top management should co-ordinate functional departments from a company-wide perspective. The Reports intended to have the controller play a role in providing top management with information necessary for their co-ordination (Oota et al., 1951). Nevertheless, the committee members recognized that the information provided by the controller should be used not to control but to co-ordinate functional departments. One of the committee members stated that "the term 'control'

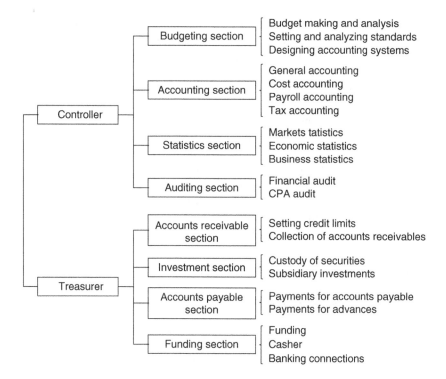

Figure 9.2 Separation between controller and treasurer.

Source: *On Internal Control in Companies* (1951) and *Guidelines for the Implementation of Internal Control* (1953).

may sound like coercion. But we intend harmonized development of the company as a whole" (Oota et al., 1951, p. 72).

Reports concerning the controller at the headquarters did not demand the centralization of the management accounting function. One of the committee members explained that "since we mainly addressed the controller at the headquarters, we did not get into the details about cost control at the factory" (Kurosawa et al., 1953, pp. 78–79). The committee recognized that, even if budgetary control was implemented, "in most cases, people who are far from the front line of production and sales could not understand the sources of budget variances" (Kurosawa et al., 1953, p. 80). Information provided by the controller was not seen as an instrument for ensuring complete transparency about functional departments. The committee expected factory accountants to closely communicate with factory people and enhance transparency. The chairperson of the committee mentioned the case of Mitsubishi Electric in the pre-war period and indicated that "the factory costing manager was an engineer. He scrutinized standards and actual results every day. Once he found the increase of material costs he talked to someone" (Kurosawa et al., 1953, p. 81).

This raises the question: what effect did the Reports have on the structure of the management accounting function at that time? According to the case studies of 25 major companies (Kigyo Kenkyukai, 1955), the majority of companies maintained the existing accounting department and also created a new department which was in charge of budgeting and/or planning. Different companies named the new department in different ways; for instance, 'administration' (*kanri* in Japanese), 'planning and control' (*kikaku tosei*), 'investigation' (*chosa*) or 'integrated production' (*seisan togo*).[4] The functions of financial reporting, taxation, cost accounting, and cash budgeting usually remained in the accounting department. Moreover, some companies also left the budgeting tasks in the accounting department, and others only transferred budget setting to the newly created department. The survey demonstrated that approximately 75 percent of the companies investigated had a budgeting/planning department in parallel with an accounting department. This budgeting/planning department was an archetype of the current corporate planning department (Tsumagari & Matsumoto, 1972).

Education for management accountants

Accounting qualifications in Japan

According to the comparative case study of large Japanese and British manufacturers conducted by Koike (2002), accountants in British manufacturing companies usually obtain the qualification of Certified Accountant and/or Cost and Management Accountant, which is also one of the requirements to be promoted to senior positions. In contrast, Japanese manufacturers do not require accountants to acquire a formal accounting qualification such as the Certified Public Accountants (CPA). In Japan, there is not even any widely accepted management accounting qualification such as CIMA or CMA. The Japan Industrial Management and Accounting Institute runs a management accounting course for company accountants and qualifies those who finish the course as cost accountants. This course has a long tradition, and leading accounting academics and practitioners serve as lecturers. However, it has only several dozen participants and its qualification is not widely recognized at this time.

The Japan Chamber of Commerce and Industry administers the most popular accounting competency test. The subjects in this test cover bookkeeping, financial accounting, costing, and management accounting. Only paper exams are conducted and no work experience is needed. The test is classed into four grades, mainly according to the skill levels. For example, the second grade provides the proper skills for a company accountant and the first grade covers more advanced knowledge about business administration and analysis. The number of people taking the test across all the four grades is over 400,000 a year. Approximately 20,000 people a year take the first grade test. The pass rate of the first grade is about 10 percent. Although there is no accurate data about what percentage of company accountants pass this test, some companies incorporate the passing of the first and/or second grade into their training courses for junior accountants.

In-house training for accountants

In hiring accountants, very few Japanese companies consider the advanced accounting knowledge of applicants or their major in accounting at university. Instead, some large companies provide their own in-house training program for accountants. Hiki (1997) illustrated the in-house training program for account- ants at Panasonic, a leading electronics company. The study revealed that Panasonic has developed its training programs since the 1950s. These programs offer five- to ten-year courses, in which accountants follow a step-by-step process. The first step starts immediately after someone is hired and consists of training on the general policies and systems in the accounting department. For the second step, accountants receive basic practical training in fixed asset accounting, accounting for materials, basic cost management, and so forth. The third step offers training in accounting practices, such as taxation, cash manage- ment, and intermediate cost management.

The in-house qualification exams are often linked to the in-house training program (Hiki, 1997; Ikenaga, 2005; Koike, 2002). Ikenaga (2005) illustrated the qualification exam in the in-house training program at NEC, another leading electronics company. In order to pass the exam, accountants have to study inde- pendently a wide range of accounting-related knowledge including bookkeeping, financial reporting, income tax, cost accounting, management accounting, finance, and so forth. The exam questions are prepared with reference to the first and second grades of the Japan Chamber of Commerce and Industry test. All accountants are required to pass the in-house exams for promotion to managerial positions.

However, Koike (2002) argued that these classroom training and qualification systems can develop only the basic knowledge as an accountant. In the case of Panasonic, the training courses also provide hands-on training in which account- ants need to conduct interviews with divisional and functional managers (Hiki, 1997). At NEC, in parallel with the training program, the on-the-job training (OJT) also plays an important role in developing accounting human resources. The novice accountants are usually in charge of supporting budget setting and reporting for the divisions. Experienced budgeting managers at the divisions serve as instructors and provide the OJT. Through OJT, the novice accountants are required to gain knowledge about the divisions as part of the preparation for smooth communications with the experienced managers (Ikenaga, 2005).

Koike (2002) also discussed the concept of job rotation within Japanese accounting departments. Accountants are assigned to the factory accounting department soon after joining the company. They usually work there for about five years, and are in charge of a different product every year. After leaving the factory, they are transferred to the divisional accounting department. As a divi- sional accountant, they are in charge of cost accounting certain products, and then sales accounting and cash management. Subsequently, accountants deal with profitability analyses for other products within the division, or are further transferred to the corporate accounting department. In a comparative study of large Japanese and British companies, Koike (2002) found that whereas the British accounting managers who moved quickly up to senior positions had no experience as factory accountants, all of the Japanese accounting managers went through the factory accounting departments. The British accounting managers held the view that if they needed information about the divisions an inquiry could be sent from the corporate accounting department to the divisional managers. On the other hand, the Japanese accounting managers emphasized the sharing of experiences with people at the divisions to facilitate smooth communication with them (Fujita et al., 2015; Ikenaga, 2005).

To illustrate to what extent Japanese companies value the sharing of experiences, the career track of a management accountant at Kao provides a typical example (Hiki et al., 2006). In 1971, this management accountant became the head of the newly created head office management accounting department. In order to support the research and development strategies, he implemented marketing accounting techniques to increase the effectiveness of research and development and reduce marketing costs. However, a marketing manager complained about this attitude of controlling marketing costs at a distance. Interestingly, he later became the head of the marketing department and his position turned 180-degrees from controlling to being controlled. Since Kao had long espoused direct communication as one of the corporate credos, as the marketing manager, the former management accountant encouraged brand managers to closely communicate with research and development and production departments, and shift their focus from market share to profitability. After a few years in the marketing department, Kao returned to the management accounting department. Through this rotation, his credo of 'direct communication' permeated the brand management process of the company, based on the marketing accounting techniques implemented (Hiki et al., 2006).

Placing greater emphasis on the frequent communication between management accountants and divisional and functional managers is also consistent with the idea of *koto-mae* management, which has long been held in the accounting departments of Japanese companies (Okano & Suzuki, 2007; Hiki, 1997). *Koto-mae* means before-things-happen. *Koto-mae* management relates to the monthly process of analyzing causal relationships and thinking of actions before figuring out actual financial results (Okano & Suzuki, 2007). Divisional accountants scrutinize forecasts for the next three months, which functional managers develop in the middle of every month. Then, based on the forecasts, the accountants prepare monthly estimated financial statements and provide advice to divisional managers on the challenges and actions to be addressed. The communication skills developed by accountants through the in-house training program are expected to facilitate this *Koto-mae* management (Hiki, 1997).

Summary and conclusion

Following a brief introduction to the current status of Japanese management accountants, this chapter explored the effects of the historical and educational context in Japan on Japanese management accountants and their interactions with operational managers. From the historical perspective, this chapter revealed that one of the origins of management accountants in Japan lies in the factory accountants of the 1920s. At that time, Japanese manufacturers actively transferred management accounting techniques from the United States to Japan (Hasegawa, 1936). However, since accountants at the headquarters did not have sufficient resources at that time, factory accountants mainly engaged in the implementation of these management accounting techniques. The case of Mitsubishi Electric illustrated that both factory managers and accountants, historically, had shared experiences and values as engineers, which enabled them to communicate closely with each other and adapt the management accounting techniques for their own purposes. Nowadays, the engineering-rooted belief that experiences at the actual operational sites should be valued fosters the role of management accountants as strategic partners to operational managers in Japanese companies, and facilitates the interaction between these two groups.

In the 1940s and 1950s, the governmental initiatives gradually forced headquarters accountants to pay more attention to management accounting. Particularly after World War II, the government advocated the introduction of the American-style controller to provide information for top management. This chapter demonstrated that the committee members expected that, rather than the centralized controller, factory accountants could communicate closely with factory managers and enhance transparency for top management.

Currently, the decentralized accounting departments also provide educational opportunities for junior accountants. Japanese companies emphasize the experiences of accountants at the divisions and factories more than the publicly recognized accounting qualifications, because the shared experiences can underpin their communication skills. The OJT and job rotation are also arranged in order to encourage junior accountants to actively interact with experienced operational managers.

Examination of contemporary business practice makes it rather difficult to clearly answer the question of where a management accountant sits in Japanese companies, because members of different units or departments (e.g. accounting department and corporate planning department) collectively carry out the management accounting function. These departments and their members also have various vernacular titles and, in some cases, even the people in these departments may not recognize themselves as management accountants.

This chapter offers opportunities to attract further interest from international researchers in Japanese management accountants and management accounting practices. However, the findings are subject to several limitations. First, the focus is only on the domestic accounting function. Nowadays, more and more Japanese companies transfer their sales, production, and even research and development sites, overseas and buy overseas factories and companies. Thus, there could be far less time to educate management accountants at such overseas units. Further research is required to explore whether or not, and how, this globalization might change the decentralized structure of the management accounting function and the communication between managers and management accountants.

Second, the horizontal differentiation at corporate level is also faced with some changes. Recently, some companies have changed the title of an accounting director into 'CFO' (Chief Financial Officer). This title is used with the expectation that the accounting director could more closely provide strategic advice for the CEO. However, in many cases, the differentiation between the accounting department and the corporate planning department does not help the CFO become informed about strategies and middle-range plans. To deal with this issue, Panasonic, for instance, reformed its corporate staff departments and integrated the accounting department, the corporate planning department, and the human resource department (Kawai & Matsuda, 2015). This kind of reform provides a fertile arena for further research into the role of the CFO, or senior financial managers, in Japanese companies.

Finally, so as to discuss the role of Japanese management accountants in general, this chapter focused on the practices often used in large companies. In that sense, these may be only mainstream practices. It is necessary to conduct further studies on management accountants in small and medium-sized enterprises (SMEs) (Sawabe, 2016). The SMEs do not have as many resources as the large companies to run their own training programs for management accountants. To complement their resources, the SMEs could draw on external accounting experts. Further research is necessary to illustrate the role of external experts in supporting or replacing in-house management accountants.

Notes

1 This work is supported by a Grant for International Studies Exchange from the Melco Foundation.
2 Training programs in the accounting department will be discussed in more detail later.
3 The former described the basic roles of controller and the latter explained in more detail the division of duties within the controller department and the procedures for budgetary control and internal audit.
4 This variety of names may be due to linguistic matters. The Reports did not translate 'controller' into the Japanese language. They just wrote *kontorora*, which sounds similar to controller, but for most of the practitioners *kontorora* was not suitable as a name for the department. Companies should have devised their own Japanese name.

References

Daniel, S. J. & Reitsperger, W. D. (1991). Linking quality strategy with management control systems: Empirical evidence from Japanese industry. *Accounting, Organization and Society, 16*(7), 601–618.

Fujino, M. (2010). Genka kanri shikou no houga (Emergence of cost management thinking). In K. Yamamoto (Ed.), *Genka keisan no donyu to hatten* (*Introduction and development of cost accounting*) (pp. 299–307). Tokyo: Moriyama shoten.

Fujita, Y., Saeki, T., & Matsuda, C. (2015). Kigyo rinen ga keiei wo ugokasu: Kao Kagome 2sha no torikumi (Mission-driven management: the cases of Kao and Kagome). *Kigyo Kaikei, 65*(5), 638–654.

Hasegawa, Y. (1936). *Waga kigyo yosan seido no jisshoteki kenkyu (Empirical research on budgeting systems in Japanese companies)*. Tokyo: Dobunkan.

Hiki, F. (1997). Matsushita Denki Sangyo no keiri (Management and accounting at Panasonic). In M. Sakurai (Ed.), *Wagakuni no keiri-zaimu soshiki (Accounting organizations in Japan)* (pp. 112–136). Tokyo: Zeimukeiri Kyokai.

Hiki, F., Fujino, M., & Ito, K. (2006). *Domestication and evolution of management accounting systems in a Japanese manufacturing company*. Unpublished paper presented at the European Accounting Association Annual Congress 2006, Dublin, Ireland.

Hiromoto, T. (1991). Restoring the relevance of management accounting. *Journal of Management Accounting Research, 3*, 1–15.

Hofstede, G. (1991). *Cultures and organizations: Software of the mind*. U.K.: McGraw-Hill.

Ikenaga, K. (2005). NEC no keiri buin seido to jinzai kaihatsu heno torikumi (The accounting career track system and human resouces development at NEC). *Junkan Keiri Joho, 1092*, 8–16.

Japan Industrial Management & Accounting Institute. (2003). *Nihon genka keisan kyokai no setsuritsu to ayumi (The foundation and trajectory of the Japan Cost Accounting Institute)*. Tokyo: Sangyo Keiri Kyokai.

Kato, T. (1958). Industrial engineering institute (About industrial engineering). *PR (Public Relations), 9*(2), 14.

Kato, Y., Ishikawa, K., Oura, K., & Arai, K. (2007). Wagakuni no keiei kikaku-bu no jittai chosa (Empirical analysis of management planning and control section in Japan). *Genka Keisan Kenkyu (Journal of Cost Accounting Research), 31*(1), 52–62.

Kawai, H. & Matsuda, C. (2015). Panasonic no honsha kaikaku (Reform of the headquarters). *Kigyo Kaikei, 68*(12), 1617–1630.

Kigyo Kenkyukai. (1955). *Keiei yosan tosei no jitsurei (Cases on budgetary control in Japanese companies)*. Tokyo: Diamond Sha.

Koike, K. (2002). Dentou aru dai maker no Nichiei Hikaku (Comparison of Japan and the U.K. in the traditional large manufacturers). In K. Koike & T. Inoki (Eds.), *White-collar no jinzai keisei (White-collar human resource development)* (pp. 85–108). Tokyo: Toyokeizai Shinposha.

Kurosawa, K. (1980). *Nakanishi Torao keiei keizai ronbun senshu (Collections of Torao Nakanishi's papers on business and economics)*. Tokyo: Chikura Shobo.

Kurosawa, K., Noda, N., Furukawa, E., Matsumoto, M., Nakayama, T., & Iwata, I. (1953). Naibutousei no jisshi ni kansuru tetsuduki youryo no mondaiten (Problems about Guidance for Internal Control). *Sangyo Keiri, 13*(3), 72–85.

McMann, P. J. & Nanni, A. J. (1995). Means versus ends: A review of the literature on Japanese management accounting. *Management Accounting Research, 6*, 313–346.

Ministry of International Trade and Industry (MITI). (1951). *On internal control in companies*. Tokyo: Tsusho Sangyo Chosakai.

Mitsubishi Electric. (1927). *Denki kaikei soshiki kenkyu iinkai chosa houkoku (Research committee on Electric's accounting and organization: Study Report)*.

Mitsubishi Electric. (1951). *Kengyo kaiko (Retrospective review of the company foundation)*. Tokyo: Mitsubishi Denki.

Morikawa, H. (1988). Nihon gijutsusha no "genba shugi" ni tsuite (Hands-on approach of Japanese engineers). *Yokohama Keiei Kenkyu, 8*(4), 295–306.

Nishizawa, O. (1995). *Nihon kigyo no kanri kaikei* (*Management accounting in Japanese companies*). Tokyo: Chuo Keizai Sha.

Noda, N. (1927). Mitsubishi Electric Kobe Factory ni okeru jikan kenkyu to chinritsu settei (Time study and setting wage rate in Kobe Factory of Mitsubishi Electric). In Mitsubishi Goshi Gaisha Shiryo Ka (ed.), *Shiryo Shuho* (*Report Collection*).

Noda, N. (1928). *Yosan seido an* (*Budgetary system proposal*).

Okano, H. & Suzuki, T. (2007). A history of Japanese management accounting. In C. S. Chapman, A. G. Hopwood, & M. D. Shields (Eds.), *Handbook of Management Accounting Research* (pp. 1119–1137). Amsterdam: Elsevier.

Oota, T. (1968). *Kindai kaikei sokumen shi: Kaikeigaku no 60 nen* (*Modern accounting history: 60 years of accounting*). Tokyo: Chuo Keizai Sha.

Oota, T., Furukawa, E., Noda, N., Iwata, I., & Matsumoto, M. (1951). Kigyo niokeru naibu tosei no taikou ni tsuite: Tokuni kansa kijun niokeru naibutousei tono chigai (On internal control in companies: The difference with the internal control in Auditing Standards). *Sangyo Keiri, 11*(12), 71–76.

Sakurai, M. (1997). Nihon kigyo no keiri zaimu soshiki no tokucho (Features of accounting and finance organizations in Japanese companies). In M. Sakurai (Ed.), *Wagakuni no keiri-zaimu soshiki* (*Accounting organizations in Japan*) (pp. 40–69). Tokyo: Zeimukeiri Kyokai.

Sakurai, M. (2015). *Kanri kaikei* (*Management accounting*). Tokyo: Dobunkan Shuppan.

Sawabe, N. (2016). Clinical accounting research practices in Japanese SMEs. Presentation materials presented at the 10th Conference on New Directions in Management Accounting 2016 in Brussels, Belgium.

Simon, H. A., Kozmetsky, G., Guetzkow, H., & Tyndall, G. (1954). *Centralization vs. decentralization in organizing the controller's department*. New York: The Controllership Foundation.

Toyo Keizai (1999). Keiei kikaku-bu no kenkyu (Research on corporate planning departments). *Toyo Keizai Tokei Geppo, 59*(9), 6–11, *59*(10), 22–29.

Toyoshima, Y. (2005). Kobe Mitsubishi Zosenjo no genka keisan seido no kakuritsu ni kansuru shiteki kousatsu (History of the establishment of cost accounting system at Kobe Mitsubishi Shipyard). *Shogaku Ronsou, 73*(4), 3–22.

Tsumagari, N. & Matsumoto, J. (1972). *Wagakuni no kigyo yosan* (*Budgeting in Japanese companies*). Tokyo: Japan Productivity Center.

Yoshikawa, O., Takahashi, M., & Manabe, S. (2016). Keiei senryaku sakutei niokeru keiei kikaku bumon no yakuwari: nihon kigyo no jittai chosa (The roles of the corporate planning department in strategy formulation: Survey of Japanese companies). *Kigyo Kaikei, 68*(1), 84–90.

10 Management accountants in Russia

Theoretical and practical aspects

Sergey G. Falko[1]

Introduction

Although the term 'cost accounting' has been used previously in Russia, the term 'management accounting' only appeared in the process of transitioning from a centrally controlled to a market economy. Due to its short history, no generally accepted definition of management accounting has yet been established in the Russian context; rather, various definitions can be found from different perspectives, for example, a classical Russian textbook states the following:

> Management Accounting is a subsystem that provides management units with the information necessary for planning, directing and controlling the activities of the organization. This process includes identification, measurement, collection, analysis, preparation, interpretation, transmission and reception of information necessary for the management of the organization to carry out its functions.

> (Sheremet, 2002: 17)

Although execution of accounting procedures is essential for companies regulated by the Ministry of Finance in Russia, which dictates the classification of costs, accounting rules and the cost of production, and so on (Federal Law of Accounting, 2011), management accounting per se is still usually performed on a voluntary basis, at the request of management. It is not regulated by the state, although an attempt was made to do so by the Ministry of Economic Development and Trade in the early 2000s, and some efforts to regulate management accounting are made by professional association managers, chief financial officers, controllers, and others.

As a result of the mandatory status of accounting, management accounting in Russia is primarily based on financial accounting data. It is typically organized according to the accounting structure (for example, the management accounting department in SMEs) and is responsible for providing information, such as concerning the cost or profitability of products to assist decision-making. The focus on supporting corporate decision-making is also reflected in more recent definitions of management accounting like, for example, that developed by the well-known

Russian management accounting expert Svetlana Nikolaeva: "Management accounting is a system for collecting, processing and managing organizational information to make reasonable management decisions" (Nikolaeva & Shebek, 2004: 16). This definition also reveals that management accounting is developing into a more independent discipline, separate from regular accounting, and organized as an independent unit, which, as a rule, follows the structure of the Directorate for Economy. The main focus of this definition is on making reasonable management decisions. For this reason, management accounting should utilize tools that enable a transparent calculation of costs that can be objectively interpreted.

However, management accountants have neither accepted nor applied direct costing as a primary method to calculate the "partial cost price", that is, excluding fixed indirect costs (Nikolaeva & Shebek, 2004: 183–189). The first reason for this phenomenon in Russia is the fact that it is much more important for accountants to prepare accurate reports concerning taxes, and to receive no comments from the regulator for the reporting period. Therefore, the chief accountant is more concerned with compliance with regulation than with objective measurement of the costs of production and profitability. While the accountant is a bookkeeping specialist working on an accounting system in accordance with the current legislation in Russia, the management accountant is a specialist that performs the functions of management accounting, which are not regulated by government directives. According to Russian law, the chief accountant, in contrast to management accountants, must necessarily sit within the organizational structure of the enterprise (Sheremet, 2002; Nikolaeva & Shebek, 2004).

The second reason is that the monopolies of most Russian companies are operating within the domestic market. This does not only refer to natural monopolies, which in principle do not require direct costing, target-costing, ABC-costing, and so on; in the context of restrictions on the supply of many types of industrial and consumer goods to Russia, some Russian companies have acquired an 'artificial monopoly'. Consequently, they form the basis of prices for the full calculation with the addition of the maximum possible rate of return, which sometimes reaches 200–300 per cent (Nikolaeva & Shebek, 2004: 186). In such situations, managers make decisions based on intuition, emotions, immediate benefits, or the interests of stakeholders. Therefore, modern methods and tools of management accounting, actively used in advanced economies and markets, have slowly diffused across Russian enterprises (Falko, 2014; Nikolaeva, 2004).

In the next section, the history of the development of the theory and practice of management accounting in Russia throughout the period from the early twentieth century to the present time will be discussed, in addition to prospects for its future development and integration with controlling.

Brief history of management accounting and management accountants in Russia before the revolution of 1917

The term 'management accounting' first appeared in accounting theory and practice in Russia in the early 1990s. However, this does not mean that management accounting was absent in earlier Russian enterprises. In the late nineteenth and early twentieth centuries industry was actively developing in Russia, and attracting foreign investment. In order to manage the firms operating in actively developing industries, foreign engineers, who had specific knowledge about engineering and production management, became involved. A content analysis of books and articles published before 1917 reveals that a lot of the knowledge at that time in the field of management accounting had been borrowed from German specialists (Charnovsky, 1911). For example, the idea and method of ABC-costing, proposed by German engineer Albert Fink, were already known in Russia at that time. Additionally, cost classifications by type of resources used (the division of costs into 'fixed' and 'variable') was already known and being applied in practice. This meant that pre-revolutionary Russia already knew about and was using methods such as direct-costing and break-even analysis.

Furthermore, Taylor's (1911) ideas were highly thought of in pre-revolutionary Russia, leading enterprises to employ a standard method of accounting, better known internationally as the 'standard-costing' method for calculating costs. Thus, the basic ideas and tools of management accounting in this period were not only known in Russia, but also applied in practice. However, due to the dominance of cost accounting issues in corporate practice at that time, the term 'cost accounting' was used instead of the term 'management accounting'.

The period before 1917 was characterized by the use of simple approaches to cost accounting and planning systems. However, by the end of the nineteenth century, the grouping of fixed and variable costs was already being practiced in Russian accounting.

Figure 10.1 shows the typical organizational structure of Russian industrial enterprises before the 1917 revolution, with the positioning of the accounting, cash desk, finance, and costing departments (Charnovsky, 1911). As can be seen from the descriptions of the functions, classical accountants worked in the accounting department. They were not engaged in management accounting issues (i.e. costing); these tasks were assigned to management accountants (i.e. the costing department).

Beginning of the transition to a market economy after 1917

A detailed history of the development of management accounting in Russia is given in many studies (e.g. Annaraud, 2007; Sokolov & Bikmukhametova, 2015; Sokolov Y., 1996).

Table 10.1 shows the key steps in the development of the Soviet Russian accounting system (Annaraud, 2007).

To understand the problems faced by Russian accountants in the Soviet period (1918–1991), it is necessary to first understand the difference between a market and a centrally regulated planned economy. The main differences are shown in Table 10.2. As can be seen from Table 10.2, in the centrally planned and regulated economy of Russia there was no objective need for management

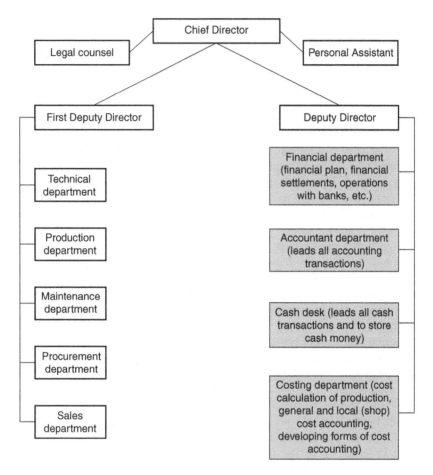

Figure 10.1 Positioning of the accounting, cash desk, finance, and costing departments in the organizational structure of Russian industrial enterprises pre-1917.

accountants; all 'traditional' accounting functions were performed by accountants. The main functions of accounting departments were accounting and reporting, as well as monitoring execution plans and collective ownership maintenance. Profit and financial performance were not in the foreground of their role. Accountants could overrule director authorization if they believed that their actions threatened collective ownership. The accountant in Russia at this time can thus be described as a 'watchman' of collective ownership. In the Soviet era, due to the relevance of accountants' work to collective ownership, any nominee for the position of chief accountant at a large enterprise had to be agreed by the Ministry of Finance. Accountants received certification after completing training courses at the Ministry of Finance, or at accredited financial and economic universities in the USSR.

Table 10.1 Key steps in the development of the Soviet Russian accounting system

Years	Key steps
1917–1918	Adaptation of accounting principles to a new economic era
1918–1929	Development and implementation of accounting principles that were applicable to a country with a socialist system and for private business (NEP)[a]
1929–1953	Rise of socialism, deformation of accounting principles
1950s	Standardization of accounting documentation
1960s	Development of a new accounting theory
1950–1980s	Application of technology to accounting
1992–1995	Development of a completely new chart of accounts applicable to a country utilizing market economy principles (cost accounting, taking into account market relations)
1996 onward	Development of integrated production cost accounting and a pro-western accounting system (Sokolov, 2015)
1998–2001	Issuance of more than 15 significant accounting regulations

Note
a New Economic Policy (NEP) along with state-owned enterprises were allowed to open small and medium private businesses.

When the country began to move from administrative to market principles of price regulation in 1991, companies began to gain economic independence and could generate information on costs and revenues from different angles for administrative purposes. As a consequence, Russian enterprises realized that management accounting tools were useful for managing organizations. As the Soviet school accountants did not meet the new requirements of management accounting knowledge, in the early 1990s top Russian managers began to recognize a need to attract foreign management accountants.

Factors affecting the advancement of management accounting and the preparation of management accountants in Russia

Due to significant economic developments in Russia, it became necessary to develop management accounting as corporate practice, and to train management accountants in accordance with new requirements. At the same time, research began to investigate the factors influencing management accounting practices in Russia. For example, Lebedev (2014) studied seven factors affecting the promotion of management accounting in Russia; the study was based on the work of Bhimani (1996) and Shields (1998), and included the following descriptions of selected factors:

Academics whose writings influence academic debate as well as corporate practice, such as whether full or variable costing should be used, relevant costs for decisions, and who, in some countries, 'champion' particular practices.

Table 10.2 Main differences between market and centrally regulated planned economies

Characteristics/ mechanisms	Market economy	Centrally regulated planned economy
Coordination	Economic actors with separate plans	Centralized economic plan
Coordinating body	Markets	State
Ownership of the means of production	Private property of economic entities	Collective ownership
Prices	Formed by the markets	Set by the state
Allocation of profits	Economic principle	Covering needs/Collective
Consumer choice	Free consumer choice	Centrally regulated consumption
Role of the state	"Night watchman state" (according to Adam Smith)	Planning, distribution, coordination

Source: adapted from Ellman (2014).

Educating students and employees from a certain management accounting perspective, and the influence that textbooks and teaching cases have on the development and diffusion of management accounting practices.

Governmental intervention and regulation of cost-based pricing and profits to ensure a desired type and level of competition, particularly when there were supply-demand imbalances in a national economy and, during WWI and WWII, to adequately allocate resources and reduce war profiteering.

Professional associations that advocate particular management accounting practices.

Consultants who advocate particular management accounting practices and/ or help firms to design and implement practices.

Technology, in particular the computerization of accounting systems, which enables more information to be collected, processed, and communicated, cheaply and quickly.

The transfer of management accounting ideas and practices across national boundaries by academics, education, consultants, and multi-national businesses (Shields, 1998).

To analyse the impact of these factors on the rise of management accounting, Lebedev (2014) used the following sources: consultants and educators in the field of management accounting; content analysis of professional magazines; and the websites of consulting companies. Lebedev also used a scale to assess the

Table 10.3 Degree of influence of different factors on the rise of management accounting in Russia

Factor (1)	Initial influence (2)	Current influence (3)
Academics	Insignificant	Moderate
Education	Moderate	Moderate
Government intervention and regulation	Insignificant	Insignificant
Professional associations	Insignificant	Insignificant
Consultants	Significant	Significant
Technology	Moderate	Moderate
Transfer of practices across national boundaries by academics, education, consultants, and multi-national businesses	Insignificant	Moderate

degree of influence, which was composed of three levels: insignificant, moderate, and significant. The results of the study are summarized in Table 10.3, where the factors are listed in column 1, the extent to which each factor initially shaped the concept of management accounting is described in column 2, and the estimated current influence of each factor in column 3.

As Table 10.3 shows, the most important factors influencing the rise of management accounting were consultants, technology, and education. However, without training highly qualified management accountants it would have been almost impossible to promote management accounting. Surprisingly, the study revealed that such educational management accounting programmes did not exist at either a Bachelor's or Master's level in the leading financial and economic universities in Russia; and business schools and IT and consulting companies offer only 'block seminars' (72 hours) and medium-term (less than 600 hours) retraining programmes in the field of management accounting. Although 'professional associations' were judged to have been insignificant in the promotion of management accounting, associations are very active in attempts to improve the qualifications of management accountants, for example, the association of financial directors (http://клуб-финансовых-директоров.рф), or the association of professional accountants (www.npabs.ru). However, it is still not necessary to gain certification to become a management accountant or controller in Russia. Although many Russian companies have the official position of 'Economist for management accounting', which is located in the department of the director of economics, and not in the accounting department, the government list of specialist positions does not include the position of management accountant.

Nevertheless, in order to secure employment in their field, while there is no mandatory certification, management accountants must meet certain professional standards. These standards were developed by the Ministry of Labour in cooperation with universities, consulting firms, and professional associations, and include professional, personal, and social competence requirements, such as bookkeeping skills, analytical ability, and communication skills. Accordingly, applicants will have an advantage if they can provide evidence of these skills, for example, a certificate from a respectable business school, university, or association, confirming their advanced training in management accounting.

Unfortunately, chartered management accountants (CMA) certificates and those of other foreign associations in the field of management accounting are neither well-known nor established in Russia. However, in 2015 the Ministry of Labour of the Russian Federation (RF) adopted a professional standard in the field of controlling for machine-building enterprises, which was designed by the Russian Association of Controllers (www.controlling.ru). In this standard, many competencies are incorporated, which, according to the professional community, are consistent with many competencies of management accountants. Moreover, in 2016, the Ministry of Labour of the RF announced a competition for the drafting of professional standards for the field of management accounting.

Management accounting versus controlling, and management accountant versus controller

Since the economic transition began in Russia, many directors and managers of newly created or privatized enterprises of the former USSR began studying Western management theory and practice. Within the framework of the TACIS[2] programme, funded by the European community, a large number of professionals have been trained in Russia and abroad. Overall, approximately €103 million has been allocated to Russia, including €54 million for management education, in order to fund the improvement of management institutions, the restructuring of enterprises and regional economies, and the development of individual managers' capabilities (http://europa.eu/rapid/press-release_MEMO-92-54_en.htm).

Education of managers, professionals, and management accounting professors took place mainly in the UK, Germany, France, and the USA; as such, there were challenges with regard to the terms used in the field of management accounting in Russia. Some experts used the term 'management accounting' (in the USA and England), and others used the term 'controlling' (in Germany). Less frequently used terms include 'contrôle de gestion' (in France) and 'il controllo di gestione' (in Italy). Although these terms were relatively new to Russian enterprises, they shared a similar meaning (Falko, 2008). In the early 1990s, the hierarchy of terms dictated the following: management accounting was part of bookkeeping, and controlling was part of management accounting. Therefore, controlling was a part of the administrative account, and executed control functions. Often, experts in the field of management accounting sat within the bookkeeping department. The terms 'controller' and 'controlling' were very seldomly used in business practice, and used synonymously with the terms 'management accountant' and 'management accounting'. From a Russian perspective, controlling was a synonym for management accounting in the German language. Over the last decade, however, understanding of the role of management accounting changed, and management accounting came to be understood as a constituent of controlling. This is also reflected in the contents of classic textbooks on management accounting and controlling, where many similarities can be found between explanations of the two concepts (e.g. Drury, 2002; Falko, 2008; Nikolaeva & Shebek, 2004; Sheremet, 2002). Table 10.4 presents the main elements of management accounting and controlling, and shows that both terms cover very similar content. The main difference is that controlling is more focused on managerial decision-making.

In Russia, many companies that utilize the concept of controlling focus on cost accounting, performance measurement, and reporting to management. Currently, the advanced German-speaking concept of controlling, as discussed by a number of scholars (Horváth et al., 2015; Weber & Schäffer, 2016) is almost never used by Russian companies. In this context, a question arises as to how the understanding of controlling has evolved in Russian business, and in the minds of academics.

Initially, controlling was perceived as just a component of bookkeeping. However, this limited conception of controlling did not last long. In the early 1990s, controlling was still identified as an administrative tool, similar to profit and loss accounting in Russia. Table 10.5 presents the evolutionary stages of controlling and management accounting functions in Russia, and the spheres of responsibility of controllers and management accountants.

By the middle of the 1990s, the majority of enterprises understood the controlling function to include budgeting, operational planning, and expenses management. Since the turn of the twentieth century, the understanding of the controller as the supplier and interpreter of important information for managers and coordinators of the enterprises' operative activities has prevailed (Falko, 2008; Karminskiy et al., 2009). While the function per se developed in the direction of business partnering, the majority of controllers themselves has neither become partners of managers in Russian enterprises, nor are they involved in the process of strategic management, yet (Falko, 2014). The majority of Russian companies has implemented only registration-analytical functions of controlling (Malikova & Mitrokhin, 2005). Accounting, statistical and administrative reporting serve as the sources of all data; benchmarking is almost never used. Coordination and integration functions are realized in very few enterprises, and even where they are, only the operative level of management is affected, not the executive level (Falko, 2010).

Controller and management accountant education in Russia

Controlling is one of the disciplines studied as a management tool. It was through such study that controlling came to Russia from the West, specifically from Austria, Germany, and Switzerland. In the middle of the 1990s, the texts written by the German founders of controlling (like Hahn, Vollmuth, Mann, Horváth, Dehyle, Weber) were translated into Russian, and quickly gained

Table 10.4 Comparison of classic textbook content on management accounting and controlling

Management accounting (1)	Controlling (2)
Cost classification Allocation of overheads Cost summary schedule (costing) Activity Based Costing (ABC costing)	Cost management (cost element, ABC costing, target costing, benchmarking, working capital management, standard costs, direct costing and so on) Cost centre accounting Product costing
Cost-Volume-Profit (CPV) analysis	CPV analysis focused on decision-making
Decision models	Methods of management decision-making
Investment accounting (evaluation)	Investment analysis focused on decision-making
Budgeting	Forecasting, planning and budgeting
Standard costs	
Variance analysis	Variance analysis focused on decision-making
Performance measurement	Specific and integrated key performance indicators
Linear programming in management accounting	Economic and mathematical models, expert assessments
Strategic planning and administrative control	Integrated system of strategic and operational planning, monitoring and information support

Table 10.5 Evolutionary stages of controlling and management accounting functions, areas of responsibility, and degree of influence of controllers and management accountants

Evolutionary stages of controlling	Functions	Areas of responsibility and degree of influence		
		Management accounting/management accountant	Controlling/controller
Early 1990s	Cost accounting by type and for cost centre	Significant	Moderate
First half of 1990s	Cost and profit accounting by type, for cost centre, products and services	Significant	Moderate
Second half of 1990s	Planning, budgeting, cost management, reporting	Moderate	Significant
End of 1990s, and beginning of twenty-first century	Supplier and interpreter information for managers, coordinator and integrator of operational activities	Insignificant	Very significant
First decade of twenty-first century	Developer and supplier of methods to support top management in strategic management	Practically absent	Significant
In the near future	Business partners of managers	Absent	Moderate

Sources: Falko (2008, 2014).

popularity. It is not surprising, therefore, that the majority of Russian enterprises use the German model of controlling, rather than the Anglo-Saxon concept of management accounting (Falko, 2008; Karminskiy et al., 2009).

The first class of Russian controllers graduated in 2000 from the Department of Engineering Business and Management at Bauman Moscow State Technical University (BMSTU) (www.bmstu.ru). The reason why controllers emerged from a technical university is threefold. First, the Russian Association of Controllers (RAC) was established at BMSTU in 1999, which provided help with curriculum development and teacher training. Second, controlling is much closer to the mental modelling practiced by engineers, as many controllers in Russia and Western Europe had an engineering background. Third, after the Russian default in 1998, Russian industrial enterprises have shown interest in modern management concepts, in particular in management accounting and controlling. For many years, BMSTU had close ties with industrial companies and, therefore, quickly reacted to this new demand.

Today, Bachelor's and Master's of controlling are granted by many Russian universities, including for example, in Moscow, St. Petersburg, Kazan, Krasnodar, Novosibirsk, Samara, Ufa, and Yekaterinburg. The relevant departments of these universities are called 'Management Accounting and Finance', 'Planning and Controlling', 'Financial Accounting and Controlling', 'Accounting, Analysis and Audit', or 'Economics and Management'. Russian university departments are usually much larger than their European equivalent and teach a large spectrum of disciplines, which explains the heterogeneity of their names. In general, Russian universities offer two controlling areas as specializations:

1   controlling and management accounting (Bachelor's);
2   controlling (Master's).

The Bachelor's specialization covers operational controlling training, the functions and tasks of which coincide with the functional scope of management accounting. The Master's specialization covers strategic controlling training. Table 10.6 compares these two basic educational specializations. It shows that the Bachelor's controlling training is very similar to management accounting programmes.

The Master's programme is more focused on developing competences in information analytics and methodology to support managers and functional units. However, it is radically different from the management accounting educational programme (see Table 10.7).

Preparation of highly qualified management accountants in Russia is currently carried out on the basis of Masters' programmes. Table 10.7 shows some examples of academic disciplines that train students in management accounting and controlling (see, for example, www.fa.ru/priemka/magistr/list/Pages/2016/uuik.aspx).

Table 10.6 Comparison of basic disciplines in controlling training programmes[a]

Names of the basic disciplines Bachelor's	Names of the basic disciplines Master's
(1)	*(2)*
Mathematics	Decision-making theory
Statistics	Econometric theory
Methods of management decision-making	Project management
Information technologies in management	Controlling and quality management
Fundamentals of management	Logistics controlling
Marketing	Marketing controlling
Accounting and analysis	Purchase controlling
Financial management	Finance controlling
Cost management	R&D and innovation controlling
Human resource management	Human resource controlling
Economic analysis of financial activity	Cost and result management controlling
Management accounting	Production controlling
Finance	Project controlling
Analysis of accounting reports	Management decision-making
Tax and taxation	Risk controlling
Business planning	Controlling of projects and project portfolio
Fundamental controlling	Strategic controlling
Investment analysis	Investment controlling
Budgeting	Strategic management
Audit	Eco-controlling

Note

a Comparison of the basic disciplines based on the author's of the study material, conducted at leading universities in Moscow at the request of university administration.

Table 10.7 Examples of academic disciplines

Main disciplines	Elective courses
• Modern concepts of management accounting and controlling	• Management accounting in trade
• Financial Accounting (Advanced Level)	• Management accounting in the service industry
• Administrative aspects of IFRS	• Management accounting in industries
• Methods and means of information protection in electronic document management systems	• Management accounting in insurance companies
• Strategic management accounting and analysis	• Management accounting in the public sector (public administration sector)
• Controlling tax calculations	
• Budgeting in management accounting systems	
• Integrated reporting: principles of drawing	

Controlling practice in Russia

Initially, commercial banks had the greatest interest in controlling when they belonged to the emerging sectors of the Russian market economy. In leading private banks, the special divisions that performed specific controlling tasks were often labeled the 'planning and economy department', 'finance and analytics', or something similar. As the examples show, the new and vague term 'controlling' was not used in everyday language (Karminskiy et al., 2009; Falko, 2010). After the default on payments in 1998, controlling lost its leading position in banks, and even reached a state of stagnation, in both theoretical and practical terms (Falko, 2010).

However, Russian industrial enterprises and businesses in the sphere of services, construction, some educational institutions and trading organizations, began to take an interest in controlling at the beginning of the twenty-first century. Typically, controlling arose in divisions such as economics, financial analysis and reporting, information and analytics departments, and was hierarchically overseen by the departments of economy and finance, or sometimes accounting departments. Currently, there are also cases of controlling services emerging in the IT department structure.

In Table 10.7, examples of the positioning and structure of controlling departments in Russian companies of various branches and sizes are shown. It also shows (see column four) that the function of management accounting is present in many different industries. Interestingly, in many cases, the introduction of controlling began with the implementation of management accounting. Therefore, management accountants operate in many Russian controlling departments.

In large enterprises, controlling departments usually report directly to the CEO, or to the Deputy General Director for Economics and Finance (CFO). In rare cases, controlling is subordinate to the Chief Accountant. In the fourth column of Table 10.8 it can be seen that, in SMEs, controlling departments have functions that are very close to management accounting. In a number of large businesses, such as nuclear, or Russian companies with foreign partners, the controlling function is clearly separated from the management accounting function. In small Russian retail and service enterprises, management accounting and controlling are absent, as all management problems are solved by the Director of the enterprise.

Prospects for the development of management accounting in Russia

In 2005, Malikova and Mitrokhin (2005) conducted a survey investigating the importance of different management accounting and controlling tasks in Russia. The results of the questionnaire are shown in Table 10.9 below.

As can be seen in Table 10.9, one of the most important management functions is information and analytical support. The cost-benefit accounting function is recognized by managers as the least significant function. Recent studies on

Table 10.8 Examples of positioning and structure of controlling departments within companies

Company name	Position in company	Subordination	Structure of controlling department (division)	Sources
Enterprise for manufacturing of optics and mechanics (St. Petersburg)	Head Economist	General Director (CEO)	Planning; Budgeting (*Cost accounting Division submits CFO*)	Tichonenkova and Filinov (2006); Falko (2008)
Nuclear industry enterprises (Glazov, Central Russia)	Deputy CEO of Controlling	General Director (CEO)	System analysis; IT; Document management	Dedov (2008)
Insurance company (Moscow)	Director of Controlling Department	Deputy CEO – Financial Controller	Analysis of business units; Reporting; Forecasting; Development of management accounting; Supporting M&A decisions	Falko (2008)
Electric power industry company (Krasnodar, South Russia)	Head of Controlling Department	Deputy CEO – Director for Economics and Finance	Cost accounting; Internal reporting; Development of management accounting	Asadulin (2009)
Middle commercial bank (Volgograd, South Russia)	Head of Planning and Analysis Division	Chief Accountant	Income-expenditure analysis; Planning; Reporting (directly to CEO)	Gunkina (2005)
Mercantile business "Retail trade sporting equipment" (Moscow)	Head of Controlling Department	CFO	Reporting; Coordination IT and Business – Unity; Management accounting methodology; Special analysis	Chaplygin (2012)
Production of lathes (Moscow)	Head of Controlling Department	Deputy CEO	Management accounting; Decision-making support by planning; Control and Reporting	Vetrov and Ogarev (2006)
University (Vladivostok, Far East Russia)	Head of Economic Analysis and Strategic Planning Department	First Vice-Rector	Economic analysis; Forecasting; Management accounting; Strategic planning; Reporting	Malzeva and Nijazova (2002)

Table 10.9 Importance of managerial functions

Management accounting and controlling functions	Importance* (%)
Information and analytical function	35–45
Control function	20–25
Planning function	15–25
Coordination function	10–20
Accounting function	10–15

Note
* Shows rounded interval estimate of the importance of the function.

this topic conducted as part of the MBA programme[3] have revealed a 55 percent increase in the importance of information-analytical functions. In addition to analytical information and advice on the subject, managers also expect to be informed of what conclusions can be drawn, and what decisions can be taken. In addition, the importance of the traditional functions of management accounting, such as cost accounting, accounting, control and analysis of deviations has decreased significantly. From this, it can be concluded that the traditional functions and tasks of management accounting do not currently satisfy the Russian managers, and the role of the controller as a 'provider of numbers' is no longer sufficient. Managers need more than numbers; they also need an explanation of the situation, and proposals for its improvement.

In order to meet these expectations and to develop the role of the controller into a value-adding profession, efforts to implement 'advanced' management accounting techniques have intensified (Falko, 2014; Sokolov & Bikmukhametova, 2015). As these 'advanced' management accounting techniques were imported from American and German sources, the term 'controlling' also began to diffuse throughout Russia (Malikova & Mitrokhin, 2005).

Currently, Russian companies have both management accounting and controlling departments, where the controlling department is responsible for the identification of appropriate conditions, prevailing methods and accounting tools, calculation, planning, budgeting, and so on, and the management accounting department implements all of these functions in practice. Thus, controlling is responsible for the method and maintenance of management processes and tools, and management accounting for the correct use of these methods and tools in practice. Although the controlling and management accounting departments should be headed by different superiors, from a theoretical perspective, in reality, in the majority of Russian companies, controlling and management accounting departments are under the same directorate, and subordinate to the Deputy General Director for Economics and Finance. This positioning of controlling contributes to both organizational and methodical operational risks, as well as the risk of intentional misrepresentation of information. Thus, the prospects for the development of management accounting in Russia lie in its integration with controlling to ensure rapid and effective reporting to managers, and consultation on financial and economic problems.

Conclusion

In Russia, the term 'management accounting' began to be used in both theory and practice in the early 1990s. However, cost accounting, understood as the grouping of fixed and variable costs, was already being applied in Russia at the end of the nineteenth century (Charnovsky, 1911; Sheremet, 2002; Nikolaeva, 2004; Sokolov & Bikmukhametova, 2015). By 1991, the country had moved from administrative to market principles of price regulation. At this stage, companies gained economic independence and could generate data to explain costs and revenues from different angles, for administrative purposes.

Accounting in Russia is essential for companies regulated by the Ministry of Finance, which determines the classification of costs, rules of accounting, and the cost of production. Management accounting is carried out on a voluntary basis, that is, at the request of management, and is not regulated by the state. However, Russian enterprises have only gradually realized the importance of management accounting and controlling tools. Many companies that do utilize the concept of controlling focus on cost accounting, performance measurement and reporting to management. Against the background of this chapter, it can be concluded that management accounting and controlling in Russian companies are more or less synonymous, but management accounting is a constituent of controlling from a structural perspective. However, the Bachelors controlling training programme is very similar to educational programmes for management accounting, whereas the basic disciplines of the Masters programme are more focused on the development of competences in the field of information-analytical and methodological support to managers and functional units. Future prospects for the development of management accounting in Russia involve integration with controlling, as well as operative consulting and providing managers with information relating to financial and economic problems faced by the business.

Notes

1 Head of the department of economics and production organization (BMSTU) and executive director of the Russian Association of Controllers (RAC).
2 TACIS – Technical Assistance for the Commonwealth of Independent States.
3 See, for example, www.fa.ru/business_education/Pages/mba_programs.aspx; https://busedu.hse.ru/?tab=business&format=181579431; www.rea.ru/ru/org/faculties/bizschool markent/Pages/mba1.aspx.

References

Annaraud, K. (2007) Accounting in Russia: Challenges for the hospitality stakeholders. *Journal of Hospitality Financial Management, 15*(2), pp. 2–19.

Asadulin, R. (2009) *Development of integrated indicators system efficiency management the regional power grid company*. Dissertation, Cand. Ekon. Sciences: BMSTU, Moscow. Russian.

Bhimani, A. (1996) *Management accounting: European perspectives*. Oxford: Oxford University Press.

Chaplygin, Y. (2012) Business intelligence as a controlling tool in large companies. *Management and Business Administration, 1*, 188–193. Russian.

Charnovsky, N. (1911) *Organization of industrial metal processing*. Moscow: ITU. Russian.

Dedov, O. (2008) *Methodology and practice of controlling large industrial enterprises*. Moscow: PH Alpina Business Books. Russian.

Drury, C. (2002) *Management and cost accounting* (5th edition). Moscow: UNITY. Russian.

Ellman, M. (2014) *Socialist planning*. Cambridge: Cambridge University Press.

Falko, S. (2008) *Controlling for leaders and specialists*. Moscow: PH Finance and Statistics. Russian.

Falko, S. (2010) Adverse conditions: Controlling in Russia. *Finance: The Executive Magazine for Emerging Europe*, Autumn, 58–59. Russian.

Falko, S. (2014) Transformation of tools organization and enterprise management in modern conditions. *Innovation in Management, 1*, 16–21. Russian.

Federal Law of Accounting (6 December 2011), N 402-FZ. Available from: http://base.garant.ru/70103036/#ixzz4IKVFMKWb, accessed 3 November 2016. Russian.

Gunkina, T. (2005) Practice of controlling in the "Russian South Bank". *Controlling, 13*, 16–23. Russian.

Horváth, P., Gleich, R., & Seiter, M. (2015) *Controlling* (13th edition). Munich: Vahlen.

Karminskiy, A., Falko, S., Zewaga, A., & Ivanova, N. (2009) *Controlling* (2nd edition). Moscow: PH Finance and Statistics. Russian.

Lebedev, P. (2014) Evolution of the management accounting concept in Russia: In a search of identity. 19th International Scientific Conference; Economics and Management, ICEM, 23–25 April 2014, Riga, Latvia, pp. 580–584.

Malikova, S. & Mitrokhin, I. (2005) Controlling and management accounting in Russia (study results). *Controlling, 13*, 24–32. Russian.

Malzeva, G. & Nijazova, M. (2002) From the automation of accounting to controlling: Development of controlling in VSUES experience. *Controlling, 4*, 44–49. Russian.

Nikolaeva, O. & Scishkova, T. (1997) *Management accounting*. Moscow: URSS. Russian.

Nikolaeva, S. & Shebek, S. (2004) *Management accounting*. Moscow: CBA. Russian.

Sheremet, A. D. (ed.) (2002) *Management accounting*. Moscow: FBK-PRESS. Russian.

Shields, M. D. (1998) Management accounting practices in Europe: A perspective from the States. *Management Accounting Research, 9*, 501–513.

Sokolov, A. & Bikmukhametova, C. (2015) Cost accounting in Russia: Historical aspects. *Asian Social Science, 11*(11), 385.

Sokolov, Y. (1996) *Accounting: From the beginnings to the present day*. Moscow: Audit. Russian.

Taylor, Frederick Winslow. (1911). *Shop management*. McGraw-Hill.

Tichonenkova, E. & Filinov, A. (2006) Construction of an integrated information space as the basis for the development of the concept of controlling in OAO "LOMO". *Controlling, 19*, 36–41. Russian.

Vetrov, S. & Ogarev, H. (2006) The practice of controlling at the lathes factory "Krasny Proletariy". *Controlling, 18*, 30–38. Russian.

Weber, J. & Schäffer, U. (2016) *Introduction to Controlling* (15th edition). Stuttgart: Schaffer-Poeschel.

11 An assessment of the current state of the management accounting profession in South Africa

Philippus L. Wessels and Leon P. Steenkamp

Introduction

In South Africa as a previous British colony, the evolution of the accounting profession has been closely influenced by the accounting professions in the United Kingdom (UK). The spread of accounting knowledge from Britain to many parts of the globe, through the expansion of British business, showed how accounting knowledge followed business (Verhoef, 2014, p. 194). British imperialism was not only responsible for changing borders around the world; it also introduced the British model of accounting associations in British colonies, including South Africa (Chua & Poullaos, 2002; Cooper & Robson, 2006). Currently, the management accounting profession in South Africa is not regulated by any Act (compared to the public accounting profession that is regulated by the Auditing Profession Act (Republic of South Africa, 2005) and the Chartered Accountants Designation (Private) Act (Republic of South Africa, 1993)). Consequently, the management accounting profession has struggled to find a foothold in South Africa compared to other countries such as Canada and the UK. Currently the management accounting profession is mainly represented by two accounting bodies in South Africa, namely the South African Institute of Chartered Accountants (SAICA), a South African enacted and regulated professional body, and the Chartered Institute of Management Accountants (CIMA), a UK-based accounting body with a regional office in South Africa.

The purpose of this chapter is to explore the past and present state of the management accounting profession in South Africa to determine specific issues that may affect the future development of the management accounting profession. In the first part the history of the accounting professions in South Africa is discussed, as well as the current status and profile of the management accounting profession, including educational pathways. The chapter concludes with a discussion of some of the main issues that may affect the future development of the management accounting profession in South Africa.

History of accounting professions in South Africa

Following the discovery of diamonds and gold in South Africa in the last quarter of the nineteenth century, international interest in the South African economy exploded, attracting a variety of professionals, including accountants from the UK, to participate in the new business opportunities (Verhoef, 2013, p. 165). In 1894, members of the British Society of Accountants and Auditors and the Institute of Chartered Accountants in England and Wales established the first organised body of accountants of South Africa, the Institute of Accountants and Auditors in the South African Republic, with 65 members (Verhoef, 2014). In 1904, the Colony's Legislative Council passed an ordinance incorporating the Transvaal Society of Accountants. It was the first law to be passed in any British dominion regulating the accounting profession and mandated the society to keep a register of all public accountants in the province, thus effectively monopolising the accounting profession in the Transvaal (Verhoef, 2013, p. 169).

In 1921, the various provincial bodies in South Africa established the South African Accountants Societies' General Examining Board which was tasked with providing uniform conditions for admission, examinations and regulations. Their work culminated in government passing an act in 1927 which allowed for public accountants in practice in South Africa to use the designation 'Chartered Accountant (SA)' or 'CA(SA)'. In 1945, the first national coordinating body, the Joint Council of the Societies of Chartered Accountants (SA), was formally approved. However, some accountancy organisations, including the Institute of Cost and Works Accountants and the Society of Incorporated Cost Accountants, were excluded from the 'mainstream' societies claiming legitimate standing (Verhoef, 2013, pp. 176–177). Their claims for legitimate standing were based on having long-term public experience, recognition in other countries, and the good character of their members. Although their submissions were considered, reasons for their continued exclusion were quoted as the 'Government was not throwing the doors wide open to all and sundry nor succumbing to the pressure of less reputable societies' and that the proposed act 'seemed more designed for the purpose of protecting public interest' (ibid., p. 177) than regulating industry accountants.

Until the 1950s, accounting education was provided mainly by technical colleges and correspondence schools. In 1950, the public accounting profession entered into an agreement with universities in terms of which specified university examinations would be accepted in lieu of intermediate requirements, and the public accounting society administered a final, uniform qualifying examination (Venter & De Villiers, 2013, p. 1256). In 1951, the Public Accountants and Auditors Act allowed for the establishment of a register of public accountants and auditors who were entitled to engage in public practice and established the right of all who passed the qualifying examination to be admitted and to have the right to use the designation CA(SA). In January 1981, the South African Institute of Chartered Accountants (SAICA) was established (SAICA, 2016a). Currently, the CA(SA) designation is highly sought after in the business community, with 19 per cent of all business job advertisements specifying the CA(SA) designation as a prerequisite for potential appointment (Venter & De Villiers, 2013, p. 1259).

Although the development of management accounting as a profession was heavily influenced by academic institutions and businesses in Europe and the

USA, South Africa indirectly contributed to the importance and acceptance of management accounting principles after the South African War (1899–1902) exposed significant defects in the administration of the British army which precipitated several parliamentary inquiries. The South African War awakened in the British government an appreciation of the importance to military success of well-developed, frequently rehearsed, habitual systems of cost accounting in the field. Although the British army was not a pioneer in the development of cost accounting techniques, its experiences unambiguously established that the management technologies of business also had an important role to play in government administration, particularly contributing towards military success (Funnell, 2005, p. 308). This led to the adoption of a system of responsibility accounting based upon cost accounts for the entire army (ibid., p. 313).

During the early part of the twentieth century, management accountants affiliated with the Institute of Cost and Works Accountants (ICWA) that worked in South Africa organised themselves informally as associations (especially in Cape Town). The Institute formally established its first branch of ICWA in 1955 with the establishment of an office in Johannesburg, South Africa (CIMA, 2015a). Currently CIMA South Africa in Johannesburg functions as the hub for the African region.

In the next section the typical profile of management accountants in South Africa is discussed as well as the various educational pathways that exist for potential candidates to qualify as management accountants.

Profile of management accountants in South Africa

Professional bodies are often seen as the mechanism through which specific conceptions of being an accountant, and what accountants can do, are spread around the world. Professional bodies are frequently heavily involved in turf wars between occupations, and this can be fought not just in terms of rights to practice in specific domains (e.g. public accounting and management accounting) but also in terms of educational credentials and requirements (Cooper & Robson, 2006, p. 420). As mentioned in the previous section, in South Africa, two professional accounting bodies are actively involved in training and representing management accountants, namely SAICA and CIMA. CIMA defines its mission to help people and businesses succeed in the public and private sectors with their members working in industry, commerce and not-for-profit organisations and focus on developing skills for strategic advice, managing risk and making key decisions (CIMA, 2016a) while SAICA defines its mission to 'promote and lead the chartered accountancy profession so as to create sustainable value for its members and other stakeholders by delivering highly competent professionals relevant to the markets they serve' (SAICA, 2016b).

Accountants working in industry have a different sense of their responsibilities than those working in large public accounting firms, who again have different values than those who work in smaller public companies or those in the public, voluntary or community sectors (Cooper & Robson, 2006, p. 416) and should therefore focus on different core disciplines in their education. CIMA regards itself as the world's largest and leading professional body of management accountants delivering financially trained business leaders and attempts to maintain and promote public confidence in management accounting (CIMA, 2016a) whilst SAICA places considerable emphasis on management accounting and financial management training in their educational requirements as to prepare and attract students with future careers as management accountants (Shuttleworth, 2014, p. 338).

As the dominant accounting designation in South Africa, a vast percentage of members with a CA(SA) designation are employed in business organisations (i.e. outside of public practice) compared to those in public practice (see Table 11.1).

Almost 48 per cent of all CAs in South Africa do not work for public practice (accounting firms) but are employed as managers and accountants in private industry. Of the CAs employed in industry in 2014, 933 worked as management accountants (compared to 271 in 2001), 4,971 worked as financial managers (compared to 2,617 in 2001), 3,382 worked as general managers (compared to 2,255 in 2001) and 607 worked as internal auditors (compared to 357 in 2001). CAs working as management accountants increased by 244 per cent compared to an increase of around 90 per cent in in total CAs employed in industry from 2001 to 2014 (SAICA, 2003, 2014). The number of black chartered accountants has increased from 1,336 in 2001 (6.7 per cent of all members) to 8,697 in 2014 (23 per cent of all members).

In 2014, CIMA South Africa had 1,446 members and 3,864 registered students (CIMA, 2014). In 2005, CIMA had a total of 1,170 members (Wessels, 2006). The growth in CIMA membership in South Africa was a mere 24 per cent over almost 10 years. In 2014 about 60 per cent of the members and students were black (CIMA, 2015a).

In 2014, about 14,302 (91 per cent) CAs worked in private businesses in varying roles compared to 1,446 CIMA members (9 per cent), clearly confirming that the management accounting/financial management profession is still dominated by CAs in South Africa.

Table 11.1 Profile of CA(SA) in practice/business

Chartered accountants in South Africa		
	2014	*2001*
Members in business	14,302	7,508
Members in public practice	9,622	5,554
Total members	**37,834**	**19,875**
Members in South Africa	30,497	15,528
Foreign members	7,337	4,347

Sources: SAICA (2014, p. 27); SAICA (2003, p. 3).

Education and pathways joining the accounting profession in South Africa

The entry requirements to become a CA(SA) or an ACMA (Associate Chartered Management Accountant) are different as SAICA requires an accredited university degree, while CIMA directly allows students without tertiary education to join their profession as registered students.

As the CA(SA) qualification is a South African designation, all education requirements are set by SAICA. However, to become an ACMA, students have to meet the education requirements and pass the examinations set by the British Accounting body, CIMA (UK).

To become a CA(SA) in South Africa a candidate has to complete at least three years of study at one of the 15 SAICA-accredited universities, obtain a Certificate in the Theory of Accounting (CTA) as a fourth year at an accredited university (with focus areas on Accounting, Auditing, Taxation and Financial Management), enter into a training contract with a SAICA-registered training office for three years, and, during these three years, pass two qualifying examinations, namely the Initial Test of Competence (ITC) and the Assessment of Professional Competence (APC) set and administered by SAICA (SAICA, 2016c). It takes seven years to qualify as a CA: four at university and three in practice (Venter & De Villiers, 2013, p. 1254). In the past, SAICA offered two training paths: one for training in public practice (TIPP) and one for training outside public practice (TOPP), the latter focusing specifically on the needs of members in private business. This has since been abolished in favour of one uniform stream. The prescribed SAICA syllabus covers four primary disciplines: Financial Accounting (virtually all of the International Financial Reporting Standards); Auditing (all of the International Standards on Auditing); South African Taxation (income, capital gains and value added tax); and Cost Accounting and Financial and Risk Management. These syllabi require in-depth knowledge of the topics in these four disciplines as CAs(SA) are considered to be experts in Financial Accounting, Taxation and Auditing. In addition to the primary disciplines, a working knowledge of company and commercial law and accounting information systems is also required.

CIMA offers two accounting qualifications: CIMA Certificate in Business Accounting (an entry-level accounting qualification available to students with little or no accounting background) and the CIMA Professional Qualification. To become an Associate Chartered Management Accountant (ACMA) a student should either pass the CIMA Certificate in Business Accounting or be exempted due to prior postgraduate studies, pass 12 examinations set by CIMA with focus areas in Strategic Management, Risk Management and Financial Management, and submit a CIMA career profile for assessment of their personal work-based practical experience and skills development based on a minimum of three years' verified relevant work-based practical experience (CIMA, 2016b).

CIMA grants students with appropriate postgraduate studies in South Africa exemptions for some of the UK examinations. Currently, 13 universities in South

Africa are registered with CIMA and students receive some exemptions; however, students that complete their qualifications at other institutions (including colleges) may also qualify for exemptions (CIMA, 2016b). However, only five universities in South Africa offer degree programmes with Management Accounting as the main field of study (see Table 11.2).

A typical degree programme in Management Accounting is structured as a three-year undergraduate programme with extensive coverage of Financial Accounting, Management Accounting and Financial Management. Most universities also include studies on Taxation, Auditing and Law in the later years of these programmes with limited exposure in operations, marketing and strategy. A fourth-year postgraduate degree programme in Management Accounting typically includes courses on Financial Accounting, Financial Management, Business Strategy, Managerial Accounting, Risk Management as well as a research component. Although the syllabi for Management Accounting degree programmes appear similar to that of SAICA, the Financial Accounting and Taxation syllabi are typically not covered in the same depth, but with a stronger focus on topics that management accountants could expect to find in ordinary business settings.

From the relevant research (see Table 11.2), it is evident that most universities in South Africa focus on accounting designations offered by SAICA (15 universities in total compared to 5 universities offering relevant management accounting degrees registered with CIMA). Venter and De Villiers (2013, p. 1266) concluded that South African university accounting departments mainly implement and maintain rules and structures to accommodate SAICA requirements, because the accounting academic managers are themselves CAs with strong professional identities, and they derive their status and financial benefits

Table 11.2 Comparison of SAICA-accredited universities and those offering dedicated management accounting studies

University	SAICA accredited	CIMA	MA studies
Monash South Africa	Yes	Yes	
Nelson Mandela Metropolitan University	Yes	Yes	Diploma
North-West University	Yes	Yes	Degree
Rhodes University	Yes	Yes	
Stellenbosch University	Yes	Yes	Degree
University of Cape Town	Yes	Yes	
University of Fort Hare	Yes	No	
University of Free State	Yes	Yes	Degree
University of Johannesburg	Yes	Yes	Diploma
University of Kwazulu-Natal	Yes	Yes	Degree
University of Limpopo	Yes	Yes	
University of South Africa	Yes	Yes	Degree
University of Pretoria	Yes	Yes	
University of the Western Cape	Yes	No	
University of the Witwatersrand	Yes	Yes	

Source: SAICA (2016c); CIMA (2016b).

from their association with SAICA. However, they recommend that these departments should also build alliances with other professional bodies, such as CIMA, which are represented in South Africa and are trying to expand their membership and influence.

Although the accounting professions in South Africa place considerable emphasis on management accounting and financial management training, little research has been conducted in South Africa on students' awareness of the different entry routes into the management accounting profession. One option is to follow the CA route and then work as a management accountant in commerce and industry, without necessarily registering as a chartered management accountant (ACMA). As a rule in South Africa, students tend first to obtain a relevant accredited degree and/or postgraduate degree, after which they may follow various gateway routes to become management accountants (Shuttleworth, 2014, p. 339).

Tasks performed by management accountants

Before the specific opportunities and risks facing the management accounting profession in South Africa are discussed, the current role and tasks performed by management accountants in the current South African business environment will be analysed.

As many management accountants are CAs, they start their careers at audit and accounting firms. Many CIMA members also follow a similar career path. Because of this, they have a solid grounding in controls and systems, as well as compliance work.

Management accountants therefore perform many tasks in developing systems, implementing controls and overseeing the accounting and operational systems, more so than in other parts of the world. At higher levels in organisations, they are tasked with reporting on these systems.

When economies are ranked by ease of doing business, South Africa ranks seventy-third out of 189 economies (The World Bank, 2016, p. 6). This is partly due to the high administrative burden of doing business. Because of their good understanding of systems and well-developed financial literacy, management accountants in South Africa are co-opted to assist with compliance work. South African management accountants are for example involved in reporting on Broad-Based Black Economic Empowerment.

Management accountants are involved with or overseeing the operational aspects of business. They are therefore logical choices to assist with strategic decisions at the highest levels of business.

Challenges facing the management accounting profession in South Africa

A number of opportunities and risks that may impact either the education of future management accountants or for existing management accountants have been identified and are discussed below.

Management accounting education

*Current perceptions of the management accounting profession
in South Africa*

In a research study targeting prospective students in South Africa, Shuttleworth (2014) deduced that although many students (66 per cent of respondents) were aware that they could become a CA(SA), only 40 per cent of them were aware of the fact that they could become a CIMA member and even fewer (only 10 per cent) had received any career guidance on how to qualify as one. Evidently, only a small percentage of the respondents had received advice from career guidance teachers on the CIMA designation, although accounting teachers had played a more significant role in informing them about the CIMA designation. All the respondents in Shuttleworth's study (2014, p. 345) concluded that tertiary institutions need to visit schools and inform both the learners and the teachers of the different career opportunities in the accounting field. They reflected that there is currently no contact and that they would welcome lecturers or even students in the management accounting field visiting schools and explaining to learners what management accountants do and the possible career opportunities for qualified management accountants. Most of the responding students lacked information on the various entry routes into the profession as well as the prerequisites to register as a CIMA member. This could partly explain the low growth in membership experienced by CIMA South Africa.

Lack of communication skills and successful completion of studies

As the CIMA examinations are set in the UK, students are expected to be proficient in English. Naidoo and Garbharran (2013) found that an inadequate knowledge of English is one of the contributing factors to the low success rate of students graduating from Management Accounting courses. Their study show that communication skills were one of the important elements in the success of students in the CMA programme. The investigation into the problem revealed that students with good communication skills or a good Grade 12 English Language symbol had a better chance of being successful in the CMA programme. The study also provided sufficient evidence to confirm that a greater proportion of enrolled students did not have the necessary communication skills to answer qualitative-type questions that regularly appear in the CIMA examinations.

Access to higher education

Even though the post-apartheid state of 1994 has established mechanisms to enhance access to and participation in higher education by especially (previously) marginalised communities, achieving equitable access and participation largely remains a mirage (Wangenge-Ouma, 2012). In the recent past, the case for increasing the level of higher education funding in South Africa has been made by student formations, university leaders and politicians, among others.

The debate has now shifted from increasing higher education subsidies to the provision of free higher education. The case for free higher education is based on two main premises: (1) social justice, i.e. increasing access for the poor, especially previously marginalised communities, to university education in the face of increasing tuition fees, and (2) growth externalities.

Given South Africa's high levels of skills shortages, free higher education is deemed necessary to get human capital investment to efficient levels (Wangenge-Ouma, 2012, p. 838). The high degree of performance inequality among schools is largely a consequence of differences in educational quality.

Business environment in South Africa

As CIMA requires payment for exemptions granted, student fees and examinations fees to be paid in British pounds, the devaluation of the South African currency of around 33 per cent in the last two years had a considerable impact on the affordability of the relevant education and access to the management accounting profession. To counter this devaluation to some extent, CIMA has capped the exemption fees for students applying with accepted South African degrees (CIMA, 2016c).

Financial crisis and the increasing importance of management accountants with relevant skills

Because information providing for managerial decision-making is one of the crucial elements of management accounting, increasing information requirements of managers can probably result in a stronger interaction and increased communication between management accountants and managers. In turn, this increased interaction can result in a higher influence of management accountants on managerial decision-making and a more powerful role within companies (Endenich, 2014, p. 127).

Pressure on ethical behaviour

A third of South African management accountants reported that they sometimes or always feel under pressure from colleagues or managers to compromise their organisation's standards of ethical business conduct, with 30 per cent reporting that they have personally observed conduct that violated organisational ethics standards, policy or the law in the previous 12 months (CIMA, 2015b). According to Transparency International's 2014 Corruption Perceptions Index, South Africa ranks sixty-seventh out of 175 countries in terms of corruption worldwide and ninth in sub-Saharan Africa (Transparency International, 2014). Research by PwC in 2016 found that 69 per cent of the businesses in South Africa were the victim of economic crime, the highest prevalence in the world (Cairns, 2016). With consistently low economic growth rates below 5 per cent (STATSSA, 2016) and no clear indication that this will improve in the near future, this is a challenge that management accountants in South Africa will continue to face.

Transformation

A major government policy that affects all businesses in South Africa is Broad-Based Black Economic Empowerment (BBBEE). This policy aims to redress the inequalities of apartheid by giving certain previously disadvantaged groups (blacks, coloureds and Indians) economic privileges that include measures such as employment preference, skills development, ownership, management, socio-economic development and preferential procurement (SA Treasury, 2014).

South Africa's businesses are required to address the inequalities of apartheid by giving previously disadvantaged groups employment preferences and skills development. This policy requires accounting professions such as SAICA and CIMA South Africa to remove barriers to entry for individuals from these groups to ensure that there is proper representation. Although some improvements have been made (for example SAICA now have 23 per cent black members compared to 7 per cent in 2001), much more needs to be done to ensure membership representation closer to that of the overall population (80 per cent black). BBBEE policy also requires business organisations to have fair representation of these disadvantaged groups in their workforce. Because of the relatively low number of qualified black management accountants, businesses struggle to meet the requirements set by this policy.

Skills shortage

South Africa has a severe shortage of employees with the required level of financial and accounting skills and knowledge (SAIPA, 2014; SAICA, 2009). This state of affairs has an impact on the growth opportunities for the profession as a whole. In addition, this is a severe constraint on the level of service existing management accountants can deliver. In many cases they will not have the support of lower-level staff to perform less challenging work, leading to less time available for value-added activities.

Opportunities for management accountants

CIMA's annual salary survey for 2014 (CIMA, 2014) shows the positive impact of professional qualifications on South African members' earning potential, salary satisfaction and the ability to realise ambitions such as moving to a new organisation, or working abroad. Respondents across the board agreed that the CIMA qualification strengthens their ability to move internationally in their career at 93 per cent, while 89 per cent agreed that the qualification creates career opportunities and 82 per cent agreed that it allows them to move across all areas of the business and outside of the finance function.

Mobility of CIMA members and students in South Africa is a strong motivator for being or becoming a management accountant, with up to 78 per cent of these respondents anticipating being in a new role within the next two years and 19 per cent planning to move abroad. Among members and students who plan to seek employment abroad, the UK is the most frequently named destination at 58 per cent, followed by the USA, Australia and Canada. Switzerland and Singapore are also popular planned destinations. Key reasons cited for moving would be a new career opportunity and improved quality of life.

Among those already working as management accountants, 42 per cent of the participants in the survey indicated that they expect to progress to finance manager, financial controller or finance director within the next three years. Among those working in assisting finance roles at the time of the survey, 43 per cent indicated that they expect to progress to management accountant.

Managerial skills, particularly leadership and strategic planning, are the skill sets students most wish to develop, while for qualified members there is a secondary focus on softer skills such as persuading and influencing, personal development and skills for developing others.

Conclusion

The dominant accounting designation in South Africa remains the CA(SA) qualification with more than 48 per cent of their members employed in industry as management accountants, financial managers and general managers. Coupled with the fact that most South African universities focus mainly on accommodating SAICA requirements at the expense of other professional accounting bodies, the dominance of the CA(SA) brand is expected to endure for the foreseeable future. Even with CIMA's commitment to 'remain at the forefront of the accounting profession's response to new business needs and keep CMA's at the forefront of the profession' (CIMA, 2016a), the brand struggles to gain wide acceptance in the South African environment. In 2009 CIMA South Africa created their transformational growth plan towards the year 2016, projecting 67 per cent growth in membership to 2,164 and 555 per cent growth in registered students (CIMA, 2009). Compared to the actual growth of 24 per cent measured between 2006 and 2014, it is clear that even with expanding its graduate recruitment strategies through increased marketing and brand awareness activity, CIMA SA struggles to compete with SAICA in attracting accounting students and members.

The current South African business environment creates a number of barriers for potential students wanting to join the accounting profession. The high cost of secondary education, high levels of poverty, unrest at some South African universities, long time-period to qualify, lack of appropriate communication skills (especially in English), low levels of literacy and the devaluation of the South African rand all contribute towards deterring potential candidates from pursuing a career as management accountants. However, the benefits in obtaining good employment, high earnings potential and the mobility to move to new organisations or to move abroad would ensure that a fair number of students would continue to pursue a career as management accountants.

References

Cairns, Patrick. (2016). Economic crime in South Africa is at 'a pandemic level'. Available: http://today.moneyweb.co.za/article?id=574469&acid=anjj%2BjmpH5YeZeuwhd4cWQ%3D%3D&adid=EzY%2FMwOY8QE8WkHj2%2BXORA%3D%3D&date=2016-03-02#.Vte7NJx96VN. Accessed: 3 March 2016.

Chua, W. F. & Poullaos, C. (2002). The empire strikes back? An exploration of centre-periphery interaction between the ICAEW and accounting associations in the self-governing colonies of Australia, Canada and South Africa, 1880–1907. *Accounting, Organizations and Society, 27*(4–5), 409–445.

CIMA (Chartered Institute of Management Accountants). (2009). Transformational growth to 2016: CIMA International Market Plan. Available: www.cimaglobal.com/Documents/Our%20locations%20docs/Southern%20Africa/agenda_13%206_africa_transformational_growth_to_2016.pdf.

CIMA (Chartered Institute of Management Accountants). (2014). *CIMA Salary Survey 2014*. South Africa.

CIMA (Chartered Institute of Management Accountants). (2015a). Six decades of success in South Africa. *The Bottom Line*, October/November, Issue 95.

CIMA (Chartered Institute of Management Accountants). (2015b). *Managing responsible business*, 2015 edition.

CIMA (Chartered Institute of Management Accountants). (2016a). Available: www.cimaglobal.com/About-us/CIMA-vision-for-management-accounting. Accessed: 3 March 2016.

CIMA (Chartered Institute of Management Accountants). (2016b). Available: www.cimaglobal.com/Study-with-us. Accessed: 29 February 2016.

CIMA (Chartered Institute of Management Accountants). (2016c). Available: www.cimaglobal.com/Our-locations/Africa/South-Africa. Accessed: 2 March 2016.

Cooper, D. J. & Robson, K. (2006). Accounting, professions and regulation: Locating the sites of professionalization. *Accounting, Organizations and Society, 31*, 415–444.

Endenich, C. (2014). Economic crisis as a driver of management accounting change: Comparative evidence from Germany and Spain. *Journal of Applied Accounting Research, 15*(1), 123–149.

Funnell, W. (2005). Accounting on the frontline: Cost accounting, military efficiency and the South African War. *Accounting and Business Research, 33*(4), 307–326.

Naidoo, S. K. & Garbharran, H. L. (2013). Communication skills as a subject in the programme cost and management accounting at a South African University. *Journal of Economics and Behavioral Studies, 5*(7), 484–495.

Republic of South Africa. (1993). Chartered Accountants Designation (Private) Act 67 of 1993. Pretoria: Government Printer.

Republic of South Africa. (2005). Auditing Profession Act 26 of 2005. Pretoria: Government Printer.

SA Treasury. (2014). Fiscal Policy. www.treasury.gov.za/documents/national%20budget/2014/review/chapter%203.pdf. Accessed: 1 March 2016.

SAICA (South African Institute of Chartered Accountants). (2003). *Group annual report 2003*.

SAICA (South African Institute of Chartered Accountants). (2009). *Skills shortage report*. Available: www.saica.co.za/News/SkillsShortageReport/tabid/1155/language/en-ZA/Default.aspx. Accessed: 3 March 2016.

SAICA (South African Institute of Chartered Accountants). (2014). *Integrated annual report 2014*.

SAICA (South African Institute of Chartered Accountants). (2016a). Available: www.saica.co.za/About/SAICAHistory/tabid/70/language/en-US/Default.aspx.

SAICA (South African Institute of Chartered Accountants). (2016b). Available: www.saica.co.za/Portals/0/about/Strategy/SAICA_Business%20Plan%20and%20Strategy%20Document%202015.pdf. Accessed: 3 March 2016.

SAICA (South African Institute of Chartered Accountants). (2016c). Available: www.saica.co.za/Training/BecomingaCA/tabid/157/language/en-ZA/Default.aspx. Accessed: 29 February 2016.

SAIPA (South African Institute of Professional Accountants). (2014). The war on talent and financial skills shortage. Available: www.saipa.co.za/articles/356772/war-talent-and-financial-skills-shortage. Accessed: 3 March 2016.

Shuttleworth, C. C. (2014). The management accountant vocational fallacy. *South African Journal for Economic Management Studies (SAJEMS), 17*(3), 336–348.

STATSSA (Statistics South Africa). (2016). Economic growth. Available: www.statssa.gov.za/?page_id=735&id=1. Accessed: 1 March 2016.

The World Bank. (2016). Doing business 2016. Economy profile 2016. South Africa. www.doingbusiness.org/data/exploreeconomies/south-africa/~/media/giawb/doing%20business/documents/profiles/country/ZAF.pdf?ver=3. Accessed: 26 July 2016.

Transparency International. (2014). SA fares poorly in the global corruption perceptions index, yet again. Available: www.corruptionwatch.org.za/sa-fares-poorly-in-the-global-corruption-perceptions-index-yet-again. Accessed: 1 March 2016.

Venter, E. R. & De Villiers, C. (2013). The accounting profession's influence on academe: South African evidence. *Accounting, Auditing and Accountability Journal, 26*(8), 1246–1278.

Verhoef, G. (2013). Reluctant ally: The development of statutory regulation of the accountancy profession in South Africa, 1904–1951. *Accounting History, 18*(2), 163–191.

Verhoef, G. (2014). Globalisation of knowledge but not opportunity: Closure strategies in the making of the South African accounting market, 1890s to 1958. *Accounting History, 19*(1–2), 193–226.

Wangenge-Ouma, G. (2012). Tuition fees and the challenge of making higher education a popular commodity in South Africa. *Higher Education, 64*, 831–844.

Wessels, P. L. (2006). The SA business and IT environment in which accountants function. *Meditari Accountancy Research, 14*(2), 131–149.

12 The role of the management accountant in the United Kingdom

Liz Warren and John Burns

Introduction

In the United Kingdom (UK), there are eight possible routes to qualify as an accountant.[1] The main professional accounting bodies are the Association of Chartered Certified Accountants (ACCA), the Chartered Institute of Management Accountants (CIMA), the Chartered Institute of Public, Finance and Accountancy (CIPFA), the Institute of Chartered Accountants in England and Wales (ICAEW), the Institute of Chartered Accountants in Scotland, Chartered Accountants Ireland (CAI), Certified Public Accountants (ACPA) and the Association of International Accountants (AIA).

The majority of qualified individuals in a management accounting role will seek a CIMA qualification, which bestows the titles Associate/Fellow Chartered Management Accountant (ACMA/FCMA) and Chartered Global Management Accountant (CGMA)[2] (CIMA, 2016). Therefore, this chapter focuses primarily on the CIMA qualification, when discussing 'professional education', and in analysing different job titles and industries within which management accountants generally operate.

CIMA (2014a, p. 8) define management accounting as situated

> at the heart of an organisation, at the crossroads between finance and management. It provides structured solutions to unstructured problems, by translating the complex into the simple and by making the simple compelling. Bringing together both financial and non-financial considerations, it is the discipline that should be used to run the organisation, to control and improve performance.

The majority of today's qualified management accountants in the UK are therefore educated and trained to provide such broad services and skills, within the boundaries of ethical codes. However, although this describes the role of qualified UK management accountants today, at least rhetorically, there have been considerable role changes over the years.

Development of the management accountant's role preceded the inception of any professional body. The official history of management accounting in the UK dates back roughly to the time of the First World War, when basic costing was widespread in industrial practice (Edwards & Boyn, 2006). That said, Fleischman and Parker (1991) gave evidence that suggested cost accounting was widely used even prior to the 1900s in the UK extraction, iron and textile industries. Such practice was said to include the utilisation of techniques normally applied in routine budgeting and costing processes. Nevertheless, whatever the origins, it was not until 1919 that 'cost accountants' gained due recognition, as well as clearer differentiation from financial accountants and auditors. And, not unrelated, 1919 was also the year in which CIMA was founded, although in its inaugural years it was called 'The Institute of Cost and Works Accountants' (ICWA). The ICWA set out to improve the fundamentals of basic cost accounting practices.

Following this formal recognition of cost accountants in the UK, further advances were subsequently made in the area of costing. For instance, between 1920 and 1930 we witnessed the emergence of standard costing and variance analysis;[3] and, from 1930 until the early 1960s, there were several improvements to basic budgeting techniques, followed by advances in discounted cash-flow techniques during the 1960s (Bhimani & Bromwich, 2010). From this point onwards, there were rather incremental changes in cost accounting techniques until the late 1980s (Johnson & Kaplan, 1987), though this was not unique to the UK and was observed in other countries such as the United States.

The developments of the management accounting field also led to changes within the ICWA body. The membership of the ICWA continued to grow, up and into the 1960s, and the significance of the professional body was acknowledged within government circles, industry and other accounting bodies. This is evidenced by the fact that the ICWA was invited by the other then dominant accounting bodies such as the ICAEW to join the debate regarding merging all the accounting bodies during the 1960s (Boyns & Edwards, 2013). Whilst this merger did not actually go ahead, the ICWA recognised that the nature of and development in the management accounting field had resulted in a prevalence of management accounting work as opposed to cost accounting work. The work of the management accountant had moved from pure recording of data to planning and control, especially in the area of budgeting; the role had therefore become a supportive one rather than administrative in nature (Wichramasinghe & Alawattage, 2007). In turn, this changing nature of the role of a UK management accountant resulted in a name change (Boyns & Edwards, 2013; Bhimani & Bromwich, 2010). The ICWA became the Institute of Cost and Management Accountants (ICMA) in 1972 (CIMA, 2009). The changing name signified the management accountant moving away from the shop floor to business specialists. Then in 1986 the ICMA received a Royal Charter[4] and rebranded as CIMA (CIMA, 2009).

Around the same time as CIMA's rebranding, an important debate began in the management accounting field. In the late 1980s and early 1990s, there were deliberations concerning whether management accounting practice comprised sufficient and appropriate techniques to support decision making within organisations (Johnson & Kaplan, 1987). The United States' (US) debate was important to the UK, because many of the techniques they referred to as inadequate were being extensively used in the UK, especially the costing systems. However, whilst the debate was required, what followed was a significant critique that the US debate did not consider some of the more advanced costing developments that were in practice in UK manufacturing (Dugdale, Jones & Green, 2006).

Nevertheless, the US debate did open up the opportunity for UK management accounting to be examined more closely. Bromwich and Bhimani (1994), for instance, conducted a comprehensive analysis of management accounting in the UK, and made some interesting and at times quite radical conclusions. For example, citing the recent survey of Bright et al. (1992), they remarked:

> over 40 percent of firms surveyed were considering the introduction of at least elements of strategic management accounting. This result may turn out to be too optimistic, but many commentators favour an extension of the role of the management accounting to encompass the cost of strategy and estimating cost structures of competitors. This may seem like something of a blue skies idea to many accountants.
>
> (Bromwich & Bhimani, 1994, p. 6)

This is an interesting observation since it reveals that, only 22 years ago, management accountants were still seen to be predominantly responsible for producing cost information (Bromwich & Bhimani, 1994) to assist decision making, while any strategic element to their role was thought to be difficult even to comprehend. Fleischman and Parker (1991), on the other hand, argued that a more strategic-oriented form of management accounting was not as novel in the UK as some were arguing, but rather a re-emergence of similar and overlapping practices from as far back as the industrial revolution.

The struggle to grasp a potentially more strategic role for management accountants needs to be considered in the context of embedded and long-established roles in such activities as data collection, performance analysis and basic cost calculations (Burns, Warren & Oliveira, 2014). The rhetoric suggested a significant leap for accountants from traditional 'bean counters' to so-called strategic 'business partners' (Bromwich & Bhimani, 1994). And following widespread debate, in the 1990s we began to see more strategic-oriented management accounting techniques such as strategic management accounting (Bromwich, 1990; Roslender & Hart, 2002), activity-based costing (Cooper & Kaplan, 1988a, 1988b), the balanced scorecard (Kaplan & Norton, 1992), and value added management (Stern, Stewart & Chew, 1995). In addition, around this time, it became more common to see organisations re-engineering their finance departments (Bhimani & Bromwich, 2010), effectively making clearer differentiation between more traditional and routine accounting roles and the new strategically focused 'business partnering' role (Parker, 2002), or at least more business analysis (Yazdifar & Tsamenyi, 2005).

So, in summary, we have briefly presented the evolution of management accounting in the UK in terms of: (1) its origins in the basic cost accounting techniques which emerged out of expanding informational needs of growing organisations during the Industrial Revolution; (2) a steady but not overly-fast extension of such techniques from the 1920s until the 1990s; and (3) a resurgence of innovations in the management field from the 1990s onwards until the present day. Alongside this development in management accounting practices, there has also been parallel development in the expected (or intentionally promoted and created, even) role for management accountants. In particular, the last two decades or so have highlighted a shift in the roles of many professional management accountants from traditional 'bean counter' to 'business partner' who is viewed as an important contributor to high-level, operational and strategic, problem-solving and decision-making processes. The remaining part of this chapter will cover four distinct but connected issues, namely: (1) identifying and discussing the most influential drivers of such change within the UK management accounting profession, from a political economy position: (2) examining the current requirements of the professional bodies in terms of education; (3) presenting the demographic information of current CIMA members: and (4) a brief look at future challenges for UK management accountants.

Key drivers of changes to UK management accounting practices

Dominant sectors have changed dramatically over the past 170 years[5] in the UK and, in turn, this has impacted the make-up of the skill set and resources of its work force. Examining Figure 12.1 it can be seen that the agriculture and manufacturing sectors have significantly declined since the 1961 census (ONS, 2013), and the service industry now dominates. The UK has especially repositioned away from producing physical products towards offering relatively more intangible services.

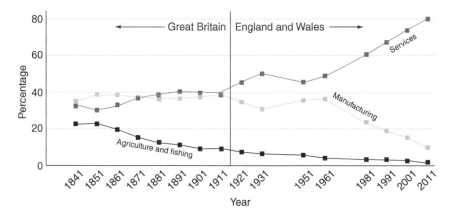

Figure 12.1 Industry change in Great Britain.
Source: ONS (2013).

Whilst it is not our intention here to attempt to provide a detailed historical analysis of management accounting or indeed the role of management accountants (for this, see Edwards, Boyns & Anderson, 1995; Edwards & Boyns, 2006), we can comment modestly on how changes to the UK's political and economic situation might in fact have influenced both.

Lowry (1990) examined the changing nature of the UK's manufacturing industry over time, highlighting the said decline in its significance compared to the services industry, but also raised some issues concerning its impact on the role of management accountants. It was clear that CIMA's initial focus on training with UK management accountants was based on manufacturing; however, with the decline in that sector the result was CIMA's membership base reduced in the 1970s and 1980s (Tiley, 2010). Many of Lowry's observations probably remain just as relevant to management practices in the UK at the present time. He identified six main factors for influencing the roles of management accountants in the service industry, namely: (1) smaller sized companies; (2) absence of inventory to value; (3) narrow conceptualisation of control; (4) non-standard output; (5) a reluctance to learn from other disciplines; and (6) a high level of ambiguity. However, since Lowry's (1990) work, there has arguably been an advance in the conceptualisation of control (point 3 above), in a clear understanding of non-standard output (point 4 above) and in the interdisciplinary nature of management accounting knowledge (point 5 above). The management accounting training in the UK has evolved since the decline in membership base in the 1970–80s and provided more flexible training, which has resulted in the training no longer focusing primarily on the manufacturing sector.

A good example of one of the UK's larger service sectors is financial and insurance. This sector, in 2014, represented 8 per cent of the gross value added (GVA) of the UK economy (Tyler, 2015), which equated to £126.9 billion. The core challenge for banks has been to create sustainable success as with most other businesses. However, as Pennington (2010) argues, the banks have different business models and there is a need to provide confidence that these models will deliver the increased value whilst also alerting the consumers that there are appropriate risk mitigations in place at the same time. Both Pennington (2010) and Brickman et al., (2016) argued that the banks have to ensure there is a detailed understanding of suitable performance measurements and incentives to direct the appropriate type of risk taking required, in order to meet the challenges following the financial crisis of 2008.

The UK training for management accountants can be argued to now provide the fundamentals necessary to support this type of sector with guidance on more flexible pricing models that are considered to optimise both customer and channel profitability and to ensure business models aid market positioning, benchmarking, regulatory adherence and risk management (CIMA, 2014a). However, it is not just the nature of industry that has influenced the management accounting field, the scope of the political economy of the UK can also be argued to have played a role.

Political/economic influences of change

Management accounting in any country, and the roles of accountants, can be influenced by multiple national and international drivers of change, many of which are included in this book, such as globalisation and technology. However, analysing the political economy of a nation can expose institutional changes by examining the political and social changes within. Every nation state has its own political policies and/or macro incentives which can influence variance across management accounting practices and roles of accountants.

One such politically infused influence on the changing nature of management accounting is the phenomenon of financialisation. According to Palley (2007: 2), financialisation is 'a process whereby financial markets, financial institutions and financial elites gain greater influence over economic policy and economic outcomes [...] transforms the functioning of economic systems at both the macro and micro levels'. Davies and Walsh (2015) argued that changes in the UK political environment fast-tracked the process of financialisation, when compared to that in other economies, as the UK Treasury particularly pursued policies that handed more control to the financial sector. This was also evident in recent times from the increased liberalisation and privatisation of corporations and industries; the UK's financialisation process was a national phenomenon in its own right (Epstein, 2005; Froud, Johal, Leaver & Williams, 2006). During the 1970s, there was a considerable paradigm shift amongst political circles, when relatively more power was transferred to the Treasury, mostly at the expense of the Department of Trade and Industry. These changes not only promoted free market forces but also constituted deliberate policy changes to advantage the financial sector. The impact of such changes transformed the financial sector and also non-financial corporations too, which began increasingly to create more shareholder value (Davies & Walsh, 2015).

Financialisation in the UK was fast-paced and, in turn, possibly impacted the general perception about accountants across society. Accountants in general profited through the financialisation process (Arnold, 2009). More specifically, accountants were perceived by society as constituting an important part of the financialisation process (Arnold, 2009), in particular *management* accountants. Management accountants were able to advise private enterprises about ways to increase their shareholder value, and the stock of management accountants rose accordingly. Management accountants increasingly became sought[6] after for senior and director-level positions, because their acumen and understanding was viewed to be closely aligned with contemporary organisational strategising. For example, even the CFO role has expanded in the past 10 years, moving from accounting regulation and overseeing the bean counting to a role that is strategically aligned with new business models, requiring a wider business understanding, one which crosses geographical boundaries (Groysberg, Kelly & MacDonald, 2011). The numbers are now seen as downgraded compared to issues such as mergers and acquisitions and risk management (Groysberg et al., 2011), areas in which UK management accountants are becoming more influential.

Another politically grounded influence on the changing nature of management accounting and roles of accountants is liberalisation. Particularly over the last three decades, UK politics has been underpinned by ideologies which endorse competitive pressures within the economy and seek efficiencies in all manner of organisations, whether public or private sector. Moreover, an increased focus on identifying value added activities and cost savings has become a pivotal role for modern-day management accountants. The UK has normally boasted market-based economies (Rubery, 2015), although in the 1960–70s there was a period of more planned-economic policy. However, from the 1970s, under Margaret Thatcher's rule, free market forces again came to the fore and, in particular, there began a significant spate, in the UK, of privatisation. The general requirement for efficiency and cost savings increased during the 1980–90s, as the UK became a global leader in liberalising state-owned industries and utilities, including electricity, the railways and airport authorities (IEA, 2012; Warren, 2014).

Many private sector organisations prioritise issues surrounding accountability, because of the influence of stakeholders, shareholders, the capital markets and regulators, all of whom require effective controls (Parker, 2003). Regulation has significantly impacted the role of the management accountant, and it became especially significant in the late 1980s and early 1990s within the UK (Warren & Brickman, 2017), as many utilities were subject to a privatisation process; for example, British Steel, the water industry, the electricity industry, British Coal and British Rail. The trend of privatisation continued, with a more recent example of a company undergoing privatisation being the Royal Mail. Regulation became a prominent part of business life in the newly privatised industries, because it was meant to counteract the supposed imperfections of competition (Crowther, Cooper & Carter, 2001).

The central features of the regulatory model in the UK were based on the Littlechild Report of 1983, the foundations of which embraced concepts of independence, forward-looking incentive-based regulation with a focus on consumers and their welfare, strong legal and well-defined appeal rights, private ownership, emphasis on competition and light-touch regulation (Stern, 2014). These regulatory characteristics significantly influenced organisations and their accounting processes and reports. However, despite regulation beginning as a light-touch mechanism, over time its influence from an accountancy perspective became more noteworthy (see Warren (2014) for an example of how regulation influenced the use of investment appraisal in the privatised electricity industry). Regulators evolved to exert a strategic impact on the way organisations operate, shaping organisation's internal metrics. This is evidenced in a report by CIMA (2014a), which argues that one of the core practice areas of a management accountant is external reporting, which of course includes reporting on regulatory compliance reports.

In addition to the regulatory aspects of liberalisation in the UK, management accountants have also been required to fulfil the traditional aspects of their job, as privatised companies demand greater efficiencies. Parker (2003: 77) argued that '[t]he efficiency gains are expected to be in allocative efficiency, as prices are more closely related to long-run marginal costs of supply and technical efficiency, as costs of production are minimised'. Efficiency is of course central to the management accountant's role. Therefore, the UK's urgent need to push forward a privatisation policy helped to establish not only the importance of the traditional skills of the management accountant, but also helped to expand the role to include elements that were more strategic.

Next, it would appear reasonable to suggest that fragmentation of company structure has also exerted pressures on the management accounting profession. The emphasis on greater competition within UK industry, via the privatisation process, has led to changes to the ways in which companies have evolved. Competition has encouraged companies to scale up, to become vertically integrated and to move into conglomerate style corporations (Rubery, 2015). The changing nature of companies has redirected management philosophy and thinking. Within the UK, changes in company structures and management are arguably a key factor behind the increased use of outsourcing/offshoring, because the sovereign bounded entity no longer exists (Davies, Diekman & Tinsley, 1994).

The disappearance of the sovereign bounded entity, in conjunction with the drive for greater competition, has also been reflected in management accounting processes, as benchmarking of production costs became more important, in particular the calculation of internal costs versus external costs. This change was documented by Ackroyd and Proctor (1998), who observed British manufacturing companies during the 1990s. They noted that just as manufacturing was now exposed to external benchmarking and outsourcing, so too were the services within these conglomerates. For instance, services such as accounting and IT became fragmented, with many traditional management accounting techniques and processes being absorbed by new software solutions, or being outsourced or restructured into shared service centres.[7]

Societal/cultural drivers of change

The increasing influence and need for accounting knowledge resulting from policy changes, organisational structures and changing business models have resulted in changes to societal perceptions of the accounting field in general. Accounting as a sector is considered a very respectable job in the UK and, in 2014, 335,000 people were members of a professional accounting body, with an additional 166,000 student members (FRC, 2015). Of these, 77,551 were members of CIMA (qualified management accountants) and 56,684 students were training to be qualified management accountants (FRC, 2015). In the UK, the role of the accountant in general is seen as prestigious, and this is reflected in the average annual salary received for the role, as illustrated in Table 12.1.

The average salary of a CIMA member at associate level £64,891 can be compared with the average salary in the UK for full-time employees, which is estimated at £27,000[8] (ONS, 2016). The role attracts both males and females; however, the profession is predominantly male with only 36 percent of CIMA members being

Table 12.1 Average salaries for those studying and qualified management accountants

Level of qualification/member status of the CIMA qualification	Average salary
Operational level (exam level)	£30,735
Management level (exam level)	£31,904
Strategic level (exam level)	£34,436
Exams completed	£39,546
CIMA member (ACMA, CGMA)	£64,891
CIMA member (FCMA, CGMA)	£110,073

Source: CIMA (2014a).

female in 2014 (FRC, 2015). However, the overall ratio of male/female occupation is not reflective of the changing face of the industry; for instance, under the age demographic of 35 years, the male/female split is approximately 50/50 (CIMA, 2016). Considering the potential financial rewards, it is probably unsurprising that accounting is an attractive career in the UK; this was confirmed by a Deloitte report (2014) which stated that the number one reason for potential employees choosing any professional job in London was the financial package offered.

In view of the many changes to political policy discussed earlier, UK boards tend to employ individuals who are able to understand current processes and understand the financial complications of running a business. Overall, CIMA members hold 112 board positions at 91 different FTSE 350 companies; 43 of these are within 34 FTSE 100 companies and 69 are within 57 FTSE 250 companies (CIMA, 2014a); 28 per cent CGMA designation holders are in c-suite or senior management roles; and a further 11 per cent are in controllership roles (CIMA, 2018).[9]

This is not a recent development within the UK; Armstrong (1987) claimed that accountants and financial specialists dominated UK firms' management structures from as early as the 1960s. *The Director* (1965 as cited in Armstrong, 1987) commented that 'qualified accountant' was the most significant academic or professional qualification held by board members within the UK. An accounting professional qualification provided the gravitas sought after for roles on a board and it is therefore important to examine the rigorous process that qualified CIMA individuals must complete to gain their recognition.

The education of UK management accountants

Academic

With the accounting qualification seemingly delivering new and very positive career prospects, including elevation to the boardroom, there has been a significant commitment to the provision of such qualifications. Typically, the majority of accountants begin their professional career by pursuing a degree. According to Financial Reporting Council (FRC), 54 per cent of students wishing to train as management accountants, including studying for the CIMA qualification, hold an accounting degree, and 45 per cent hold another business-relevant degree (FRC, 2015). Many UK universities offer a 3–4 year bachelor's degree in accounting, and the UK now has the highest proportion of accounting graduates in the European Union. In 2000, this proportion was 26 per cent, but by 2014 it had increased to around 41 per cent (Deloitte, 2014). To an extent it would seem that some UK universities tailored their accountancy programmes to the broader changes in the UK economy, and as confidence grew about offering considerable employment in the areas of banking, finance, insurance and professional services (Deloitte, 2014), in particular to support the expanding service sector.

Professional training

To complete their professional training and become CGMA-qualified, a student has to succeed in three stages of exams, namely: (1) operational; (2) management; and (3) strategic management accounting. In addition, to gain *full* professional membership they must also provide evidence of three years' relevant work experience. Some students gain exemptions for particular exams, depending on prior qualifications, including the subjects studied for a university degree. Recent data released by CIMA (December 2015) indicates that there were 50,191 students engaged across all stages of becoming a qualified CGMA member, a figure which is broken down into the respective stages in Table 12.2.

As part of the professional training of a management accountant studying through the CIMA qualification, there is a requirement that students are well prepared for practice. This effectively means they must be trained in a variety of areas such as: cost transformation and management; external reporting; financial strategy; internal control; investment appraisal; management and budgetary control; price, discount and product decisions; project management; regulator adherence and compliance; resource management; risk management; strategic tax management; and treasury and cash management (CIMA, 2014). Thus, whilst there may be some debate concerning the nature and appropriateness of such expertise, it would seem that the profession still (is assumed to) require a highly technical skill set.

Table 12.2 Total number of CIMA students in the UK

Student level	Totals
Certificate	14,919
Operational	14,260
Management	7,524
Gateway	681
Strategic	8,930
Exam Complete	3,877
Total	**5,0191**

Source: information supplied by CIMA, December 2015

Roles available to qualified management accountant in the UK

One of the key issues explored in this chapter, from the outset, is the *role* of the management accountant. There have been, as we have explained, claims and rhetoric at least that management accountants are moving away from traditional roles to more strategic-oriented roles. So, as part of our research, we decided to (acquire and) investigate data on the current 'mapping' of CIMA members (i.e. both qualified fellows and students). First, we explored the top 20[10] job titles for a qualified management accountants at the associate level, as at December 2015, as shown in Table 12.3. As can be seen, in the UK job titles are still in general more aligned with traditional aspects of the management accountant's role, whereas business partnering featured as only the tenth most used title. The same focus (i.e. top 20 job titles) but for fully qualified management accountants gave the results presented in Table 12.4.[11] So, at fully-qualified (i.e. fellowship) level, we can see more senior job titles, including more directorship roles that we have previously referred to.

Next, we explored the top 20 industries or sectors where qualified UK management accountants work, as at December 2015, as shown in Table 12.5. As can be seen, the service sector dominates in terms of the need for management accountants' skills, which is not really surprising in view of the size of the UK's service sector economy. We can see from Tables 12.3–12.5 where UK management accountants are currently positioned, but what does the future hold?

Table 12.3 Top 20 job titles for qualifying management accountants at associate level

Job title	Number
Finance Manager	4,078
Management Accountant	3,823
Financial Controller	3,717
Finance Director	2,386
Accountant	1,333
Director	1,018
Financial Accountant	809
Financial Analyst	795
Head of Finance	674
Finance Business Partner	642
Finance Analyst	589
Business Analyst	553
Managing Director	515
Senior Finance Manager	405
Financial Director	403
Senior Management Accountant	403
Project Accountant	394
Commercial Finance Manager	358
Senior Accountant	295
Group Financial Controller	291

Source: information supplied by CIMA, December 2015.

Table 12.4 Top 20 job titles for fully qualified management accountants, fellow level

Job title	Number
Finance Director	561
Director	315
Managing Director	263
Financial Controller	229
Financial Director	125
Finance Manager	98
Chief Financial Officer	82
Group Finance Director	71
Director of Finance	63
Accountant	51
Consultant	49
Chief Executive	48
Chairman	45
Head of Finance	44
Partner	44
Management Accountant	33
Group Financial Controller	33
CFO	32
CEO	27
Company Secretary	24

Source: information supplied by CIMA, December 2015.

Outlook for the UK management accountant

A report by Deloitte (2014) predicted that 35 per cent of UK accounting jobs, at that time, have and were continuing to be at risk of disappearing. Whilst some of these roles were argued to be associated with financial accounting and more clerical-type accounting, they also relate to basic costing roles associated with management accounting (see Figure 12.2). Unsurprisingly, Deloitte cites the considerable advances in digital technology as having a key influence on the nature of these predictions.

However, technology does not present the only risk to tomorrow's management accountants in the UK. Another key threat to indigenous management accountants, for instance, is outsourcing, as more organisations appear to be attracted to the low cost arbitrage of overseas services (Nicholson & Aman, 2008). Since the 1990s, more management accounting procedures are being carried out by outsourcing companies outside of the UK, particularly in the areas of compliance and control, including budgeting, forecasting, regulator reporting, risk management, cost management and treasury (Nicholson & Aman, 2008).

This could seem to suggest that although management accountants should maintain their mastery of their role's traditional aspects (Baldvinsdottir et al., 2010;

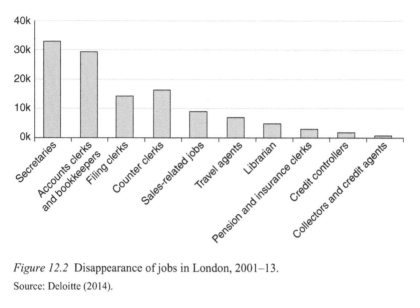

Figure 12.2 Disappearance of jobs in London, 2001–13.
Source: Deloitte (2014).

Table 12.5 Top 20 industries/sectors where fully qualified UK management accountants
work

Industry/sector	Associate	Fellow	Total
Business services	5,784	435	6,219
No employer	5,203	688	5,891
Holding and other investment offices	3,103	198	3,301
Banks and licensed deposit takers	2,859	64	2,923
Health services	2,201	90	2,291
Exec, legislative and general government, not finance	2,126	122	2,248
Education services	1,610	139	1,749
Communications	1,446	66	1,512
Wholesale trade? Non-durable goods	1,377	107	1,484
Food and kindred products	1,329	61	1,390
Wholesale trade – durable goods	1,218	97	1,315
Non-depository credit institutions	1,223	58	1,281
Chemicals and allied products	1,204	72	1,276
Industrial and commercial machinery and computer equipment	1,114	83	1,197
Transportation equipment	1,067	76	1,143
Electric, Gas and Sanitary Services	934	36	970
Electronic and Electrical Equipment and Components, not Computers	758	60	818
Insurance Agents, Brokers and Service	749	22	771
Miscellaneous Retail	736	34	770
Real Estate	706	54	760

Source: information supplied by CIMA, December 2015.

Burns et al., 2014), repositioning might also be sensible in the future. And, with this in mind, it is probably some comfort that Deloitte's recent research has suggested that two of the most essential skills' requirements for employees in the future is problem solving and a professional qualification, as shown in Table 12.6.

It is clear from the data presented so far in this chapter that the role of the management accountant underscores a solid and respectable career. That said, there is still debate regarding the expertise of the role going into the future. Although the purpose of the chapter was not to debate the role of the business partner or some of the directions that the professional bodies are apportioning the role, it is clear that in the UK there is still a considerable way to go before the future direction will be agreed. Despite the new job titles and the push by the professional bodies to increase the functions and responsibilities of the UK management accountant, industry must not forget the essentials; a good management accountant should have the following skills to complete any task/project successfully:

IT proficiency; ability to assist IT experts and statisticians in the design and development of information systems, integrating the latest technologies;

Broad business understandings: a broad commercial acumen, to help financially-astute colleagues assess performance and make decisions;

Communication: ability to relate management accounting information to its various users, in a way that is understood by them;

Interpersonal: strong interpersonal skills, as well as the competence for nurturing relationships and trust with colleagues across the organisation;

Conviction: show strong conviction and persuasion, to push ideas through, and the ability to deal with differences in personalities, levels of seniority, and mindsets.

(Burns et al., 2014, p. 5)

Table 12.6 Essential skills' requirements of employees (%)

Digital know-how	16
Management	15
Creativity	13
Entrepreneurship	10
Problem solving	9
Negotiation	9
Professional qualifications	8
Processing, support, etc.	6
Social perceptiveness	5
Persuasiveness	5
Cultural know-how and languages	4

Source: adapted from Deloitte (2014).

The skills of the management accountant remain in high demand; however, the biggest question facing the future role of the management accountant is how far the boundaries of responsibility extend. Should management accountants focus on developing new systems and techniques to generate higher efficiencies and provide information that assists better decision making, or is there scope to push the strategic boundaries and the role of the business partner?

Conclusion

Within this chapter, we have seen that the development of the management accounting role in the UK has not been shaped solely by the profession itself, but by the political and economic direction of the country. Historical developments have been key factors, as government policy changes in the 1970s initiated the change process, ultimately providing the impetus behind the professional status of accounting. There are of course risks facing the future of UK management accountants; however, there are also numerous opportunities as attested to by the actions of professional bodies, which are currently highlighting the strong business acumen of management accountants above the tasks of financial accountants.

Acknowledgements

The authors would like to thank CIMA for the data provided (in particular the help from Rebecca McCaffry, the data team and Paul Turner) and the useful comments from Karen Brickman and Professor David Otley

Notes

1 This chapter will focus on qualified/qualifying management accountants – although it is possible to hold the title Management Accountant without being formally qualified.
2 The title CGMA is bestowed on CIMA accountants due to CIMA's joint venture with the American Institute of Certified Public Accountants (AICPA).
3 The first texts books in this area were also published in the UK around this time.
4 Royal charter: a formal document issued granting a right or power to an individual or a body by a monarch.
5 Data taken from the 1941 census – the first recorded census that had full data of individual and the latter part of the industrial revolution.
6 Evidence will be presented later in the chapter.
7 This chapter will not examine shared services evolution; the reader should refer to Chapter 15 by Will Seal.
8 £27,000 is the gross annual earning for individuals who have been in the same role for 12 months minimum.
9 Information supplied directly from CIMA. The authors would like to acknowledge the support and data provided by CIMA.
10 Does not include those allocated as 'unspecified'.
11 Does not include those allocated as 'unspecified'.

References

Ackroyd, S. & Proctor, S. (1998). British manufacturing organisation and workplace industrial relations: Some attributes of the new flexible firm. *British Journal of Industrial Relations, 36*(2), 163–183.

Armstrong, P. (1987). The rise of accounting controls in British capitalist enterprises. *Accounting, Organizations and Society, 12*(5), 415–436.

Arnold, P. (2009). Institutional Perspective on the Internationalization of Accounting. In C. Chapman, S. Cooper & P. Miller (Eds.), *Accounting, organizations and institutions: Essays in honour of Anthony Hopwood* (Chapter 3). Oxford: Oxford University Press.

Baldvinsdottir, G., Burns, J., Nörreklit, H. & Scapens, R. (2010). Professional accounting media: Accountants handing over control to the system. *Qualitative Research in Accounting and Management, 7*(3), 395–414.

Bhimani, A. & Bromwich, M. (2010). *Management accounting: Retrospect and prospect.* London: CIMA.

Boyns, T. & Edwards, J. (2013). *A history of management accounting: The British experience.* New York: Routledge.

Brickman, K., Otley, D. & Warren, L. (2016). The impact of incentives on risk-taking behaviour: Evidence from the UK financial services industry. EAA conference, Maastricht, May 2016.

Bromwich, M. (1990). The case for strategic Management Accounting: The role of accounting information for strategy in competitive markets. *Accounting, Organizations and Society, 13*(1–2), 27–46.

Bromwich, M. & Bhimani, A. (1994). *Management accounting: Pathways to progess.* London: CIMA.

Burns, J., Quinn, M., Warren, L. & Oliveira, J. (2013). *Management accounting.* Maidenhead: McGraw-Hill.

Burns, J., Warren, L. & Oliveira, J. (2014). Business partners: Is it all that good? *Controlling and Management Review.* http://link.springer.com/article/10.1365/s12176-014-0907-6.

CIMA. (2009). The bottom line. www.cimaglobal.com/Documents/ImportedDocuments/The_Bottom_Line_February_March_2009(1).pdf, accessed 7 March 2016.

CIMA.(2014a). *Global management accounting principles.* London: CIMA.

CIMA. (2014b). CIMA salary survey results. www.cimaglobal.com/About-us/Press-office/Press-releases/2014/2014-CIMA-Salary-Survey-results/Press release, accessed 11 January 2016.

CIMA. (2016). The CGMA designation. www.cimaglobal.com/Members/CGMA, accessed 7 March 2016.

Cooper, R. & Kaplan, R. (1988a). How costing distorts product costs. *Management Accounting*, April, 96–103.

Cooper, R. & Kaplan, R. (1988b). Measure costs right: Make decisions right. *Harvard Business Review*, September, 130–135.

Crowther, D., Cooper, S. & Carter, C. (2001). Regulation – the movie: A semiotic study of the periodic review of UK regulated industry. *Journal of Organisational Change, 14*(3), 225–238.

Davies, A. & Walsh, C. (2015). The role of the state in the financialisation of the UK economy. *Political Studies.* doi:10.1111/1467_9248.12198.

Davies, G., Diekman, K. & Tinsley, C. (1994). The decline and fall of the conglomerate firm in the 1980s: The deinstitutionalization of an organisational form. *American Sociology Review, 59*(4), 547–570.

Deloitte. (2014). *London futures agiletown: The relentless march of technology and London's response*. London: Deloitte.

Dugdale, D., Jones, T. & Green, S. (2006). *Contemporary management accounting practice in the UK manufacturing*. London: CIMA.

Edwards, J. & Boyns, T. (2006). The development of cost and management accounts in Britain. In S. Chapman, A. G. Hopwood & M. D. Shields (Eds.), *Handbook of management accounting research. Vol. 2* (pp. 969–1034). London: Elsevier.

Edwards, J., Boyns, T. & Anderson, M. (1995). British cost accounting development: Continuity and change. *The Accounting Historians Journal, 22*(2), 1–41.

Epstein, E. (2005). Introduction. In G. Epstein (Ed.), *Financialization of the world economy* (pp. 3–16). Cheltenham: Edward Elgar.

Fleischman, R. & Parker, L. (1991). *What is past is prologue: Cost accounting in the British Industrial Revolution 1760–1850*. New York: Garland Publishing.

FRC (Financial Reporting Council). (2015). *Key facts and trends in the accounting profession*. London: FRC.

Froud, J., Johal, S., Leaver, A. & Williams, K. (2006). *Financialization and strategy: Narrative and numbers*. London: Routledge.

Groysberg, B., Kelly, K. & MacDonald, B. (2011). The new path to the C-Suite. *Harvard Business Review*. March.

ICAEW. (2011). Key facts about ICAEW chartered accountants. www.icaew.com/en/join-us/become-an-icaew-chartered-accountant/key-facts-about-icaew-chartered-accountants, accessed 21 February 2016.

IEA. (2012). The soft 'renationalisation' of the energy sector. www.iea.org.uk/blog/the-%E2%80%98soft-renationalisation%E2%80%99-of-the-energy-sector, accessed 8 February 2016.

Johnson, H. T. & Kaplan, R. S. (1987). *Relevance lost: The rise and fall of management accounting*. Boston, Mass: Harvard Business School Press.

Kaplan, R. S. & Norton, D. P. (1992). The balanced scorecard as a strategic management system. *Harvard Business Review, 4*, 53–79.

Lowry, J. (1990). Management accounting and service industries: An exploratory account of historical and current economic contexts. *ABACUS, 26*(2), 159–184.

Nicolson, B. & Aman, A. (2008). *Offshore accounting: The case of India*. London: ICAEW.

ONS (Office for National Statistics in the UK). (2013). 170 years of industrial change across England and Wales. www.ons.gov.uk/ons/rel/census/2011-census-analysis/170-years-of-industry/170-years-of-industrial-changeponent.html, accessed 18 January 2016.

ONS (Office for National Statistics in the UK). (2014). Annual survey of hours and earnings: 2014 provisional results. www.ons.gov.uk/ons/rel/ashe/annual-survey-of-hours-and-earnings/2014-provisional-results/stb-ashe-statistical-bulletin-2014.html, accessed 11 January 2016.

ONS (Office for National Statistics in the UK). (2016). Annual survey of hours and earnings: 2016 provisional results. www.ons.gov.uk/employmentandlabourmarket/peopleinwork/earningsandworkinghours/bulletins/annualsurveyofhoursandearnings/2016provisionalresults.

Palley, T. (2007). *Financialization: What it is and why it matters*. Working paper series, no 153. UMASS.

Parker, D. (2003). Performance, risk and strategy in privatised, regulated industries: The UK experience. *International Journal of Public Sector Management, 16*(1), 75–100.

Parker, L. D. (2002). Re-inventing the management accountant. Transcript of the CIMA address delivered at Glasgow University, 15 March 2002. CIMA.

Pennington, M. (2010). *The global banking sector: Current issues*. London: CIMA.

Roslender, R. & Hart, S. (2002). *Marketing and management interfaces in the enactment of strategic management accounting practices: An exploratory investigation*. London: CIMA.

Rubery, J. (2015). Change at work: Feminisation, flexibility, fragmentation and financialization. *Employee Relations, 37*(6), 633–644.

Simons, P. (2007). Transforming finance. *Financial management*, pp. 36–37.

Stern, J. (2014). The British utility regulation model: Its recent history and future prospects. *Utilities Policy, 31*, 162–172.

Stern, J., Stewart, N. & Chew, D. (1995). The EVA Financial Management system. *Journal of Applied Corporate Finance, 8*(2), 32–46.

Tiley, C. (2010). CIMA: A history of innovation. www.cfoinnovation.com/story/1259/cima-history-innovation, accessed 8 March 2016.

Tyler, G. (2015). Financial services: contribution to the UK economy. House of Commons, standard note SN/EP/06193. http://researchbriefings.files.parliament.uk/documents/SN06193/SN06193.pdf, accessed 8 March 2016.

Warren, L. (2014). Management control, regulation and investment uncertainty in the UK electricity generation industry. In Otley, D. & Soin, K. (Eds.), *Management control and uncertainty*. Basingstoke: Palgrave Macmillan.

Warren, L. & Brickman, K. (forthcoming, 2017). External data sources – Industry benchmarks. In E. Harris (Ed.), *Performance, Management and Control* (Chapter 9). Abingdon: Routledge.

Wichramasinghe, D. & Alawattage, C. (2007). *Management accounting change: Approaches and perspectives*. Abingdon: Routledge.

Yazdifar, H. & Tsamenyi, M. (2005). Management accounting change and the changing roles of management accountants: A comparative analysis between dependant and independent organizations. *Journal of Accounting and Organizational Change, 1*(2), 180–198.

13 Management accountants in the United States

Evolving to meet the changing needs of practice

Kip Krumwiede and Raef Lawson

The emergence of management accountants/controllers in the U.S.[1]

Early years (1800–1865)

The history of cost accounting in the U.S. can be traced back to the New England textile industry of the early 1800s, where the development of large-scale manufacturing required cost information for a variety of managerial purposes.[2] Mill owners and managers needed to address issues such as make or buy, evaluating efficiency, analyzing prices to determine if they covered costs, expanding production capacity, etc. Their cost reports were not so helpful because they used simple averaging and allocation methods and usually ignored depreciation. The formation of railroad empires in the 1840s, with their ton-mile (later cost/ton) as a basic cost measure led to the emergence of accounting from bookkeeping.

The gilded age (1866–1899)

The job of management accountant in the U.S. emerged largely during the Industrial Revolution era. Previts and Merino (1998) discuss how after the American Civil War (1861–1865), the steel industry boomed due largely to demand from railroads moving westward. Albert Fink, a German-born civil engineer who worked for the U.S. Louisville and Nashville Railroad, often referred to as the "Father of Cost Accounting" in America, invented a form of activity-based costing. He divided costs into four categories: (1) maintenance and overhead that did not vary with the volume of traffic; (2) station personnel expenses that varied only with volume of freight; (3) fuel and other operating expenses which varied with the number of train miles run; and (4) fixed charges for interest. Using his cost model he converted costs in each category to a cost per ton-mile basis, monitored costs per ton-mile for the entire railroad, and determined the reasons for cost differences among the subunits.

Important developments in cost accounting took place as the industrial revolution began in the nineteenth century. Cost-focused Andrew Carnegie pioneered the use of cost accounting in his steel mills and used a large staff in his cost department. The assignment of the growing pool of overhead cost on the basis of prime cost or direct labor emerged along with assigning costs to cost centers based on routed steps. Industrial engineering began to influence management accounting in the 1890s as Fredrick Taylor developed his concept of "scientific management." Taylor's more systematic view of work led other industrial engineers to link work measurement to its costs.

Early profession (1900–1945)

The stock market crash of 1929 led to public outcry for more oversight of the business sector and had a significant impact on accounting practice. The importance of independent audits and accountants' role as professionals with obligations to stockholders was reemphasized (Previts & Merino 1998). Following the 1929 stock market crash, the U.S. Congress enacted the Securities Act of 1933 and the Securities Exchange Act of 1934, which created the Securities Exchange Commission (SEC). As a result, external financial reporting eclipsed management accounting as a priority in the United States, leading to stagnation of the latter field. It is for this reason that Johnson and Kaplan in 1987 stated that all in U.S. managerial accounting was known by 1925.

With the emergence of large industrial firms with multiple departments, businesses needed to develop cost systems. Most firms had bookkeeping departments under the supervision of the treasurer or secretary of the company (McKinsey, 1925). The bookkeepers mostly compiled financial data to be used in the collection and payment of debts and provided financial data to the "public accountant" who compiled the financial statements for creditors and investors. Gradually the head bookkeeper developed into a chief accountant, often independent from the secretary or treasurer and reported directly to the president of the company. As time passed, the chief accountant developed into a controller who became one of the chief executives of the company and became an "investigator, advisor and guide of the operations of his company" (McKinsey, 1925).

Typically, cost accountants focused more on tracking costs for financial reporting and engineers identified relevant costs for decision making. Because the main purpose of cost accounting was to support financial accounting, custody for cost accounting was given to the financial accountants. Cost information was primarily used for evaluating cost of inventories and financial reporting. Thus, the accounting department began to focus primarily on reporting for external users, a situation that exists to this day.

The scientific management movement of the late nineteenth century contributed significantly to the development of management accounting in the U.S., leading to the introduction of standard costing in the first decade of the twentieth century. Donaldson Brown, an engineering trained financial executive at DuPont and then at General Motors in the 1920s developed management accounting systems and techniques to manage the decentralized structure of these huge companies, including the return on investment (ROI) model, return on equity, flexible budgeting and financial forecasting (Johnson & Kaplan, 1987).

Economists and engineers are often given credit for originating most of the concepts and practices associated with modern management accounting (Johnson & Kaplan, 1987; Previts & Merino, 1998). Engineers such as Frederick Taylor, known as the father of scientific management, helped drive the need for more efficient and systematic production. Standard costing emerged to provide the information needed by engineers engaged in making production more efficient. The term "standards" was used instead of "estimates" based on the idea they were scientifically determined through time and motion studies. Another use of standard costing also emerged. Engineers started using variances between standard and actual performance for cost control. Variances were used to identify areas of focus, such as material prices (Johnson & Kaplan, 1987).

Around 1910 the rapid progress that cost accounting had experienced in the previous century suddenly came to a screeching halt and cost accounting entered a "dark age." The usage of cost accounting expanded, but the concepts and methods used were frozen for the next three-quarters of a century. One reason may have been collecting and processing the cost and other operating information required to support more advanced costing methods was just too difficult and expensive for the widening range of products being produced, thereby making it difficult to justify cost accounting's benefits. Instead, cost accountants used various simplified costing procedures that twentieth-century accountants adopted to measure the cost of inventories (and cost of goods sold) for financial reports (Johnson & Kaplan, 1987).

Meanwhile, economists began to show interest in applying microeconomic analysis to decision methods used in businesses, a field that became known as "managerial economics." Broadly defined, managerial economics is the application of economic concepts and economic analysis to the problems of formulating rational managerial decisions. One of the first to contribute was John Maurice Clark.

In 1923 Clark published *Studies in the Economics of Overhead Costs.* In his book, Clark discussed fixed and variable costs; joint, sunk, differential and residual costs; short and long run fluctuations; and a number of other issues from the economist's point of view. He also advocated that different costs should be used for different purposes, such as decision making versus financial reporting. It is considered one of the major contributions to cost accounting literature (Johnson & Kaplan, 1987). For example, Clark (1923, 235) states:

> if cost accounting set out, determined to discover what the cost of everything is and convinced in advance that there is one figure which can be found and which will furnish exactly the information which is desired for every possible purpose, it will necessarily fail, because there is no such figure.

The field of managerial economics continued its contributions to management accounting in the 1950s when economist Joel Dean introduced the use of Net Present Value, Discounted Cash Flow and Internal Rate of Return into the capital budgeting and project evaluation arena.

Post World War II (1945–1979)

Another cause for the slow development of management accounting in the U.S. was the lack of demand for better cost or management accounting information due in large part to the lack of competition for the major goods and services it provided. The period following World War II was one of generally high demand for products. The Du Pont ROI model dominated the performance management arena. The focus was on ROI and efficiency, and standard costs and variance analysis replaced actual costing. Costing and other management accounting practices remained largely unchanged through the early 1980s. In this pre-electronic age, where American manufacturing dominated the world, firms found it relatively easy to generate adequate profit margins and there was little demand for enhanced costing methods. Full absorption costing and cost-based pricing were the norm.

In 1977, the U.S. government enacted the Foreign Corrupt Practices Act (FCPA) which added to the responsibilities of U.S. management accountants. The Act legally requires companies to implement effective systems of internal control systems. The recent increased prosecution of companies under the FCPA has made compliance with the Act of great importance.

Renaissance of management accounting (1980–1999)

The 1980s were a major turning point in management accounting practice in the U.S. Much of the impetus for this change was the increased competitiveness of foreign manufacturers, which were developing sophisticated production systems and often also had lower input costs and output of higher quality.

Two events took place in 1984 that brought new life to the U.S. management accounting community. Eli Goldratt (co-author of "The Goal" promoting of Theory of Constraints) made a presentation at the NAA (now the IMA) Annual Conference discussing why "cost accounting is the number one enemy of pro-ductivity." That same year, Robert Kaplan (1984) of Harvard University pub-lished an article in the *Harvard Business Review* entitled "Yesterday's Accounting Undermines Production." These events set off a firestorm of activity among academics and consultants who were determined to find a way to restore the field of cost accounting to make it more relevant with the ever more complex and competitive global business environment.

Another important event was publication of Johnson and Kaplan's book *Relevance Lost* (1987). Their main thesis was that cost and management accounting systems in Western (mostly U.S.) firms were no longer providing rel-evant information for decision making and control. Their book helped fuel a drive toward more "relevant" accounting and performance measurement systems. Cooper and Kaplan (1988) introduced a new paradigm of cause-and-effect cost modeling, a revival of Albert Fink's ideas from the 1860s, and called it "Activity-Based Costing" or simply ABC. Further, a new focus on quality and nonfinancial measures emerged.

Early twenty-first century

Fraudulent reporting scandals at firms such as Enron, WorldCom and others in the late 1990s and early 2000s and the downfall of Arthur Andersen prompted increased debate regarding the ethical practice of accountancy in the U.S. A consequence of this was the passage of the 2002 Sarbanes-Oxley Act (SOX) by the U.S. Congress to protect shareholders and the general public from accounting errors and fraudulent practices by companies, as well as improve the accuracy of corporate disclosures. Additionally, SOX requires management at U.S. listed public companies to choose an internal control framework and then assess and report on its design and effectiveness annually. Both the Chief Executive Officer (CEO) and the Chief Financial Officer (CFO) of public companies must certify that they have evaluated the company's internal controls, that the company's financial statements are accurate and comply with the requirements of the exchange acts, and that the information reported is fairly presented (McMullen, Sanchez & Stout, 2011). Making false statements carries a penalty of up to 20 years in jail. The bulk of the responsibility for implementing, maintaining and evaluating the internal control framework typically falls on the accounting department.

One aspect of the American economy that distinguishes it from those in other countries is the relatively low level of government-owned entities. Owners (e.g. shareholders) expect management to allocate resources wisely and put significant pressure on management to run the business both legally and in a way that maximizes shareholder value. Controllers and financial managers have a fiduciary duty to report significant deviations from company policy in the areas of business ethics, compliance and financial reporting to the organization's CFO, Chief Audit Executive (CAE) and senior management. This fiduciary duty can be very challenging.

A key improvement in performance measurement by management accountants was an understanding of the need for both financial and nonfinancial measures to evaluate performance. Due to limitations in financial measures, the balanced scorecard and strategy maps based on the work of Kaplan and Norton (2004) became quite popular in the U.S. Gartner Group notes that over 50 percent of large U.S. firms have adopted the balanced scorecard approach (Balanced Scorecard Institute, 2016).

U.S. management accounting today

Today, approximately 20 percent of U.S. companies use ABC to some extent somewhere in their value chain (Stratton, Desroches & Lawson, 2009). Although those using ABC find it beneficial for decision making, with the introduction of many new costing approaches, the practice of management accounting has not kept pace with its theory.

In 2003 IMA and Ernst & Young published the results of a survey indicating that 98 percent of senior financial executives believed that the cost information they provided management for decision making was inaccurate while less than

20 percent indicated that they planned to do anything about it. There has been little evidence since then that the situation has improved. A major factor appears to be a lack of a demand for better cost information on the part of top-level management. Decision makers appear to either be oblivious to the fact that they are basing their decisions on irrelevant cost information or to be primarily focused on short-run performance measures. Additionally, they often do their own analysis for decision making (Johnson & Kaplan, 1987).

In the mid-2000s, there was a strong debate among academics and professionals in U.S. firms about whether costing systems should be more complex (Sharman, 2003a, 2003b; van der Merwe & Keys, 2002) or leaner (Fullerton, Kennedy & Widener, 2013; Grasso, 2005). However, neither approach has been implemented to a significant degree. Traditional costing methods are still the most prevalent.

Despite the potential benefits of lean accounting, Grasso (2006) reports that management accountants struggle to implement lean because it is very different than the traditional inventory reporting model. They tend to associate the lean philosophy with production and manufacturing only and have trouble abandoning traditional management accounting methods.

Resistance to change is a major issue affecting U.S. management accountants. Despite the recent development of more advanced costing systems, 80 percent of U.S. companies still use traditional (simple) costing methods. This is despite only 23 percent of companies being satisfied with their decision-support information and 35–45 percent believing their costing information is significantly distorted (Clinton & White, 2012).

Differences in culture and information systems are also reasons for the failure to adopt more advanced costing methods in the U.S. (MacArthur, 2006; Krumwiede & Suessmair, 2007). For example, after Germany-based Daimler-Benz merged with U.S.-based Chrysler Corporation in 1998, Daimler had difficulty getting Chrysler to use its detailed GPK system (Krumwiede, 2005). Chrysler had a much simpler costing system and very different culture and resisted the reporting requirements. This resistance to management accounting innovation is common in the U.S. where accountants often do not see the need for such sophisticated costing systems.

Strategic planning in the U.S. has been greatly influenced by the work of Michael Porter (1985), who suggested that firms must first identify their place in their industry's "value chain" before developing their strategy and planning. Unfortunately, operational and capital budgets for U.S. companies are often developed with little consideration of organizational strategy. Instead, they are based on short-term financial targets set by owners or investors and are developed top-down with little input from lower levels or thoughtful consideration of the firm's strategy. As a result, financial planning and analysis practices are consistently rated as one of the greatest concerns of finance professionals. For example, Clinton and White (2012) found "new budgetary procedures" to be one of the highest priorities initiatives of management accountants. Nevertheless, the majority of U.S. finance professionals still feel the traditional budgeting process is useful, especially for operational control and resource planning (Shastri & Stout, 2008).

A recent report by IMA found 64 percent of the management accountants surveyed (almost all from the U.S.) said they use spreadsheets in some way for revenue forecasting (IMA, 2016). Although many U.S. companies have implemented enterprise resource planning (ERP) systems, few accountants take advantage of the many features they offer such as greater automated budgeting capabilities and costing methods. Because the complexity of ERP systems makes implementation quite difficult, the goal for most U.S. accountants is to do the minimum required to enable the system to provide the same MA and financial reporting capabilities provided by the previous legacy system.

Clinton and White (2012) found that 66 percent of the respondents to their survey rated the role of cost management in their organization's overall strategic goals as important or very important as compared with 80 percent in a similar 2003 study. There are numerous reasons for this situation. Compared to other countries, U.S. firms are driven more by financial accounting and short-term profit pressures (Chow, Shields & Wu, 1999). Investment appraisal decisions tend to be based on ROI and payback period. Carr and Tomkins (1998) find U.S. firms place much lower priority on having precise answers to questions, have executives with shorter tenures and outlooks, use less thoroughness in decision making, and are more focused on short-term profit and dividend payouts. They tend to be slow to change or improve their management accounting systems and practices.

The evolving role of management accountants

Business partner

In recent years the role of U.S. accounting and finance professionals working in businesses and other organizations in the U.S. has expanded into many aspects of management decision making, employing both financial and nonfinancial information. With the expansion of the field of management accounting, the role of the management accountant is evolving from being a recorder and reporter of information to that of "business partner" with the senior management of an organization helping to achieve a company's strategy. The term "business partner" was first used by Lianabel Oliver (1991) in the U.S. to describe the expanding strategic role of CFOs. The idea became increasingly popular in the U.S. as the need grew for accounting information to help plan and implement strategy. Today, CFOs are increasingly expected to increase organizational value by having a strategic orientation and partner with other functional areas in the strategic decision making of the company (Siegel & Sorensen, 2002). In a recent IMA study, 76 percent of the financial executives indicated adding value is a high priority for their position (Lawson, 2013). These professionals are increasingly being asked to provide both financial and nonfinancial data.

Further, management accountants in the U.S. are increasingly being asked to partner with operations to provide both financial and nonfinancial data and analysis to enhance organizational decision making. For example, over two-thirds of U.S. senior finance and accounting leaders are being asked to lead, support, or measure (i.e. govern) innovation efforts in their organizations. And the more importance placed on innovation in the organization, the more comfortable the accounting and finance leaders are leading innovation efforts (Stroh, 2015).

On the positive side, their increasing support of strategic decision making is raising the profile of the management accountant within many U.S. organizations. It has led to more interaction with nonfinancial managers which in turn enhances the perception of the value of the finance function. On the downside, staff reductions in the name of short-term profitability have often stretched the finance team's ability to support this expanded role. Besides the inability to implement innovative management accounting techniques, there have been instances when internal controls over financial reporting has been compromised, either intentionally or unintentionally, leading to fraudulent reporting. These issues require management accountants in the U.S. to possess a wide array of skills to meet the expectations of their internal and external customers.

Required competencies of U.S. management accountants

The *Practice Analysis of Management Accounting* (Siegel & Kulesza, 1996) was the first national study of what management accountants in the U.S. actually do. The most important knowledge, skills and abilities (KSAs) were work ethic, analytical/problem-solving skills, interpersonal skills and listening skills. More recently, a study by the American Productivity and Quality Center (APQC, 2015) and the IMA found that companies are expecting more out of accounting graduates but not getting people with the skills they need. Their survey found the following competencies have the largest skill gaps: leadership; planning, budgeting and forecasting; strategic thinking and execution; cost management; internal financial reporting and performance management; and change management.

Status of management accountants in their organizations

Throughout the early 1900s, U.S. engineers and accountants made advances in cost accounting. However, "independent public accountants viewed cost accountants as employees and technicians, not as professionals, and the cost-accounting area remained tangential to the movement for professional status throughout the Progressive Era" (Previts & Merino, 1998, p. 180). Meanwhile, a commission was formed by Congress to investigate and report on whether large corporations had abused their power to negatively impact the nation's economic well-being. The fact that no accountants were invited reflects the lowly status of accountants at the time (Previts & Merino, 1998, p. 184).

Unfortunately, today many U.S. firms are driven by financial accounting and short-term external reporting pressures (Chow, Shields & Wu, 1999). As such, the evolution of the strategic role of the management accountant is taking place in an environment in which there is usually a stronger emphasis on financial reporting and weaker emphasis on management accounting relative to other countries. Clinton and White (2012) in their study of management accounting practice in the U.S. note: "Management accountants are clearly valuable strategic partners, but the longitudinal perspective presented by this study over a nine-year period does not show growth in the management accountant's role or initiative in cost management" (p. 43).

Cokins, Cherian, and Schwer (2015) similarly find common weaknesses in management accountants at U.S. companies. These include not understanding the decision making needs of the business they serve, emphasizing reporting needs and "hitting the numbers" over user needs, hesitance to report all relevant information to protect their jobs, resistance to change, being too busy doing reports to have time to add value, and an often combative culture between accounting and other managers. Their study highlighted how non-financial executives often view financial personnel at their organizations. Among the opinions expressed by non-accountants interviewed were:

> The paradox, which continues to puzzle me, is how chief financial officers and controllers can be aware that their management accounting data is flawed and misleading yet not take action to do anything about it.

> [Accountants are too] rigid because they want to be consistent across divisions. But if divisions are different, you can't give them all the same data because they have different data needs!

Typical profile of a US management accountant

Based on a recent study of IMA members (Krumwiede, 2016), the median age for management accountants is 47, about 60 percent male, 99 percent have a Bachelor's degree, and 55 percent have a graduate degree. The percentage of female management accountants is expected to continue to increase. U.S. management accountants have an average of 20 years of experience and 9 years with their current employer. The time with current employer has steadily decreased over time as it is much easier for them to change companies in today's online job market. Seventy-three percent have at least one professional certification.

Professional associations for U.S. management accountants

Institute of Management Accountants (IMA)

An important player in the development of management accounting in the U.S. has been the Institute of Management Accountants (IMA). World War I led to the advent of "cost plus" government contracts. The need to monitor and control the cost of these contracts led to more formalization of cost accounting practices. In 1919, Major J. Lee Nicholson, a cost accounting consultant who had led this formalization effort as a Major in the U.S. Army's Ordinance Department, founded the National Association of Cost Accountants (NACA) in Buffalo, New York. The purpose was to "promote knowledge and professionalism among cost accountants and foster a wider understanding of the role of cost accounting in management."[3] In 1925, the *NACA Bulletin* was introduced to provide articles and research on cost accounting issues. Prior to this there was a lack of detailed writings about management accounting methods (Previts & Merino, 1998).

Because the professional accounting associations of the day did not value the cost accounting area, NACA provided leadership in the cost area (Previts & Merino, 1998). Membership was open to all those interested in cost accounting and included many nonaccountants such as engineers. NACA published bulletins which brought cost accounting ideas to many businesses that needed to be convinced of the merits of more sophisticated costing methods. The timing was good because the Federal Trade Commission (FTC) and Department of Commerce were anxious to gather cost information so that businesses could earn "fair returns" on their investments. And accountants were usually the ones who tracked these costs.

In 1957, the name of the NACA was changed to the National Association of Accountants (NAA), recognizing that its membership extended beyond just cost accountants. In 1991, the organization's name was changed again to the Institute of Management Accountants (IMA), to signify its broader goals as an association for accountants and financial professionals working inside organizations.[4]

The IMA has played a key role in the history of management accounting in the U.S. The biggest occurred in 1972, when the IMA created the Certified Management Accountant (CMA®) certification to provide the first credential focused on the management accounting professional. This credential provided professional accountants working in companies an alternative to the CPA certification. As such, it helped to increase the stature of management accountants and management accounting in the profession (Previts & Merino, 1998). Also in 1972, IMA issued its first Statement on Management Accounting (SMA), *Concepts for Contract Costing*.

Another significant event occurred in 1983 when IMA issued its *Standards of Ethical Conduct of Management Accountants*, the first code of ethics for management accountants in the U.S. Today, these standards are taught to nearly all accounting and business students in their MA principles course. In 1992, IMA became a founding member of the Committee of Sponsoring Organizations of the Treadway Commission (COSO), a private-sector organization dedicated to improving the quality of financial reporting. In 1999, IMA relaunched and renamed its flagship magazine, *Strategic Finance*, and *Management Accounting Quarterly* debuted as an online journal focused more on MA academic research.

Today, the IMA has over 80,000 members. It provides many resources for management accountants in the U.S. including IMA's *Strategic Finance* magazine, *Management Accounting Quarterly, IMA Educational Case Journal* (IECJ), local chapter meetings, and online chat groups, webinars and news. Through its IMA Research Foundation, it funds both academic and practice-based research on issues of importance to management accounting professionals working in business.

Other associations

Besides NACA, an early association for cost accounting was the industry section of the AICPA (Sorensen, 2009). The American Institute of Certified Public Accountants (AICPA) and its predecessors have a history dating back to 1887. In 1916, there was a membership of 1,150. In 1936, the Institute agreed to restrict its future members to CPAs. In the 1957, the name was changed to its current name of the American Institute of Certified Public Accountants.[5] Today, the AICPA has over 400,000 members, most of whom work as public accountants.

A more recent professional association for management accountants in the U.S. is the joint venture between the Chartered Institute of Management Accountants (CIMA) and the American Institute of Certified Public Accountants (AICPA). This joint venture included a new designation for management accountants, the Chartered Global Management Accountant (CGMA), as well as conferences, online resources and a monthly magazine.

An organization for management accountants who rise to top management, or aspire to do so, is the Financial Executives International (FEI). FEI is an advocate for the views of corporate financial management. Its more than 10,000 members include CFOs, treasurers and controllers at companies from every major industry. It provides professional development through peer networking, career management services, conferences, research and publications. Members participate in the activities of 74 chapters in the U.S.[6]

Certifications for U.S. management accountants

Because the U.S. constitution gives states "residual powers" to oversee professional licensing and education, early efforts to organize accountants involved building separate state professional organizations (Previts & Merino, 1998). After various early accounting associations and states failed to unite to control and certify the growing ranks of accountants, the first CPA certificates were awarded in 1896 and 1897. Only a high school or equivalent education was required. In the early 1900s, several states passed CPA legislation and CPAs began forming separate professional associations. The CPA exam and licensing continue to be managed by states' boards of accountancy.

Because the content of the CPA exam is primarily geared toward public accounting, the CMA was established by the NAA (now IMA) as an alternative certification focusing on management accounting. To date, more than 50,000 CMA certificates have been awarded. The content of the CMA and other professional exams in the U.S. have evolved over time to encompass the skills needed by today's management accountants (Van Zante, 2010). Early topics no longer tested include linear programming, decision tree analysis and financial statement assurance. The exam initially consisted of five 3.5-hour exams including many topics covered by the CPA exam. The content of the exam was subsequently revised; the current exam is two 4-hour exams with much less overlap with the CPA exam. Newer topics added include top-level planning and analysis, internal controls, risk management and international financial reporting standards. In addition, all the major accounting certification exams including the CMA, CPA and CIA have increased ethics content in their exams as well as in the continuing education requirements (Bates et al., 2008).

A new CGMA credential was introduced in 2012 and for the first three years, was offered for a fee as an add-on designation, in which approximately 30,000 Certified Public Accountants (CPAs) were grandfathered into the program. In 2015, AICPA/CIMA introduced the CGMA exam for U.S. CPAs and which will soon be available to non-CPAs. The program includes three preparation phases; the exam consists of a one-part, 3-hour strategic case study.

Education for U.S. management accountants

Before WWI, it was relatively rare for most people to complete high school in the U.S. Although many professional accountants wanted to require at least a high school diploma for CPA certification, state legislators were reluctant to incorporate any education requirements (Previts & Merino, 1998). Thus it was common for accountants to not even have a high school diploma.

Accounting education in the U.S. has struggled to provide the necessary skills to students as the profession has evolved, creating a "skills gap" (Sorensen, 2009; Lawson et al., 2014). Numerous committees and commissions have called for change in accounting education, starting with the Ford Foundation and Carnegie Commission in 1959 (Gordon & Howell, 1959; Pierson, 1959). Additional calls for change came from the Trueblood Commission (Trueblood, 1963), the Bedford Committee (Bedford et al., 1986), and the Accounting Education Change Commission (Sundem, 1999), among others. Yet despite these recommendations, U.S. accounting education continues to largely focus on preparation for entry-level requirements in the field of accounting. Additionally, accounting education remains largely focused on preparing students for careers in public accounting/auditing, despite several attempts to align academic curricula with the demands and responsibilities of accounting practice (Lawson et al., 2014).

Throughout the first half of the twentieth century, college cost accounting texts emphasized the use of cost accounting for internal and external financial reporting. Then, in 1962, Charles Horngren published the first text that melded many of the managerial economics concepts with the half-century old cost accounting concepts to create a new type of cost accounting text entitled, *Cost Accounting: A Managerial Emphasis* (Horngren, 1962). The text emphasized the use of cost information for operational planning and control as well as for decision support. Almost by itself, his textbook changed the field. His objective was to demonstrate to faculty and students alike how the most important role of accounting within a company was as a management tool for making wiser decisions.

The greater emphasis on external financial reporting in the U.S. extends into academia. CPA firms hire a large proportion of the upper echelon accounting students in the U.S. Limited financial resources, along with the need to meet state education requirements for CPA certification, has led many schools to focus their programs in the areas of financial reporting and audit. However, new hires at CPA firms typically only stay with those firms two to four years, then move on to jobs with client companies. The lack of essential management accounting competencies has contributed to the tension between expectations as a strategic business partner and accountants' tendency to focus on financial reporting. Because their experience is primarily in public accounting, they tend to focus on financial reporting in their new company roles and let other departments – such as marketing, engineering and purchasing – take the lead in the area of decision analysis, an area where management accountants are increasingly expected to play an important role.

Conclusion

The management accounting profession in the U.S. today is at a crossroads. A strong focus on external financial reporting in the U.S. has resulted in an environment where financial accounting and audit tend to overshadow management accounting, both in academia and in practice. This focus threatens the "business partner" role that management accountants in the U.S. are being asked to fill and leads to numerous adverse consequences. In academia, many schools are failing to adequately prepare their students for their eventual careers in management accounting (Lawson et al., 2014). It has also resulted in a significant "gap" between academic management accounting research and practice (Hopwood, 2007; Kaplan, 2011; Merchant, 2012; Scapens, 2012; Tucker & Lawson, 2016). These issues have the potential to impact management accounting practice, including the failure, previously mentioned, of U.S. companies to adopt better management accounting techniques and engage in innovation practices, resulting in a failure to take advantage of potential profitability increasing and value creating opportunities.

There are efforts being made to counteract this trend, however. Professional associations such as the IMA promote the importance of the skills needed through certification and continuing education programs, media campaigns, support and endorsement of academic programs that teach the needed business and analytical skills, and conducting research aimed at help management accountants fulfill their role.

Companies are starting to ask U.S. education systems to do more to prepare accounting graduates for careers in today's world. For instance, the CFO of U.S. accounting firm PricewaterhouseCoopers LLP, said a lack of science, technology, engineering and mathematics education in primary and secondary school discourages students from going into related careers and makes accounting students less inclined to develop more technical competency. In response, this firm has increased its training to focus more on these and other business and leadership skills.[7]

Hopefully these efforts will lift the status of management accountants within the U.S. accounting education environment to help prepare them for careers in companies. Better training in strategic management, technical skills, strategic cost and risk management, and operational and decision support should help management accountants better fulfil the business partner role they are being asked to assume.

Notes

1 We appreciate the contribution of Douglas T. Hicks to this section.
2 For more information on the evolution of management accounting in the U.S., see Johnson and Kaplan (1987), Fleischman and Tyson (2007) and Sorensen (2009).
3 For more information about IMA's history, see www.imanet.org/about-ima/our-history.
4 For more information about the IMA, see the IMA website, www.imanet.org.
5 For more information, see the AICPA website, accessed December 23, 2016, www.aicpa.org/About/MissionandHistory/Pages/History%20of%20the%20AICPA.aspx.
6 For more information, see the FEI website, www.financialexecutives.org.
7 "The Plain-Vanilla Accountant Goes out of Style," *The Wall Street Journal*, May 19, 2015.

References

American Productivity and Quality Center (APQC). 2015. The skills gap in entry-level management accounting and finance, www.imanet.org/-/media/e1800c9dbb5b4c6eb25ad247f234ea50.ashx?la=en, accessed December 23, 2016.

Balanced Scorecard Institute. 2016. Balanced Scorecard Basics, http://balancedscorecard.org/Resources/About-the-Balanced-Scorecard, accessed September 1, 2016.

Bates, H. L., B. E. Waldrup & C. H. Calhoun. 2008. Ethics Education in U.S. accounting practice: A status report. Allied Academies International Conference. *Academy of Accounting and Financial Studies, Proceedings, 13*(1): 7–12.

Bedford, N., E. E. Bartholomew, C. A. Bowsher, A. L. Brown, S. Davidson, C. T. Horngren, et al. 1986. Future accounting education: Preparing for the expanding profession. *Issues in Accounting Education, 1*(1): 168–195.

Carr, C. & C. Tomkins. 1998. Context, culture, and the role of the finance function in strategic decisions: A comparative analysis of Britain, Germany, the U.S.A and Japan. *Management Accounting Research, 9*, 213–239.

Chow, C. W., M. D. Shields & A. Wu. 1999. The importance of national culture in the design of and preference for management controls for multi-national operations. Accounting, *Organizations and Society, 24*(5,6) (July/August), 441–461.

Clark, John Maurice, 1923. *Studies in the economics of overhead costs*. Chicago, Illinois: University of Chicago Press.

Clinton, D. & L. White. 2012. The role of the management accountant: 2003–2012. *Management Accounting Quarterly, 14*(1), Fall, 40–74.

Cokins, G., J. Cherian & P. Schwer. 2015. Don't be stuck in the last century. *Strategic Finance, 97*(4) (October), 26–33.

Cooper, Robin & Robert S. Kaplan, 1988. Measure costs right: Make the right decisions. *Harvard Business Review, 66*(5) (September), 96–103.

Fleischman, R. & T. Tyson. 2007. The history of management accounting in the U.S. In C. S. Chapman, A. G. Hopwood & M. D. Shields (Eds.), *Handbook of Management Accounting Research*. Amsterdam: Elsevier.

Fullerton, R. R., F. A. Kennedy & S. K. Widener. 2013. Management accounting and control practices in a lean manufacturing environment. *Accounting, Organizations and Society, 38*, 50–71.

Gordon, R. A. & J. E. Howell. 1959. *Higher education for business*. New York: Columbia University Press.

Grasso, L. 2005. Are ABC and RCA Accounting Systems compatible with lean management? *Management Accounting Quarterly, 7*(1) (Fall), 12–27.

Grasso, L. 2006. Barriers to lean accounting. *Cost Management, 29*(2), 6–19.

Hopwood, A. G. 2007. Whither accounting research? *The Accounting Review, 82*(5), 1365–1374.

Horngren, Charles T. 1962. *Cost accounting: A managerial emphasis*. Englewood Cliffs, NJ: Prentice-Hall.

Institute of Management Accountants (IMA). 2016. The new world of revenue management: How CFOs are embracing today's revenue models to bring more value to the business, www.imanet.org/docs/default-source/thought_leadership/external-reporting-and-disclosure-management/the-new-world-of-revenue-management.pdf?sfvrsn=2.

Johnson, H. T. & R. S. Kaplan. 1987. *Relevance lost: The rise and fall of management accounting*. Boston, MA: Harvard Business School Press.

Kaplan, R. S. 1984. Yesterday's accounting undermines production. *Harvard Business Review*, July/August, 95–101.

Kaplan, R. S. 2011. Accounting scholarship that advances professional knowledge and practice. *The Accounting Review, 86*(2), 367–383.

Kaplan, R. S. & D. P. Norton. 2004. Strategy Maps. *Strategic Finance, 85*(9), 26–35.

Krumwiede, K. R. 2005. Rewards and realities of German cost accounting. *Strategic Finance*, April, 27–34.

Krumwiede, K. R. 2016. 2015 U.S. Salary Survey, Institute of Management Accountants, www.imanet.org/insights-and-trends/salary-surveys.

Krumwiede, K. & A. Suessmair. 2007. Comparing U.S. and German cost accounting methods. *Management Accounting Quarterly, 8*(3) (Spring 2007), 1–9.

Lawson, R. 2013. Evolving Role of the Controller, Institute of Management Accountants, www.imanet.org//-/media/f02e5645dd5140fd8b3254997e76c68a.ashx?as=1&mh=200&mw=200.

Lawson, R. L., E. Blocher, P. C. Brewer, G. Cokins, J. E. Sorensen, D. E. Stout, et al. 2014. Focusing accounting curricula on students' long-run careers: Recommendations for an integrated competency-based framework for accounting education. *Issues in Accounting Education, 29*(2), 295–317.

MacArthur, J. B. 2006. Cultural influences on German versus U.S. management accounting practices. *Management Accounting Quarterly, 7*, 10–16.

McKinsey, J. O. 1925. Modern tendencies in accounting practice. *Journal of Accountancy, 39*(4) (April), 299–308.

McMullen, Dorothy A., Maria H. Sanchez & David E. Stout. 2011. Initial Public Offerings and the role of the management accountant. *Management Accounting Quarterly, 12*(2) (Winter), 11–23.

Merchant, K. A. (2012). Making management accounting research more useful. *Pacific Accounting Review*, 24(3), 1–34.

Oliver, Lianabel. 1991. Accountants as Business Partners. *Management Accounting* (June), 40–42.

Pierson, F. C. 1959. *The education of American businessmen: A study of university-college programs in business administration*. New York: McGraw-Hill.

Porter, M. E. 1985. *Competitive advantage*. New York: The Free Press.

Previts, Gary J. & Barbara D. Merino. 1998. *A history of accountancy in the United States: The cultural significance of accounting*. Columbus, OH: Ohio State University Press.

Scapens, R. W. 2012. Commentary: How important is practice-relevant management accounting research? *Qualitative Research in Accounting and Management*, 9(3), 293–295.

Sharman, P. A. 2003a. The case for management accounting. *Strategic Finance* (October), 43–47.

Sharman, P. A. 2003b. Bring on German cost accounting. *Strategic Finance* (December), 30–38.

Shastri, K. & D. E. Stout. 2008. Budgeting: Perspectives from the real world. *Management Accounting Quarterly, 10*(1) (Fall), 18–25.

Siegel, G. & C. S. Kulesza. 1996. The practice analysis of management accounting. *Management Accounting, 77*(10), 20–28.

Siegel, G. & J. E. Sorensen. 2002. *How to become a business partner*. Montvale, NJ: Institute of Management Accountants.

Sorensen, J. E. 2009. Management accountants in the United States: Practitioner and academic views of recent developments. In Christopher S. Chapman, Anthony G. Hopwood & Michael D. Shields (Eds.), *Handbook of Management Accounting Research*. Amsterdam: Elsevier.

Statton, William, Denis Desroches & Raef A. Lawson. 2009. Activity-based costing: Is it still relevant? *Management Accounting Quarterly, 10*(3) (Spring), 31–40.

Stroh, P. J. 2015. Advancing innovation: Galvanizing, enabling, and measuring for innovation value. Montvale, NJ: IMA®.

Sundem, G. L. 1999. *The Accounting Education Change Commission: Its history and impact*. Accounting Education Series, Volume 15.

Trueblood, R. M. 1963. Education for a changing profession. *Journal of Accounting Research, 1*(1), 86–94.

Tucker, B. & R. Lawson. 2016. Moving academic management accounting research closer to practice: A view from US and Australian professional accounting bodies. In M. J. Epstein & M. A. Malina (Eds.), *Advances in Management Accounting*, Volume 27 (pp. 167–206). Bingley: Emerald Group Publishing.

Van der Merwe, A. & D. E. Keys. 2002. The case for resource consumption accounting. *Strategic Finance, 83*(10) (April), 30–36.

Van Zante, Neal R. 2010. IMA's professional certification program has changed. *Management Accounting Quarterly* (Summer), 48–51.

Part II

Global factors influencing the role of management accountants

14 IT and the management accountant

Albrecht Becker and Rafael Heinzelmann

Introduction

Management accountants' work has always been mediated by technologies. Early precursors of management accounting in ancient Sumer/Mesopotamia (Ezzamel & Hoskin, 2002) or Egypt (Ezzamel, 2009) used various media to record transactions and methods of calculation. From the fourteenth century onwards, monasteries and the Christian church, universities and educational institutions began to develop and use ever more sophisticated techniques of measuring and recording performance-related information (Hoskin & Macve, 1986, 1996; Quattrone, 2004). In the nineteenth century mechanical calculation machines were developed and used by accountants, soon followed by the development of cash registers and the tabulator operating with punched cards, the 'Hollerith machine' and its competitors (McMickle, 2014 [1996]). After the Second World War, mainframe computers and later personal computers took over and the triumph of spreadsheet software – Visicalc, Lotus1–2–3 and MSExcel – followed (McMickle, 2014 [1996]). In the late 1980s the first integrated enterprise resource planning (ERP) systems were developed (Pollock & Williams, 2009) and included accounting modules (e.g. Granlund, 2011). The newest frontier are cloud-based services and mobile devices (ACCA & IMA, 2015; Strauss, Kristandl & Quinn, 2015). Working with these new technologies and tools always changed the work of management accountants (or their predecessors) and management accounting. While in the late nineteenth century when the accounting profession took shape these changes seem to have been accompanied by resistance and fear (McMickle, 2014 [1996]), today technological changes are met in a much more accepting and proactive manner, at least by the accounting profession (e.g. ACCA & IMA, 2015; CIMA, 2008). The accounting profession embraces new information technology in its discourse and attempts to mobilize it for their project of advancing the business partner role of management accountants.

In this chapter we concentrate on the more recent developments in the relation of IT and management accounting. In a first step we give an overview of existing research on the impact of ERP systems on management accountants' work, occupational roles and self-understandings. We then look into what is known about the impact of the latest information technological developments comprising cloud computing and mobile devices on management accounting. Concluding, we will then outline some topics and directions for future research on the relation between information technologies, management accounting and management accountants.

ERP systems and management accountants' work

Enterprise resource planning (ERP) systems are integrated software packages representing an organization's core processes, functions and formal account-ability structures. Modern ERP systems exhibit a client-server architecture with a core databank system and a periphery of functional and specialized systems (modules) drawing on this same core stock of data for their specific tasks. A client-server architecture provides the prerequisite for system and information integration across the whole organization. ERP systems comprise modules for financial and management accounting, e.g. SAP-FI (financial accounting) and SAP-CO (management accounting). Implementing ERP standard software pack-ages means changing organizational processes and structures, most often adapt-ing the latter to the former. An ERP system thus is far more than only a representation of an existing organization and its processes in the information system. Therefore, most research on accounting and ERP systems studies whether and how management accounting which has become an IT-enabled organizational practice changes when new ERP systems are implemented (Caglio, 2003; Dechow & Mouritsen, 2005; Dechow, Granlund & Mouritsen, 2007; Granlund, Mouritsen & Vaassen, 2013; Quattrone & Hopper, 2005; Sánchez-Rodríguez & Spraakman, 2012; Scapens & Jazayeri, 2003).

The design of ERP systems constitutes a major structuring force for manage-ment accountants' tasks and roles. This is specifically visible when these systems restrain management accounting in performing its tasks. A good example is pro-vided in the study of Dechow and Mouritsen (2005). They describe two cases where organizations implementing SAP "by the basic system set-up had given primacy to the logistics based representation of the firm through nonfinancial information over an accounting based representation of the firm through finan-cial information" (Dechow & Mouritsen, 2005, p. 703). This restricted the pro-duction of relevant financial and accounting data representing, for example, factory-specific cost accountabilities. As a consequence, the organization had to invent workarounds to repair these deficiencies. In the end this led to a situation in which management accounting became subservient to financial accounting and the logistics function.

Standard ERP systems comprise standard tools for management accounting. As customization encounters narrow boundaries due to time and resource restric-tions as well as the attempt to preserve system integrity, often management accounting has to confine its tools to the pre-set standard tools included in the ERP system. As Granlund (2011, p. 7) states, "solutions are not designed starting from specific requirements, but most choices have been pre-made by software vendors." This leads in some cases to management accountants and companies supplementing standard systems with – or even substituting them for – additional management accounting information systems (e.g. Granlund & Malmi, 2002; Heinzelmann, 2015; Hyvönen, 2003; Hyvönen, Järvinen & Pellinen, 2006). In both cases, sticking with the system standard or supplementing/substituting standard modules, ERP systems and their management accounting modules aim at standardizing monitoring, reporting and control procedures. Research has looked at this standardization through ERP systems from different angles. While some studies have described how the implementation of ERP systems have empowered management accountants to act in a more business partner-like role (Caglio, 2003; Goretzki, Strauss & Weber, 2013; Lindvall & Iveroth, 2011; Lodh & Gaffikin, 2003; Sánchez-Rodríguez & Spraakman, 2012; Scapens & Jazayeri, 2003), others have found ambiguous or even the opposite effects (Dechow & Mouritsen, 2005; Heinzelmann, 2012; 2016a, Jack & Kholeif, 2008; Quattrone & Hopper, 2005), or at least report serious resistance from managers toward a stronger role of management accountants (Wagner, Moll & Newell, 2011).

Several studies demonstrate that the implementation of ERP systems and related modules for management accounting tend to free management accountants from data gathering and entry as well as routine reporting tasks (e.g. Sánchez-Rodríguez & Spraakman, 2012). This provided management accountants in many cases described in the literature with the capacities as well as the opportunity for enacting a role as business partner and becoming "hybrid accountants" (Burns & Baldvinsdottir, 2005). Caglio (2003), for example, finds evidence for this hybridization of management accountants' roles following the implementation of an ERP system in the Italian case company, 'Pharmacom.' The CFO and the accounting function were drivers of the ERP implementation as they perceived it as an opportunity to enhance their status in the organization where they were perceived as non-value-adding 'bean counters'. The high amount of standardization of accounting procedures led, on the one hand, to constraining management accountants' scope for action and specifically limited their "discretion in applying the procedures for the collection, elaboration and provision of information" (Caglio, 2003, p. 141). On the other hand, it increased management accounting's perceived reliability and quality of service. Moreover, the high degree of system integration and the dominant role of the accounting function in the customization and implementation of the ERP system led to a high amount of collaboration and interdependence between management accounting and other functions. Overall, Caglio (2003, p. 142) concludes that: "In sum, accountants, as a consequence of the introduction of the ERP system, have experienced a phenomenon of 'hybridization,' deriving from the enlargement of their set of practices and legitimated competencies."

In a study of Canadian companies, Sánchez-Rodríguez and Spraakman (2012) demonstrate that ERP systems can drive accounting toward a greater standardization and automatization of activities. They found specifically that routine tasks in transaction processing, bookkeeping and compiling the chart of accounts were standardized and automatized. This left management accountants a significantly increased amount of capacity and time for more analytical tasks and also increased the availability and significance of non-financial information. Similarly, Lodh and Gaffikin (2003) and Scapens and Jazayeri (2003) find that when ERP systems are implemented management accountants' activities become stronger IT-based and IT-enabled. They also argue that through reducing the number of routine tasks management accountants' roles become enriched and change toward the model of the business partner. In a case study of Ericsson, Lindvall and Iveroth (2011) describe how the implementation of SAP/R3 paved the ground for standardizing as well as centralizing the finance and accounting function in a shared service center; this was made possible by the functionalities and core features of the ERP system allowing for data integration, centralization and standardization. Lindvall and Iveroth (2011) report that against this backdrop the management accountants were perceived as more proactive and customer-oriented in the company.

Heinzelmann's (2012, 2016a) study, however, demonstrates that implementing the same standard ERP system may lead to completely different effects on management accountants and management accounting in different contexts. He studied, inter alia, the implementation of SAP R/3 in the British subsidiary of an Austrian industrial company. The separation between the SAP FI and SAP CO modules represents a core component of the Germanic accounting model, i.e. the clear separation between the financial accounting and the management accounting function. Its promotion by the headquarters challenged the established role differentiation between management and financial accounting in the subsidiary. This initially created dissatisfaction due to the implicated challenge of management accountants' professional self-understanding and because the company's top-down approach was experienced as a coercive process, restraining local management accountants' scope for action. For example, all changes in cost centers now needed approval by and had to be implemented by headquarter staff. Over time, however, management accountants' sense-making changed in line with the new system. They began appreciating the new costing system as it allowed for a more detailed understanding and for 'drilling down' to deeper levels of costs incurrence. Heinzelmann (2012, 2016a) observed that the management accountants not only adopted the new vocabulary of management and cost accounting derived from SAP and the Germanic accounting tradition, but also enacted a role more distanced from operations and strategic processes that is characteristic of the Germanic model of 'Controlling' (Ahrens, 1999; Becker & Messner, 2005; Heinzelmann, 2016b; Messner et al., 2008). The management accountants now interacted with other functions predominantly mediated by the information system and they increasingly began to perceive operations as an organizational reality external to their sphere of influence. In this case the ERP system subjected management accountants to enacting a more distant role from functional management which seems to be clearly in tension with the ideal of the business partner.

From the studies reported above, with the exception of Caglio (2003), it is not always clear whether the role change and the occupational positioning of management accountants vis-à-vis other occupational groups such as functional managers and IT-managers is the result of a conscious strategy. Goretzki et al. (2013) report a case where the CFO and later CEO of a German company strategically mobilized a new ERP system and its new functionalities, among other 'allies', for positioning the management accounting function and the management accountants explicitly as business partners. Management accountants were able to position themselves as gatekeepers not only of improved and integrated management accounting information but also of the ERP system itself. Such strategic utilization of ERP systems and related knowledge and competencies is also propagated by the management accounting profession (e.g. CIMA, 2008).

This strategy of the profession and of individual CFOs, management accountants or accounting departments is, on the one hand, driven by a general professional project of strengthening the management accounting profession (see Chapter 4 of this volume). On the other hand, there are also concerns that management accounting's relevance may be challenged and thus its legitimacy come under threat as ERP systems may lead to the diffusion of management accounting information, tools and techniques (Caglio, 2003; Granlund, 2011), i.e. that 'every manager may become a management accountant'. This is the case, for example, in one of the cases Quattrone and Hopper (2005) describe ('Think Pink'). Here, the SAP system is designed and used in a way which allows a large number of decentralized managers inputting and manipulating data. The central management accounting function partly lost control over the system so that "everyone is an accountant now" (Quattrone & Hopper, 2005, p. 761). In a slightly different way, management accountants lose control and are disempowered in the cases reported by Dechow and Mouritsen (2005), where SAP was implemented following a logistics-driven logic which made it more or less impossible to produce management accounting data that could be linked to accountabilities of plant managers. Consequently, the accounting and control function was weakened inside the organization not making it possible for the management accountant to draw on the business partner role.

Wagner et al.'s study (2011) presents a case of resistance from managers to intended management accounting change and increased control by management accounting. They study the reconfiguration and implementation of an ERP system in a US Ivy League university. They show how initially the central administration including the accounting function used the ERP implementation project to gain more control over the decentralized units through standardization and integration of accounting. However, over time and due to strong resistance from departments that were used to do their budgeting and accounting by themselves the system was reconfigured and the previous rather decentralized organizational setup and use of accounting was reinstated.

Not surprisingly, research on the interplay of management accounting and processes of design, implementation and practicing of ERP systems has not resulted in a simple and unambiguous picture. As accounting and information systems are practiced in their specific organizational contexts (Hopwood, 1983), we should not expect to find uniformity in this field, either. What we can see, however, is that ERP systems have the potential to provide some specific challenges to management accounting and management accountants who are acting toward these challenges in diverse ways in specific situations. First, ERP systems provide the opportunity for automatizing a range of routine management accounting activities that have traditionally been associated with the 'bean counter' stereotype of accountants, such as collecting and inputting data and routine reporting (Järvinen, 2009). Second, availability of data for non-accountants often is improved, thus providing the opportunities for managers to challenge data accuracy and competencies of management accountants as well as increasing the demands put on them in terms of real-time data provision and a widened scope of analyses. Third, management accountants face the challenge to become more IT knowledgeable, be it just to be able to work with a new ERP system or to involve themselves in development and customization activities. Moreover, business intelligence tools are seen to provide a new challenge for management accountants' competence development (CIMA, 2008). As the studies cited above demonstrate, the implementation of new ERP systems and the related challenges have often resulted in what has been termed 'hybridization' of management accountants (Burns & Baldvinsdottir, 2005; Caglio, 2003), i.e. the inclusion of legitimate tasks, responsibilities and competencies that previously had been in the domain in other professional or occupational groups. In the case of management accountants this can mean two things: (1) including more managerial tasks because management accountants have been freed from routine accounting tasks and can act more like a business partner; and/or (2) including more IT tasks and competencies because management accountants may be deeply involved in ERP systems design and implementation. Also, it has been observed that management accountants and CFOs very consciously have mobilized ERP implementation projects to advance their occupational status within their organizations (see the example in Goretzki et al., 2013). We should be wary, however, of perceiving these instances of management accountants' increase in competencies and status as something following quasi-naturally from the potentials of ERP systems. Research has also found cases of resistance to attempts at extending management accountants' influence (Wagner et al., 2011) and examples of systems design (Dechow & Mouritsen, 2003) and implementation processes (Quattrone & Hopper, 2003) which resulted in management accountants losing power and influence or challenging the project of the business partner (Heinzelmann, 2012, 2016a).

Mobile and cloud computing

Mobile and cloud computing technologies have been introduced over the last years into organizations in different ways, most obvious probably in organizing relations with customers or clients. Cloud-based services which are at the same time accessible through all kinds of mobile devices are, for example, widely used in the entertainment industry. Today, cloud-based information technology and mobile devices have arrived in the domain of accounting. Probably because cloud and mobile computing have only recently been taken up more systematically in management accounting practice there is currently hardly any published research on these topics available. In the field of management accounting, the only exception so far seems to be a number of articles and a CIMA technical report by Strauss, Kristandl and Quinn (Kristandl, Strauss & Quinn, 2015; Strauss, Kristandl & Quinn, 2015; Strauss, Quinn & Kristandl, 2015) based on the 'WHU Controller Panel' (www.whu-on-controlling.com/en/network/whu-controller-panel). There are, however, some discussions in professional organizations such as CIMA and IMA on the impact of these new technologies on management accountants and finance professionals.

While ERP systems involve significant investments and are therefore more common in larger organizations, cloud-based solutions are usually less costly and therefore of high interest to SMEs (Murphy, 2015). Strauss, Kristandl and Quinn (2015) report that the scalability, cost efficiency and ease of system administration are the main reasons their respondents from SMEs named for adopting cloud-based solutions. Software-as-a-service (SaaS) solutions are attractive because the costly and resource-intensive activities of system maintenance and updating are outsourced to the service provider who amortizes investments over a large number of users (Murphy, 2015; on outsourcing the management accounting function, see Chapter 2 of this volume). Practically oriented articles such as Brands and Smith (2015), Howell (2015) and Murphy (2015) also expect that the pattern of providing and accessing management accounting data and reports will change and that mobile devices will be increasingly used. Therefore, issues of data/IT governance and security are in these authors' view the latest and probably most serious issues management accountants will have to deal with. Strauss, Kristandl and Quinn (2015), on the one hand, support this view as they find that security issues are the main concerns management accountants have regarding cloud computing. On the other hand, their results show that only a small number of respondents report frequent use of mobile devices for accessing management accounting and finance data. Their results also seem to frustrate the dreams uttered often in the professional literature that "Collaboration improves business performance by allowing teams to access work documents from any location and from almost any platform" (Brands & Smith, 2015; see also ACCA & IMA, 2015). Strauss, Kristandl and Quinn (2015, p. 7) rather find that patterns of decision making and collaboration have not changed in a significant way after introducing cloud technologies and mobile devices and conclude that "our research suggests that the role of the management accountant has not changed much as a result of cloud technologies."

"Moving to the cloud" (Howell, 2015) is expected to put pressure on management accountants to stay up-to-date on their knowledge of information systems, IT governance and data security. The professional literature unanimously urges management accountants to develop their IT-literacy and competencies (Brands & Smith, 2015). Moreover, we may expect that the development toward real-time data availability and extended possibilities of on-demand analyses will make a problem stand out more pronounced that has already been identified in relation to ERP systems: On the one hand, greater availability of and access to data for functional managers may threaten the reputation, legitimacy and standing of management accountants. On the other hand, it creates specific dangers because these data and reports always have to be interpreted and contextualized:

> Nonetheless, although SoMoClo [social, mobile and cloud technologies] offers great opportunities to make financial data more readily available to the wider business, that does not mean that users will automatically be empowered or have the necessary expertise or context to interpret and use that data.
>
> (ACCA & IMA, 2015, p. 23)

Moreover,

> The expansion of dashboards, data analysis, and other tools that management increasingly relies on creates risk for organizations: The information appears reliable but may be incorrect. Management accountants' skills are needed to assess that this information is indeed reliable.
>
> (Murphy, cited in Brands & Smith, 2015)

The management accounting profession, therefore, sees this as a major opportunity for management accountants to deepen and stabilize their aspired role of business partner.

Summarizing, it is fair to say that a lot of what the professional literature predicts and/or projects as necessary or desirable for management accountants seems plausible and understandable. In fact, however, we have very little reliable knowledge about the effects of cloud and mobile technologies' impact. From the perspective of management accounting research this may, on the one hand, be disappointing. On the other hand, it provides a whole new and promising field of empirical research.

Conclusions and directions for further research

Summarizing what we know about IT and management accountants we can tentatively conclude the following. In terms of management accountants' tasks information technology has the – often realized – potential to automatize and thus free management accountants from routine operational tasks such as data gathering, data inputting and preparing routine reports. This is independent from the question whether it is an ERP system running on the organization's own servers or a cloud-based solution. Further, management accountants seem to be often involved in customization and implementation of ERP systems or in the selection of service providers. The proximity to IT-related issues requires often that management accountants acquire qualifications in the IT field. Potentially, management accountants can also use the capacities freed through automatization to concentrate more on their aspired business partner role. The literature very explicitly sees not only the opportunity but also a kind of functional necessity for this new role as managers should not be left alone with their new possibilities of data access brought about by information systems. The newer developments toward cloud-based computing and mobile devices ('SoMoClo') could aggravate this possible issue. Overall, the majority of studies on management accounting and ERP systems seems to suggest that the phenomenon of hybridization and enacting a business partner role following system implementation is more prevalent than the sometimes uttered apprehension of de-valuing management accounting. We have, however, cited some studies which showed that ERP system implementation may under certain conditions also lead to disempowering management accounting. How this tendency will realize in the case of SoMoClo is currently just not known.

Consequently, a first conclusion regarding directions for further research is a very general call for more research on the interrelation, or interaction, of information technologies and management accounting. We emphasize that this research should study the practice of management accounting in an environment that is deeply imbued with different information technologies (Granlund, 2011). In most organizations information technology plays a major role whether it is SAP or some small software package running on the management accountant's personal computer. To understand how management accounting practice and information technology interact it may be helpful to use an ethnographic or related methodology, thus acknowledging the importance of context and embeddedness of these practices as well as focusing on the interplay of management accounting and information technology. Taking a sociomateriality perspective (Orlikowski & Scott, 2008) or an actor-network and STS (Science and Technology Studies) perspective (Bijker, Hughes & Pinch, 1987; Latour, 2005; Law, 1992) might be specifically helpful.

Research on the relation of management accounting and information systems has often touched upon the issue of professional identity of management accountants, though mostly framed as hybridization (e.g. Caglio, 2003) or moving toward a business partner role (e.g., Scapens & Jazayeri, 2003; Goretzki et al., 2013) rather than explicitly in terms of professional identity (a notable exception is Heinzelmann, 2012, 2016a). In these studies, changing roles or professional identities are mostly analyzed as an issue of the management accountants involved, e.g. in terms of qualification and competencies. It might, however, be an interesting direction for further research to look more into the potential lines of inter-professional conflict over jurisdictions (Abbott, 1988) and the boundary work entailed (Gieryn, 1983; Lamont & Molnár, 2002). The research available on cloud-based and mobile computing and management accounting demonstrates that issues of IT governance, for example, will be of increasing importance, as well as issues of customization, selection of providers of cloud-based services. These issues touch on questions of jurisdictions, responsibilities and accountabilities. It seems plausible that more or less severe inter-professional or inter-occupational conflicts may arise between management accountants and IT personnel. This again should impact the possibilities and constraints for management accounting in a strongly IT-based environment. These issues may be amplified by developments in the context of 'Big Data' analysis, translated as 'business analytics' into the context of business organizations (Acito & Khatri, 2014; Manyika, Chui, Brown et al., 2011) where management accounting's role and jurisdictional claims seems even more open for challenge.

In research on IT and management accounting artefacts such as IT tools, graphical and numerical representations etc. are strikingly absent. From Strauss, Kristandl and Quinn (2015) we know that reports and information from cloud-based systems are almost exclusively presented to users in a mixed graphic and numerical format which is suited for mobile devices like smartphones or tablets. On the other hand, we know that among management accountants but also many managers Excel spreadsheets are very popular and are widely used, despite the fact that special interfaces have to be designed to connect them to standard ERP or similar software (Morato & Weber, 2016). Therefore, the tools and representations themselves seem to matter and make a difference. For example, we know from accounting history how new forms of representing information paved the way for developing modern accounting and double-entry bookkeeping (Hoskin & Macve, 1986, 1988; also Quattrone, 2009). Another example is the study by Pollock and D'Adderio (2012) who demonstrate the performative capacity of a specific four by four matrix, the 'magic quadrant' of the industry analyst firm Gartner Inc. It literally constructs IT-market segments. These are just some more or less randomly picked examples from a wide range of literature drawing on Foucauldian studies (Miller & Power, 2013) and social studies of technology (STS; cf. Bijker et al., 1987; Latour, 1999) to argue we should not forget the technologies themselves when we talk about IT and management accounting. Specifically, when management accounting knowledge is increasingly disseminated within an organization using specific graphical formats displayed on mobile devices we might ask how this constructs a specific accounting reality. Is this a different reality from the one created by spreadsheets? How does a new format impact management accountants and their tasks? Does it change the role of interpreter of accounting information claimed by management accountants? Does it change management accountants' powers to involve themselves in decision making?

A last area where we see potential for interesting research on the relation of management accounting and information systems regards the development of the systems themselves. In parallel to the observation Pollock and Williams (2009) in their study on the development of enterprise-wide ERP systems we can state that basically all the research studies on IT and management accounting are studies of implementation and sometimes customization of standard systems. In the same way as Pollock and Williams state a lack of systematic research on the genesis and construction of standard ERP systems in general, we observe a lack of studies on the construction of management accounting-related system components. We see this as a severe gap in our knowledge not least because the systems in question are based on specific techniques of calculation which are not always self-evident, as, for example, the case reported by Heinzelmann (2012, 2016a) demonstrates.

To summarize, we have identified at least four promising areas for further research into the relation between management accounting practice, management accountants and information technology. It seems plausible that this list is not exhaustive, not least because of the rapid developments in organizational practice. What seems as obvious as astonishing, however, is the fact how little we still know about the issue regarding the fact that for many years now management accounting has been a practice highly influenced by IT.

References

Abbott, A. (1988). *The system of professions: An essay on the division of expert labor.* Chicago: University of Chicago Press.

ACCA & IMA. (2015). *SoMoClo technologies: Transforming how and where business takes place.* London and Montvale, New York: Association of Chartered Certified Accountants and Institute of Management Accountants.

Acito, F. & Khatri, V. (2014). Business analytics: Why now and what next? *Business Horizons, 57*(5), 565–570.

Ahrens, T. (1997). Talking accounting: An ethnography of management knowledge in British and German brewers. *Accounting, Organizations and Society, 22*(7), 617–637.

Ahrens, T. (1999). *Contrasting involvements: A study of management accounting practices in Britain and Germany.* London: Routledge.

Becker, A. & Heinzelmann, R. (2013). *Management Accounting und Controlling: Ausbildungstraditionen in Großbritannien und im deutschsprachigen Raum Jahrbuch für Controlling und Rechnungswesen 2013* (pp. 73–100). Vienna: LexisNexis.

Becker, A. & Messner, M. (2005). After the scandals: A German-speaking perspective on management accounting research and education. *European Accounting Review, 14*(2), 417–427.

Bijker, W. E., Hughes, T. P. & Pinch, T. J. (eds.) (1987). *The social construction of technological systems: New directions in the sociology and history of technology.* Cambridge, MA: MIT Press.

Brands, K. & Smith, P. (2015). Raise your technical intelligence. *Strategic Finance*, (May 2015). Retrieved from http://sfmagazine.com/post-entry/may-2015-raise-your-technical-intelligence.

Burns, J. & Baldvinsdottir, G. (2005). An institutional perspective of accountants' new roles: The interplay of contradictions and praxis. *European Accounting Review, 14*(4), 725–757.

Caglio, A. (2003). Enterprise resource planning systems and accountants: Towards hybridization? *European Accounting Review, 12*(1), 123–153.

CIMA. (2008). *Improving decision making in organsations: Unlocking business intelligence.* London: Chartered Institute of Management Accountants.

Dechow, N. & Mouritsen, J. (2005). Enterprise resource planning systems, management control and the quest for integration. *Accounting, Organizations and Society*, 30(7–8), 691–733.

Dechow, N., Granlund, M. & Mouritsen, J. (2007). Interactions between modern information technology and management control. In T. Hopper, D. Northcott & R. W. Scapens (Eds.), *Issues in Management Accounting* (pp. 45–63). London: Prentice Hall.

Ezzamel, M. (2009). Order and accounting as a performative ritual: Evidence from ancient Egypt. *Accounting, Organizations and Society, 34*(3–4), 348–380.

Ezzamel, M. & Hoskin, K. (2002). Retheorizing accounting, writing and money with evidence from Mesopotamia and ancient Egypt. *Critical Perspectives on Accounting, 13*(3), 333–367.

Gieryn, T. F. (1983). Boundary-work and the demarcation of science from non-science: Strains and interests in professional ideologies of scientists. *American Sociological Review 48*(6), 781–795.

Goretzki, L., Strauss, E. & Weber, J. (2013). An institutional perspective on the changes in management accountants' professional role. *Management Accounting Research, 24*(1), 41–63.

Granlund, M. (2009). On the interface between management accounting and modern information technology: A literature review and some empirical evidence. Working Paper, University of Turku.

Granlund, M. (2011). Extending AIS research to management accounting and control issues: A research note. *International Journal of Accounting Information Systems, 12*(1), 3–19.

Granlund, M. & Malmi, T. (2002). Moderate impact of ERPS on management accounting: A lag or permanent outcome? *Management Accounting Research, 13*(3), 299–322.

Granlund, M. & Mouritsen, J. (2003). Special section on management control and new information technologies. *European Accounting Review, 12*(1), 77–83.

Granlund, M., Mouritsen, J. & Vaassen, E. (2013). On the relations between modern information technology, decision making and management control. *International Journal of Accounting Information Systems, 4*(14), 275–277.

Heinzelmann, R. (2012). *Diverging identities and professions in European management accounting*. Unpublished doctoral dissertation, Innsbruck.

Heinzelmann, R. (2015). Managing conflicting logics of beyond budgeting and enterprise resource planning systems. Beta. *Scandinavian Journal of Business Research, 29*(1), 27–48.

Heinzelmann, R. (2016a). Accounting logics as a challenge for ERP system implementation: A field study of SAP. Working Paper, NHH Norwegian School of Economics.

Heinzelmann, R. (2016b). Comparing professions in UK and German-speaking management accounting. *Accounting in Europe, 13*(1), 103–120.

Heinzelmann, R. & Becker, A. (2013). Controlling und ERP-Systeme: State of the Art und Forschungsperspektiven. *Jahrbuch für Controlling und Rechnungswesen 2014* (pp. 147–172). Vienna: LexisNexis.

Hopwood, A. G. (1983). On trying to study accounting in the contexts in which it operates. *Accounting, Organizations and Society, 8*(2–3), 287–305.

Hoskin, K. & Macve, R. H. (1986). Accounting and the examination: A genealogy of disciplinary power. *Accounting, Organizations and Society, 11*(2), 105–136.

Hoskin, K. & Macve, R. (1996). The Lawrence Manufacturing Co.: A note on early cost accounting in US textile mills. *Accounting, Business and Financial History, 6*(3), 337–361.

Howell, J. (2015). Moving to the cloud. *Strategic Finance*, June 2015. Retrieved from http://sfmagazine.com/post-entry/june-2015-moving-to-the-cloud.

Hyvönen, T. (2003). Management accounting and information systems: ERP versus BoB. *European Accounting Review, 12*(1), 155–173.

Hyvönen, T., Järvinen, J. & Pellinen, J. (2006). The role of standard software packages in mediating management accounting knowledge. *Qualitative Research in Accounting and Management, 3*(2), 145–160.

Jack, L. & Kholeif, A. (2008). Enterprise resource planning and a contest to limit the role of management accountants: A strong structuration perspective. *Accounting Forum, 32,* 30–45.

Järvinen, J. (2009). Shifting NPM agendas and management accountants' occupational identities. *Accounting, Auditing and Accountability Journal, 22*(8), 1187–1210.

Kristandl, G., Quinn, M. & Strauß, E. (2015). Controlling und Cloud Computing: Wie die Cloud den Informationsfluss in KMU verändert. *Zeitschrift für KMU und Entrepreneurship, 63*(3–4), 281–304.

Lamont, M. & Molnár, V. (2002). The study of boundaries in the social sciences. *Annual Review of Sociology, 28,* 167–195.

Latour, B. (1999). On recalling ANT. *The Sociological Review, 47*(S1), 15–25.

Latour, B. (2005). *Reassembling the social: An introduction to actor-network-theory.* New York: Oxford University Press.

Law, J. (1992). Notes on the theory of the actor-network: Ordering, strategy, and heterogeneity. *Systems Practice, 5*(4), 379–393.

Lodh, S. C. & Gaffikin, M. J. (2003). Implementation of an integrated accounting and cost management system using the SAP system: A field study. *European Accounting Review, 12*(1), 85–121.

Lindvall, J. & Iveroth, E. (2011). Creating a global network of shared service centres for accounting. *Journal of Accounting and Organizational Change, 7*(3), 278–305.

Manyika, J., Chui, M., Brown, B., Bughin, J., Dobbs, R., Roxburgh, C. & Byers, A. H. (2011). *Big data: The next frontier for innovation, competition, and productivity.* McKinsey Global Institute.

McMickle, P. L. (2014 [1996]). Computing technology in the West: The impact on the profession of accounting. In M. Chatfield & R. Vandermeersch (Eds.), *The history of accounting: An international encyclopedia* (pp. 145–150). London: Routledge.

Messner, M., Becker, A., Schäffer, U. & Binder, C. (2008). Legitimacy and identity in Germanic management accounting research. *European Accounting Review, 17*(1), 129–159.

Miller, P. & Power, M. (2013). Accounting, organizing, and economizing: Connecting accounting research and organization theory. *Academy of Management Annals, 7*(1), 557-605.

Morato, R. & Weber, J. (2016). Rouven Morato im Dialog mit Jürgen Weber: "Wir ziehen Daten live und in Farbe raus, um sie im System darzustellen." *Controlling and Management Review, Sonderheft 1* (2016), 24–30.

Murphy, G. (2015). Should the cloud be in your future? *Strategic Finance,* April 2015. Retrieved from http://sfmagazine.com/post-entry/april-2015-should-the-cloud-be-in-your-future.

Orlikowski, W. J. & Scott, S. V. (2008). Sociomateriality: Challenging the separation of technology, work and organization. *The Academy of Management Annals, 2*(1), 433–474.

Pollock, N. & D'Adderio, L. (2012). Give me a two-by-two matrix and I will create the market: Rankings, graphic visualisations and sociomateriality. *Accounting, Organizations and Society, 37*(8), 565–586.

Pollock, N. & Williams, R. (2009). *Software and organizations: The biography of the enterprise-wide system or how SAP conquered the world.* London and New York: Routledge.

Quattrone, P. (2004). Accounting for God: Accounting and accountability practices in the Society of Jesus (Italy, XVI–XVII centuries). *Accounting, Organizations and Society, 29*(7), 647–683.

Quattrone, P. (2009). Books to be practiced: Memory, the power of the visual, and the success of accounting. *Accounting, Organizations and Society, 34*(1), 85–118.

Quattrone, P. & Hopper, T. (2005). A ["]time-space odyssey": Management control systems in two multinational organisations. *Accounting, Organizations and Society, 30*(7–8), 735–764.

Sánchez-Rodríguez, C. & Spraakman, G. (2012). ERP systems and management accounting: A multiple case study. *Qualitative Research in Accounting and Management, 9*(4), 398–414.

Scapens, R. W. & Jazayeri, M. (2003). ERP systems and management accounting change: Opportunities or impacts? A research note. *European Accounting Review, 12*(1), 201–233.

Strauß, E., Kristandl, G. & Quinn, M. (2015). *The effects of cloud technology on management accounting and decision making.* Research executive summary series, 10(6). London: Chartered Institute of Management Accountants.

Strauß, E., Quinn, M. & Kristandl, G. (2015). Möglichkeiten und Grenzen eines IT-gestützten Controlling- und Reportingsystems für mittelständische Unternehmen mit mobilen Endgeräten. *Controlling, 27*(6), 313–317.

Wagner, E. L., Moll, J. & Newell, S. (2011). Accounting logics, reconfiguration of ERP systems and the emergence of new accounting practices: A sociomaterial perspective. *Management Accounting Research, 22*(3), 181–197.

15 Agent or victim?

Shared services and management accounting

Will Seal

Introduction

Although there are many variations of shared service models (SSM),[1] this chapter focuses on the captive shared service organization (CSSO) which may be defined as "wholly owned subsidiaries that provide services, in the form of back office activities, to the parent company" (Oshri, 2011, p. 1). Similarly, Strikwerda defines the CSSO as "an accountable entity in the internal organization of a firm or institution, tasked to deliver specialized services to operational units (business units, divisions) on the basis of a service level agreement" (2014, p. 3). Strikwerda argues that the philosophy of the CSSO challenges the multi-divisional corporation (M-form) which traditionally was free to decide on issues such as how to source its business support services. This focus on the role of the CSSO in the M-form is also reflected in Sako's (2006) distinction between vertical disintegration of services and corporate unbundling. In her paper, the CSSO may be depicted as the outcome of a 'horizontal' restructuring as the M-form moves corporate support functions, including finance and accounting, out of its semi-autonomous divisions into new corporate units that are sometimes specialized or multi-functional (Sako, 2006).

Much of the small and emergent academic literature on the CSSO draws on an eclectic mix of economic, organizational and strategic theories (Davis, 2005; Sako, 2006; Gospel & Sako, 2010; Helper & Sako, 2010; Oshri, 2011; Seal & Herbert, 2013a; Bondarouk, 2014) from which it is difficult to develop a single compelling explanation. In contrast with some of the more sceptical views on the CSSO in the academic literature, practitioner sources (Quinn et al., 2000; Schulman et al., 1999) have created a positive rhetoric that identifies a number of key characteristics of the CSSO. First, the CSSO is customer-oriented, with the customer being the M-form's operating business units; the CSSO has a high morale because (in contrast to support services in the old M-form) delivering business services is its core business. The level of services are determined by the operating units with the allocation of budgets based on demand and costs per unit calculated and managed via a service level agreement (SLA). Service demand is documented in the SLA together with the CSSO's accountability for the quality of services and cost of its services (Strikwerda, 2014). Finally, the SSM is located optimally from an operational perspective. Yet, in practice, many of the positive features identified above either are not put into practice (e.g. lump sum allocation rather than re-charging based on demand) or driven by cost saving (e.g. location based on low cost labour arbitrage rather than optimal operationality). Indeed, although the practitioner rhetoric associated with the CSSO evokes images of innovation and progress, it is argued in this chapter that, in many ways, the work processes in the CSSO are not new but rather represent an expansion of tried and tested factory forms of control into service work (Seddon, 2005, 2008). Indeed, if there is novelty then it might lie in the deployment of more totalizing modes of technological control (Bain & Taylor, 2000).

With a more sceptical take on the CSSO, there are many possible issues emerging from the SSC phenomenon: scope (which services), relationship with head office/corporate HQ, location (domestic, inshore, offshore, backshoring), accountability (e.g. SLA, charging cost allocation), trends and developments in the CSSO (e.g. transaction versus transformational). Although the chapter will touch on some of these issues, the main focus will be on the role of management accounting. It is submitted that the phenomenon of corporate unbundling raises a number of fundamental questions for the role of accounting in organizations. Is management accounting primarily the agent of change or the victim? This question is prompted by another question: is accounting a secondary support function as suggested by Porter's (1985) value chain concept or does it lie at the heart of the corporation's governance structures and processes? Strikwerda (2014) submits that just as the CSSO challenges the principles and practices of the M-form then management accounting has been resistant to the development of networked organizations. In short, since he argues that it has a vested interest in preserving the traditional M-form with its systems of cost, profit, investment centres and transfer prices, any move away from the traditional structures may cast management accounting as the victim of the CSSO model. Yet against this victim narrative, the chapter will also argue that although many accounting activities are 'packed off' to either specialist or multi-functional CSSOs, the practices of calculation (Miller, 2001) and control at a distance (Robson, 1992) associated with management accounting can also be deployed in the new structures making it the agent rather than the victim of these types of organizational changes.

The research questions mean that the chapter is structured into three main sections. The first section reviews the mainstream view that accounting along with other support services is largely the victim of the change to the CSSO. The second section takes an alternative view arguing that management accounting is the agent of organizational change. Finally, there is some discussion which synthesises these positions.

Management accounting as a 'victim' of the CSSO

Some motives for unbundling

The managerial discourse for the CSSO is written from the point of view of the parent company where the most obvious advantage for the parent company is that by concentrating service activities in one site, specially chosen for the purpose, the company can reduce costs. Some authors have suggested that an 'easy' 25–30 per cent reduction in costs is possible with the promise of progressive pressure on the CSSO as it itself may be threatened by outsourcing to an even lower cost location (Quinn et al., 2000). But it is also argued that there are more than cost advantages. It is often claimed in the consultancy literature that the CSSO should provide better service than the old service departments. There was always a danger that employees in the business units saw themselves as fulfilling low status 'back office functions'. The CSSO can focus its core competencies, standardize processes and apply the best technology appropriate to a service business. The appropriate technology may involve ERP systems combined with other technologies used in call centres which link voice, video and data interaction capability (Schulman et al., 1999). The standardization and technology may mean that the CSSO can possibly employ cheaper junior staff but the scale and new focus of the organization should also enable it to recruit and concentrate top experts and professionals.

Yet, the managerialist conceptualizations of SSCs suffer from a number of limitations. There is an understandable narrowness of perspective and a lack of reflection on concepts such as cost and efficiency. How are the costs and benefits measured and if efficiency is enhanced, how can that be tested? In the formation of a CSSO in a large electricity company, Herbert and Seal (2012) found that the consultancy narrative had resonance with key actors although the rationalization of the SSO was largely justified on reductions in headcount from which cost savings were assumed to flow. The authors also noted that any savings could only have been assessed with data supplied from the divisions who had an obvious scope for political posturing. The language and outlook of the consultancy discourse seemed to represent native categories in the eyes of the managers in both the SSO and its user departments. They all suggested that the key motivation for the SSO was economic or at least cost-saving. So that although from a research perspective, the SSO needs to be interpreted via broader and more reflective perspectives, the chosen framework should acknowledge the pressures and opportunities of acting in a twenty-first century capitalist environment (Marglin, 1974; Edwards, 1979). In short, it should be broad enough to understand as well as critique the functionalist perspective.

Yet, as will be argued later, it is difficult to demonstrate either theoretically or empirically that the delivery of support services through a remote SSC can provide better information for decision making. Perhaps a consultant/provider-dominated discourse cannot be expected to countenance the awful possibility that the entire SSM project not only fails to provide better information but may even lead to either a loss of intellectual capital or at least its relocation away from where it might be most productively deployed. These issues are beginning to be explored in the academic literature (Gospel & Sako, 2010; Maatman et al., 2010).

The academic literature has tried to understand the CSSO by drawing on strategic and contractual theories. For example, building on Porter (1985), Gospel and Sako (2010) argue that it may be possible to classify corporate activities into primary value adding activities and support activities which may be either tightly or loosely coupled to the primary activities. Drawing on Teece's (2009) concept of dynamic capabilities, Gospel and Sako submit that "operational capabilities are more widely diffused in the firm and outsourceable, whilst dynamic capabilities are more concentrated and not subject to outsourcing" (2010, p. 8). This typology of capabilities suggests how service functions may be divided up into those which are to be sent to the CSSO or outsourced and those which are to be retained 'on site'. As much of the terminology implies, corporate unbundling usually has a strong *spatial* dimension. At the most mundane level, it implies a change from a user of support services just being able to 'pop their head round the door', or walk down the corridor or even visit a location in the same building. The physical manifestation of unbundling involves moving support services to a special building, off-site or even off-shore. The spatial reordering may also be a matter of lay-out in specialized buildings with a grouping together of 'end-to-end' process teams and a working environment which some critical researchers have characterized as 'service factories' (Taylor & Bain, 1999).

In terms of geographical location, the usual assumption is that capitalist firms will have incentives to move activities to low-cost sites and that improvements in information and communication technology enable services to be relocated just, as in an earlier phase, manufacturing was relocated. Although they may face political constraints on offshoring and outsourcing, non-profit making governmental organizations may also pursue the shared services option. In the public sector, however, the rhetoric may be different with talk about 'achieving cost reduction without damaging the front-line'. As well as cost reduction, Gospel and Sako (2010) identified value adding motives. Citing their own empirical evidence, Gospel and Sako found in one case that internal HR managers are freed up "to concentrate on less routine matters" (2010, p. 6) and, in another, the unbundling enables a "further release of internal managers to concentrate on more value-adding activities" (2010, p. 18).

Impact on professional support services

Given that many of the advocates and allies of the CSSO come from a general management or operations perspective, it might be thought that some professional services are more likely to resist the CSSO than others. Human resource (HR) management might be expected to be particularly resistant given a presumption of a human face. These concerns are reflected in Cooke's views that the restructuring of the HR function "may create (temporary) confusion in the ownership of responsibilities and the need for new skills from line managers and employees" resulting in "a tangible reduction in the quality of services and an increased level of user dissatisfaction with the delivery of HR services" (2006, p. 214). Yet there are common challenges for *all* professional groups some of which are reflected in wider labour market trends expressed in terms such as 'hollowing out' and 'hourglass economy' (Sissons, 2011). Workers in the CSSO may face problems in career progression, getting stuck in entry-level processing.

Rothwell et al. (2011) found that professional service functions in organizations (such as accounting or human resources) may be subject to a narrowing or bottleneck effect: metaphorically, to become 'hourglass' shaped, due to a concentration of work at the lower transactional end of the scale mainly at the expense of the middle. IT-enabled self-service support and enquiry facilities appeared to be connected to a reduction in the professional headcount. In addition, process re-engineering and call-centre style workflow processing appear to create a widening divide between a smaller group of elite professionals engaged in higher-level diagnostic and design work, with a large mass of technician level staff that were delivering the support services and transactional processing.

Other research on the impact of CSSOs drew on Weber's (1958) famous image of the Iron Cage (Seal & Herbert, 2013b) as it set out the threats to the professional nature of accounting work posed by the processes of rationalization. Once processes were re-engineered and standardized, there was a much reduced need for higher-level accounting in the CSSO. Furthermore, the standardized and simplified processes made it easier to train and monitor accounting staff, and replace some professionally qualified accountants with technician and clerical level workers. The organization hierarchy was flattened by eliminating all of the financial director (FD) roles in the 30 or so business units as Business unit FDs were replaced with more junior, newly or part-qualified accountants, who could be supervised by a new regional layer of just three regional FDs. The CSSO also increased the level of control at a distance as, with the standardized systems of the SSC, local managing directors and editors were now exposed to a new level of scrutiny due to the greater levels of transparency in the accounts. Local managers could no longer hide behind inconsistencies and confusion in accounting methods and local idiosyncrasies and there was no longer sufficient accounting staff to run 'shadow' accounting systems. In short, although it was functionally separate from corporate head office, the calculations enabled by the CSSO had changed the balance of power towards the corporate centre (Seal & Herbert, 2013b). In another case study, Herbert and Seal (2012) reported that there was pressure on management accountants to justify their existence through outputs to 'customers' who have the power to demand value for money and relevance. Although the CSSO did not employ an activity-based charge back mechanism, the new organizational distance created a new relationship between the accountants in the businesses and those working in the CSSO as one became a 'buyer' of accounting services, and the other a 'supplier'.

Given these challenges to the role of the 'accountant in business', we might see the professional bodies as potential resisters to the CSSO phenomena. Indeed, although the cultural traits of the accountant are not normally associated with face-to face facility in comparison with say the HR function, the profession has tried to carve out new roles for itself by claiming jurisdiction over particular calculative practices, particularly decision making (CIMA, 2008). In practical terms, this response involved the promotion of softer skills and the notion of the business partner which emerged first in the human resource literature (CIMA, 2008). The latter has seen new variants of the divisionalized corporation with shared service centres as well as the outsourcing of a range of business support services. Organizations are under pressure to manage complexity, reduce cost and utilize their finance professionals in areas where they can add most value. The management accounting function is expected to complete its transformation from a transaction-processing focus to a fully fledged 'business partner' with a high decision support capability (CIMA, 2008, 2009b).

Challenge to professional notions of the 'career' posed by corporate unbundling

Rothwell et al. (2011) argued that corporate unbundling challenges the professional worker in first-world countries. Hitherto, protected by barriers to entry based on structured formation and progression, and secured by knowledge that is independent of organizational bonds, these professionals had a degree of perceived occupational security that had defied the apocalyptic predictions of late-twentieth and early-twenty-first century career theorists (Handy, 1989; Baruch & Pieperl, 1997; Marchington et al., 2005; Wright, 2008). However, aside from the professional accounting work protected by statutory regimes, this past sense of security may yet prove to be ill-founded in the future. Rothwell et al. (2011) also noted anecdotal concerns about the emergence of a *development gap* (CIPD, 2004). For example, the next generation of high-level business partners may fail to acquire both the required 'nuts and bolts' experience of accounting routines and the inculcation into professional 'life'.

There may also be a problem if a significant number of technician-level workers experience problems in career progression. In one case history, *OilCo*, Rothwell et al. (2011) noted that the company had chosen to have an honest dialogue with their young mid-career workers in developing countries in which the management was explicit about the lack of opportunities for career progression within the company. A further scenario might emerge in *developed countries* where, if the technician level jobs are relocated overseas, the opportunities for workers in developed countries to become senior managers may be damaged because they cannot acquire technical competences or experience the practices of professional life.

Overall, the imperative of cost reduction that is driving the reorganization, reconfiguration, redesign, relocation, commoditization and marketization of support services could, over time, lead to a hollowing out of professional skill-sets (Rothwell et al., 2011). This is particularly problematic for those individuals who previously would have regarded themselves as professionals fulfilling what were integral, if not necessarily core functions in organizations, but now find themselves fulfilling a narrower, more programmed role, and in a more transactional relationship with their employing organizations. The consequence may be an 'hourglass' profession whereby the middle, comprised typically of recently qualified professionals, will be competing for tough-to-get promotion or aiming to leave with their experience 'passport stamped'.

The Rothwell et al. (2011) study found that workers in off-shore centres were well-qualified and motivated and that the top of the pyramid at the CSSO was actually very small. They argued that with a picture of offshore workers who are highly motivated, technically skilled and keen to embrace responsibility, professional workers in first-world countries faced a wake-up call. But the CSSO combined with IT-enabled self-service support and enquiry facilities appeared to be connected to a reduction in the professional headcount. In addition, process re-engineering and call-centre style workflow processing appear to create a widening divide between a smaller group of elite professionals engaged in higher-level diagnostic and design work, with a large mass of technician level staff that were delivering the support services and transactional processing, hence the 'hourglass' structure.

Management accounting as 'agent'

There are a number of ways of portraying management accounting as an agent. One emergent approach draws on actor-network theory which sees management accounting as an actant that both initiates and supports moves towards horizontal organizational relationships such as the CSSO. Drawing on Callon (1998), Kastberg (2014) argues that management accounting helps to frame the SSM relationships. Emphasizing other work by Callon and Muniesa (2005), Seal (2016) focuses on the calculative nature of the CSSO. Seal's (2016) work ties in with other approaches which show that the discourses and institutional logics of the traditional management accounting practices are supportive of the command-and-control philosophy of the CSSO (Seddon, 2005, 2008). The institutional logics of management accounting may be teased out in the more critical texts on the CSSO, particularly those that include organizational 'voices' beyond the managers and consultants. Such an approach easily leads into a critical discourse as workers in the business units are often forced to move or lose their jobs completely. Dissident voices may be also found both in texts by non-managerial stakeholders such as employers and customers but also by considering criticisms from specific service functions, especially human resources (Farndale et al., 2009). Furthermore, if the CSSO is conceptualized as a special type of call centre then an academic discourse can draw on the research on call centres and the extended organization (Colling, 2000; Marchington et al., 2005). These perspectives introduce a far more complex view of contemporary trends in service work as being "underpinned by dual logics of rationalization and customer-orientation … [which] potentially lie in contradiction to each other" (Korczynski, 2004, p. 98).

Perhaps it is not surprising that critical views can be found when non-managerial voices are heard. Yet, it may be possible to criticize the CSSO even from an efficiency-perspective by building on dissident voices within the consultancy/practitioner community. In particular, the ideas of Seddon[2] (2005, 2008) are based on looking at the CSSO in the context of more general notions of lean production, Taylorism and systems theory. Seddon's critique of the 'command-and-control' philosophy of management is similar to Armstrong's critique (2002) in that they both point out the problems caused by separating management from knowledge of process or *context-free managerialism*.

The critical stance in these instances comes not from dissident voices outside management but from a critique that argues that corporate unbundling is not always the most efficient strategy. Seddon criticizes the CSSO as follows:

> Unfortunately, most service centres are managed solely on production data, measuring activity rather than anything relating to purpose. Service centres appear as costs in top management's accounts. This is why managers are attracted by the idea of outsourcing. They hand over calls to an agency, whether in the same country or, more recently, in low wage countries abroad, and pay per call for the service. The result is simply to outsource waste.
>
> (2005, p. 29)

The key critique is that shared service managers "know about volumes and activity but little or nothing about the real nature of the work" (Seddon, 2005, p. 29). It is not fault of the managers but rather that the design of the work process into front office/back office or primary and support inevitably fragments the end-to-process leading to 'failure demand' – activity created by mistakes in the system. Even more worrying is the notion that the service work itself has been de-graded in order to make it 'fit' into the abstract, context-free, managerialist mould (Armstrong, 2002). In general, if we (i.e. both practitioners and researchers) seek "(t)o understand the organizational forms we observe around us, we need to understand the work practices that these forms are designed to support" (Adler, 2007, p. 1313).

In the managerialist discourse, knowledge is seen as separable in a way that is similar to Tayloristic division between 'brain and brawn'. Yet even from an efficiency perspective this simplistic view may be challenged. First, it ignores the dynamics of knowledge acquisition and deployment at the operational level of the organization which is a feature of lean production (Womack et al., 1990). Second, it ignores the danger that the lack of expertise in the CSSO may lead to the generation of so-called 'failure demand' which is "the demand caused by a failure to do something or do something right for the customer" (Seddon, 2005, p. 26).

Seddon's work (2005, 2008) is an excellent example of how the insights of the consultant can contribute to the development of a critical discourse on the CSSO. Seddon's work is informed by the practical experience of the consultant together with an explicit conceptual framework. The conceptual basis for his critique of 'service factories' is lean production or what he terms a 'systems approach' (Seddon, 2005, 2008). Despite its reputation for work intensification and increased exploitation, lean production *can* be given a radical twist (Adler, 2007). From a lean perspective, the work processes and customer relationships associated with the CSSO are more reminiscent of mass – rather than lean – production. The organization is restructured through the CSSO but the command-and-control and separation between managerial and shop floor work is actually reinforced.

The critical perspective on the CSSO may be linked to the logics of 'traditional' management accounting based on practices such as standard costing and a hierarchical/silo orientation which are inimical to lean and value stream approaches (Johnson, 2006; Hansen & Mouritsen, 2007). In short, although the rhetoric of the CSSO is one of process and empowerment, the practice is actually much closer to the traditional command-and-control traditions supported by traditional management accounting (Johnson, 2006). But perhaps it is not so much particular practices that portray an image of management accounting as the agent of the CSSO but rather the traditional mindset based on cost saving and shareholders rather than on value adding and customers. Perhaps the way to avoid both agent and victim roles is to change both mindsets and practices as will be discussed below.

Reconciliation: changing management accounting roles and mindsets in the new organizational structures

Although broadly supportive of the CSSO, Herbert and Seal (2012) report that management accounting and management accountants (MAs) need not be passive victims of the CSSO. Herbert and Seal (2012) argued that the CSSO caused three broad dimensions of change: (1) to the roles of MAs retained in divisions; (2) to the roles of MAs moving to the CSSO; and (3) through the creation of new relationship between the two groups, as one becomes a 'buyer' of accounting services, the other a 'supplier'. The MAs retained in divisions testified that they had been freed from the tedium of transaction processing and now enjoyed more 'space' to enhance the overall role of the management accounting function. The term 'business partner' was used by interviewees as an expression of the notion of finance playing a proactive role in planning, decision-making and control within strategic and operational teams (see Baldvinsdottir et al., 2009; Gospel & Sako, 2010). Herbert and Seal (2012) found that there was pressure on the MAs in the CSSO to justify their existence through outputs to 'customers' who have the power to demand value for money and relevance. Conversely, having lost their core accounting transaction processing function to the CSSO, the divisional MAs were under pressure to justify themselves as business partners. A common expectation of MAs throughout the corporation was for them to manage *intra-firm* relationships around a market-oriented SSO, albeit with *internal* rather than external customers. Thus, as a consequence of the CSSO with its hybrid practices, there was a need for MAs to adapt to outward-facing roles in selling and negotiating their accounting services.

As mentioned earlier, the redesign of systems and business processes that accompanies the migration of accounting work to a CSSO is often combined with the introduction of corporate-wide ERP systems. Indeed, research has shown that ERP systems can change the balance of tasks undertaken by management accountants in ways similar to those associated with the SSM. For example, the elimination of routine accounting jobs can, at least potentially, enhance a more value adding role for the management accountant (Scapens & Jazayeri, 2003).

To their credit, professional accounting bodies are aware of the challenges posed by new organizational structures and advocate the development of new skills and roles (Burns & Baldvinsdottir, 2007; Baldvinsdottir et al., 2009; ACCA, 2009a, 2009b; CIMA, 2008). The professional emphasis is more on decision making and the management accountants see themselves as business partners rather than corporate policemen. Many of these developments are described in Chapter 17 of this book.

Some conclusions

This chapter has reviewed research on the corporate unbundling of support services. It has been argued that cost management is involved in the logics of the unbundling decision (mode of delivery, location, etc.) and in the management control of the unbundled services. Outsourcing and in-sourcing via shared services have both changed the administrative structures and processes of multidivisional organizations as corporate expertise is moved to new locations and delivered in different ways. This type of unbundling also has potential implications for the professional worker, especially the accountants who are traditionally charged with cost management responsibilities. Indeed, there is even an element of the 'biter bitten', as management accountants as workers in traditional cost management roles are becoming 'victims' of unbundling. Given that much of the academic research on unbundling has focused on the HR function, we would urge that a complementary research effort needs to be undertaken with respect to the accounting and finance function. Such an academic research effort should also serve to challenge the consultancy discourse that currently dominates the unbundling agenda.

Notes

1 The SSM refers to the general model in the context of the wider organization. The acronyms for shared services centre (SSC) or captive shared service organization (CSSO) refers to a specific sub-unit or specific site.
2 Seddon has academic links and thus straddles both academic and consultancy camps.

References

ACCA. (2009a). *The Finance Professional 2020*. London: ACCA.

ACCA. (2009b). *Accountants for Business 2009*. London: ACCA.

Adler, P. S. (2007). The future of critical management studies: A paleo-Marxist critique of labour process theory. *Organization Studies, 28*(9), 1313–1345.

Armstrong, P. (2002). Management, Image and Management Accounting. *Critical Perspectives on Accounting, 13*, 281–295.

Bain, P. & Taylor, P. (2000) Entrapped by the "electronic panopticon"? Worker resistance in the call centre. *New Technology, Work and Employment, 15*(1), 21–28.

Bangemann, T. O. (2005). *Shared services in finance and accounting*. Aldershot: Gower.

Baldvinsdottir, G., Burns, J., Norreklit, H. & Scapens, R. (2009). The management accountant's role. *Financial Management*, May, 34–35.

Baldvinsdottir, G., Burns, J., Nørreklit, H. & Scapens, R. W. (2009). The changing roles and changing discourse of the management accountant: 1980-2008. Working Paper.

Baruch, Y. & Pieperl, M. (1997). High flyers: Glorious past, gloomy present, any future? *Career Development International, 2*, 354–358.

Bergeron, B. (2003). *Essentials of shared services.* New Jersey: Wiley.

Bondarouk, T. (Ed.). (2014). *Shared services as a new organizational form.* Bingley: Emerald Group Publishing.

Burns, J. & Baldvinsdottir, G. (2007). The changing role of management accountants. In T. Hopper, D. Northcott & R. Scapens, (Eds.), *Issues in management accounting*, 3rd edition (pp. 117–132). Harlow: Pearson Education.

Callon, J. (1998). Introduction: The embeddedness of economic markets in economics. In M. Callon (Ed.), *The laws of the markets* (pp. 1–57). Oxford: Blackwell.

Callon, J. & Muniesa, F. (2005). Markets as collective calculative devices. *Organization Studies, 26*(8), 1229–1250.

Chandler, A. D. (1962). *Strategy and structure: Chapters in the history of the American industrial enterprise.* Cambridge, Mass: MIT Press.

Chartered Institute of Personnel and Development. (2004). *Managing the careers of professional knowledge workers.* London.

CIMA. (2008). *Improving decision making in organisations: The opportunity to reinvent finance business partners*, July. London: CIMA.

CIMA. (2009a). *Finance transformation: The evolution to value creation*, October. London: CIMA.

CIMA. (2009b). *Management accounting tools for today and tomorrow.* London: CIMA.

Colling, T. (2000). Personnel management in the extended organization. In S. Bach & K. Sisson (Eds.), *Personnel management: A comprehensive guide to theory and practice*, 3rd edition (pp. 70–90). Oxford: Blackwell.

Cooke, F. L. (2006). Modelling an HR shared services center: Experience of an MNC in the United Kingdom. *Human Resource Management, 45*(2), 211–227.

Davis, T. (2005). Integrating shared services with the operations and strategies of MNEs. *Journal of General Management, 31*(2), 1–17.

Edwards, R. (1979). *Contested terrain: The transformation of the workplace in the twentieth century.* New York: Basic Books.

Gospel, H. & Sako, M. (2010). The unbundling of corporate functions: The evolution of shared services and outsourcing in human resource management. *Industrial and Corporate Change, 19*(5), 1–30.

Farndale, E., Paauwe, J. & Hoeksema, L. (2009). In-sourcing HR: Shared service centres in the Netherlands. *The International Journal of Human Resource Management, 20*(3), 544–561.

Frenkel, S., Tam, M., Korczynski, M. & Shire, K. (1998). Beyond bureaucracy? Work organisation in call centres. *International Journal of Human Resource Management*, December, 957–979.

Handy, C. (1989). *The age of unreason.* London: Random House.

Hansen, A. & Mouritsen, J. (2007). Management accounting and changing operations management. In T. Hopper, D. Northcott & R. Scapens (Eds.), *Issues in management accounting*, 3rd edition (pp. 3–25). Harlow: FT-Prentice Hall.

Helper, S. & Sako, M. (2010). Management innovation in supply chain: Appreciating Chandler in the twenty-first century. *Industrial and Corporate Change, 19*(2), 399–429.

Herbert, I. P. & Seal, W. B. (2012). Shared Services as a new organisational form: Some implications for management accounting. *British Accounting Review, 44*(2), 83–97.

Johnson, H. T. (2006). Lean accounting: To become lean, shed accounting. *Cost Management, 20*(1), 6–17.

Kastberg, G. (2014). Framing shared services: Accounting, control and overflows. *Critical Perspectives on Accounting, 25*(8), 743–756.

Korczynski, M. (2004). Back-office service work: Bureaucracy challenged? *Work, Employment and Society, 18*(1), 97–114.

Korczynski, M. & Ott, U. F. (2004). When production and consumption meet. *Journal of Management Studies, 41*(4), 575–599.

Korczynski, M., Shire, K., Frenkel, S. & Tam, M. (2000). Service work in consumer capitalism: Customers, control and contradictions. *Work, Employment and Society, 14*(4), 669–687.

Maatman, M., Bondarouk, T. & Looise, J. K. (2010). Conceptualising the capabilities and value creation of HRM shared service models. *Human Resource Management Review, 20*(4), 327–339.

Marchington, M., Grimshaw, D., Rubery, J. & Willmott, H. (Eds.) 2005. *Fragmenting work: Blurring organizational boundaries and disordering hierarchies.* Oxford: Oxford University Press.

Marglin, S. (1974). What do bosses do? The origins and functions of hierarchy in capitalist production. *Review of Radical Political Economy, 6*, 33–60.

Miller, P. (2001). Governing by numbers: Why calculative practices matter. *Social Research, 68*(2), 379–396.

Oshri, I. (2011). *Offshoring Strategies: Evolving Captive Center Models.* Cambridge, MA: MIT Press.

Phillips, N., Lawrence, T. & Hardy, C. (2004). Discourse and institutions. *Academy of Management Review, 29*(4), 635–652.

Porter, M. (1985). *Competitive advantage: Creating and sustaining superior performance.* New York: Free Press.

Quinn, B., Cooke, R. & Kris, A. (2000). *Shared Services: mining for corporate gold.* Harlow: Pearson Educational.

Robson, K. (1992). Accounting numbers as "inscription": Action at a distance and the development of accounting. *Accounting, Organizations and Society, 17*(7), 685–708.

Rothwell, A. T., Herbert, I. P. & Seal, W. B. (2011). Shared Service Centres and professional employability. *Journal of Vocational Behavior, 70*(1), 241–252.

Sako, M. (2006). Outsourcing and offshoring of business services: Implications for productivity. *Oxford Review of Economic Policy, 22*(4), 499–512.

Scapens, R. & Jazayeri, M. (2003). ERP systems and management accounting change: Opportunities or impacts? A research note. *European Accounting Review, 12*(1), 201–233.

Schulman, D., Dunleavy, J., Harmer, M. & Lusk, J. (1999). *Shared Services: adding value to the Business Units.* New York: John Wiley.

Seal, W. (2010). Managerial discourse and the link between theory and practice: From ROI to value-based management. *Management Accounting Research, 21*(2), 95–109.

Seal, W. (2016). Accounting and the firm as impure calculating devices: Making, unmaking and remaking a black box. Paper presented to Management Control Association, Salford, 19 February.

Seal, W. & Herbert, I. (2011). Organisational change and the transformation of the management accounting function. In Abdel-Kader (Ed.), *Review of Management Accounting Research* (pp. 3–21). Hampshire: Palgrave-Macmillan.

Seal, W. & Herbert, I. (2013a). Cost management and the provision of support services. In F. Mitchell, H. Norreklit & M. Jakobsen (Eds.), *The Routledge Companion to Cost Management* (pp. 199–214). Abingdon: Routledge.

Seal, W. & Herbert, I. (2013b). Shared service centres and the role of the finance function: Advancing the Iron Cage? *Journal of Accounting and Organizational Change*, 9(2), 188–205.

Seddon, J. (2005). *Freedom from command and control*, 2nd edition. Buckingham: Vanguard Press.

Seddon, J. (2008). *Systems thinking in the public sector*. Axminster: Triarchy Press.

Sissons, P. (2011). *The hourglass and the escalator: Labour market change and mobility*. London: The Work Foundation.

Strikwerda, J. (2014). Shared Services: From cost savings to new ways of value creation and business administration. In T. Bondarouk (Ed.), *Shared Services as a new organizational form* (pp. 1–15). Bingley: Emerald.

Taylor, P. & Bain, P. (1999). An assembly line in the head: Work and employee relations in a call centre. *Industrial Relations Journal, 30*(2), 101–117.

Teece, D. (2009). *Dynamic capabilities and strategic management*. Oxford: Oxford University Press.

Weber, M. (1958). *The Protestant ethic and the spirit of capitalism*. New York: Scribner.

Womack, J. & Jones, D. T. (1996). *Lean thinking: Banish waste and create wealth for your corporation*. New York: Simon and Schuster.

Womack, J. P., Jones, D. T. & Roos, D. (1990). *The machine that changed the world*. New York: Rawson Associates.

Wright, C. (2008). Reinventing human resource management: Business partners, internal consultants and the limits to professionalization. *Human Relations, 6*, 1063–1098.

16 The relationship between management and financial accounting as professions and technologies of practice

Alan J. Richardson[1]

Introduction

Management accounting as a distinct profession emerged after World War I and developed a technology of practice distinct from financial accounting. In part, its emergence reflected the importance of operational efficiency in the war effort and the development of specialists in budgeting and costing (Loft, 1986; cf. Boyns & Edwards, 1997, 2006). However, it also arose as a distinct profession because of the exclusionary practices of existing accounting associations who wished to maintain the purity of public accounting in the face of increasing numbers of salaried accountants. Recently there have been calls to unify these branches of accounting thought and professional organization, but important questions are raised by these trends.

Management accounting information is needed to support financial reporting and, as financial reporting became more future-oriented and investor focused, the assumptions underlying budgeting and operational planning became input to financial accounting policies and estimates (Taipaleenmäki & Ikäheimo, 2013; Ahmed & Duellman, 2013). This has led to calls for the unification of financial accounting and management accounting as technologies of practice. But management accounting has expanded its areas of practice to support strategy implementation, competition on the basis of quality and social impact, and stakeholder management. If merging these technologies of practice occurred would it represent the continued dominance of the shareholder view of accounting underlying financial reporting or would a new synthesis be needed that reflects a broader set of stakeholders and issues in organizations?

Membership in management accounting associations is growing faster than membership in financial accounting associations creating potential usurpatory challenges to the hegemony of financial accounting in the market for professional credentials. Management accountants have developed a distinct identity and regard their careers as independent of financial accounting (Richardson & Jones, 2007; Weaver & Whitney, 2015). If a merger of professional associations occurred, would it be a merger of equals or would the merged association reinstate the traditional dominance of financial accountants over management accountants?

This chapter explores these two macro pressures on the future of management accounting. First, I explore the relationship between financial and management accounting as professions. In many countries, each technology of practice is represented by separate professional associations. I explore the rationale for the creation of separate professional bodies and the trend towards consolidation of the profession. Second, I consider the relationship between financial accounting and management accounting as technologies of practice. I identify specific junctures at which management accounting and financial accounting diverged in the conceptualization of the stakeholders to whom they oriented their techniques and the decision-models that their information supports. Third, I examine the call for integrating financial and managerial accounting around a shared focus on shareholder value and risk, based on a common database. I conclude the chapter by addressing the question of whether or not management accounting has a future as a distinct profession and technology of practice.

Financial and management accounting as professions

The creation of associations of public accountants began in the UK in the late 1800s, spreading throughout the Commonwealth and internationally. The early associations were largely signalling devices to distinguish higher status public accountants from others. In time, the distinction between designated accountants versus those not affiliated with an association was argued to reflect the difference between "qualified" and "unqualified" accountants leading to the development of tests of competence and, ultimately, programmes of training to justify this distinction (Hoskins & McVie, 1986; Anderson et al., 2005). These associations used both ascriptive and cognitive criteria to restrict access to credentials and, in general, succeeded in raising the economic and social status of their members.

The problem with this form of "exclusionary" closure is that it does not prevent others from forming their own associations and implementing a strategy of "usurpatory" closure, i.e. attempting to take privilege from those who had structured the profession (Parkin, 1982; Coronella et al., 2015). We thus see competing accounting associations in many countries and attempts by entrenched associations to limit the creation of new associations (or at least their intended domain of practice) through lawsuits, registration systems, and unification proposals (Richardson, 1997; Walker & Shackelton, 1998).

Following World War I, accountants were increasingly employed in industry in part to provide information to produce financial statements for equity markets but also to manage control systems in organizations that covered vast geographic distances (e.g. transportation companies), had extensive hierarchies (e.g. public sector organizations and large scale enterprises), or operated as conglomerates with many unrelated businesses where management accounting information replaced prices to guide the allocation of capital (Johnson, 1983; Chandler & Daems, 1979). Accountants in industry also were concerned about professional development and recognition. Eventually they started organizations to fulfil these functions which in some cases grew into designation granting associations.

Abbott (1988: 230) asserts that cost accounting "has been without question the most contested information jurisdiction in American history". This contest was mostly between accountants, engineers, economists and, more recently, information technologists. By the late 1920s, however, accountants had largely succeeded in claiming this domain in the UK and its colonies (although countries such as Germany displayed a greater engineering influence over management accounting, see Armstrong, 1985; MacArthur, 2006) and it is in this period that management accounting associations arose. For example, the Institute of Cost and Works Accountants in the UK and the National Association of Cost Accountants in the US were formed in 1919 and the Society of Cost Accountants of Canada was launched in 1920.

Richardson (2002: 116) demonstrates that the independence of management accounting from financial accounting during these formative years was illusory

> because of: (1) the use of financial accounting criteria to judge the quality of management accounting systems, (2) the assignment of management accountants to subordinate positions in organizational units whose primary purpose was financial accounting, (3) the dominance of financial accounting in the market for educational materials, (4) the judgment of the labor market that a financial accountant could replace a management accountant (but not vice versa), and (5) the need for a young profession to gain and retain the support of established interests in society.

There remained an implicit hierarchy among accountants long after management accountants began forming their own associations.

Given the status of management accountants as employees within organizations, these associations did not seek registration or licensing of all management accountants as is common with public accounting associations. In addition, since management accountants were not in direct competition with each other in the marketplace, these associations were less concerned with closure. In fact, management accounting associations sought to expand their scope of practice and their membership. These associations, for example, became involved in the scientific management movement and in Canada expanded their title to include industrial engineers, a term used for efficiency experts (i.e. their name was changed in 1930 from the Society of Cost Accountants of Canada to the Society of Cost Accountants and Industrial Engineers; see also Latzer, 1955). More recently, management accounting associations redefined their members as business consultants and strategic decision-makers rather than just cost or management accountants (e.g. Russel et al., 1999; Richardson & Jones, 2007; Suddaby & Viale, 2011). This trend towards a strategic focus was supported by the rise of personal computing and enterprise resource systems that made accounting information readily available to managers throughout the organization, turning management accountants into coaches to ensure appropriate use of this information rather than simply information providers (Granlund & Malmi, 2002).

The creation of management accounting associations across nations is not uniform. Based on the list of professional associations in IFAC I identified 186 professional accounting associations (as of 2015). On average there were 1.65 associations in each country; code law countries averaged 1.46 professional associations while common law countries averaged 2.08 professional associations (t = 1.88, p < 0.05). Typically, if only one association existed it tended to be an association of auditors. Where multiple associations existed, often there were competing associations of public accountants but usually only one management accounting association in each country.

These statistics suggest that management accounting as a distinct profession is a culturally specific phenomenon. It is related to the Anglo-Saxon, common-law heritage of the profession and the rise of industrial economies. Within those contexts, management accounting succeeded in competition with other management information providers because of its connection to the production of financial statements for equity markets; where this information was not crucial (e.g. bank-based capitalist systems and systems based on relationships, Rajan & Zingales, 1998), engineers and economists tended to be more successful in claiming this domain. Further international research is needed to understand these differences and the processes that generate them. The first part of this book contributes to our understanding of local variations in management accounting practice in a range of countries.

Throughout history there has been a trend towards consolidation of the accounting profession through voluntary mergers and statutory registration processes. Although these merger activities typically focus on bringing together public accountants both to facilitate regulation by the state and to provide market power to practitioners (Richardson & Kilfoyle, 2012), often the goal is to consolidate the entire profession – bringing management accountants and financial accountants together in one organization – or at least, to register all accountants as a way of preventing the entry of "unqualified" public accountants from cognate areas of practice into the audit market. The issue underlying the process is one of professional "drift" where members of one association, nominally focussed on one aspect of accounting, shift their occupational roles into related areas (e.g. a person trained as an auditor becomes the controller of a former client) without changing their professional affiliation. As will be discussed below, there may also be a "cognitive drift" where the technical domain of one profession encroaches on that of another profession (Walker, 2004; Suddaby et al., 2015). Over time these professional and cognitive drifts undermined the distinctions between accounting associations resulting in duplication of professional development services and conflict over professional boundaries.

The process of professional drift of accountants is, in part, an unintended consequence of the structure of public accounting firms (Greenwood & Empson, 2003). These firms historically employed a steep hierarchical structure with relatively few partners compared with the number of accountants who train in the firm and provide the labour on which audits were based (the rise of digital records and statistical auditing has changed the need for this level of skilled labour). After junior accountants achieved their designation they had to fight for these limited partner positions or make the transition into industry. The profession thus tended to overproduce financial accountants to meet the entry-level skill needs of the public accounting firms and this oversupply of labour migrated into cognate fields with a public accounting designation where they would compete with accountants who held a management accounting designation. This competition in the labour market encouraged merger talks within the profession.

The initial wave of profession formation in accounting occurred within national boundaries but always mindful of the implications of events in one country for the aspirations of associations in other countries (Poullaos & Sian, 2010; Sian & Pollaos, 2010; Parker, 2005). This transformed into a concern with mutual recognition of credentials and licences across national borders to simplify migration of skilled labour and the flows of capital (Peek et al., 2007).[2] Concern with these issues was amplified after the negotiation of the General Agreement on Trade in Services within the World Trade Organization during the Uruguay Round of negotiations (1986–1994) (Arnold, 2005). A natural projection of this trend is the proposed creation of transnational credentials such as the failed XYZ credential (Shafer & Gendron, 2005) or the more recent Certified Global Management Accountant (CGMA) designation offered as a joint venture of the AICPA and CIMA. Alternatively, the opening of trade in services between nations may encourage individual professional associations to seek to globalize their credentials. The UK's ACCA is currently implementing this strategy with aggressive recruitment campaigns in various countries. The aspirations of these global players was one of the motivations for the merger of financial and management accounting associations in Canada to create a professional association with sufficient scale to compete in an international credential environment (see Chapter 3).

A dilemma facing the profession is that a "unified" profession, i.e. where all accountants use a single designation, does not change the fact that accountants perform a diverse set of tasks and require differentiated professional development opportunities and guidance. The US AICPA for many years resisted the creation of post-designation specialties arguing that they would be divisive to the profession, but after 20 years of debate finally allowed specialty designations (Chiasson et al., 2006). This tension between the desire for a single professional identity while allowing diversity in practice has been faced by medicine and law (among other professions) (Richardson, 1987; Richardson & Jones, 2007). At issue is the form of segmentation within the profession and how those segments will be related to each other.

This thumbnail history of the accounting profession shows that management accounting was organized as a profession late in the process of separating accounting from other professional fields. The management accounting profession was initially defined as much by what it was not than what it was – i.e. it referred to accountants who were not in public practice – but beyond this it included tax, internal control, internal audit, performance measurement, management control etc. The motivation to consolidate financial and management accounting professional associations appears to be driven by three factors.

1 Management accounting associations provided an organizational basis from which practitioners could attempt usurpatory closure in response to the exclusionary closure of public/financial accounting associations. Consolidation of the profession represents a new boundary for exclusionary practices while reducing the risk of usurpatory closure.

2 Financial accounting associations overproduced audit-trained practitioners to meet the labour needs of public accounting firms but these "excess" practitioners migrated into management accounting roles pushing their audit/financial accounting professional body to provide services beyond their original mandate. I refer to this as a process of "professional drift". This process undermined the differentiation of financial versus managerial accounting associations and created inefficient duplication of services.

3 The creation of international trade in services has created the demand for transnational professional associations. To the extent that scale of professional associations is necessary for competition and nationalism is still a motivation behind professional association formation, financial and management accounting associations may merge to compete against other international associations entering their domestic market.

Financial and management accounting as technologies

The relationship between financial and managerial accounting as technologies is complex. On the one hand, management accounting systems provide the cost data and inventory valuations that are used to support financial reporting and, in this sense, are subordinate to financial reporting (Richardson, 2002). There is no question that management accountants and financial accountants share a common knowledge base at a basic level (Richardson, 1992). On the other hand, management accountants have been urged to act as internal consultants within organizations focusing on strategic initiatives and performance measurement/management rather than routine costing processes (Russell et al., 1999). There is also a well-recognized tension between the information needed for stewardship versus investment decision-making (Beyer et al., 2010). Management accounting focuses on the stewardship or implementation aspects of management actions while financial accounting focuses on the investment uses of information. Management accounting is thus simultaneously a profession that supports financial reporting while attempting to develop beyond this narrow scope.

Complicating this relationship is the idea that financial reporting should provide stakeholders with insight into the metrics that managers use to run the business. This can be taken to imply that managers should and do manage by the numbers (Geneen, 1984; Papadakis et al., 1998) but some have suggested that financial statements are "too late, too aggregated and too distorted" (Johnson & Kaplan, 1991) to be used to run organizations. Even so, there is pressure for management accounting systems to become isomorphic with the needs of financial reporting (Johnson, 1991; Weißenberger & Angelkort, 2011). The key question is thus whether or not management accounting and financial accounting represent two distinct technologies of practice or whether they are converging on a single information set that can support managerial decision-making and investor decision-making. I identify two historical junctures at which management accounting has diverged from the information needs of financial reporting and then return to consider the current state of this relationship.

The discussion that follows is biased towards developed economies. The link between management accounting technologies and the institutional context within which it is practiced is still developing (Hopper et al., 2009). The assumptions underlying the discussion below are that management accounting and financial accounting technologies reflect the separation of ownership and control, i.e. they have different primary stakeholders, but that both are evolving within a "rationalized" industrial society. This implies that individuals are using accounting technologies to make decisions that advance their individual interests and to improve the efficiency of resource use. The primacy of this institutional logic as a determinant of organizational structure and practice is subject to considerable debate. Where ownership and control are not separate, or where the ostensible goal of management is not the efficient allocation and use of resources, then the observations below may not reflect local management accounting practice.

The first major break in the relationship between financial and management accounting as technologies was the "marginal cost" revolution notably championed by Horngren both in his academic work (e.g. Horngren and Sorter, 1961; Sorter & Horngren, 1962; Horngren, 1995) and his textbooks (e.g. Horngren, 1962). The concept of marginal cost has a long history in economics dating to the late 1800s but received significant impetus after World War II with the refinement of game theory and expected value analysis. Prior to Horngren's work, Clark (1923) made the point that overhead costs were usually fixed and therefore irrelevant to most managerial decisions: only opportunity costs are relevant. Horngren's contribution was to apply these concepts to accounting practice differentiating the "full cost" information used in financial reporting from the opportunity cost information used in managerial decision-making.

Horngren intended to realign cost accounting to fit the decision needs of managers, essentially "inventing" management accounting as a discipline.

> This book's goal is to put cost accounting in focus as a highly developed quantitative device for helping managers select and reach their objectives. Ample attention is devoted to accounting systems and procedures for data accumulation, but stress is given to the concepts that make modern cost accounting dynamic and vital. In short, the major theme of the book is "different costs for different purposes".
>
> (Horngren, 1962, p. vii)

The decision-making focus of management accounting meant that not all costs were relevant to every decision and some cost concepts, such as opportunity cost, relied on information outside the accounting system itself.

This change in focus meant that management accounting systems no longer integrated with the financial accounting system (Richardson, 2002). They might contain information that would not be considered "auditable" either because it was not based on transaction data or it was future-oriented information specific to particular decisions (e.g. projections) (cf. Joseph et al., 1996). Two related areas of practice that have not been fully integrated into management accounting are cost analysis and estimation, and cost-benefit analysis. The cost estimation domain is still dominated by engineers and non-accountants and largely based on learning curves and historical cost information (e.g. parametric costing). Cost-benefit analysis, on the other hand, is dominated by economists and is more common in the public sector where the objective function under which managers' work is more complex and subjective than the profit maximization models used in business settings. These domains include technologies of practice that would allow management accounting to further expand away from financial reporting.

A related development was the introduction of standard costing and variance analysis. Standard costing substitutes a "norm" for what a cost "should" be in place of actual costs. The choice of a standard-cost might be informed by knowledge of planned changes in technology and learning curves. The use of standard costs simplifies accounting in long-chain production processes and highlights variations from expectations that facilitates management-by-exception (Brownell, 1983). After World War II, standard costing and variance analysis were common components of cost accounting courses. These techniques establish a baseline for performance evaluation and managerial decision-making that is distinct from the transaction-based records underlying financial reporting.

The second break in the relationship between financial accounting and management accounting as technologies was the strategic revolution (Bromwich, 1990; Langfield-Smith, 1997). Johnson and Kaplan (1991) goaded management accountants into renewing the relevance of their technique to management decision-making. This work focused attention on the role of management accounting in implementing strategy and providing the incentive systems that guide strategic behaviour (MacDonald & Richardson, 2002). A key technical development was the balanced scorecard and strategy maps (Kaplan & Norton, 1996, 2001, 2004).

At the same time there was a change in the focus of financial accounting that reinforced the divergence of perspectives. Initially financial reports were intended as "general purpose" documents for multiple stakeholders. As formal standard-setting processes were put in place to guide the development of financial reports, however, it was found to be impossible to produce general purpose reports that were internally consistent. The search for a conceptual framework for financial reporting led standard-setters to focus on equity valuation models, "value relevance" (Barth et al., 2001; Holthausen & Watts, 2001) and equity market reactions to new accounting standards as a test of their relevance (Hines, 1989; Young, 2006). Management, however, must be mindful of multiple stakeholders and management accountants provide data to support this broader perspective on the long-run success of organizations (Ratnatunga et al., 2015).

The increasingly distinct sets of stakeholders that are the focus of financial reporting and management accounting, respectively, encourages a divergence of practice in each area (cf. Ball, 2004).

The Institute of Management Accountants (IMA, 2008) in the US has adopted the strategic perspective, stating:

> Management accounting is a profession that involves partnering in management decision making, devising planning and performance management systems, and providing expertise in financial reporting and control to assist management in the formulation and implementation of an organization's strategy.

The sketch of the development of management accounting as a technology of practice suggests that management accounting is distinct from financial accounting in:

1   focusing on opportunity costs to support management decision-making and encouraging different information for different decisions within the same firm;
2   providing information relevant to a wide group of stakeholders rather than being focused on information relevant to the decision-model of shareholders; and
3   varying management accounting practice according to the strategy of the organization, particularly in the choice of performance measures to drive strategy implementation and the construction of information specific to the decision-needs of local managers.

Integrating financial reporting and management accounting

The call for a single system of accounting for both managerial decision-making and stakeholder reporting has deep roots. It is based on three considerations. First, in equity-focused economies, the claim is made that managers should always act in the best interests of shareholders, i.e. their decisions should focus on maximizing shareholder value. Financial statements provide a means by which shareholders monitor management and are often used to build compensations systems intended to align management interests with those of shareholders. But more than this, it is argued that shareholders should be able to see the information on which managers make their decisions in order to differentiate between good/poor outcomes and good/poor decisions, i.e. to separate skill from luck. This suggests that the information system used by management should be a more detailed and real time version of the information provided to shareholders and not an information system based on a different logic of practice (cf. Berliner & Brimson, 1988; Bhimani, 2009; Hemmer & Labro, 2008). This logic also challenges financial accounting standard setters to move away from "arbitrary" standards and to adopt those that have proven to be "value relevant". So if financial statements are built on information that drives shareholder value and managerial compensation and performance evaluation is contingent on financial statement outcomes, why would managers use a different set of information in decision-making?

A related trend in both management and financial accounting is a focus on risk (Power, 2004; Hayne & Free, 2014). The concept of risk draws attention to possible future outcomes and contingencies for the organization and whether or not the organization can withstand shocks (business resiliency), react constructively to challenges (contingency planning), and innovate to meet new challenges (innovativeness). The financial statements with their traditional backward perspective have been inadequate to provide insights into this aspect of corporate performance. Recent experiments in corporate reporting such as sustainability reporting (and related reports on corporate social responsibility, environmental and social impact, and intellectual capital) begin to provide more useful data on these dimensions but, in this case, the assumption is that management is developing information systems to support business resilience and investors would find disclosure of this information value relevant.

This argument for integration suggests that the merger of management accounting and financial accounting as technologies of practice is most likely in publicly listed companies operating within strong shareholder rights jurisdictions.

Second, the development of information technologies that allow real-time data capture and report creation has been suggested to remove the need for separate systems for managerial decision-making. Kaplan and Johnson (1987: 193) suggested that financial reports were "too aggregate, too distorted and too late" to be useful for managerial decision-making. This critique, in part, suggests the conditions under which financial reporting could be used for management decision-making, i.e. if it was available in disaggregate form, made theoretically sound distinctions between cost categories and used theoretically appropriate allocation methods (including not allocating true joint costs), and was available in real time. Hopper et al. (1992) report a pilot study in which they examined whether or not financial accounting systems dominated management accounting systems. They found that among their small sample both financial accounting and management accounting relied on the same database but processed and formatted the information in distinct ways. While this suggests a level of integration around "primitive" accounting data, both systems can maintain their independence. However, if the underlying "primitive" system is based on the ontology of financial accounting (i.e. limited to transaction-based, auditable information), it remains unclear if the potential of management accounting information could be realized. The existence of "vernacular accounting systems" alongside the formal accounting systems of organizations suggests that this form of integration may not entirely meet the information needs of managers (Kilfoyle et al., 2013).

Finally, the move to market-based information under IFRS weakens the requirement that financial statements be based on transaction data and opens up the possibility that the "opportunity cost" information recommended for managerial decision-making could be consistent with the information reported in financial statements (Taipaleenmäki & Ikäheimo, 2013; Ahmed & Duellman, 2013). As Ball (2006) notes, however, the "fair value" provisions of IFRS are among the most controversial aspects of global standards and are an area where significant domestic variation in application will occur.

Weißenberger and Angelkort (2011) use the transition of management accounting systems in Germany from stand-alone to integrated management accounting/financial accounting systems to explore the potential benefit of integration. They do not find a direct technical benefit from the change but do report a positive relationship between the change and the effectiveness of the controllership function within the firm based on the creation of a single "language" for talking about both investor issues and management issues. Although not tested, presumably a similar benefit would have been found if the financial reporting system moved to the management accounting conceptual foundation. Typically, however, integration is taken to imply the abandonment of a distinct management accounting system in favour of the compliance-based financial accounting system. The hegemony of financial reporting remains powerful.

Conclusion

Management accounting as a distinct profession and body of knowledge is a relatively recent addition to and differentiation of the accounting profession as a whole. It is a creation largely of Anglo-Saxon countries and distinct management accounting associations outside this context are less common. The existence of distinct associations of management accountants is threatened by professional drift (associations following the movement of their members into related fields) and cognitive drift (increasing overlap of the knowledge base of professions in cognate jurisdictions) which generates competition and conflict between professional associations. The trend is to resolve these issues through the consolidation of the profession.

Management accounting as a technology of practice focuses on the decision needs of managers and on supporting managers as they implement strategy and manage a diverse stakeholder population. There are calls for greater convergence of financial and managerial information technologies. While there are significant reasons to maintain the distinction between management and financial accounting, the continuing hegemony of financial reporting and audit-focused professional associations within the profession means that these calls must be taken seriously. All of this raises the question: is there an independent future for management accounting as a technology and profession?

To the extent that management accounting has become a technology of practice that extends beyond investment-focused information and seeks to anticipate changes in the information needs of diverse stakeholders, there remain incentives to develop this technology. The challenge will be whether the convergence of financial and managerial accounting as professions allows them to continue diverging as technologies of practice.

Notes

1 I would like to acknowledge the research assistance of Andrew Leboeuf and Belinda Cancian, the support of the University of Windsor Outstanding Scholars Program, and the helpful comments of the editors.
2 This is an underresearched and theorized aspect of the professional organizations literature, but see Iredale (2001).

References

Abbott, A. (1988). *The system of professions: An essay on the division of labor.* Chicago: University of Chicago Press.

Ahmed, A. S. & Duellman, S. (2013). Managerial overconfidence and accounting conservatism. *Journal of Accounting Research, 51*(1), 1–30.

Anderson, M., Edwards, J. R., & Chandler, R. A. (2005). Constructing the "well qualified" Chartered Accountant in England and Wales. *The Accounting Historians Journal, 32*(2), 5–54.

Armstrong, P. (1985). Changing management control strategies: The role of competition between accountancy and other organisational professions. *Accounting, Organizations and Society, 10*(2), 129–148.

Arnold, P. J. (2005). Disciplining domestic regulation: The World Trade Organization and the market for professional services. *Accounting, Organizations and Society, 30*(4), 299–330.

Ball, R. (2004). Corporate Governance and Financial Reporting at Daimler-Benz (DaimlerChrysler) AG: From "Stakeholder" toward a "Shareholder Value" Model. In A. Hopwood, C. Leuz, & D. Pfaff (Eds.), *The Economics and Politics of Accounting: International Perspectives on Research, Trends, Policy, and Practice.* Oxford: Oxford University Press.

Ball, R. (2006). International Financial Reporting Standards (IFRS): Pros and cons for investors. *Accounting and Business Research, 36*(Sup. 1), 5–27.

Barth, M. E., Beaver, W. H., & Landsman, W. R. (2001). The relevance of the value relevance literature for financial accounting standard setting: Another view. *Journal of Accounting and Economics, 31*(1), 77–104.

Berliner, C. & Brimson, J. A. (Eds.). (1988). *Cost management for today's advanced manufacturing: The CAM-I conceptual design.* Cambridge, MA: Harvard Business School Press.

Beyer, A., Cohen, D. A., Lys, T. Z., & Walther, B. R. (2010). The financial reporting environment: Review of the recent literature. *Journal of Accounting and Economics, 50*(2), 296–343.

Bhimani, A. (2009). Risk management, corporate governance and management accounting: Emerging interdependencies. *Management Accounting Research, 20*(1), 2–5.

Boyns, T. & Edwards, J. R. (1997). The construction of cost accounting systems in Britain to 1900: The case of the coal, iron and steel industries 1. *Business History, 39*(3), 1–29.

Boyns, T. & Edwards, J. R. (2006). The development of cost and management accounting in Britain. *Handbooks of Management Accounting Research, 2*, 969–1034.

Bromwich, M. (1990). The case for strategic management accounting: The role of accounting information for strategy in competitive markets. *Accounting, Organizations and Society, 15*(1–2), 27–46.

Brownell, P. (1983). The motivational impact of management-by-exception in a budgetary context. *Journal of Accounting Research*, 456–472.

Chandler, A. D. & Daems, H. (1979). Administrative coordination, allocation and monitoring: A comparative analysis of the emergence of accounting and organization in the USA and Europe. *Accounting, Organizations and Society, 4*(1): 3–20.

Chiasson, M., Gaharan, C., & Mauldin, S. (2006). A history of the development of the AICPA's Specialty Designation Program. *The CPA Journal, 76*(1), 64.

Chua, W. F. & Poullaos, C. (2002). The Empire strikes back? An exploration of centre–periphery interaction between the ICAEW and accounting associations in the self-governing colonies of Australia, Canada and South Africa, 1880–1907. *Accounting, Organizations and Society, 27*(4), 409–445.

Clark, J. M. (1923). The economics of overhead costs. *Journal of Political Economy, 31*(5), 606–636.

Coronella, S., Sargiacomo, M., & Walker, S. P. (2015). Unification and dual closure in the Italian accountancy profession, 1861–1906. *European Accounting Review, 24*(1), 167–197.

Geneen, H. S. (1984). The case for managing by the numbers. *Fortune, 110*(7), 78–81.

Granlund, M. & Malmi, T. (2002). Moderate impact of ERPS on management accounting: A lag or permanent outcome? *Management Accounting Research, 13*(3), 299–321.

Greenwood, R. & Empson, L. (2003). The professional partnership: Relic or exemplary form of governance? *Organization Studies, 24*(6), 909–933.

Hayne, C. & Free, C. (2014). Hybridized professional groups and institutional work: COSO and the rise of enterprise risk management. *Accounting, Organizations and Society, 39*(5), 309–330.

Hemmer, T. & Labro, E. (2008). On the optimal relation between the properties of managerial and financial reporting systems. *Journal of Accounting Research, 46*(5), 1209–1240.

Hines, R. D. (1989). Financial accounting knowledge, conceptual framework projects and the social construction of the accounting profession. *Accounting, Auditing and Accountability Journal, 2*(2): 72–91.

Holthausen, R. W. & Watts, R. L. (2001). The relevance of the value-relevance literature for financial accounting standard setting. *Journal of Accounting and Economics, 31*(1), 3–75.

Hopper, T., Kirkham, L., Scapens, R. W., & Turley, S. (1992). Does financial accounting dominate management accounting? A research note. *Management Accounting Research, 3*(4), 307–311.

Hopper, T., Tsamenyi, M., Uddin, S., & Wickramasinghe, D. (2009). Management accounting in less developed countries: What is known and needs knowing. *Accounting, Auditing and Accountability Journal, 22*(3), 469–514.

Horngren, C. T. (1962). *Cost accounting: A managerial emphasis*. Englewood Cliffs, NJ: Prentice-Hall.

Horngren, C. T. (1995). Management accounting: This century and beyond. *Management Accounting Research, 6*(3), 281–286.

Horngren, C. T. & Sorter, G. H. (1961). "Direct" costing for external reporting. *Accounting Review, 36*(1), 84–93.

Hoskin, K. W. & Macve, R. H. (1986). Accounting and the examination: A genealogy of disciplinary power. *Accounting, Organizations and Society, 11*(2), 105–36.

IMA (Institute of Management Accountants). (2008). Definition of management accounting. www.imanet.org/docs/default-source/research/sma/definition-of-mangement-accounting. pdf?sfvrsn=2.

Iredale, R. (2001). The migration of professionals: Theories and typologies. *International Migration, 39*(5), 7–26.

Johnson, H. T. (1983). The search for gain in markets and firms: A review of the historical emergence of management accounting systems. *Accounting, Organizations and Society, 8*(2), 139–146.

Johnson, H. T. (1991). Managing by remote control: Recent management accounting practice in historical perspective. In P. Temin (Ed.), *Inside the business enterprise: Historical perspectives on the use of information* (pp. 41–70). Chicago: University of Chicago Press.

Johnson, H. T. & Kaplan, R. S. (1991). *Relevance lost: The rise and fall of management accounting*. Harvard Business Press.

Joseph, N., Turley, S., Burns, J., Lewis, L., Scapens R., & Southworth, A. (1996). External financial reporting and management information: A survey of UK management accountants. *Management Accounting Research, 7*(1), 73–93.

Kaplan, R. S. & Johnson, T. H. (1987). *Relevance lost*. Brighton, MA: Harvard Business School Press.

Kaplan, R. S. & Norton, D. P. (1996). *The balanced scorecard: Translating strategy into action*. Brighton, MA: Harvard Business Press.

Kaplan, R. S. & Norton, D. P. (2001). *The strategy-focused organization: How balanced scorecard companies thrive in the new business environment*. Brighton, MA: Harvard Business Press.

Kaplan, R. S. & Norton, D. P. (2004). *Strategy maps: Converting intangible assets into tangible outcomes*. Brighton, MA: Harvard Business Press.

Kilfoyle, E., Richardson, A. J., & MacDonald, L. D. (2013). Vernacular accountings: Bridging the cognitive and the social in the analysis of employee-generated accounting systems. *Accounting, Organizations and Society, 38*(5), 382–396.

Langfield-Smith, K. (1997). Management control systems and strategy: A critical review. *Accounting, Organizations and Society, 22*(2), 207–232.

Latzer, P. J. (1955). Cost accountant and industrial engineer. *The Accounting Review, 30*(2), 348–350.

Loft, A. (1986). Towards a critical understanding of accounting: The case of cost accounting in the UK, 1914–1925. *Accounting, Organizations and Society, 11*(2), 137–169.

MacArthur, J. B. (2006). Cultural influences on German versus US management accounting practices. *Management Accounting Quarterly, 7*(2): 10–12.

MacDonald, L. D. & Richardson, A. J. (2002). Alternative perspectives on the development of American management accounting: Relevance lost induces a renaissance. *Journal of Accounting Literature, 21*, 120.

Papadakis, V. M., Lioukas, S., & Chambers, D. (1998). Strategic decision-making processes: The role of management and context. *Strategic Management Journal, 19*(2), 115–147.

Parker, R. H. (2005). Naming and branding: Accountants and accountancy bodies in the British Empire and Commonwealth, 1853–2003. *Accounting History, 10*(1), 7–46.

Parkin, F. (1982). Social closure and class formation. In A. Giddens & D. Held (Eds.), *Classes, power, and conflict* (pp. 175–184). London: Macmillan Education.

Peek, L., Roxas, M., Peek, G., McGraw, E., Robichaud, Y., & Villarreal, J. C. (2007). NAFTA professional mutual recognition agreements: Comparative analysis of accountancy certification and licensure. *Global Perspectives on Accounting Education, 4*, 1–27.

Poullaos, C. & Sian, S. (Eds.). (2010). *Accountancy and empire: The British legacy of professional organization.* Abingdon: Routledge.

Power, M. (2004). *The risk management of everything: Rethinking the politics of uncertainty.* London: Demos.

Rajan, R. G. & Zingales, L. (1998). Which capitalism? Lessons form the east Asian crisis. *Journal of Applied Corporate Finance, 11*(3), 40–48.

Ratnatunga, J., Michael, S. C., & Wahyuni, D. (2015). Societal role expectations of management accounting professionals: An Australian study. In M. J. Epstein & J. Y. Lee (Eds.) *Advances in Management Accounting,* Volume 25 (pp. 29–48). Bingley: Emerald Group Publishing.

Richardson, A. J. (1987). Professionalization and intraprofessional competition in the Canadian accounting profession. *Work and Occupations, 14*(4), 591–615.

Richardson, A. J. (1992) Accounting Competence: Canadian Experiences. In K. Anyane-Ntow (Ed.), *International Handbook of Accounting Education and Certification* (pp. 263–278). Oxford: Pergamon.

Richardson, A. J. (1997). Social closure in dynamic markets: The incomplete professional project in accountancy. *Critical Perspectives on Accounting, 8*(6), 635–653.

Richardson, A. J. (2002). Professional dominance: The relationship between financial accounting and managerial accounting, 1926–1986. *The Accounting Historians Journal, 29*(2), 91–121.

Richardson, A. J. & Jones, D. B. (2007). Professional "brand", personal identity and resistance to change in the Canadian accounting profession: A comparative history of two accounting association merger negotiations. *Accounting History, 12*(2), 135–164.

Richardson, A. J. & Kilfoyle, E. (2012). Merging the profession: A historical perspective on accounting association mergers in Canada. *Accounting Perspectives, 11*(2), 77–109.

Russell, K. A., Siegel, G. H., & Kulesza, C. S. (1999). Counting more, counting less. *Strategic Finance, 81*(3), 38.

Shafer, W. E. & Gendron, Y. (2005). Analysis of a failed jurisdictional claim: The rhetoric and politics surrounding the AICPA global credential project. *Accounting, Auditing and Accountability Journal, 18*(4), 453–491.

Sorter, G. H. & Horngren, C. T. (1962). Asset recognition and economic attributes: The relevant costing approach. *The Accounting Review, 37*(3), 391–399.

Suddaby, R., Saxton, G. D., & Gunz, S. (2015). Twittering change: The institutional work of domain change in accounting expertise. *Accounting, Organizations and Society, 45*, 52–68.

Suddaby, R. & Viale, T. (2011). Professionals and field-level change: Institutional work and the professional project. *Current Sociology, 59*(4), 423–442.

Taipaleenmäki, J. & Ikäheimo, S. (2013). On the convergence of management accounting and financial accounting: The role of information technology in accounting change. *International Journal of Accounting Information Systems, 14*(4), 321–348.

Walker, S. P. (2004). Conflict, collaboration, fuzzy jurisdictions and partial settlements: Accountants, lawyers and insolvency practice during the late 19th century. *Accounting and Business Research, 34*(3), 247–265.

Walker, S. P. & Shackleton, K. (1998). A ring fence for the profession: Advancing the closure of British accountancy 1957–1970. *Accounting, Auditing and Accountability Journal, 11*(1), 34–71.

Weaver, S. C. & Whitney, D. (2015). The global growth of the CMA: IMA's highly respected certification is becoming more in demand by professionals around the world. *Strategic Finance, 96*(11), 26–29.

Weißenberger, B. E. & Angelkort, H. (2011). Integration of financial and management accounting systems: The mediating influence of a consistent financial language on controllership effectiveness. *Management Accounting Research, 22*(3), 160–180.

Young, J. J. (2006). Making up users. *Accounting, Organizations and Society, 31*(6), 579–600.

17 Every light has its shadow

Some reflections on the "business partner" role

Lukas Goretzki, Martin Messner and Erik Strauss

Introduction

Much has been written about the 'changing role' of the management accountant, both in the academic and practitioner literatures. Of particular interest has thereby been the so-called 'business partner' role and the advantages and opportunities that go along with this alleged 'modern ideal type' of the accountant. The present book shows that 'business partnering' is indeed a global trend that affects management accountants in different countries and continents. Many 'success stories' can be told where management accountants have developed from bean-counters to real partners of management. However, a closer analysis of the business partner role and of the factors that facilitate its emergence suggests a more nuanced, and partly critical, assessment of this role model. Based on a discussion of potential challenges and negative consequences of the business partner role, this chapter provides some ideas for future research that might complement the current academic discourse.

Factors facilitating management accountants' role change

Previous research shows that management accountants' role change is facilitated by a variety factors, ranging from strategic aspects such as a firm's increasing customer-orientation (e.g. Granlund & Lukka, 1998) to more micro-level aspects such as top management support for management accountants' change efforts (e.g. Goretzki, Strauß & Weber, 2013). From a conceptual perspective, these factors can be divided into structural and agentic factors (see also Järvenpää, 2001 for a similar distinction).

Structural factors

Management accounting constitutes a 'corporate profession' which builds upon both a professional and an organizational identity (e.g. Abbott, 1988; Hiller, Mahlendorf & Weber, 2014). Whereas the professional identity is based on a shared, abstract knowledge base that goes along with a particular behavior and societal status, the organizational identity is based on the specific organizational context in which the accountants work (e.g. Abbott, 1988). These identities are not necessarily in line with each other and might suggest at times different courses of actions. In such a case, it can happen that management accountants adapt their professional identity to the contextual requirements of their organization, in order to be able to meet the organizational role expectations they face. In other words, the organizational context can affect management accountants' roles and changes to these roles.

Although the organizational context in which management accountants perform their tasks varies between industries and countries, prior research identified one major global trend that seems to be a significant facilitator of the emergence of the business partner role, i.e. decentralization (Burns and Baldvinsdottir, 2005; Byrne & Pierce, 2007; Granlund & Lukka, 1998). Locating management accountants closer to operational managers increases the interaction between these two parties, enables management accountants to gather experience and know-how in the "battle field" (Granlund & Lukka, 1998), and, thereby, enhances their business-orientation (Granlund & Lukka, 1998; Järvenpää, 2007).

Decentralization is also often accompanied by the introduction of a standardized accounting or ERP system, which has been identified as another important factor facilitating role change (e.g. Caglio, 2003; Coad & Herbert, 2009). This kind of information system typically leads to the standardization of data formats and to the codification of accounting practices. As a consequence, management accountants are unburdened from many routine tasks that can be summarized under the label of "information gathering" (e.g. Burns and Baldvinsdottir, 2005; Caglio, 2003; Järvenpää, 2001, 2007). This enables them to focus more strongly on the interpretation and consolidation of data (e.g. Caglio, 2003). However, ERP systems also contribute to the diffusion of accounting knowledge through the organization as they enable managers to access accounting information more easily (e.g. Byrne & Pierce, 2007; Caglio, 2003; Järvenpää, 2007, 2009). As a result, accountants lose their 'information monopoly' and have to find alternative ways of adding value to the organization. One response is to increase interaction with managers, providing more business-oriented services and participating in managerial decision-making.

In addition to the reduction of routine work, standardization of accounting information reduces the complexity of accounting systems and fosters the homogenization between financial and management accounting which is also affected by the diffusion of international financial reporting standards, such as IFRS which promote the management approach (Weißenberger & Angelkort, 2011). As a result, management accountants have to put less effort into the consolidation of information but are expected to "talk in IFRS [even] at the divisional level" (Lantto, 2014, p. 351).

Furthermore, the increased business orientation of management accountants is also affected and positively supported by the development of new accounting innovations, which support business managers (e.g. Byrne & Pierce, 2007; Järvenpää, 2007, 2009). For example, it is argued that the invention of activity-based costing or the balanced scorecard changed management accountants' tasks (Järvenpää, 2001) from providing "boring budget figures" to providing "innovative financial expertise" (Busco, Quattrone & Riccaboni, 2007, p. 138).

Agentic factors

Roles are defined as "conceptions of appropriate goals and activities for particular individuals or specified social positions" (Scott, 2008, p. 55) that "arise as common understandings develop that particular actions are associated with particular actors" (Berger & Luckmann, 1967, p. 73). Accordingly, actors in their organizations implement the abovementioned structural factors such as major technological and organizational changes. However, agents can, although they are embedded in this kind of structure, also be the initiators of role change (e.g. Burns & Baldvinsdottir, 2005), which makes agentic factors also an important category of factors facilitating management accountants' change toward increased business orientation.

For instance, extant research identifies top managers as important facilitators of management accountants' role change. In particular, top managers' expectations and their support can influence management accountants' willingness and ability to change their role (e.g. Järvenpää, 2007, 2009; Wolf, Weißenberger, Wehner & Kabst, 2015). If top managers "neither have a positive attitude toward business partnering nor expect controllers to participate in their decision-making, controllers will inevitably remain in their traditional roles and carry out traditional tasks" (Wolf et al., 2015, p. 27) because this role script seems to be regarded as appropriate. In addition to voicing their expectations, top managers may more actively support role change (e.g. Burns & Baldvindottir, 2005; Järvenpää, 2007, 2009; Goretzki et al., 2013). This can take the form of providing accountants with resources that are required for changing their role (e.g. Järvenpää, 2007). The active support of top managers can also appear in the form of shaping management accountants' own meanings of their role by emphasizing the importance of business partnering, encouraging management accountants to act as business partners, giving them opportunities to be visible as business partners within the organization and, finally, advertising the new role model within the entire organization (Burns & Baldvinsdottir, 2005; Goretzki et al., 2013). Alternatively, top managers could also perform the new role model by themselves and, thereby, assimilate it with official values of the firm, which might provide legitimacy for the new role (Järvenpää, 2007). In addition to supporting the willingness to change, top managers might also try to improve the ability of management accountants to change their role. Managers can, for example, offer corporate education programs that train already employed management accountants or can adapt corporate hiring policies to recruit only people that have the required skills for performing the business partner role (e.g. Järvenpää, 2009).

Overall, both kinds of factors play an important role in facilitating the new role script called business partner. What this role script actually incorporates will be explained in the next section.

Business partner – the new role model for management accountants

Management accountants' role change toward the 'business partner' is typically characterized by a change in their main tasks, from traditional scorekeeping activities such as information gathering to tasks like strategy formulation, systems development, organizational (re-)designing or change management (Siegel & Sorensen, 1999; Burns & Baldvinsdottir, 2005); advising managers and taking part in decision-making (Granlund & Lukka, 1997, 1998); and providing managers with business-relevant information for decision-making (Busco et al., 2007; Hopper, 1980; Järvenpää, 2007; Sathe, 1983).

It is somewhat surprising that the academic and practitioner literatures describe the business partner role in terms of rather abstract tasks instead of precise bundles of activities (e.g. Siegel & Sorensen, 1999; Sorensen, 2009). Although these abstract task descriptions might support the creation of a (perceived) shared understanding about the role model of the business partner, they might also cause ambiguity about what business partners do or don't do. Consequently, management accountants may start to interpret all their activities and tasks as being business partner tasks even though they could be summarized under a different role model because the interpretation of roles is highly subjective (e.g. Mahlendorf, 2014). For example, Coad and Herbert (2009) illustrate that management accountants described their role model as business partner whereas their primary activity was still reporting monthly performance against budget, which is traditionally seen as a characteristic of the scorekeeping role model. Their case also reflects a situation where management accountants "engage in a struggle for recognition in a context where tensions emerge from the confrontation between idealized occupational aspirations and situated possibilities" (Morales & Lambert, 2013, p. 228). This ambiguity of tasks and the possibility to interpret similar tasks differently caused first calls for "standard measurements" for the different role models in research (e.g. Mahlendorf, 2014), i.e. researchers suggested to agree on a certain set of tasks that is exclusively related to a specific role model like the business partner or watchdog. Simultaneously, it was also problematized that some roles were perceived as more prestigious which could distort the results of a standard measurement (Mahlendorf, 2014).

Watson (2008) shows that discursively available social identities or role models influence individual actors' identity work. Role models like the business partner can in this sense shape an individual actor's aspirational identity, which is "a story-type or template in which an individual construes him- or herself as one who is earnestly desirous of being a particular kind of person and self-consciously and consistently in pursuit of this objective" (Thornborrow & Brown, 2009, p. 356). Normative role scripts like the business partner do not, however, simply equip management accountants with discursive resources that – in a 'neutral' way – enable them to position themselves within the organization as a particular type of person (cf. Goretzki et al. 2013). They also constitute 'moral benchmarks' against which management accountants compare their actual role within the organization. Abstract role models like the business partner do in this sense exert normative pressure (cf. DiMaggio & Powell, 1983) on management accountants to comply with these scripts for legitimate behavior (Scott, 2008). Looking especially at the normative discourse it is often mentioned that only as 'true' business partners who are engaged in, for instance, strategic planning, decision-making or process improvement do management accountants 'really' add value to management. Basic tasks or 'grunt work' like standard reporting, in contrast, are often described as non-value adding activities that can (or should) be performed by IT systems or shifted to shared-service centers. Accordingly, management accountants who 'still' spend most of their time on routine activities that are discursively associated with apparently 'outdated' and stigmatized as non-value adding role models like the bean-counter would sooner or later lose their legitimacy and consequently their raison d'être within the organization. What can hence be observed in this context is an increasingly strong 'partner or perish culture' that virtually forces management accountants (and other staff professions) to submit themselves to the business partner ideal.

The normative discourse typically focuses on the positive and rewarding aspects of the business partner social identity (cf. Morales & Lambert, 2013). Research, however, has shown that (aspirational) identities are often fragile and associated with feelings of uncertainty and insecurity. For instance, considering identity as social phenomenon, the achievement of an aspirational identity is "subject to the potential of being socially denied or disconfirmed" (Knights & Clarke, 2014, p. 336). Accordingly, as 'aspirants' (cf. Thornborrow & Brown, 2009) who try to establish or stabilize an aspirational identity like the business partner, management accountants "are continuously engaged in forming, repairing, maintaining, strengthening or revising the constructions that are productive of a precarious sense of coherence and distinctiveness" (Alvesson & Willmott, 2002, p. 626; Goretzki & Messner, 2014; Morales & Lambert, 2013). But what happens if management accountants realize that they are not able to establish their aspired-for identity? Below, we critically reflect upon the normative discourse on business partnering. More specifically, we focus on those aspects that can render such an aspirational identity precarious or even conflictual. In addition, we will emphasize some issues illustrating that a business partner role is not per se in each and every situation beneficial for an organization.

Potential challenges in becoming a business partner

The study by Morales and Lambert (2013) provides valuable insights on what can be referred to as the 'dark side' of the business partner discourse. Based on an ethnographic study the authors show that management accountants situationally relate specific types of tasks to different role models, namely the 'demeaning' bean-counter and the 'rewarding' business partner role. In light of this "moral division of labour" (Morales & Lambert, 2013, p. 229), management accountants confronted with the business partner discourse might feel that basic or routine tasks do not fit to or even contradict their aspirational identity. As a result, such tasks constitute "dirty work" (Hughes, 1951) that management accountants might consider demeaning and negatively affecting their status as a professional group. As a result, management accountants would try to avoid and delegate such "unclean tasks" (Morales & Lambert, 2013, p. 230) and focus on those activities that they regard to be in line with their aspired-for identity. The study also shows that tasks or activities that from the management accountants' perspective are 'theoretically' in line with the business partner ideal can in some situations still turn into dirty work if "audiences reposition them within practices reinforcing a devalued identity" (Morales & Lambert, 2013, p. 230). An illustrative example for such 'polluted tasks' (p. 2013) is the participation of management accountants in management meetings. Participating in, for instance, sales or operations meetings is basically in line with the business partner discourse as it allows accountants to get closer to management. However, if they (feel that they) do not have a voice in these meetings or are only used as 'scapegoats,' then this particular task would quickly turn into a form of dirty work that does not support the aspired-for identity. The study in this vein nicely shows how in specific situations particular activities can render management accountants' aspirational business partner identity fragile or even threaten it. Activities that management accountants regard as dirty work can lead to uncertainty, insecurity and frustration. The study by Morales and Lambert (2013) emphasizes the situational nature of both the stability as well as the fragility of the business partner identity on the micro-level.

In addition to the fact that specific tasks are in certain situations considered to be threatening the business partner identity, the accounting literature shows that managers (as important counterparts) play a crucial role in management accountants' identity work. The entrenchment of an aspirational identity depends to an important extent upon how managers actually see their management accountants and what they allow them to do (Goretzki & Messner, 2014; Morales & Lambert, 2013). The business partner discourse portrays management accountants as proactive and powerful actors who are supposed to influence what other organizational actors (including managers) do.

Despite the prominence of the 'partner' metaphor in the practitioner-oriented literature and its apparent potential to support value creation, previous research that looked at the relationship between management accountants and other actors provides evidence on competition and conflict resulting from management accountants' endeavors to become more influential (e.g. Armstrong, 1985; Ezzamel & Burns, 2005; Vaivio, 1999; Whittington & Whipp, 1992). Armstrong (1985), for instance, focuses on the top management level and – more specifically – the relationship between accountants, engineers and personnel staff. He argues that there is a competition between these professional groups over providing strategies to control labor. Resulting from the respective control strategy adopted by a firm, the professional group representing this particular control strategy may find its way to management hierarchies and hence increase its influence. Other studies looked in more detail at the professional competition between management accountants and sales and marketing managers (Ezzamel & Burns, 2005; Vaivio, 1999; Whittington & Whipp, 1992). Taking up a marketing-centered perspective, Whittington and Whipp (1992), for instance, argue that the dominant position of management accountants within the firm depends on a professional apparatus conferring on them not only technological competence but also a kind of ideological credibility. The authors argue that "the accountancy profession has extended beyond its hard technological core (centred on the provision of quantitative information) to claim a competence in management in general" (p. 53). Furthermore, they critically state that "[a]ccountants have projected themselves to the top by promoting the managerial problems which accounting is best suited to solve, while systematically denigrating the expertise of competing professional groups" (p. 53). The authors also point to inter-professional competition and suggest that to "steal back from the accountants some of the legitimacy of numbers" (p. 61), marketing also needs to build up a professional ideology. As a result, it can be argued that when trying to position themselves as influential actors, management accountants have to compete with other professional groups. This, however, may lead to conflicts, which could eventually interfere with a successful implementation of a partnership strategy.

Considering the competition between management accountants and other actors, previous research also shows that management accountants do not always emerge as 'winners.' Vaivio (1999), for example, presents a case study in which the abstract knowledge of the management accountants could not prevail against the local knowledge of the case company's sales people. He shows how the so-called 'quantitative customer,' namely the calculative entity presented by the management accountants was substituted by the 'sales customer,' that is, the analytical entity determined by the sales people who were consequently able to succeed in this 'knowledge competition.' Similarly, Ezzamel and Burns (2005) present a case study on professional competition between management accountants and buyers and merchandizers. In the case company, management accountants were not able to implement a specific control tool, namely Economic Value Added®. Similar to Whittington and Whipp (1992), Ezzamel and Burns (2005) pay special attention to the management accountants' calculative toolbox that was basically supposed to increase their influence on sales and marketing activities. Based on their case material the authors show how sales and marketing people challenged this toolbox and tried to keep the management accountants out of their daily business.

Existing literature hence points to tensions between management accountants' abstract knowledge and operational managers' local knowledge about, for example, markets, customers and organizational processes. What existing studies hereby indicate is that the struggle for influence between management accountants and other professional groups can impede the entrenchment of a business partner identity. A potential result is that management accountants' endeavors to establish their aspired-for identity become more difficult and uncertain.

Potential downsides of the business partner role

It is widely acknowledged in the literature that the business partner role can create a role conflict for management accountants, especially for those located in business units (e.g. Maas & Matejka, 2009). In the following we will focus on such business unit management accountants. They are, on the one hand, expected to act as 'corporate watchdogs' and make sure that managers' decisions and actions are economically reasonable and in line with certain policies, rules or regulations. On the other hand, they are supposed to support their managers as local business partner and in this sense to be deeply involved in decision-making and control practices. This results in the widely known 'involvement versus independence dilemma' (cf. Sathe, 1982). But how do business unit management accountants actually deal with such conflicts and what are the implications for the organization?

As mentioned above, the business partner discourse propagates a closer involvement of management accountants in management, which should enable them to contribute to the value creation process. From existing research we know, however, that management accountants' involvement in decision-making processes may positively affect their willingness to participate in unethical behavior (Hartmann & Maas, 2010). Research shows that business unit management accountants typically identify themselves with their business unit rather than the head office (Maas & Matejka, 2009). In other words, they are likely to see themselves as local business partners rather than corporate watchdogs. As a result, they may compromise their functional responsibilities and support their managers by, for instance, participating in budgetary slack building (Maas & Matjeka, 2009, p. 1249). Social pressure further facilitates their willingness to engage in such unethical practices (Hartmann & Maas, 2010).

In the previous section we argued that management accountants' aspirations to become more strongly involved in operational agendas can lead to professional competition and conflict within the organization. Being afraid of losing power, line managers might not be willing to cooperate with management accountants. The latter would hence in the first place need to prove themselves as trusted partners and develop certain strategies to gain internal legitimacy. Lambert and Sponem (2005) observe in this context that management accountants sometimes mobilize their accounting expertise to manipulate profits and frame such an unethical behavior as a kind of 'confidence-building measure' (Lambert & Sponem, 2005, p. 736). Fauré and Rouleau (2011) provide evidence that management accountants sometimes even teach their managers in 'creative accounting.' Drawing on these and other studies it can be argued that the business partner role model and the associated need to prove themselves as loyal partners to their managers might induce management accountants to compromise their functional duties (Burns, Warren & Oliveira, 2014; Maas & Matejka, 2009) and – in extreme cases – even to violate their professional ethos (cf. Lambert & Sponem, 2005; Puyou & Faÿ, 2013).

Even if management accountants do not actively demonstrate unethical behavior and are not willing to do so, there is still a risk that they could 'go native' and lose their independent view and critical distance to management (Burns et al. 2014). This might, in turn, threaten their role as "critical actors" who "challenge established mindsets of managers" (Messner, Clegg, and Kornberger, 2008, p. 76). Also, if management accountants are too deeply involved in the decision-making process they might not be able or willing to 'put a brake' "on unfounded corporate optimisms" (Baldvinsdottir, Burns, Nørreklit & Scapens, 2009, p. 34), which might also have negative effects for an organization. In light of the above mentioned, Burns et al. (2014) "question whether the business partner role is necessarily a good thing for organisations" (p. 37). Baldvinsdottir et al. (2009) go even one step further and make a case for management accountants' traditional qualities. They argue that, especially in volatile times, firms might benefit from "the traditional qualities of the management accountant instead of the more glamorous aspects of business partnering" (p. 34) to "ensure long-term performance and proper conformance" (p. 35).

Conclusion

In this chapter, we discussed the business partner role which constitutes a dominant role model for management accountants and which typically implies changes in the collaboration between accountants and line managers (cf. Morales & Lambert, 2013). More specifically, we reviewed empirical papers that are informative about the practices associated with this specific role model. Our analysis shows that prior research associates the business partner role with rather abstract (meta-)tasks like 'supporting managers' and 'participating in decision-making.' Additionally, we looked at research on role change processes and identified factors that on the organizational and individual level facilitate role and identity transformations. The most important factors in this respect seem to be decentralization, IT systems, change agents and external normative discourses. Finally, we shed some critical light on the business partner role and argued based on existing research that, somewhat contrary to the normative discourse, business partnering might also have negative effects for the organization and the value creation process.

Considering the notable quantity of studies on the role of the management accountant, it seems fair to ask whether there is space for future research on this topic. We believe that there is and, in the following, will try and outline some avenues for such future research.

As mentioned above, the discursively available business partner role script defines specific skills that management accountants should acquire so as to be able to put this ideal into practice. In the same vein, creating a more nuanced understanding of the tasks that might or might not belong to the business partner role would help us better understand what 'the' business partner actually is (see also Mahlendorf, 2014). Generating a common and more distinct bundle of business partner tasks could help overcome contradictory academic results and identify those characteristics of management accountants that most strongly influence their role within the organization. Furthermore, researchers could examine in more detail how different disciplinary practices and forms of 'identity regulation' (Alvesson & Willmott, 2002) influence how management accountants prepare themselves for becoming business partners. It would be interesting to compare these mechanisms with those related to other role models such the "producer of truthful knowledge" described by Lambert and Pezet (2010). In this context, it could be interesting to study how management accountants discipline themselves to become business partners.

We mentioned above that the business partner discourse presents management accountants as potentially influential actors. However, as staff professionals, management accountants may neither have the knowledge nor the hierarchical power to have influence on, for instance, line managers (cf. Goretzki & Messner, 2014). Additionally, although expected to act as change agents, they are embedded in a structural context that is difficult to change. The question therefore emerges how management accountants can actually exert influence on their organization. Future research could examine in more detail the strategies or tactics that management accountants use in order to perform the business partner role despite the constraints that they face in their organization (cf. Daudigeos, 2013).

References

Abbott, A. (1988). *The system of professions: An essay on the division of expert labor.* Chicago: University of Chicago Press.

Alvesson, M. & Willmott, H. (2002). Identity regulation as organizational control: Producing the appropriate individual. *Journal of Management Studies, 39*(5), 619–644.

Armstrong, P. (1985). Changing management control strategies: The role of competition between accountancy and other organisational professions. *Accounting, Organizations and Society, 10*(2), 129–148.

Baldvinsdottir, G., Burns, J., Nørreklit, H. & Scapens, R. (2009). The management accountant's role. *Financial Management, 9*, 33–34.

Berger, P. & Luckmann, T. (1967). *The social construction of reality.* New York: Anchor Books.

Burns, J. & Baldvinsdottir, G. (2005). An institutional perspective of accountants' new roles: The interplay of contradictions and praxis. *European Accounting Review, 14*(4), 725–757.

Burns, J., Warren, L. & Oliveira, J. (2014). Business partnering: Is it all that good? *Controlling & Management Review, 58*(2), 36–41.

Busco, C., Quattrone, P. & Riccaboni, A. (2007). Management accounting: Issues in interpreting its nature and change. *Management Accounting Research, 18*(2), 125–149.

Byrne, S. N. & Pierce, B. (2007). Towards a more comprehensive understanding of the roles of management accountants. *European Accounting Review, 16*(3), 469–498.

Caglio, A. (2003). Enterprise resource planning systems and accountants: Towards hybridization? *European Accounting Review, 12*(1), 123–153.

Coad, A. & Herbert, I. (2009). Back to the future: New potential for structuration theory in management accounting research? *Management Accounting Research, 20*(3), 177–192.

Daudigeos, T. (2013). In their profession's service: How staff professionals exert influence in their organization. *Journal of Management Studies, 50*(5), 722–749.

DiMaggio, P. J. & Powell, W. W. (1983). The iron cage revisited: Institutional isomorphism and collective rationality in organizational fields. *American Sociological Review, 48*(2), 147–160.

Ezzamel, M. & Burns, J. (2005). Professional competition, economic value added and management control strategies. *Organization Studies, 26*(5), 755–777.

Fauré, B. & Rouleau, L. (2011). The strategic competence of accountants and middle managers in budget making. *Accounting, Organizations and Society, 36*(3), 167–182.

Goretzki, L. & Messner, M. (2014). The "business partner" as a fragile aspirational identity: A field study of management accountants' identity work. Paper presented at the 7th Workshop on Management as Social and Organizational Practice, Paris.

Goretzki, L., Strauß, E. & Weber, J. (2013). An institutional perspective on the changes in management accountants' professional role. *Management Accounting Research, 24*(1), 41–63.

Granlund, M. & Lukka, K. (1997). From bean-counters to change agents: The Finnish management accounting culture in transition. *LTA, 3*(97), 213–255.

Granlund, M. & Lukka, K. (1998). Towards increasing business orientation: Finnish management accountants in a changing cultural context. *Management Accounting Research, 9*(2), 185–211.

Hartmann, F. G. & Maas, V. S. (2010). Why business unit controllers create budget slack: Involvement in management, social pressure, and machiavellianism. *Behavioral Research in Accounting, 22*(2), 27–49.

Hiller, K., Mahlendorf, M. D. & Weber, J. (2014). Management accountants' occupational prestige within the company: A social identity theory perspective. *European Accounting Review, 23*(4), 671–691.

Hopper, T. M. (1980). Role conflicts of management accountants and their position within organisation structures. *Accounting, Organizations and Society, 5*(4), 401–411.

Hughes, E. C. (1951). Mistakes at work. *The Canadian Journal of Economics and Political Science/Revue canadienne d'Economique et de Science politique, 17*(3), 320–327.

Järvenpää, M. (2001). Connecting management accountants' changing roles, competencies and personalities into the wider managerial discussion: A longitudinal case evidence from the modern business environment. *Liiketaloudellinen Aikakauskirja*, 431–458.

Järvenpää, M. (2007). Making business partners: A case study on how management accounting culture was changed. *European Accounting Review, 16*(1), 99–142.

Järvenpää, M. (2009). The institutional pillars of management accounting function. *Journal of Accounting and Organizational Change, 5*(4), 444–471.

Knights, D. & Clarke, C. A. (2014). It's a bittersweet symphony, this life: Fragile academic selves and insecure identities at work. *Organization Studies, 35*(3), 335–357.

Lambert, C. & Pezet, E. (2010). The making of the management accountant: Becoming the producer of truthful knowledge. *Accounting, Organizations and Society, 36*(1), 10–30. doi:10.1016/j.aos.2010.07.005.

Lambert, C. & Sponem, S. (2005). Corporate governance and profit manipulation: A French field study. *Critical Perspectives on Accounting, 16*(6), 717–748.

Lantto, A.-M. (2014). Business involvement in accounting: A case study of international financial reporting standards adoption and the work of accountants. *European Accounting Review, 23*(2), 335–356.

Maas, V. S. & Matejka, M. (2009). Balancing the dual responsibilities of business unit controllers: Field and survey evidence. *The Accounting Review, 84*(4), 1233–1253.

Mahlendorf, M. D. (2014). Discussion of the multiple roles of the finance organization: Determinants, effectiveness, and the moderating influence of information system integration. *Journal of Management Accounting Research, 26*(2), 33–42.

Messner, M., Clegg, S. & Kornberger, M. (2008). Critical practices in organizations. *Journal of Management Inquiry, 17*(2), 68.

Morales, J. & Lambert, C. (2013). Dirty work and the construction of identity. An ethnographic study of management accounting practices. *Accounting, Organizations and Society, 38*(3), 228–244.

Puyou, F.-R. & Faÿ, E. (2013). Cogs in the wheel or spanners in the works? A phenomenological approach to the difficulty and meaning of ethical work for financial controllers. *Journal of Business Ethics, 128*(4), 863–876.

Sathe, V. (1982). *Controller involvement in management.* Englewood Cliffs: Prentice Hall.

Sathe, V. (1983). The controller's role in management. *Organizational Dynamics, 11*(3), 31–48.

Scott, W. R. (2008). *Institutions and organizations: Ideas and interests* (3rd ed.). Thousand Oaks: Sage.

Siegel, G. & Sorensen, J. E. (1999). *Counting more, counting less. Transformations in the management accounting profession: The 1999 practice analysis of management accounting.* Institute of Management Accountants.

Sorensen, J. E. (2009). *Management accountants in the United States: Practitioner and academic views of recent developments.* Handbooks of Management Accounting Research, Vol. 3, pp. 1271–1296. Amsterdam: Elsevier.

Thornborrow, T. & Brown, A. D. (2009). "Being regimented": Aspiration, discipline and identity work in the British parachute regiment. *Organization Studies, 30*(4), 355–376.

Vaivio, J. (1999). Examining "the quantified customer." *Accounting, Organizations and Society, 24*(8), 689–715.

Watson, T. J. (2008). Managing identity: Identity work, personal predicaments and structural circumstances. *Organization, 15*(1), 121–143.

Weißenberger, B. E. & Angelkort, H. (2011). Integration of financial and management accounting systems: The mediating influence of a consistent financial language on controllership effectiveness. *Management Accounting Research, 22*(3), 160–180.

Whittington, R. & Whipp, R. (1992). Professional ideology and marketing implementation. *European Journal of Marketing, 26*(1), 52–63.

Wolf, S., Weißenberger, B. E., Wehner, M. C. & Kabst, R. (2015). Controllers as business partners in managerial decision-making: Attitude, subjective norm, and internal improvements. *Journal of Accounting and Organizational Change, 11*(1), 24–46.

18 Sustainability as a fundamental challenge for management accountants

Stefan Schaltegger

Introduction

Sustainability issues and problems have exercised a growing influence on society, governments, markets and companies for the last three decades. Apart from the Deep Water Horizon oil platform accident of BP in 2010 (Balmer, 2010, 2011) and similar publically discussed cases which have occupied media it is the multitude of stakeholder pressure-related (Jaegersberg & Ure, 2011), regulatory (Porter & van der Linde, 1995), financially (Carroll & Shabana, 2010), operationally (Mills et al., 2008) and strategically relevant (Graafland & van de Ven, 2006), social and environmental issues relating to health and safety (Schaltegger & Herzig, 2011), reporting (Burritt & Schaltegger, 2010), efficiency improvement (von Weizsäcker et al., 2009), procurement (Beske et al., 2015), reputation (Jones & Rubin, 1999), and innovation driving (Hansen et al., 2010) sustainability issues filtered into daily business practices which require an adequate coverage of social and environmental topics and their economic relevance in management accounting (Bennett et al., 2013).

In spite of the need for adequate middle and top management support, recent empirical surveys among large companies in economically developed countries show a dreary picture with accounting, management control and finance departments being the least involved business functions in sustainability management practices (Schaltegger et al., 2013a). One reason for this weak involvement of management accountants in sustainability management practice may be the inadequacy of conventional management accounting methods to deal with sustainability challenges and issues. With the increasing importance of sustainability topics for the economic success of companies (Dao et al., 2011; Carroll & Shabana, 2010) and the inadequacy of conventional management accounting methods to provide useful decision support (Kaplan & Johnson, 1987) particularly for sustainability related challenges (Maunders & Burritt, 1991) it is not astonishing that management requires additional, new and fundamentally different information to improve its decision making and communication processes. To better understand the business relevance of sustainability issues calls (in addition) for new types of information which are physical, qualitative or future oriented (Burritt et al., 2002) and which serve a broad range of addressees in the company such as production, communication or R&D managers (Schaltegger et al., 2015).

The emergence of environmental, social and sustainability management accounting has so far mainly been driven by non-management accountants (Bennett, Schaltegger & Zvezdov, 2012) who have started to take over roles and tasks which actually would match well the key job profile of management accountants (Schaltegger & Zvezdov, 2015). While sustainability accounting is mainly supported with accounting systems which have been developed and established in parallel to conventional management accounting, the need to integrate these systems has been emphasized more recently (Maas et al., 2016). While the heterogeneity of roles of management accountants (e.g. Lambert & Sponem, 2012; Goretzki et al. 2013; Morales & Lambert, 2013) has been discussed with regard to a wide range of tasks, less is known about the specific sustainability related challenges and requirements for management accountants. It may now still be the right time for management accountants to also engage in the emerging field of sustainability management accounting.

What can be understood by 'sustainability management accounting'?

Whether a company can be sustainable or not has been contested (Gray, 2010) and as a result the notion of sustainability management accounting is challenged. Sustainability management accounting needs to address the strategic integration of all three perspectives of sustainability: social, environmental and economic, and to contribute to solving problems of unsustainability at a societal level which is beyond the usual scope of companies, even though often largely influenced by business activities. While some discussions are rather philosophical representing differences between critical and pragmatic scholars (Baker & Schaltegger, 2015) the sustainability challenge to management accounting may result largely from practical difficulties such as the high complexity of sustainability problems, the simultaneous interactivity of multiple variables measured in different units, by different methods, at different times, for different periods, in different entities and for different stakeholders (Schaltegger & Burritt, 2015).

Elkington's (1998) triple bottom line challenge to accounting has been taken up by groups either to expand the indicators of corporate performance through sustainability accounting and reporting (e.g. the Global Reporting Initiative, United Nations Global Compact, Integrated Reporting), or to incorporate additional social and environmental considerations in performance measurement and management. Measuring and managing sustainability performance requires considering fundamental aspects of corporate sustainability including: content (social, ecological and economic perspectives); linkages between these perspectives; time, particularly present and future orientation; and stakeholder participation. More recently planetary boundaries have been emphasized as a key aspect to which sustainability management should direct its attention (Whiteman et al., 2013) while the United Nations has issued the UN Development Goals (UN, 2015) as a set of reference themes which need to be addressed in the global context. Global issues are thus ever more related to companies and seen as management requirement, which in turn challenges management accounting and accountants to reconsider their role, methods and processes.

The pragmatic proposition that management accountants and accounting could be a useful support for managers to develop companies towards sustainability (Schaltegger & Burritt, 2000) has been mirrored in a large number of publications and a variety of methods developed. In this view, the pragmatic approach forward is to further develop and reinvent management accounting step by step by tackling small 'manageable' issues with new, changed or adapted methods and then enlarge and interlink the approaches over time. Given the complexity of sustainable development such a practice-oriented approach may be the only way forward (Baker & Schaltegger, 2015; Schaltegger & Burritt, 2015). In addition, such a step-by-step development of focused management accounting approaches has been observed in case studies on environmental management accounting (Herzig et al., 2012).

Sustainability management accounting can thus be seen as the result of an emerging goal-oriented approach to account for a variety of social and environmental issues with the goal of enabling the company organization to contribute to sustainable development. In this view, sustainability management accounting is an umbrella term which covers diverse management accounting approaches dealing with partial aspects of sustainability, such as carbon accounting, water accounting, eco-efficiency accounting, material flow cost accounting, etc.

Admittedly, such an approach creates an incomplete picture which may be considered patchy and there is no guarantee that this approach will always serve as a starting point to develop an encompassing sustainability-oriented management accounting. This approach may in various cases also end with partial views, incomplete methods, narrow insights and undesired effects. The effect of a narrow focus on partial accounts of sustainability such as eco-efficiency accounts may mean further aspects of corporate sustainability escape management attention. Managers may miss the need for and value of development of a more encompassing accounting scope of performances. A core challenge for research and practice is thus to find approaches to support an ongoing development of management accounting for improved sustainability contributions.

While trade-offs in sustainability contexts are sometimes emphasized (Hahn et al., 2010) the aim of a pragmatically informed sustainability management accounting can only be to support management to overcome trade-offs or to create win situations for all stakeholders involved (Baker & Schaltegger, 2015; Burritt & Schaltegger, 2010). This may be difficult and in some cases impossible in the short run, but often collaboration with stakeholders helps towards finding innovative solutions (Hansen et al., 2010; Schaltegger et al., 2013a).

The most critical problems facing humanity today are complex sustainability problems, such as climate change or poverty, characterized by high levels of uncertainty, multiple perspectives and multiple interlinked processes from local to global scales (Lang et al., 2012). For a successful resolution to emerge complex problems usually require more than one perspective and inter- and transdisciplinary approaches to management (Schaltegger et al., 2013a). For example, carbon management accounting as a foundation approach for understanding climate change impacts requires the expertise of scientists, management accountants and controllers, engineers, policy makers, etc. The suggested way to address such complexity is through transdisciplinary teams which are less about producing highly specialized knowledge but more about knowledge useful to solve a real problem at hand (Apgar et al., 2009). In this context, management accounting moves away from an expert system which can only be understood by (highly) specialized experts with particular accounting training to a broader solution-oriented and faceted information management approach involving a wider set of information providers, addressees and users. This raises the question of what role management accountants have in today's corporate practice of sustainability management.

Current involvement and role of management accountants

Managers are increasingly challenged to make decisions that are influenced by social and environmental aspects of business. Informed decisions depend on the timely preparation and interpretation of information – expertise that belongs to the domain of management accountants (CIMA, 1981). Furthermore, management accountants frequently advise top and middle management and may thus have a significant influence whether and how sustainability is considered in an organization (Pierce & O'Dea, 2003). Hence, the role of management accountants in sustainability management accounting may be a significant one.

Contrary to the potential of and need for involving management accountants in sustainability management, a literature review, however, reveals that management accountants are not sufficiently, if at all, involved in managing environmental and sustainability information (e.g. Mathews, 1997; Wilmshurst & Frost, 2001; Schaltegger & Zvezdov, 2015). While the role and involvement of management accountants in conventional accounting (Burns & Baldvinsdottir, 2007; Byrne & Pierce, 2007; Goretzki et al. 2013; Morales & Lambert, 2013) has been examined deeply, little attention has been paid to empirically analysing the role of management accountants in sustainability management accounting practice. Recent comparative empirical studies examining the involvement of different business functions in the sustainability management practice of large companies in 11 developed countries show that the management accountants, controllers and corporate finance are much less involved than any other business function (Figure 18.1).

A qualitative in-depth study based on interviews with management accountants in the UK and Germany, however, reveals that accountants are not completely uninvolved but, rather, focus on a gatekeeping role between the company-internal providers of sustainability information and top management, while neglecting expert roles such as deciding on what sustainability information should be collected, designing the respective sustainability management accounting systems and collecting data (Schaltegger & Zvezdov, 2015). This raises the question of who shapes and practices sustainability management accounting in companies at present.

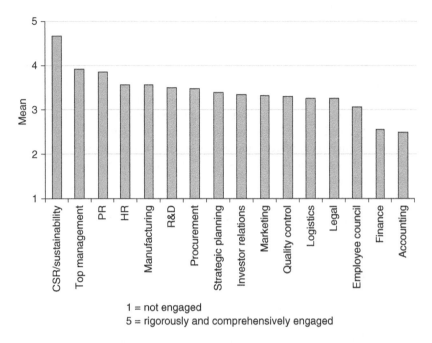

1 = not engaged
5 = rigorously and comprehensively engaged

Figure 18.1 Engagement of business functions in corporate sustainability management practice.

Source: Hörisch and Windolph (2014, p. 27).

Who shapes sustainability management accounting in practice?

Sustainability issues tend to influence every business function of an organization. For example, customer demand has motivated marketing managers to develop new green and fair-trade products and services for the market. Likewise, technical innovations such as energy efficient production processes are encouraging production managers to consider sustainability. Procurement needs to audit against social and environmental risks in the supply chain of purchased products, and the sustainability preferences particularly of highly qualified potential and current employees have motivated HR departments to deal with sustainability as part of developing the employee attractiveness of the organization.

Hence, to support the necessity for managers to gather, communicate and use sustainability information has grown in importance (Burritt, 2012; Burritt & Schaltegger, 2010; Melville, 2010; Petrini & Pozzebon, 2009). Given the different purposes various business functions need sustainability information for it is not astonishing to find a wide range of varying types of sustainability information processed in an organization.

Figure 18.2 provides an overview of various management roles and types of sustainability information that managers receive in order to fulfil their various sustainability roles and to respond to stakeholder pressures.

The findings demonstrate different information needs with regard to sustainability relating to different roles of functional managers. What works well for one manager in a particular business function and what sustainability information creates value may be of little use to another and thus not worth the effort collecting the respective information. Contingency theory addresses this aspect also with regard to information management (Chapman, 1997; Donaldson, 2001). Organizations can be seen as open systems with various and varying

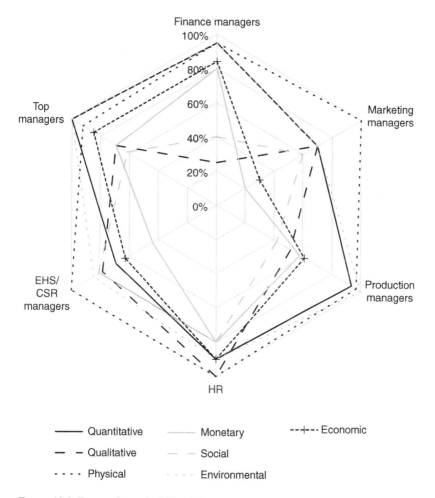

Figure 18.2 Types of sustainability information collected and used by different management roles.

Source: similar to Schaltegger et al. (2015, p. 339).

information needs. Contingency theory views management and management accounting from a fundamentally different perspective than conventional management accounting schools. General solutions and principles cannot be applied to organizations and not all management roles and situations should be assessed identically. As there is in practice no single best way for all departments and managers to achieve certain targets, the best approach to solve specific sustainability problems and what sustainability information is most relevant is contingent upon circumstances and must be differentiated according to management roles. Contingency theory highlights that managers do in practice search for solutions in given situations. Translating contingency theory to management accounting for sustainability issues thus suggests that differences can be observed reflecting the individual needs of managers. As a consequence, there are different systems and tools that help achieving certain goals that different departments and managers in different roles require and pursue.

As explained by the pragmatic approach to sustainability management accounting, the collection, communication and use of sustainability information has not just emerged as a decentralized pattern but also differs remarkably between management roles with regard to content and information type. Whereas, for example, marketing managers are particularly interested in physical information (e.g. on environmental impacts) but much less in monetary sustainability information (e.g. costs of pollutions prevention or savings of energy efficiency measures), HR managers gather and use quantitative, monetary and social information (in addition to physical and environmental information) to a much higher extent. Other large differences include finance managers who focus on quantitative environmental and monetary information as opposed to HR managers who place high importance on qualitative sustainability information. Apart from differences, however, an empirical investigation (Schaltegger et al., 2014) shows that common sustainability information requirements exist for all management roles, too.

The findings (see Figure 18.2) reveal that physical and environmental information is of high relevance to all business functions and management roles identified, indicating that they may be considered fundamental for sustainability-oriented decision making in general and thus should build the basis for any sustainability management accounting system.

Considering management accounting as a supportive function to serve a broad range of decision makers in the organization suggests that the role of management accountants for sustainability management accounting may be discussed in the light of the sustainability information types used by all business functions.

What could the role of management accountants be for sustainability management accounting?

While some may not see a problem if different managers have their own, specific sustainability information methods and databases, this can be both a source of information management inefficiency and even more a source of risk for internal decision making, conflicts and external communication. Although marketing, procurement and production managers will use physical environmental for different purposes and contexts, it may be crucial in many cases that they rely on the same harmonized information basis which does not entail conflicts or is even contradictory to the information available to other managers. If public relations, marketing and the corporate responsibility department use different information on, for example, carbon emissions, energy use or toxic materials processed, this may cause irritations and long adjustment processes in projects where different departments are involved, or may even be addressed in media if conflicting information is communicated.

Many reasons exist why the collection of certain information may lead to remarkably different figures (e.g. Schaltegger & Burritt, 2000). The scope of information collection may vary from production sites to company-wide, supply chain or product life cycle views (Gibassier & Schaltegger, 2015). Similarly, decisions are needed what is part of a certain information property, such as whether 'CO$_2$ emissions' means only emissions of CO$_2$ or emissions of all substances which contribute to climate change, the latter mostly being measured in CO$_2$ equivalents (e.g. one kilogram of methane released is usually assessed to contribute more than 30 times more to climate change than one kilogram of CO$_2$).

With a growing number of business functions dealing with sustainability-related decisions it is thus necessary to harmonize sustainability information which is relevant for many decision makers and to standardize its collection, communication and use. This is where the supportive and fundamental role of management accountants lies in designing and implementing a company-wide sustainability management accounting system which serves a broad range of business functions and managers.

Rather than aiming to design a hugely comprehensive sustainability management accounting system which may take years to complete and be overly complex, a pragmatic perspective on sustainability management accounting suggests establishing a partial accounting system focused on key sustainability information useful to many different management functions in the company. Once established and creating benefits, it can and should be further developed to support more comprehensive sustainability thinking and acting in the organization.

As shown in the last section, the empirical findings of what sustainability information is required and used most broadly by all or most business functions reveal that physical and environmental information followed by quantitative information is of high relevance to all management roles identified. Examples for this kind of information are tons of CO$_2$ emissions, use of freshwater in cubic metres and toxic waste in kilograms.

The sustainability management accounting approach which addresses this kind of information most directly is environmental management accounting (EMA). Burritt et al. (2002) introduced a comprehensive framework of EMA which provides an overview of EMA tools and which are most suitable and designed for different decision situations (Table 18.1).

Table 18.1 EMA framework

| | | Environmental Management Accounting (EMA) | | | |
| | | Monetary Environmental Management Accounting (MEMA) | | Physical Environmental Management Accounting (PEMA) | |
		Short-term focus	Long-term focus	Short-term focus	Long-term focus
Past-oriented	Routinely generated information	1 Environmental cost accounting (e.g. variable costing, absorption costing, and activity based costing)	2 Environmentally induced capital expenditure and revenues	9 Material and energy flow accounting (short-term impacts on the environment – product, site, division and company levels)	10 Environmental (or natural) capital impact accounting
Past-oriented	Ad-hoc information	3 Ex post assessment of relevant environmental costing decisions	4 Environmental life cycle (and target) costing Post investment assessment of individual projects	11 Ex post assessment of short-term environmental impacts (e.g. of a site or product)	12 Life cycle inventories Post investment assessment of physical environmental investment appraisal
Future-oriented	Routinely generated information	5 Monetary environmental operational budgeting (flows) Monetary environmental capital budgeting (stocks)	6 Environmental long-term financial planning	13 Physical environmental budgeting (flows and stocks) (e.g. material and energy flow activity based budgeting)	14 Long-term physical environmental planning
Future-oriented	Ad-hoc information	7 Relevant environmental costing (e.g. special orders, product mix with capacity constraint)	8 Monetary environmental project investment appraisal Environmental life cycle budgeting and target pricing	15 Relevant environmental impacts (e.g. given short run constraints on activities)	16 Physical environmental investment appraisal Life cycle analysis of specific project

Source: Burritt et al. (2002, p. 43).

The EMA framework differentiates management information into: physical and monetary dimensions (thus distinguishing monetary environmental management accounting – MEMA – and physical environmental management accounting – PEMA); the time frame of decision making – past, present and future; length of time frame – short- or long-run; and routineness of the information supplied – regular or ad hoc (Burritt et al., 2002). The framework can serve as a guide for decision makers in all functions of a company and for identification of the information properties that are relevant to corporate decision makers and to how these properties are related to EMA tools for collecting and managing environmentally related information. Such a framework can provide the foundation for comparing the scope, range and potential variability of environmental management accounting structures and processes in practice.

Based on the framework each manager can identify their decision situation, the kind of information required and the most adequate EMA tool(s). On a more general level, some decision situations and types of information may be more relevant for certain management roles than other types of information. Table 18.2 provides a generic overview of hypothesized typical information needs for different management roles (similar to Schaltegger et al., 2001). For each management role a rationale is put forward as to why certain types of environmental information and decision situations may be of highest interest.

While Table 18.2 provides some indication of what kind of tools may be relevant and supportive for which management role, this may particularly change in larger projects where different business functions are involved and interdepartmental transdisciplinary collaboration is required. For example, all management roles listed in Table 18.2 will at one stage be somehow involved in the development of a new production site. These collaboration processes may lead to an enlarged set of EMA tools applied or a selection and focus on some tools which are considered most important by the managers with most power. Contingency factors, such as the national and local legal situation, current topics in media and politics, the power of certain societal stakeholders, the strategy of the corporation, industry standards, isomorphic pressures, etc. may also influence the choice of tools implemented.

In sum, the conceptual and empirical literature shows that for different business functions, management roles and decision situations different types of information may be relevant. However, when observing implementation processes over time, case study-based empirical analyses reveal certain common patterns on what basis EMA and the development of EMA in corporate practices substantiate (Herzig et al., 2012).

The basis for most environmental information relevant to decision makers in a company is material and energy flow accounting which provides past-oriented information on short-term impacts on the environment on product, site, division and company levels (cell no. 9 in the framework in Table 18.1). Also the overview in Table 18.2 reveals a high relevance of PEMA, the physical environmental management accounting tools (right side in the EMA framework). While this fundamental role of physical information may be astonishing at first glance,

Table 18.2 Management roles and relevant EMA tools

Relevant EMA users	Rationale for link with accounting tools	Relevant EMA tools
Top managers	Main concern is with aggregate financial and strategic information about the company's overall investment and financial performance as well as with corporate reputation and legitimacy.	• MEMA (regular and ad hoc, long-term, past and future) • PEMA: physical information relating to reputation and legitimacy of the corporation • Cells 2, 4, 6 and 8 in Table 18.1
Finance managers	Focus is on short- and long-term investment and financial performance measures at the corporate, segmental and product levels, etc. Includes measures of costs of quality, health and safety and human resources management.	• MEMA (regular and ad hoc, long- and short-term, past and future) • Physical information providing the basis for financial implications (taxes, etc.) • Cells 1, 2, 3, 4, 5, 6, 7 and 8 in Table 18.1
Corporate communication and PR managers	Information about stakeholder claims. Physical and financial information on the company's environmental impacts and efforts for pollution reduction and prevention.	• MEMA and PEMA (regular and ad hoc, long-term, past and future) • Cells 2, 4, 6, 8, 10, 12, 14 and 16 in Table 18.1
Human resource managers	Main emphasis is on short-term physical information about employee numbers and types, allocation to segments of the business, turnover, satisfaction, morale and financial information about employee rewards.	• MEMA and PEMA (regular and ad hoc, short-term, past and future-orientated) • Cells 1, 3, 5, 7, 9, 11, 13 and 15 in Table 18.1
Legal managers	Main concern is with physical information about compliance with legislation and regulation and financial penalties for non-compliance.	• PEMA (regular and ad hoc, short-term, past and future) • Cells 9, 11, 13 and 15 (and some concern for 1, 3, 5 and 7) in Table 18.1

Environmental, health and safety managers	Emphasis on physical measures of material and energy flows and stocks and related processes and products, and their impacts upon the environment.	• PEMA (regular and ad hoc, long- and short-term, future and past) • Cells 9, 10, 11, 12, 13, 14, 15 and 16 in Table 18.1
Quality managers	Main focus is on physical information about technical product attributes, and aspects of personnel and technology that provide the customer service or product.	• PEMA (regular and ad hoc, long- and short-term, past and future-orientated) • Cells 9, 10, 11, 12, 13, 14, 15 and 16 (regarding environmental quality management) in Table 18.1
R&D managers	Focus on information about the technical feasibility and environmental impacts of newly designed products, services and operations.	• PEMA (ad hoc, long-term, future) • Cell 16 in Table 18.1
Procurement managers	Requires information about quality and environmental properties of the goods and services purchased, and information about prices.	• MEMA and PEMA (regular and ad hoc, short-term, past and future) • Cells 1, 3, 5, 7, 9, 11, 13 and 15 in Table 18.1
Production managers	Main concern is with short-term information about material and energy flows and production scheduling.	• PEMA (regular, short-term, past and future) • boxes 9, 11, 13 and 15 in Table 18.1
Logistics managers	Based on physical measures e.g. on distribution means and storage facilities and related environmental impacts.	• PEMA (regular and ad hoc, long- and short-term, past and future) • Cells 9, 10, 11, 12, 13, 14, 15 and 16 in Table 18.1
Marketing and sales (and product management)	Information on operational market conditions (e.g. pricing, competitor activities) and customer demands.	• MEMA and PEMA (regular and ad hoc, short-term, past and future) • Cells 1, 3, 5, 7, 9, 11, 13 and 15 in Table 18.1

Note
Numbers relate to cells in Table 18.1.

it becomes more obvious when unravelling the basis of financially relevant corporate environmental and social issues. Even managers whose role is financially oriented need information on the quantitative, physical basis to calculate, estimate or check the monetary relevance of the non-financial issue. For example, the financial relevance of CO_2-emissions depends not only on the costs per tonne of CO_2 but also on the quantity emitted. This shows that physical environmental and social sustainability information is not just relevant for management roles with a key task to improve the environmental and social performance of the company but also for management roles with a 'pure' financial focus.

For managers with sustainability jobs, in turn, financial information may be important to support activities and projects with a primary social or environmental purpose. For example, the reduction of water discharges may require either an improvement of the sewage plant or an investment in closed-water loop production equipment. The latter conforms to a pollution prevention approach and can reduce production costs at the same time. As this is often not known by managers whose role is not related to environmental protection or production system development, the financial arguments and calculations may be helpful to support the superior approach.

Revealing the interlinkages between physical and monetary environmental management accounting and the process of enlarging the information basis for discussions with an extended range of management roles or even with external stakeholders shows that the introduction of EMA and sustainability management accounting is not a question of a 'one-for-all-times' top management decision but rather an emergent process based on interactions between different business functions, managers and stakeholders. These interactions may be facilitated by management accountants acting as information system and transfer organizers (e.g. Tushman & Scanlan, 1981).

For example, once the initial physical material and energy flow accounting (cell no 9 in the framework in Table 18.1) is introduced by functional managers it can be established as a routinely generating information system by management accountants supporting the functional managers. The interaction between these roles may be the basis for further developing the EMA system over time to create long-term information. As a consequence, EMA expands towards the support of long-term oriented decision making (expansion towards cell no. 10). Furthermore, for some management roles such as in finance a link to monetary information related to environmental issues is crucial and will lead to an expansion of the EMA system to include monetary information (thus including cells no. 1 and 2).

Although the existing case study-based research provides indication that sustainability management accounting is a pragmatically developed approach which does not follow a predefined 'one right way' further research is needed to understand better what motivates different management roles to engage in sustainability management accounting and what obstacles exist. To receive a better understanding of these issues may be particularly relevant for management accountants whose role to support all business functions with sustainability management accounting systems, methods, data and indicators. Therefore, they require a good insight into why and when managers in different business functions are interested and engaged in actively using sustainability information to be effective in their job.

Conclusions

For the last two decades, sustainability issues have been increasingly influential on the economic success of ever more companies. As conventional management accounting has not been able to provide the relevant information needed to successfully manage sustainability challenges a range of new measurement and management tools have been developed to create, analyse and communicate sustainability information. While management accountants and controllers have in the main been very little involved in sustainability management of large companies, sustainability management accounting has been largely developed and practiced by non-management accountants in almost every corporate department. This development reflects a pragmatic perspective on sustainability accounting, with the identification of key sustainability issues and the choice of a set of adequate tools required to assist managers with responsibility for achieving purposive sustainability goals in their business functions and for the company as a whole. This includes a contingent specification of what sustainability performance entails in the context of the organization, its business environment and social setting. Such specification in the context of vexed, highly complex and intertwined sustainability problems requires transdisciplinary approaches and the involvement of a broad range of actors in the company as well as from external stakeholders, with the effect of opening up the boundaries between management and financial accounting and reporting. This pragmatic interaction-based process of developing sustainability management accounting in business functions has lead and may lead in many cases to a focus on a number of prioritized aspects of sustainability (such as eco-efficiency of production, health and working conditions in the supply chain, etc.) in the future. If improved without missing the overall goal of sustainable development, these partial developments can contribute to improving overall sustainability performance. Based on the identification of key sustainability issues the requirements and management accounting tools for which data need to be gathered, aggregated, communicated and used in different decision settings can be specified. One proposed unifying approach is sustainability management control (Schaltegger, 2011) which aims to establish explicit links between different issues, indicators and management areas to coordinate activities and actors towards improving the overall sustainability performance of the company and its contributions to sustainable development at large.

Given the novelty and difference of sustainability issues to conventional financial issues management accountants are challenged to redefine and further develop their role as coordinators and organizers of processes and system developments for the management of sustainability information as integrated part of the overall measurement and information management system of the company.

As a consequence, the skill sets of management accountants need to be developed in order that they can build beyond conventional management accounting to address sustainability issues. Apart from related educational and training challenges this may require a new and fundamentally broader understanding of the role of management accountants than in the past.

References

Apgar, J. M., Argumedo, A. & Allen, W. (2009). Building transdisciplinarity for managing complexity: Lessons from indigenous practice. *International Journal of Interdisciplinary Social Sciences, 4*(5), 255–270.

Baker, M. & Schaltegger, S. (2015). Pragmatism and new directions in social and environmental accountability research. *Accounting, Auditing and Accountability Journal, 28*(2), 263–294.

Balmer, J. (2010). The BP Deepwater Horizon débâcle and corporate brand exuberance. *Journal of Brand Management, 18*(2), 97–104.

Balmer, J., Powell, S. & Greyser, S. (2011). Explicating ethical corporate marketing. Insights from the BP Deepwater Horizon catastrophe: The ethical brand that exploded and then imploded. *Journal of Business Ethics, 102*(1), 1–14.

Bennett, M., Schaltegger, S. & Zvezdov, D. (2012). *The practice of corporate sustainability accounting.* London: ICAEW.

Bennett, M., Schaltegger, S. & Zvezdov, D. (2013). *Exploring corporate practices in management accounting for sustainability.* London: Institute for Chartered Accountants of England and Wales (ICAEW).

Beske, P., Johnson, M. & Schaltegger, S. (2015). 20 years of performance measurement in sustainable supply chain management. What has been achieved? *Supply Chain Management. An International Journal, 20*(6), 664–680.

Burns, J. & Baldvinsdottir, G. (2007). The changing role of management accountants. In T. Hopper, R. Scapens & D. Northcott (Eds.), *Issues in Management Accounting* (pp. 117–132). London: Prentice Hall.

Burritt, R. L. (2012). Environmental performance accountability: Planet, people, profits. *Accounting, Auditing and Accountability Journal, 25*(2), 370–405.

Burritt, R. & Schaltegger, S. (2010). Sustainability accounting and reporting: Fad or trend? *Accounting, Auditing and Accountability Journal, 23*(7), 829–846.

Burritt, R., Hahn, T. & Schaltegger, S. (2002). Towards a comprehensive framework for environmental management accounting: Links between business actors and environmental management accounting tools. *Australian Accounting Review, 12*(2), 39–50.

Byrne, S. & Pierce, B. (2007). Towards a more comprehensive understanding of the roles of management accountants. *European Accounting Review, 16*(3), 469–498.

Carroll, A. B. & Shabana, K. M. (2010). The business case for corporate social responsibility: A review of concepts, research and practice. *International Journal of Management Reviews, 12*(1), 85–105.

Chapman, C. (1997). Reflections on a contingent view of accounting. *Accounting, Organizations and Society, 22*(2), 189–205.

CIMA (Chartered Institute of Management Accountants). (1981). *CIMA Official Terminology.* London: CIMA.

Dao, V., Langella, I. & Carbo, J. (2011). From Green to Sustainability: Information Technology and an Integrated Sustainability Framework. *The Greening of IT, 20*(1), 63–79.

Donaldson, L. (2001). *The contingency theory of organizations*. London: Sage.

Elkington, J. (1998). *Cannibals with forks: The triple bottom line of 21 century business*. Gabriola Island, BC, Canada: New Society Publishers.

Gibassier, D. & Schaltegger, S. (2015). Carbon management accounting and reporting in practice: A case study on converging emergent approaches. *Sustainability Accounting, Management and Policy Journal, 6*(3), 340–365.

Goretzki, L., Strauß, E. & Weber, J. (2013). An institutional perspective on the changes in management accountants' professional role. *Management Accounting Research, 24*(1), 41–63.

Graafland, J. & van de Ven, B. (2006). Strategic and moral motivation for Corporate Social Responsibility. *Journal of Corporate Citizenship, 2006*(22), 111–123.

Gray, R. (2010). Is accounting for sustainability actually accounting for sustainability … and how would we know? An exploration of narratives of organisations and the planet. *Accounting, Organizations and Society, 35*(1), 47–62.

Hahn, T., Figge, F., Pinkse, J. & Preuss, L. (2010). Trade-offs in corporate sustainability: You can't have your cake and eat it. *Business Strategy and the Environment, 19*, 217–229.

Hansen, E. G., Grosse-Dunker, F. & Reichwald, R. (2010). Sustainability innovation cube: A framework to evaluate sustainability-oriented innovations. *International Journal of Innovation Management, 13*(4), 683–713.

Herzig, C., Viere, T., Schaltegger, S. & Burritt, R. (2012). *Environmental Management Accounting: Cases of South-East Asian companies*. Abingdon, UK/New York: Routledge.

Hörisch, J. & Windolph, S. (2014). Overview of the aggregate results of the International Corporate Sustainability Barometer. In S. Schaltegger, S. E. Windolph, D. Harms & J. Hörisch (Eds.), *Corporate sustainability in international comparison: State of practice, opportunities and challenges* (pp. 21–33). Dordrecht: Springer.

Jaegersberg, G. & Ure, J. (2011). Barriers to knowledge sharing and stakeholder alignment in solar energyclusters: Learning from other sectors and regions. *Journal of Strategic Information Systems, 20*(4), 343–354.

Jones, K. & Rubin, P. (1999). Effects of harmful environmental events on reputations of firms. Available at SSRN: http://ssrn.com/abstract=158849 or http://dx.doi.org/10.2139/ssrn.158849.

Kaplan, R. S. & Johnson, H. T. (1987). Relevance lost: The rise and fall of management accounting. Boston: Harvard Business School Press.

Lambert, C. & Sponem, S. (2012). Roles, authority and involvement of the management accounting function: A multiple case-study perspective. *European Accounting Review, 21*(3), 565–589.

Lang, D., Wiek, A., Bergmann, M., Stauffacher, M., Martens, P. & Moll, P. (2012). Transdisciplinary research in sustainability science: Practice, principles, and challenges. *Sustainability Science, 7*(S1), 25–43.

Maas, K., Schaltegger, S. & Crutzen, N. (forthcoming 2016). Integrating corporate sustainability performance measurement, management control and reporting. *Journal of Cleaner Production*.

Mathews, M. R. (1997). Twenty-five years of social and environmental accounting research: Is there a silver jubilee to celebrate? *Accounting, Auditing and Accountability Journal, 10*(4), 481–531.

Maunders, K. T. & Burritt, R. L. (1991). Accounting and ecological crisis. *Accounting, Auditing and Accountability Journal, 4*(3), 9–26.

Melville, N. P. (2010). Information systems innovation for environmental sustainability. *MIS Quarterly, 34*(1), 1–21.

Mills, E., Shamshoian, G., Blazek, M., Naughton, P., Seese, R., Tschudi, W. & Sartor, D. (2008). The business case for energy management in high-tech industries. *Journal of Energy Efficiency, 1*(1), 5–20.

Morales, J. & Lambert, C. (2013). Dirty work and the construction of identity: An ethnographic study of management accounting practices, *Accounting, Organizations and Society, 38*(3), 228–244.

Petrini, M. & Pozzebon, M. (2009). Managing sustainability with the support of business intelligence: Integrating socio-environmental indicators and organisational context. *Journal of Strategic Information Systems, 18*(4), 178–191.

Pierce, B. & O'Dea, T. (2003). Management accounting information and the needs of managers: Perceptions of accountants and managers compared. *The British Accounting Review, 35*(3), 257–290.

Porter, M. E. & Linde, C. van der (1995). Green and competitive: Ending the stalemate. *Harvard Business Review, 73*(5), 120–133.

Schaltegger, S. (2011). Sustainability as a driver for corporate economic success: Consequences for the development of sustainability management control. *Society and Economy, 33*(1), 15–28.

Schaltegger, S. & Burritt, R. (2000). *Contemporary environmental accounting: Issues, concepts and practice.* Greenleaf Publishing.

Schaltegger, S. & Burritt, R. (2015). Business cases and corporate engagement with sustainability: Differentiating ethical motivations. *Journal of Business Ethics, 126*, 1–19.

Schaltegger, S. & Herzig, C. (2011). Managing supplier requirements with HSE accounting: The case of the mechanical engineering company Bisma Jaya, Indonesia. *Issues in Social and Environmental Accounting, 5*(1/2), 82–105.

Schaltegger, S. & Synnestvedt, T. (2002). The link between "green" and economic success: Environmental management as the crucial trigger between environmental and economic performance. *Journal of Environmental Management, 65*(4), 339–346.

Schaltegger, S. & Zvezdov, D. (2015). Gatekeepers of sustainability information: Exploring the roles of accountants. *Journal of Accounting and Organizational Change, 11*(3), 333–361.

Schaltegger, S., Beckmann, M. & Hansen, E. (2013a). Transdisciplinarity in Corporate Sustainability: Mapping the Field. *Business Strategy and the Environment, 22*(4), 219–229.

Schaltegger, S., Burritt, R., Zvezdov, D., Hörisch, J. & Tingey-Holyoak, J. (2015). Management roles and sustainability information: Exploring corporate practices. *Australian Accounting Review, 25*(4), 328–345.

Schaltegger, S., Hahn, T. & Burritt, R. (2001). Environmental management accounting: Overview and main approaches. In M. Bennett & J. J. Bouma (Eds.), *Environmental Management Accounting and the Role of Information Systems.* Springer-Kluwer.

Schaltegger, S., Harms, D., Hörisch, J., Windolph, S. E., Burritt, R., Carter, A. et al. (2013b). *International Corporate Sustainability Barometer: A Comparative Study of 11 Countries*, with prefaces from E. U. von Weizsäcker and John Elkington. Lüneburg: CSM.

Schaltegger, S., Lüdeke-Freund, F. & Hansen, E. (2012). Business cases for sustainability: The role of business model innovation for corporate sustainability. *International Journal of Innovation and Sustainable Development, 6*(2), 95–119.

Schaltegger, S., Windolph, S. E., Harms, D. & Hörisch, J. (2014). *Corporate sustainability in international comparison: State of practice, opportunities and challenges.* Heidelberg: Springer.

Searcy, D. & Elkhawas, C. (2012). Corporate sustainability ratings: An investigation into how corporations use the Dow Jones Sustainability Index. *Journal of Cleaner Production, 35* (November), 79–92.

Tushman, M. L. & Scanlan, T. J. (1981). Boundary spanning individuals: Their role in information transfer and their antecedents. *Academy of Management Journal, 24*(2), 289–305.

UN (United Nations, General Assembly). (2015). Transforming our world: The 2030 agenda for sustainable development (Seventieth session; agenda items 15 and 116; A/RES/70/1). Retrieved from https://sustainabledevelopment.un.org/content/documents/21252030%20Agenda%20for%20Sustainable%20Development%20web.pdf.

von Weizsäcker, E. U., Hargroves, K., Smith, M., Desha, C. & Stasinopoulos, P. (2009). *Factor five: Transforming the global economy through 80% improvements in resource productivity.* London: Earthscan.

Whiteman, G., Walker, B. & Perego, P. (2013). Planetary boundaries: Ecological foundations for corporate sustainability. *Journal of Management Studies, 50*, 307–336.

Wilmshurst, T. D. & Frost, G. R. (2001). The role of accounting and the accountant in the environmental management system. *Business Strategy and the Environment, 10*(3), 135–147.

19 The influence of the economic crisis on the tasks and roles of management accountants

Sebastian D. Becker and
Matthias D. Mahlendorf

Introduction

Crises pose substantial threats to organizations (Ury & Smoke, 1991), lead to high degrees of uncertainty (Rosenthal, Charles, & 't Hart, 1989; Rosenthal & 't Hart, 1991), and offer very little time to respond (Hermann, 1963). To address these threats adequately, decision-makers need to first understand the financial and non-financial impacts of a crisis. After such an analysis, they can then develop countermeasures whose envisaged effects need to be calculated, planned, and implemented. Management accountants (MAs) routinely handle these tasks owing to their access to the data necessary for such analyses and since they are usually responsible for planning and budgeting. Given their expertise, MAs may thus be helpful in crisis situations and instrumental in organizational efforts to assess and counteract these. Hence, it seems likely that they are highly affected by an economic crisis. Previous management accounting and control research, however, has offered few insights in this respect. It is therefore the aim of this chapter to investigate whether and how an economic crisis in general, with the particular example of the economic crisis that began in 2008 under study, changes the tasks and the roles of MAs.

To offer insights into this question, we review previous studies and draw on data collected in interviews as well as through a content analysis of practitioner articles. In section 2, we briefly present the limited extant literature on the consequences of an economic crisis on the tasks and roles of MAs. Section 3 details the research methods we used for collecting and analysing our data. We present and discuss our findings in section 4. Section 5 summarizes and concludes the chapter.

Previous literature

Given the large impact of economic crises on organizations (Furman & Stiglitz, 1998), it is important to better understand an organization's response to these external influences. Despite calls for research on the effect of external economic crises on management accounting and control (e.g. Hopwood, 2009; Van der Stede, 2011), few papers have thus far studied this question.[1] The majority of such studies have analysed the changes to management accounting practices, often focusing on budgeting practices (e.g. Becker et al., 2016), which is not surprising given their centrality for management accounting and control. Becker et al. (2016), for example, provided evidence that during a crisis, budgeting becomes more important for planning and resource allocation, but less relevant for performance evaluation. In addition, two studies have investigated how the information flow changes within an organization impacted by an economic crisis (Ezzamel & Bourn, 1990; Olofsson & Svalander, 1975).

Endenich (2014) compared the impact of economic crises in Spain and Germany. By examining changes in the tasks and roles of MAs, he found that management accounting departments analyse potential ways of reducing costs related to investments, production processes, and human resources following the onset of a crisis. Further, tasks typically centre on ensuring liquidity as well as on more continuous forms of budgeting through shorter-term planning ranges (see also Asel, Posch, & Speckbacher, 2011) and rolling forecasts. The study also found an increase in the interaction of MAs with management and a resulting rise in MAs' importance and appreciation.

Research method

To develop additional insights into changes to the tasks and roles of MAs in response to economic crises, we drew on two types of data. First, we analysed interviews conducted for a previous research project on the impact of the 2008 economic crisis on budgeting (Becker et al., 2016). To better understand the data collected from archival and survey sources, we additionally conducted 11 semi-structured interviews with MAs[2] working in a representative set of industries affected by the economic crisis. By using an interview guide, we encouraged interviewees to speak about the impact of the economic crisis on their companies' management accounting and control practices. Of relevance for this study's research question, interviewees also alluded to several issues relating to how their tasks and roles changed throughout the crisis. The interviews lasted between 30 and 60 minutes and were tape-recorded to ease further analysis of the data (see Becker et al., 2016 for an overview of interviewees).

In addition, to provide a broader picture of practitioners' views of the crisis, we reviewed articles published in the most important practitioner magazine for German-speaking countries, the *Controller Magazin*, as a secondary source of data. Many of its articles are written by an active community of practitioners, consultants, and academics reporting about particular companies, their management accounting and control practices, or the management accounting function more generally. These articles represent a valuable source of the changes practitioners have seen in particular organizations (Hsie & Shannon, 2005).

To identify relevant articles, we searched for the keyword "crisis" in the title. When talking about an economic crisis, some articles related to the energy crisis at the beginning of the 1980s or the early 2000s recession; however, the majority of articles were concerned with the economic crisis that started in 2008. We read the relevant articles and also looked through their references, which allowed us to find further articles or reports with relevant data. In summary, we conducted a content analysis of 23 articles (numbered 1–23 in the following; see Table 19.1 in the Appendix for an overview).

Results

In the following, we first describe the impact of the economic crisis on the *tasks* of MAs. Second, we discuss how these changes affected the *roles* of MAs.

Tasks of MAs

Overall, our analyses show that the economic crisis led to substantial changes in the *emphasis* of the classical tasks of MAs as well as the introduction of new tasks in some companies (Article 7; Weber & Zubler, 2010). Moreover, some companies started doing things that other companies had been doing for a longer time. In this respect, the crisis served as a "wake-up call" for companies to improve their management accounting and control practices (Weber & Zubler, 2010; see also Endenich, 2014).

In the following, we roughly order the practices according to the urgency of the change (as mentioned in our data), starting with those practices affected immediately and subsequently discussing those practices that changed later. First, managers had to understand where the crisis hit the company most. Hence, accountants had to provide more frequent variance analyses from the start of the crisis. In addition, an imminent threat for many companies was a lack of liquidity. Relatedly, during the first months of the crisis, one of the biggest changes was in the area of cost management and budgetary planning, followed by the area of long-term planning; later, reporting tasks also became important (Weber & Zubler, 2010).

Variance analysis

When the crisis hit first, very large variances between budgeted and actual values arose for many firms, especially with respect to revenues, incoming orders, and customer payment dates. Our data suggest that variance analysis has thus become more important in companies impacted by the crisis. Sources said that companies were moving from comparing planned with actual values to comparing actual with actual values (i.e. current data compared with the previous year or previous months, see interview) or planned with forecasted values (Article 11). This forward-looking practice shows that if an expected gap becomes visible, more action is needed in order to close it.

Moreover, we learned that executives high up in the organizational hierarchy became more interested in variance analysis, exerted pressure to improve forecast accuracy, and increasingly asked questions such as "What are the reasons for the variances, how are you going to change and with which action plans?" (interviewee, retailer) (Becker et al., 2016, p. 17).

Dropping value for a cash orientation

As a consequence of the drastic declines in demand and capital availability in many industries during the crisis, managing liquidity became a vital issue for organizations threatened by the crisis (Article 16; Hopwood, 2009). Under normal circumstances, MAs may follow the dictum of value orientation. By applying concepts such as Economic Value Added (e.g. Malmi & Ikäheimo, 2003; Wallace, 1998), they would prioritize those choices that have the highest long-term payoffs – adjusted for the involved risk and cost of capital. During the crisis, however, we found that cash flow considerations seemed to have gained priority over a value orientation. Many companies were fighting hard to avoid insolvency (Article 21) and some told us that they conducted weekly or even daily liquidity meetings.

Yet, improving cash flow involves tough choices that may reduce long-term company value. In one of our interviews, an MA from a glass and ceramics manufacturer told us about the option of shutting down a melting oven that had run non-stop for several years. Such ovens have enormous energy costs that lead to negative cash flow if products cannot be sold during phases of low demand such as during the crisis. Shutting those ovens down immediately improves cash flow substantially. As a consequence, however, the cooling glass clogs parts of the machinery. Hence, the company expected vast replacement/repair costs later when the ovens were restarted. Depending on the length of the crisis, such replacement costs might be much higher than the savings from the reduced energy costs. Thus, a company has to prioritize between the risk of becoming insolvent in the short-term and the risk of destroying company value in the long-term.

In addition, the practitioner articles we found reported that firms have established comprehensive planning and control systems to manage liquidity in order to understand the consequences of payment defaults by customers (Article 5; Article 11) as well as ensure compliance with covenants (Article 9). These systems need to work alongside a more centralized cash management approach as well as the constant monitoring of working capital (Article 9; Article 17; Weber & Zubler, 2010).

Cost management

Related to the issue of ensuring liquidity is the pressure to reduce costs. The results show that within the initial phases of the economic crisis, conducting cost cutting and cost savings projects were tasks in which MAs were very much involved. For this reason, these have been described as the "standard repertoire" of MAs during economically difficult times (Article 10; Weber & Zubler, 2010). It was also mentioned, however, that cost-cutting should not be undertaken "across the board" as a hectic response to an economic crisis; rather, costs should be cut strategically (Article 8). In some firms, cost management was modernized in the sense that new IT systems were put in place (Article 9).

Planning

As mentioned above, budgetary planning and control was one of the practices most impacted by the economic crisis. There is some debate in the literature around whether organizations and MAs should engage in more or less planning when a crisis hits (see Becker et al., 2016) given that crises strongly increase uncertainty. On the one hand, changes happen so frequently that plans quickly become outdated (Hopwood, 2009; Van der Stede, 2011). On the other hand, demand for planning may increase because companies' information deficit grows (Widener, 2007). Moreover, the proportion of relevant information held by decentralized units increases (Burns & Stalker, 1961; Donaldson, 2001), because they are closer to their respective markets. Since budgetary planning and control can reduce the information asymmetry between a headquarters and its decentralized units, one would expect the planning function of budgeting to become more important in times of crisis. The recent study by Becker et al. (2016) supported this view; the findings reported below also corroborate this perspective.

Given that the development of the economic crisis was difficult to predict (Weber & Zubler, 2010), companies were reported to be planning "non-stop" to reduce their planning cycles and to incorporate newly gathered market information in order to cope with the increased uncertainty (Article 9). To do so, a planning practice adopted in most firms was forecasting or rolling forecasting. In many firms, running the forecasting process also became the "dominant" task for MAs during the economic crisis. Further, if companies had already been using (rolling) forecasts before the crisis, they often increased their frequency during the crisis (Article 7; Article 11; Article 12; Weber & Zubler, 2010). Further, companies were reported to be forecasting not only traditional key performance indicators (KPIs) such as revenue, materials costs, and overhead costs, but also the impact of early warning indicators such as the general business outlook or changes in the ability of customers to pay (Article 11; Article 12). In summary, this increase in the frequency of planning as well as the permanent review of plans and their adjustment was often called "driving by sight" (Article 9; see also Becker et al., 2016; Endenich, 2014; Hopwood, 2009).

While preparing plans and budgets anew, which often happened as a result of the economic crisis, many reports actually mentioned that companies also introduced scenarios (Article 7; Article 11; Article 12; Article 14; Weber & Zubler, 2010). An MA from an automobile supplier told us:

> [Now we also] include scenarios. We not only look at variances ex post but also dive into scenarios when preparing the plan ex ante … it may be requested to analyse what happens if revenue is plus or minus 20 percent, or … [when] the profit margin is plus or minus 5 percent.

Scenarios were needed because the magnitude of the shock was not known ex ante and because "in the crisis, [decision-makers] never knew how far things could fall" (Becker et al., 2016, p. 17). Moreover, scenarios were said to help create an awareness of issues not directly visible (Weber & Zubler, 2010). In addition, planning was reported to have become much more top-down or iterative when before it was more bottom-up, especially in the companies more strongly impacted by the crisis (Weber & Zubler, 2010). While this could have been a reflection of saving time and resources in planning, as these were already done more frequently and for shorter horizons, Weber and Zubler (2010) showed that companies did not reduce the level of detail in these plans, which could have been another route to saving time and resources in this highly resource-intensive practice. In addition, many companies impacted strongly by the economic crisis moved from preparing plans by extrapolating historical information (ex-post-plus planning) to using completely new assumptions when building budgets, a change that increased the intensity of MAs' work. Becker et al. (2016) also reported that MAs were being explicitly asked to coordinate between different business units and departments and ensure that these bodies had aligned plans to eliminate any slack.

Managerial reporting

Managerial reporting has changed in many ways as a result of the crisis impact. First, many articles mentioned that reporting cycles have shortened to allow quick overviews of the current situation (Article 6; Weber & Zubler, 2010; see also Ezzamel & Bourn, 1990). Moreover, especially at the beginning of the economic crisis, reporting also increased on the progress made in the implementation of cost-cutting and cost-saving measures (Article 9; Article 11). Second, many articles showed that the content of these reports changed in several ways. On the one hand, while KPIs regarding product and organizational performance were under focus in the pre-crisis period, focus was shifted to KPIs regarding cash management, operating cash flow, net working capital, the development of raw materials prices, and customer payments in order to constantly monitor financial solvency (Article 6) as the financing situation and customers' ability to pay deteriorated (Weber & Zubler, 2010). Given these financing problems as well as the competition for capital with other companies, some commentators also said that the capital market orientation increased to ease financing (Weber & Zubler, 2010). Moreover, there was more open information exchange with outside stakeholders to rebuild some of the trust in management lost through the crisis (Article 6; see also Van der Stede, 2011). Third, Weber and Zubler (2010) showed that the nature of information had changed. Because many KPIs could no longer be compared with past measures or other business units, they were presented relative to peers in the same industry. This presented a challenge in terms of data availability; indeed, when new KPIs were found, whether these were understandable and actionable was questionable.

New tasks related to customers, compliance, and suppliers

In addition to the changes to the classical tasks of MAs, the practitioner articles also reported that a few new tasks were added to their portfolio of responsibilities during the economic crisis. First, MAs implemented or took over *accounts receivable and claims management* (Article 10; Article 13; Weber & Zubler, 2010) to avoid having to rely on the diminishing amount of external financing. These tasks included appraising the creditworthiness of new customers as well as enforcing increased contractual protection with risky customers (Article 13). Second, MAs were asked to supply and interpret *compliance-related information* for managers owing to the additional regulations introduced during the economic crisis. This presumes an understanding of the regulations and their implications (Article 18; Article 19).

In the crisis period, troubled companies also needed to appease their suppliers. Due to cash constraints, suppliers were often paid only after several reminders. As the situation worsened, companies even needed to ask for deferred payments. In such a situation, MAs can play an important role, as they are experts on expected cash flow and can therefore become involved in negotiations with suppliers. When confronted with such a task, MAs need to be sensitive to avoid conveying the impression that the company is on the brink of bankruptcy. If suppliers notice serious financial trouble and do not trust that this liquidity shortage is only temporary, they might start to reclaim unpaid supplies and demand pre-payment for new deliveries, which has negative consequences on cash flow (Faulhaber, Landwehr, & Grabow, 2009, p. 62).

Strategic tasks and strategic planning

Strategy-related tasks were in some cases emphasized by practitioners to improve early warning systems and thus better foresee the arrival and impact of future crises (Article 2; Article 23). Further, MAs increasingly checked whether strategies were economically sustainable (Article 3), especially in companies in which MAs did not normally address these types of questions (Article 9). In particular, MAs were frequently asked to take over risk analysis and management tasks (Article 4; Weber & Zubler, 2010).

Roles of MAs

The interviews and the practitioner articles we analysed mentioned several issues related to the roles of MAs during the economic crisis. One issue was the rise in stress for MAs (Article 1). In some cases, MAs worked 20 per cent longer working hours, with 40 per cent of MAs working more than 50 hours per week in the post-crisis period compared with not more than 25 per cent before the crisis (Article 9; Weber & Zubler, 2010). Given the changes in tasks (e.g. those around planning and reporting/information supply) as well as the new tasks to be undertaken, this increase in workload seemed understandable. One accountant from a glass and ceramics manufacturing company illustrated the increased pressure as follows:

> Variances between actual and forecasted liquidity ... were tracked even closer due to the crisis. More important people called you to increase pressure to forecast correctly, better, or more precisely.

A senior controller at a car manufacturer told us:

> During a crisis, as a management accountant you are really squeezed out.

Given, however, that these tasks and the intensive demand for more and updated information were all requested by management (Article 12), MAs found themselves having an increased influence on management's decision-making. A corporate controller from a German holding company told us:

> As a young person, coming from university, you usually expect that investments will always strictly be handled based on cost-benefit criteria. When you arrive, in reality, things look quite different, of course. In large corporations, it will probably be more the case, because formalization is also much higher. But when you arrive at the Mittelstand, you see a little bit of this and a little bit of that. Let me put is as follows: Before the crisis, managers here received as much as they needed to adequately run their business. And [resource allocation] was more generous [than actually necessary]. After the crisis, applying the principles and orderly checking of whether these resources can actually be profitably invested played a bigger role.

In this company, because profitability calculations were carried out by MAs, this enabled them to position themselves as an effective partner of management, both formally and through informal communication and improved personal relationships (Article 9; Weber & Zubler, 2010). Especially in companies where MAs were previously not close to management – such as in small and medium-sized enterprises – this may have been a noticeable change in the role of MAs. Janke, Mahlendorf, and Weber (2014, p. 264), for example, quoted:

> [The CEO] visited our [i.e. the financial managers'] offices more often and said "Have a quick look. Is this possible? This can't be right! Why do we have four million less here?"

As a consequence, many practitioner articles mentioned that an adage was confirmed during an economic crisis: "bad times for the company are good times for the controller" (Article 7; Article 12; Article 13; Article 15; Article 19; Article 20; Article 22; Weber & Zubler, 2010). An MA from a technology manufacturing company illustrated the mindset that strengthened the role of MAs:

> We also used this [i.e. the crisis] as a chance. This is like taking a sauna. You enter with a little pad of fat that has accumulated over time and then you come out of the sauna strengthened, the fat is gone, the unnecessary removed, and the strong ones emerge from the crisis even stronger.

Moreover, controllers acted as "pilots" and were responsible for ensuring not only transparency in the organization but also that expected results could be met.

They further needed to recognize the crisis impact in the data (Article 3) and take the initiative to lead companies out of the crisis (Article 4).

This increased proximity to management was further said to have stimulated the role change of MAs in moving from a "bean counter" to a "business partner" role. Some practitioner articles even reported that MAs would proactively push countermeasures or stimulate innovation to tackle the economic crisis instead of blocking them as perhaps previously in their roles of "savings superintendent" or the "natural enemies" of innovation (Article 12; Article 13; Article 22). Hence, while the traditional tasks of MAs were more backward-looking and scorekeeping (e.g. Burns & Baldvinsdottir, 2007), which prevented MAs from recognizing crises early and interpreting them correctly (Article 5), MAs in times of crisis were asked to support and advise managers in coping with uncertainty (Article 9; Weber & Zubler, 2010) as well as develop instruments that could detect future crises and model their impact on their organization (Article 4). Along those lines, Janke, Mahlendorf, and Weber (2014, p. 264) quoted an MA who experienced "permanent in-depth questions from the board of directors to the controlling department – the board recognized that it has to pay more attention to risks". Moreover, along with the new focus on reducing risks in the future, MAs sometimes "got more involved in strategic processes" (Janke et al., 2014, p. 264).

Yet, given their increased proximity to management, MAs needed to improve their understanding of weak spots (e.g. in managerial initiatives) and thus question these critically (Weber & Zubler, 2010). This may be especially true because in economic crises in general, managers tend to blame external factors for their organization's situation (compared with consultants, who blame internal errors). Hence, an MA has to make management aware that it may have made mistakes (Article 4) that have led to the susceptibility of being impacted by the economic crisis or agreed certain ineffective measures. In addition, an economic crisis may lead to a perception of having lost control on the part of managers and may therefore induce them to take high risks or to behave irrationally. Again, an MA is needed to contain these developments (Article 4).

Beyond proximity to management, the data we gathered also indicated that MAs have more interaction with other departments, both formally and informally (Article 9; Weber & Zubler, 2010). For example, the implementation of countermeasures to respond to the economic crisis demanded interdisciplinary efforts in companies, leading to the development of new structures with employees from other departments (Article 6), not only market-facing units but also, for example, treasury or investor relations (Weber & Zubler, 2010).

Indeed, to have adequate resources for MAs' increased tasks, many management accounting and control departments actually *enlarged* during the crisis (Article 18), signalling that controller services are regarded as helpful and not a cost drain (Weber & Zubler, 2010). Nevertheless, in some, especially larger companies, the cost savings pressure instituted by management accounting departments themselves created pressure to reduce MA headcount as well (Article 19).

Conclusion

By drawing on data from interviews and practitioner studies, this research investigated the impact of the economic crisis on the tasks and roles of MAs. We found that crises have a substantial impact, less in terms of types of tasks but rather in terms of their emphasis. Regarding the more traditional tasks of MA, activities such as variance analysis, planning, forecasting, and reporting were conducted more frequently. Further, cash and liquidity management as well as cost management became more important and new tasks concerning strategies, customers, compliance, and suppliers were also performed.

At the same time, the roles of MAs changed. We found that managers higher up in the hierarchy requested input from MAs more often. While a consequence of this was increased pressure and stress, MAs also had the opportunity to have more impact with their work. For example, managers discussed numbers more often with their MAs and the management control system was used more in order to develop solutions by combining individual knowledge across hierarchical levels. Through this greater intraorganizational exposure, MAs moved closer to management and supported managers in decision-making more than they did before. Therefore, the economic crisis may have facilitated their often purported and aspired role change to becoming business partners.

While we mobilize academic literature from different contexts, our work is limited in the sense that our interviews and practitioner publications were all collected from German companies. Our findings may have to be qualified when applying them to other countries. Nevertheless, we are confident that MAs in other countries faced similar experiences – perhaps even stronger given that the German economy coped relatively well during the crisis.

Appendix

Table 19.1 Articles on the impact of an economic crisis on the tasks and roles of MAs published in *Controller Magazin*

1 Biel, Alfred (1983): Controlling – Ein Instrument zur Krisen-Vorsorge und Krisen-Bewältigung, Vol. 8, No. 2/1983, pp. 77–81.
2 Kropfberger, Dietrich (1983): Krisen erfolgreich beherrschen – Die Anforderungen der 80er Jahre an die Unternehmensführung, Vol. 8, No. 4/1983, pp. 185–189.
3 Remmel, Manfred (1993): Zu Standort und Krise – Eröffnungsvortrag zum 18. Congress der Controller in München, Vol. 18, No. 5/1993, pp. 247–250.
4 Sudmann, Lars, and Wolfram Lenzen (2004): Psychologie der Krise – Über die Wirkung von psychologischen Faktoren auf die Unternehmensführung und das Controlling, Vol. 29, No. 6/2004, pp. 593–600.
5 Ederer, Franz (2005): Controller im Mittelstand, Vol. 30, No. 2/2005, pp. 130–140.
6 Sendel-Müller, Markus (2008): Krisenmanagement, Verhaltensanomalien und Controlling, Vol. 33, No. 4/2008, pp. 73–77.
7 Weber, Jürgen (2009): Controller in der Krise, Vol. 34, No. 2/2009, p. 14.
8 Biel, Alfred (2009): Controlling in harten Zeiten – Interview mit Siegfrid Gänßlen, Vol. 34, No. 3/2009, p. 21.
9 Rehring, Jochen, Jürgen Weber, and Susanne Zubler (2009): Die Finanz- und Wirtschaftskrise – Einschätzungen und Maßnahmen der Controller in deutschen Unternehmen, Vol. 34, No. 5/2009, pp. 66–71.
10 Pudliszweski, Daniel, and Susanne Schneider (2009): Forderungsmanagement in Krisenzeiten – Zuckerbrot oder Peitsche als Instrumente gegenüber den Kunden, Vol. 34, No. 6/2009, pp. 77–82.
11 Kunstek, Rolf (2010): Der Einsatz der statistischen Prognose bei krisenhafter wirtschaftlicher Entwicklung, Vol. 35, No. 1/2010, pp. 30–36.
12 Weber, Jürgen (2010): Controlling und Nachhaltigkeit, Vol. 35, No. 2/2012, p. 12.
13 Weber, Jürgen (2010): Was ist nur mit den Controllern los!, Vol. 35, No. 5/2010, pp. 54–55.
14 Schmitt, Matthias (2011): Szenario-Planung: Mit Best Case und Worst Case sicher durch die Krise, Vol. 36, No. 1/2011, pp. 74–79.
15 Rehring, Jochen, Ludwig Voußem, and Jürgen Weber (2011): Die Rolle(n) der Controller – Eine Einordnung durch den WHU-Controllerindex, Vol. 36, No. 5/2011, pp. 14–19.
16 Biel, Alfred (2012): Der Controller als Change Agent – Interview mit Prof. Dr. Joachim Sandt, Vol. 37, No. 1/2012, pp. 4–9.
17 Frei, Matthias, Norbert Klingebiel, and Fabio Mazzariello (2012): Umfang und Struktur des Working Capital in Schweizer Unternehmen, Vol. 37, No. 1/2012, pp. 24–29.
18 Weber, Jürgen (2012): Controller und Compliance, Vol. 37, No. 1/2012, pp. 62–63.
19 Weber, Jürgen (2012): Controlling und Effizienz, Vol. 37, No. 3/2012, p. 37.
20 Gleich, Ronald (2012): Vom Business Partner zum Change Agent? Auf der Suche nach der neuen Rolle der Controller, Vol. 37, No. 5/2012, pp. 58–62.
21 Löhr, Sebastian, and Olaf B. Mäder (2013): Transformation – Restrukturierung – Sanierung: Eine fallstudienbasierte Analyse, Vol. 38, No. 4/2013, pp. 72–80.
22 Weber, Jürgen (2013): Sind schlechte Zeiten für das Unternehmen gute Zeiten für Controller?, Vol. 38, No. 4/2013, p. 81.
23 Exler, Markus W., Clemens Gapp, Ottokar Kelz, Thomas Levermann, and Matthias Ortner (2014): Das Erkennen einer strategischen Krise als Managementaufgabe, Vol. 39, No. 6/2014, pp. 4–11.

Notes

1 Consistent with Becker et al. (2016), we define an economic crisis as having an external origin and resulting in "a significant downward shift and an increased economic uncertainty compared to a pre-crisis situation" (ibid., p. 2).
2 In Germany, MAs are called "Controllers".

References

Asel, J. A., A. Posch, & G. Speckbacher. 2011. Squeezing or cuddling? The impact of economic crises on management control and stakeholder management. *Review of Managerial Science, 5*(2–3): 213–231.

Becker, S. D., M. D. Mahlendorf, U. Schäffer, & M. Thaten. 2016. Budgeting in times of economic crisis. *Contemporary Accounting Research*, forthcoming.

Burns, J. & G. Baldvinsdottir. 2007. The changing role of management accountants. In T. Hopper, D. Northcott, & R. Scapens (Eds.), *Issues in management accounting* (pp. 117–222). Harlow: Pearson Education.

Burns, T. & G. M. Stalker. 1961. *The management of innovation*. London: Tavistock Publications.

Donaldson, L. 2001. *The contingency theory of organizations: Foundations for organizational science*. Thousand Oaks, Calif.: Sage Publications.

Endenich, C. 2014. Economic crisis as a driver of management accounting change. *Journal of Applied Accounting Research, 15*(1), 123–149.

Ezzamel, M. & M. Bourn. 1990. The roles of accounting information systems in an organization experiencing financial crisis. *Accounting, Organizations and Society, 15*(5), 399–424.

Faulhaber, P., N. Landwehr, & H.-J. Grabow. 2009. *Turnaround-Management in der Praxis: Umbruchphasen nutzen – neue Stärken entwickeln*, 4th edition. Frankfurt/Main: Campus Verlag.

Furman, J. & J. E. Stiglitz. 1998. *Economic crises: Evidence and insights from East Asia*. Brookings Papers on Economic Activity.

Hermann, C. F. 1963. Some consequences of crisis which limit the viability of organizations. *Administrative Science Quarterly, 8*(1), 61–82.

Hopwood, A. G. 2009. The economic crisis and accounting: Implications for the research community. *Accounting, Organizations and Society, 34*(6–7), 797–802.

Hsie, H.-F. & S. E. Shannon. 2005. Three approaches to qualitative content analysis. *Qualitative Health Research, 15*(9), 1277–1288.

Janke, R., M. D. Mahlendorf, & J. Weber. 2014. An exploratory study of the reciprocal relationship between interactive use of management control systems and perception of negative external crisis effects. *Management Accounting Research, 25*(4), 251–270.

Malmi, T. & S. Ikäheimo. 2003. Value based management practices: Some evidence from the field. *Management Accounting Research, 14*(3), 235–254.

Olofsson, C. & P. A. Svalander. 1975. The medical services change over to a poor environment. Working paper. University of Linköping.

Rosenthal, U. & P. 't Hart. 1991. Experts and decision makers in crisis situations. *Knowledge: Creation, Diffusion, Utilization, 12*(4), 350–372.

Rosenthal, U., M. T. Charles, & P. 't Hart. 1989. *Coping with crises: The management of disaster, riots and terrorism*. Springfield: Charles C. Thomas.

Ury, W. L. & R. Smoke. 1991. Anatomy of a crisis. In J. William Breslin & Jeffery Z. Rubin (Eds.), *Negotiation theory and practice* (pp. 47–54). Cambridge, MA: Program on Negotiation at Harvard Law School.

Van der Stede, W. A. 2011. Management accounting research in the wake of the crisis: Some reflections. *European Accounting Review, 20*(4), 605–623.

Wallace, J. S. 1998. EVA® Financial Systems: Management Perspectives. In M. J. Epstein, J. Y. Lee, & K. M. Posten (Eds.), *Advances in Management Accounting* (pp. 1–15). Amsterdam: Elsevier.

Weber, J. & S. Zubler. 2010. *Controlling in Zeiten der Krise: Wirkungen und Maßnahmen*. Edited by Jürgen Weber. Vol. 73, Advanced Controlling. New York: Wiley VCH.

Widener, S. K. 2007. An empirical analysis of the levers of control framework. *Accounting, Organizations and Society, 32*(7–8), 757–788.

20 The dynamics of the academic discourse on the role change of management accountants

A Finnish perspective

Kari Lukka and Marko Järvenpää

Introduction

One of the most vivid academic discourses in management accounting during the last few decades has been that on the (changing) roles of management accountants, for instance concerning their roles as bean-counters versus business partners/controllers.[1] This chapter examines that international discourse from the Finnish perspective with two aims: first, to analyse the contents and trajectory of that discourse over time and, second, to explore the anatomy and dynamics of that discourse as an example of how scholarly discourses evolve. The first mentioned purpose means a retrospective analytical 'stock-taking' of what we have actually learned in the big picture about the roles of management accountants during the last few decades. Relating to the latter aim, using this particular discourse as an illustrative example, we seek to shed light on the dynamics of scholarly discourses and especially on the value of *dialectic tensions* in advancing our knowledge. In line with classical philosophy, by dialectic we mean a form of reasoning which is based on dialogue of arguments and counter-arguments, advocating propositions (theses) and counter-propositions (antitheses) and hence including some tension. The outcome of such a dialectic process might be a synthesis of propositions (if that would turn out to be possible), the refutation of one of the arguments or a qualitative improvement of the dialogue (cf. Ayer & O'Grady, 1992).

Changing roles of management accountants have been under active debate and research during the last two decades in management accounting literature (e.g. Granlund & Lukka, 1997, 1998a; Friedman & Lyne, 1997; Järvenpää, 1998, 2001, 2002, 2007, 2009; Byrne & Pierce, 2007; Burns & Baldvinsdottir, 2005). Some early scholars (Hopper, 1980; Sathe, 1983; Mouritsen, 1996) already pointed out the different roles of accountants as well as the potential of professional role competition in organizations (Armstrong, 1985). Since the mid-1990s, the discussion has intensified and several studies have indicated observable changes in these roles, most importantly the increasing business involvement of financial managers in different formal organizational positions (management accountants, business controllers and CFOs) (Granlund & Lukka, 1997, 1998a; Järvenpää, 1998, 2001, 2002; Partanen, 2001). Early studies in the mid-1990s stressed particularly the new business partner role, which could be contrasted to the traditional roles of management accountants, especially to that of a 'bean-counter' (Granlund & Lukka, 1997, 1998a; Järvenpää, 1998, 2001). Since then, several additional studies have been carried out and viewpoints presented, including also a certain amount of criticism towards any stricter polarity of these two roles and towards the belief that a business partner/controller role can be implemented straightforwardly and easily. Indeed, the perceived claim of two almost incommensurable roles of management accountants has been a major source of inspiration and platform for motivation for numerous later studies (e.g. Burns & Baldvinsdottir, 2005; Vaivio & Kokko, 2006; Byrne & Pierce, 2007; Järvenpää, 2007, 2009; Lambert & Sponem, 2012; Goretzki, Strauss & Weber, 2013; Morales & Lambert, 2013; Hyvönen, Järvinen & Pellinen, 2015).

We conduct our study by first reviewing some of the early Finnish studies on management accountants' roles and their changes, which were inspired by some novel and exciting developments in the management accounting practices in a few leading Finnish firms as well as by the increasing emphasis on the qualitative and 'practice-near' case studies in management accounting. Thereafter we will take a look, through a few examples, at the following international discussion and debate and finally put this example area into a broader context of scholarly discourses in general. As a few Finnish-based studies published in the 1990s and early 2000s (Granlund & Lukka, 1997, 1998a, 1998b; Järvenpää, 1998, 2001, 2002) have become rather widely cited and employed as discussion partners in the trajectory of the field in focus, we will start our examination from them by seeking to clarify what those original studies actually argued.

The early Finnish pieces of research

The early pieces of research no doubt provided an image of a relatively polarized distinction between bean-counters and business partners/controllers (Granlund & Lukka, 1997, 1998a; Friedman & Lyne, 1997; Järvenpää, 1998, 2001, 2002), probably in their attempt to crystallize and sharpen the new and emerging aspects of the work requirements of management accountants (the business partnership/controllership) as compared to the traditionally established ones (corporate watchdog and especially bean-counter). However, as in our view the later readings of the early pieces on business partners/controllers have at times been even overly black and white by nature, we will start our review of these early pieces by suggesting an *integrative reading* of Figure 20.1 and Table 20.1 presented by Granlund and Lukka (1998a), which both deal with the relationship between bean-counters and (business) controllers.

The key underlying idea of Granlund and Lukka (1998a) was to depict various roles of management accountants as a *broadening continuum*, where the new orientations or accentuations of the role complex of management accountants build on the prior ones. This central idea is quite explicitly illustrated in Figure 20.1, brought in directly from the original piece.

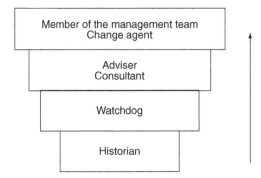

Figure 20.1 Expansion of the management accountant's job description.

Data source: Granlund and Lukka (1998, p. 187).

The surrounding text further explicates the same underlying idea:

> The transition in the role of management accountants over time, or at least the claimed need for it, is outlined in Figure [20.]1. It is crucial to understand that Figure [20.]1 is concerned with the *expansion* of the management accountant's role, with the upper roles *including* new and wider dimensions in the job description. At the lower levels, a certain kind of historiography and "watching over" is likely to prevail as the basis of all accounting, regardless of what other roles may in practice be built on (Mattsson, 1987; Olve, 1990).
>
> (Granlund & Lukka 1998a, p. 187, italics as in the original)

A bit later in the same paper, Granlund and Lukka compare the main characteristics of 'bean-counters' and controllers in a table format (see Table 20.1).

The text on the previous page of Granlund and Lukka (1998a) comments on this table as follows:

> Our analysis of current Finnish management accounting practices revealed several change tendencies. The most prominent of these appears to concern accountants' role models, going from "bean-counting" to a controller-type of operation. This development seems to be linked with the increasing decentralization of the management accounting function in particular. However, while the relative significance of "bean-counters" appears to be diminishing, there still remains a need for this kind of role model in the centralized part of the accounting function, in which consolidated corporate reporting in the standard format is the major issue, along with running the financial accounting procedures of the firm. Therefore, the ongoing change tendency in fact sharpens the division of labour within the accounting

Table 20.1 Typical characteristics of "bean-counters" and controllers compared

Character	"Bean-counter"	Controller
Temporal orientation	Emphasis on the past	Emphasis on the present and the future
Knowledge of the business in which the firm operates	Not expected	Expected
The primary aim of communication	Fulfilling of information requirements	Active attention attraction in order to get the message through
Felt scope of responsibility	Narrow; covers the production of correct accounting reports in time	Wide; covers both the production of relevant accounting figures and their application in business decisions
Cross-functional appreciation	Limited; based often on fear	High for an active and capable person
General operating style	Information collector and processor	Member of management team and a change agent

Source: Granlund and Lukka (1988, p. 202).

function as today both types of accountants are simultaneously needed. The major distinctions between the alternative role models are depicted in Table 1.

(p. 203)

In retrospect, the text relating to Table 20.1 can indeed be read to indicate a more dichotomic argument than what was originally intended – in places the wording could have been slightly different. While the continuing need of bean-counters (yet arguably in a diminishing degree) is certainly noted, the text and the table seem to actually highlight the separation of the two roles rather than their combined employment. However, the original intention of the authors was not to overly stress such separation, but instead keep to the idea of a relatively seamless continuum of these different roles, yet with evolving accentuations towards an increasing significance of the (business) controller role. An integrative reading of Figure 20.1 and Table 20.1 of Granlund and Lukka (1998a) would hence be needed to receive the message in the intended way.[2]

The original intention of the studies dealing with the distinction between bean-counters and business partners/controllers (see, for example, Granlund & Lukka, 1997, 1998a; Järvenpää, 1998, p. 298 and 346, 2002, p. 23) was actually not to argue them to be unconnected and entirely separate organizational roles, but rather to *demonstrate the direction of development potential* (i.e. path) from bean-counting aspects of management accountant's work to the direction of business partnership/controlling. This intention was based on observations from Finnish management accounting practice: there is notable evidence that bean-counting and business partnership/controllership have never been strongly separated in Finland – they have rather been considered as closely interlinked 'two sides of the same coin', where basic accounting reporting is seen as a necessary prerequisite for effective business partnership/controlling. While a breed of business controllers certainly exists in the Finnish 'wilderness' (organizations), they are not any 'heroic' or hyped supernatural characters, but relatively mundane individuals being able to not only collect information, process it, do calculations and carry out reporting, but also – and most importantly – willing to develop a good understanding of the operational and strategic business issues as well to directly collaborate with operational managers and executives around such matters. Relatedly, the findings of these early studies, based on empirics sourced from Finland, indicate how the development of the business partner/controller role has not been any dramatic revolutionary change, but mostly an evolutionary one where management accountants have gradually realized the needs and opportunities for being increasingly involved in business decision-making processes. That said, a few Finnish firms (most notably Kone and Nokia) took steps, starting already in the 1980s, into this direction at a quicker pace and earlier than many others, thereby forming models for the others to copy (Granlund & Lukka, 1997, 1998a, 1998b; Järvenpää, 1998).

In fact, the business partner/controller role has never been overly hyped in Finland, even though it has been a popular topic at executive seminars, and new competences supporting such a role have increasingly been taken into account in university curricula. Quite the contrary, arguments have consistently been presented for the importance and essence of the basic accounting reporting (e.g. Järvenpää, 1998, 2002), while at the same time business partnership/controlling was seen as a significant optional path of development for the management accounting function in Finnish firms. While this led in many firms into separation between the centralized accounting organization taking care of routine reporting (later increasingly carried out by service centres) and the decentralized business controller organization supporting business operations, representatives of the latter have never been allowed to view themselves as non-accountants – they are normally supposed to conduct, for instance, a considerable amount of routine reporting-related tasks as part of the reporting cycle of their organizations. It was, however, noticed that some people may have more resources (like skills, suitable education, motivation or experience) for one or the other of these tasks and that companies often (at least aim to) develop their management accounting function towards a more business-oriented direction in particular. It was, however, also observed that managerial expectations regarding the preferred directions of developments vary, sometimes according to organizational culture (Järvenpää, 2002, 2007, 2009).

We suggest that the strongly polarized and unconnected view of the relation of the bean-counter and business partner/controller roles was primarily a later interpretation, to some extent a self-feeding myth living its own life, detached from what was originally intended to be argued, particularly in the early studies in Finland. However, as these early Finnish studies were perhaps not quite successful in their communication to get their intended less dichotomic view across to the readers, these studies have actually likely happened to form a (more intriguing than originally intended) target and inspiration for further studies. Moreover, the worldwide consultancy-oriented hype around the business part-nering concept has further emphasized the exaggerated separation of the various roles of management accountants. In this chapter we will follow and analyse the trajectory of this research literature and thereafter draw a few wider conclusions about the dynamics in academia that this example brings forth.

Expanded discourse on management accountants' roles

In this section we will take a look at a few later studies about management accountants' roles. There are several studies, even quite recent ones, represent-ing the research area, the role change of management accountants. Such studies as Baxter & Chua (2008), Baldvinsdottir, Burns, Nørreklit & Scapens (2009), Lambert & Pezet (2011), Hyvönen et al. (2015), Puyou & Faÿ (2015), Henttu-Aho (2016) and ter Bogt et al. (2016) exemplify this. The studies sampled for a closer analysis are, however, picked from those in which, it appears, the earlier Finnish studies function as notable discussion partners and sources of motiva-tion. Vaivio and Kokko (2006) argue that there are no more bean-counters in Finland; Lambert and Sponem (2012) point to the scarcity of clear empirical evidence of business partners and argue for a considerable many-sidedness of management accountants' roles; Goretzki et al. (2013) argue that achieving a business partner's identity can be based on a notable amount of institutional work; and, in the same vein, Morales and Lambert (2013) depict a picture of the challenges of implementing business partnership. Next we will examine the research tasks, motivations, methods and main messages of these four selected papers in more detail.

Primarily motivated by the question whether the passed time might have changed something in the landscape of management accountants' work, Vaivio and Kokko (2006) developed an interesting analysis where they concluded that there were no more bean-counters in Finland, contrasting their findings to par-ticularly those of Granlund and Lukka (1997) and (1998a). The abstract of Vaivio and Kokko captures their arguments in a neat manner:

> This study places the concept of the bean counter controller under critical empirical re-examination, in a Finnish context. By interviewing Finnish controllers from several organizations in different industries, it examines whether the bean counter notion is still valid in a specific situational setting, in a typical bean counting activity – when the controller is analysing and processing performance measurements. The study does no longer recognize the narrow bean counter metaphor as being descriptive of contemporary Finnish practice. Instead, it reports how the business-oriented controller engages in organizational social networks, in order to develop the necessary cognitive and interpretive frame which allows him/her to analyse and

process information rapidly. Hence, we have to reconsider what traditional bean counting suggests in the contemporary setting.

(Vaivio & Kokko, 2006, p. 49)

However, instead of actually giving strong support to the argument of the vanished bean-counter from Finnish firms, which appears on the surface of the paper, a careful review of Vaivio and Kokko (2006) rather suggests a somewhat differing conclusion: the findings, where the authors mobilize the quite unique notion of "bean counter controller", actually seem quite directly to support only the prior findings on the wide set of business-oriented activities that the Finnish business controllers have assumed.

This differing conclusion is primarily implied by the fact that the empirics of Vaivio and Kokko (2006) were formed by eight interviews of controllers (under the titles of CFOs and Controllers), whose task orientation – based on a closer look on what they actually have stated in the interviews – obviously *needed* to be relatively business-oriented. Hence findings such as "the controller does not appear as a detached analyser of formal performance data" or "instead of an isolated accounting expert, we encountered a controller who was seeking involvement" (p. 63, see also p. 70) appear almost unavoidable, given the sample of financial managers. The consequence is that the findings presented in section 4 of Vaivio and Kokko (2006), rather than being challenging, as was likely intended, primarily only support the results of earlier research from Finland on the increasing significance of business-oriented management accounting tasks. Such surfacing tasks and orientations as being forward-looking and able to offer rough profit estimates, understanding basic relationships of the business, being constantly involved and communicating actively with operations, looking around the organization, observing the markets and securing that accounting data are interpreted correctly in management meetings have all been well-documented in earlier research as features of business-oriented management accountants' work (e.g. Granlund & Lukka, 1997, 1998a; Järvenpää, 1998, 2002). However, it is more difficult to see how they could support the argument of the vanished bean-counter role, not least as the applied sampling does not seem to even allow such findings to be easily made.[3]

In fact, if we explore the effects of some trends of development of some of the most essential issues and contingencies around management accounting in contemporary organizations (such as quickly evolving AIS technologies (ranging from accounting specific information systems, ERP-systems, consolidation packages and business analytics to technologies to handle big data) (Davenport, 2010; Granlund, 2011; Taipaleenmäki & Ikäheimo, 2013; Bhimani & Willcocks, 2014; Nykänen, Järvenpää & Teittinen, 2016), structural organizational arrangements (e.g. shared service centres and accelerating international outsourcing) (Tuomela & Partanen, 2001; Järvenpää, Lähteenmäki, Niemelä, Pellinen & Voutilainen, 2008; Hyvönen, Järvinen, Oulasvirta & Pellinen, 2012), as well as the increasing need to consider the tax aspect from the international angle (Järvenpää, Pellinen & Virtanen, 2007; Sikka & Willmott, 2010; Chen, Chen, Pan & Wang, 2015), it seems that the bean-counter tasks of accountants are not disappearing, but rather the contrary. It is indicative, for instance, that when one simply mentions transfer-pricing in executive education contexts a nearly automatic reaction of the audience is to start considering the tax aspect, even though the (more business-oriented) control of operations aspect of transfer-pricing policies and procedures is certainly also continuously relevant. In a recent Finnish survey, 60 per cent of Finnish CFO's viewed taxation as the most important issue in determining transfer prices, while only 24 per cent considered management motivation and business profitability as the most important driver in their determination (Järvenpää et al., 2007). There is evidence in abundance to argue that even though the need and wide spread of business partners/controllers is evident, so remains also that of bean-counters.

Arguing that there is only limited amount of evidence of the shift towards the business-oriented role among management accountants, Lambert & Sponem (2012) set and motivate their research task as follows:

> Historical lag may explain this role's gradual diffusion within organisations. However, drawing on multiple case-study research, we set out and explore an alternative explanation: that not all firms yearn for business partners. But if they are not business partners, then what role do management accountants play in the organisation?
>
> (Lambert & Sponem, 2012, p. 566)

They studied management accountants' work in 10 multinational companies gathering wide empirical materials consisting of 73 interviews. Four distinct styles of management accounting function emerged: discrete, safeguarding, partner and omnipotent. Management accounting functions employing discrete and partnering styles were emphasizing local management as their client, whilst those having adopted safeguarding and omnipotent styles considered the HQ as their primary customer. Further, each style was found to be associated with one main role: discrete control, socialization, decision making facilitator or centralization of power. Lambert & Sponem also found risks associated with each style – for example 'a drift in governance' was a risk for partnering style, and 'short sightedness' a risk for omnipotent style.

Lambert & Sponem (2012) nicely enriched earlier knowledge by adding more nuances into the styles/roles of management accounting function (and thereby also of management accountants), considering also the question of authority as well as the risks and unexpected benefits associated with each style, and finally questioning whether a strong controller is always the best option. They build their arguments carefully by first describing the distinction of two stereotypical roles, bean-counter and business partner, and then challenging the straightforwardness of this position through their empirics. As part of motivating their research, Lambert & Sponem note (2012, p. 566):

> Management accounting innovations, implementation of modern financial and operational control systems, software empowerment, and decentralisation of

management accountants supposedly foster a business-orientation role for management accountants (Järvenpää, 2007). Yet empirical evidence supporting fundamental shifts in these roles remains relatively scarce (Burns and Baldvinsdottir, 2005). Most research still empirically discerns the bean counter phenomenon (Vaivio, 2006).

According to their interpretation, in addition to the institutional logic of the organization, the authority of the management accounting function is an important explanatory factor of the style adopted:

> Our research suggests that in organisations where their function holds little authority, management accountants confine their activity to certain technical tasks. Yet in organisations where their function enjoys significant authority, i.e. with omnipotent and partner styles, we show that management accountants accumulate technical and advisory tasks. Our findings confirm that "accounting departments' 'core tasks' relate to bookkeeping and all remaining accounting department competencies are negotiable" (Mouritsen, 1996, p. 300). When fully empowered, accounting departments can participate in management activities or serve management teams, influencing the firm's businesses by developing 'consulting work'.
>
> (Lambert & Sponem, 2012, p. 585)

The main result of Lambert & Sponem (2012) can be anyhow viewed to be the separation of two variations in both bean-counting and business part ner/ controller role: those inclined towards bean-counters can be either modest safeguards or powerful omnipotents, those inclined towards business partners/ controllers again can be modest discrete or active partners. These observations are actually consistent with the original results such as Granlund and Lukka (1997, 1998a), yet refining them in a most interesting manner. Moreover, the findings indicate the importance of basic bean-counting work as well as the relative rarity of business partners in France, which is contrary to the claimed Finnish results of Vaivio and Kokko (2006). Lambert & Sponem (2012) concluded by encouraging further studies to "question the contemporary fascination with the business partner" (p. 587).

Goretzki et al. (2013) theorize how a new CFO in a firm can drive the institutionalization of a new role for management accountants. It draws on a single case study with 46 interviews in a German context and employs institutional theory. Again the introduction of the article starts with bringing the 'usual suspects' in, i.e. the essential elements of the bean-counter vs. business partner distinction-related literature. Arguing first that "[a]lthough not every firm seems to yearn for the 'business partner' (Lambert & Sponem, 2012) it still appears to be commonsencical to use the term 'business partner' to describe the apparently new (Vaivio, 2004) and more management-oriented (Byrne & Pierce, 2007; Järvenpää, 2007) role of the management accountant" (p. 41), they continue by stating that "the knowledge about the efforts of individual actors … for actual processes of professional role change is still scarce" (p. 42). On this basis they set out to examine the research question "how do actors drive the institutionalisation of a business-oriented role for management accountants within the organisation?" (p. 42).

The method theory (Lukka & Vinnari, 2014) employed in the analysis is the theory of institutional work, which is an actor-focused form of institutionalist analysis (e.g. Lawrence & Suddaby, 2006). It highlights the microprocesses of institutionalization, viewing the formation of new roles as a product of the purposive action of actors having an interest in achieving change. As results Goretzki et al. (2013) found three kinds of institutional work used by the CFO in supporting the emergence of business partnering role in their case firm: legitimizing the new business partnering role, (re)constructing management accountants' role identities and finally linking the intraorganizational level with the institutional environment. They argue that management accountants' role change can be seen as a product of institutional work, and that in the German context the professional community (like training in the Controller Academie) can also be an important tool for the institutional worker seeking to accomplish change towards business partnership.

The results of Goretzki et al. (2013) can be viewed as being consistent with the prior studies regarding the fundamental aspects of management accountant's role change towards business partnering (e.g. Mouritsen, 1996; Granlund & Lukka, 1998a; Järvenpää, 2007; Byrne & Pierce, 2007), legitimacy seeking (Järvenpää, 2009) and identity work (Järvinen, 2009). They make an important contribution to the prior knowledge with the help of their meticulous empirical analysis informed by the theory of institutional work by adding to our understanding of the detailed mechanisms which make a management accountant's role change (here towards business partnering) possible and eventually happen, emphasizing the role of individual actors – even just one single actor – in such processes.

Morales & Lambert (2013) examined the processes by which identity work influences accounting and organizational practices. Based on an ethnographic study (using direct field observations) they sought to shed light on "how accountants engage in a struggle for recognition in a context where tensions emerge from the confrontation between idealised occupational aspirations and situated possibilities" (p. 228). Building on the concept of "dirty work" by Hughes (1951), they differentiate between the "unclean" (tasks which are incompatible with aspirational identities) and the "polluted" (tasks that, in a more favourable context, would be associated with prestigious aspects of the job, become degrading in specific situations), which accountants often have to perform. They recognized how trying to comply with a positive role transition can help avoid unclean work, yet generate more polluted work. They suggested paying more attention especially to symbolic differentiations between prestigious and shameful aspects of work, which can enhance our understanding of accounting and identity work.

Similar to the other studies reviewed here, also Morales & Lambert (2013) start their paper by introducing the distinction between "bookkeeper role" and "business-oriented role", referring to a wide set of existing literature, including Granlund & Lukka (1998a). But they continue:

> However, these analyses neglect the moral and symbolic aspects of work, overlooking the insecurities and fragility of management accountants' sense of self, their subjectivity and identity construction. The focus on professional and political aspirations leads these studies to disregard the ways in which management accountants become subjugated as their sense of self is shaped through normative pressures.
>
> (Morales & Lambert, 2013, p. 229)

For Morales & Lambert (2013) the notion of moral division of labour by Hughes (1956) forms the central anchor notion in methodical theory. The moral division of labour highlights the symbolic aspects of work and the fragile nature of identity work within the study of organizational practices. Morales & Lambert studied management accountants who often felt they are not able to be as fully business-oriented in their work as they aspire. This created tensions in their work life. For Morales & Lambert, the earlier literature mainly depicts management accountants' role transformation towards business-orientation only as a positive, unproblematic development and, contrary to that, they provide evidence of tensions and even pain that pursuing business-orientation can create, as well as of tactics management accountants try to employ regarding "unclean" or "polluted" tasks. In practice, according to their results, this dirty work can include, for example, correcting errors, providing unused reports, needing to remain silent at meetings, justifying and validating already made decisions. As such, many of these kinds of duties seem to be very typical and commonsensical aspects of accounting work in practical working life, yet they can feel problematic from the symbolic perspective. However, "the definition of dirty work and its manifestations depend on how the moral division of labour is materialised in a specific context" (Morales & Lambert, 2013, p. 242).

The results of Morales & Lambert (2013) are well consistent with prior literature in the sense that they develop a picture of management accountants needing to often conduct bean-counter kind of tasks and their typical aspiration to carry out more business-oriented tasks. Against this backdrop, the finding of management accountants trying to avoid "dirty work" is no big surprise as such, yet the explanation through the moral and symbolic perspective is very illuminating. Perhaps the most interesting of Morales & Lambert's findings are those related to "polluted work" as it brings forth clearly the challenges that management accountants can easily face even in situations when they are formally acting in the aspired business-oriented situations. It is not only up to themselves to be able to act like business-oriented management accountants, but depends on many elements of the social game involved.

Concluding comments: dialectic tension and the dynamics of scholarly discourse

Our brief review of a few recent studies indicates how the discussion/debate on management accountants' roles and their changes has been lively and fruitful – and it seems to be still actively ongoing. The review reveals some similarities between the four studies examined, some of them naturally due to our sampling strategy. All four pieces of research build first a carefully designed tension with earlier studies, in particular regarding the dichotomy of bean-counters and business partners, which is typically staged in the reviewed papers as too simple. Vaivio & Kokko (2006) strikingly question the dichotomy with their argument of bean-counters having vanished from Finnish organisations. Lambert & Sponem (2012) and Morales & Lambert (2013) consider the earlier promises of the role transformation towards business partnership too simplistic and positive, and build relatively high tension at their point of departure. In this spirit they produce as their result a richer picture of the nuances of the style/role categories, provide examples of risks and unexpected benefits attached to them, and moreover, question the panacea of a strong controller (Lambert & Sponem, 2012). Morales and Lambert (2013) also provide evidence on the only partially successful nature, and potentially negatively perceived aspects, of the role transformation towards business orientation. Goretzki et al. (2013) again point to the scarcity of our knowledge about the significance of the efforts of (individual) actors in the processes seeking to accomplish professional role change. They took advantage of the theory of institutional work, built carefully on the earlier literature on management accountants' role transformation and added to our knowledge of the mechanisms of such change.

Taken together, this analysis indicates how scholarly discourse based on dialectic tensions – a notion that can be dated back to the Socratic dialogues documented in Plato's works – can be fruitful for the dynamics of development on a field of research. Motivating a study in relation to a felt issue in the existing knowledge stages the scene and motivates further scrutiny, leading – as exemplified in the four reviewed studies – to new interesting findings and theses on the topic. They exemplify how sometimes especially provocative prior scholarly arguments, at times even more provocatively received by the readers than originally intended, can inspire other scholars in such a way that the knowledge of a field advances fruitfully when considered overall.

In the area of the role change of management accountants, the volume of studies during the last two decades has been notable and our understanding has advanced in many significant ways. Criticism towards any stricter polarity of the roles of management accountants and towards the belief that a business partner/controller role can be implemented straightforwardly 'just like that' have been typical features of these studies during the last decade. Based on careful and profound empirical analysis and through mobilizing new method theories into this domain of research (Lukka & Vinnari, 2014), significant new advances of knowledge have been achieved. For us this seems like fruitful scholarly discussion and theory development, indicating how research is always a question of sensemaking (what do I, as a researcher, consider to be a research gap or tension when looking at the literature) and sensegiving (convicing others to accept that this research is indeed a motivated one, which might, in turn, trigger further research building on my interpretation) (Gioia & Chittipeddi, 1991; Weick, 1995; Maitlis & Christianson, 2014).

Notes

1 In Finland the business support-oriented role of management accountants is typically called 'business controller', whilst internationally the label of 'business partner' seems to be more typical. Here we use the term 'business partner/controller' to indicate that regarding the intended idea of this role, these labels have a similar referent.
2 Interestingly, some management accounting researchers have anyhow recognized this major idea of Granlund & Lukka (1998a): "Granlund & Lukka (1998) point to a continuum in the controller's roles varying between score-keeper and bean-counter via watchdog, consultant and management advisor to management team member" (ter Bogt, van Helden & van der Kolk, 2016, p. 379).
3 We thank Markus Granlund for his special contribution regarding the review of Vaivio and Kokko (2006).

References

Armstrong, P. (1985). Changing management control strategies: The role of competition between accountancy and other organisational professions. *Accounting, Organizations and Society, 10*(2), 129–148.

Ayer, A. J. & O'Grady, J. (1992). *A Dictionary of Philosophical Quotations*. Oxford: Blackwell Publishers.

Baldvinsdottir, G., Burns, J., Nørreklit, H. & Scapens, R. (2009). The image of accountants: From bean counters to extreme accountants. *Accounting, Auditing and Accountability Journal, 22*(6), 858–882.

Baxter, J. & Chua, W. (2008). Be(com)ing the chief financial officer of an organisation: Experimenting with Bourdieu's practice theory. *Management Accounting Research, 19*(2), 212–230.

Bhimani, A. & Willcocks, L. (2014). Digitisation, 'Big Data' and the transformation of accounting information. *Accounting and Business Research, 44*(4), 469–490.

Burns, J. & Baldvinsdottir, G. (2005). An institutional perspective of accountants' new roles: The interplay of contradictions and praxis. *European Accounting Review, 14*(4), 725–757.

Byrne, S. & Pierce, B. (2007). Towards a more comprehensive understanding of the roles of management accountants. *European Accounting Review, 16*(3), 469–498.

Chen, C.X, Chen, S., Pan, F. & Wang, Y. (2015). Determinants and consequences of transfer pricing autonomy: An empirical investigation. *Journal of Management Accounting Research, 27*(2), 225–259.

Davenport, T. (2010). Business intelligence and organizational decisions. *International Journal of Business Intelligence Research, 1*(1), 1–12.

Friedman, A. & Lyne, S. (1997). Activity-based techniques and the death of the bean-counter. *European Accounting Review, 6*(1), 19–44.

Gioia, D. & Chittipeddi, K. (1991). Sensemaking and sensegiving in strategic change initiation. *Strategic Management Journal, 12*(6), 433–448.

Goretzki, L., Strauss, E. & Weber, J. (2013). An institutional perspective on the changes in management accountants' professional role. *Management Accounting Research, 24*(1), 41–63.

Granlund, M. (2011). Extending AIS research to management accounting and control issues: A research note. *International Journal of Accounting Information Systems, 12*(1), 3–19.

Granlund, M. & Lukka, K. (1997). From bean-counters to change agents: The Finnish management accounting culture in transition. *Finnish Journal of Business Economics, 46*(3), 213–255.

Granlund, M. & Lukka, K. (1998a). Towards increasing business orientation: Finnish management accountants in a changing cultural context. *Management Accounting Research, 9*(2), 185–211.

Granlund, M. & Lukka, K. (1998b). It's a small world of management accounting practices. *Journal of Management Accounting Research, 10*, 153–179.

Henttu-Aho, T. (2016). Enabling characteristics of new budgeting practice and the role of controller. *Qualitative Research in Accounting and Management, 13*(1), 31–56.

Hopper, T. (1980). Role conflicts of management accountants and their position within organisation structures. *Accounting, Organizations and Society, 5*(4), 401–411.

Hughes, E. C. (1951). Mistakes at work. *Canadian Journal of Economics and Political Science, 17*(3), 320–327.

Hughes, E. C. (1956). Social role and the division of labor. *Midwest Sociologist, 17*(1), 3–7. (Reprinted in *The sociological eye. Selected papers* (pp. 304–310). New Brunswick: Transaction Publishers).

Hyvönen, T., Järvinen, J., Oulasvirta, L. & Pellinen, J. (2012). Contracting out municipal accounting: The role of institutional entrepreneurship. *Accounting, Auditing and Accountability Journal, 25*(6), 944–963.

Hyvönen, T., Järvinen, J. & Pellinen, J. (2015). Dynamics of creating a new role for business controllers. *Nordic Journal of Business, 64*(1), 21–39.

Järvenpää, M. (1998). Strateginen johdon laskentatoimi ja talousjohdon muuttuva rooli. *Publications of the Turku School of Economics and Business Administration, Series D-1*:1998, Turku.

Järvenpää, M. (2001). Connecting the management accountants' changing roles, competencies and personalities into the wider managerial discussion: A longitudinal case evidence from modern business environment. *Finnish Journal of Business Economics, 50*(4), 431–458.

Järvenpää, M. (2002). *Johdon laskentatoimen liiketoimintaan suuntautuminen laskentakulttuurisena muutoksena – vertaileva case-tutkimus.* Publications of the Turku School of Economics and Business Administration, Series A-5: 2002. Summary: Business orientation of management accounting as a cultural change: A comparative case study (PhD thesis).

Järvenpää, M. (2007). Making business partners: A case study on how management accounting culture was changed. *European Accounting Reviews, 16*(1), 99–142.

Järvenpää, M. (2009). The institutional pillars of management accounting function. *Journal of Accounting and Organizational Change, 5*(4), 444–471.

Järvenpää, M., Lähteenmäki, J., Niemelä, M., Pellinen, J. & Voutilainen, V. (2008). Hei, me mennään kunnan tilitehtaaseen! Taloushallinnon työn uudelleenorganisoinnin vaikutukset työntekijöiden kokemana. *Hallinnon tutkimus, 27*(2), 52–65.

Järvenpää, M., Pellinen, J. & Virtanen, A. (2007). *Kansainvälisen yrityksen talous.* Helsinki: WSOY Pro.

Järvinen, J. (2009). Shifting NPM agendas and management accountants' occupational identities. *Accounting, Auditing and Accountability Journal, 22*(8), 1187–1210.

Lambert, C. & Pezet, E. (2011). The making of the management accountant: Becoming the producer of truthful knowledge. *Accounting, Organizations and Society, 36*(1), 10–30.

Lambert, C. & Sponem, S. (2012). Roles, authority and involvement of the management accounting function: A multiple case-study perspective. *European Accounting Review, 21*(3), 565–589.

Lawrence, T. B. & Suddaby, R. (2006). Institutions and institutional work. In: S. Clegg, C. Hardy, T. B. Lawrence & W. R. Nord (Eds.), *The Sage handbook of organization studies* (pp. 215–254). Thousand Oaks: Sage Publications.

Lukka, K. & Vinnari, E. (2014). Domain theory and method theory in management accounting research. *Accounting, Auditing and Accountability Journal, 27*(8), 1308–1338.

Maitlis, S. & Christianson, M. (2014). Sensemaking in organizations: Taking stock and moving forward. *Academy of Management Annals, 8,* 1, 57–125.

Mattsson, H. S. (1987). *Controller*. Lund: Studentlitteratur.

Morales, J. & Lambert, C. (2013). Dirty work and the construction of identity: An ethnographic study of management accounting practices. *Accounting, Organizations and Society, 38*(3), 228–244.

Mouritsen, J. (1996). Five aspects of accounting departments' work. *Management Accounting Research, 7*(3), 283–303.

Nykänen, E., Järvenpää, M. & Teittinen, H. (2016). Business intelligence in decision making in Finnish enterprises. *Nordic Journal of Business, 65*(2), (forthcoming).

Olve, N.-G. (1990). *Controllerns roll*. Uppsala: Mekanforbundets Forlag.

Partanen, V. (2001). *Muuttuva johdon laskentatoimi ja organisatorinen oppinen. Fieldtutkimus laskentahenkilöstön roolin muutoksen ja uusien laskentainnovaatioiden käyttöönoton seurauksista*. Publications of the Turku School of Economics and Business Administration, Series A-6:2001.

Puyou, F.-R. & Faÿ, E. (2015). Cogs in the wheel or spanners in the works? A phenomenological approach to the difficulty and meaning of ethical work for financial controllers. *Journal of Business Ethics, 128*(4), 863–876.

Sathe, V. (1983). The controller's role in management. *Organizational Dynamics, 11*(3), 31–48.

Sikka, P. & Willmott, H. (2010). The dark side of transfer pricing: Its role in tax avoidance and wealth retentiveness. *Critical Perspectives on Accounting, 21*(4), 342–356.

Taipaleenmäki, J. & Ikäheimo, S. (2013). On the convergence of management accounting and financial accounting: The role of information technology in accounting change. *International Journal of Accounting in Information Systems, 14*(4), 321–348.

ter Bogt, H. T, van Helden, J. & van der Kolk, B. (2016) New development: Public sector controllership – Reinventing the financial specialist as a countervailing power. *Public Money and Management, 36*(5), 379–384.

Tuomela, T.-S. & Partanen, V. (2001). In search of strategic contribution and operative effectiveness: Developing competencies within the finance function. *Finnish Journal of Business Economics, 50*(1), 502–538.

Vaivio, J. (2004). Mobilizing local knowledge with 'provocative' non-financial measures. *The European Accounting Review, 13*(1), 39–71.

Vaivio, J. & Kokko, T. (2006). Counting big: Re-examining the concept of the bean counter controller. *Finnish Journal of Business Economics, 55*(1), 49–74.

Weick, K. E. (1995). *Sensemaking in organizations*. London: Sage.

Index

Page numbers in *italics* denote tables, those in **bold** denote figures.

Printed and bound by CPI Group (UK) Ltd, Croydon, CR0 4YY
01/05/2025
01858409-0002